Twx

H 4/96

This book contains a collection of political verses,
of social protest from medieval England. First edited by Thomas Wright in
1839, these so called 'political songs' are reissued here on behalf of the Royal
Historical Society. The collection provides a fascinating insight into
medieval responses to contemporary events. A new and wide-ranging introduction from Peter Coss offers observations on authorship, audience, the
means of dissemination and the use of the languages involved. The reader is
brought up to date on the critical study of the poems and on their significance and potentiality for the modern historian and literary scholar.
Professor Coss corrects Wright's dating where necessary and puts each item
into its full contemporary context, making these fascinating verses accessible to the modern reader.

APPENDIX

INTRODUCTION TO
1996 EDITION*

I

Political Songs was the inspiration of one of the great Victorian antiquaries. For this volume for the Camden Society, published in 1839, Wright collected together a host of scattered pieces of verse which he felt belonged under this heading and which he arranged chronologically, calling a temporary halt at the end of the reign of Edward II. As he explains in his preface, this was forced upon him by the quantity of material and the decision to provide translations. In the event, his projected second volume for the Camden Society failed to appear. Instead he published two volumes for the Rolls Series, one taking his project up to the deposition of Richard II and the other to the end of the Yorkist era.[1] Two related volumes, of satirical poetry from the twelfth century, followed from this prolific editor in 1872. In his introduction to

* I wish to thank the following for their generous help and advice in the preparation of this volume: Michael Clanchy, Françoise Le Saux, Simon Lloyd, John Maddicott, Linda Paterson, Ian Short, Thorlac Turville-Petre and Simon Walker.

[1] Thomas Wright (ed.), *Political Poems and Songs*, 2 vols. (Rolls Series, London, 1859 and 1861). Meanwhile, however, he had edited, *The Latin Poems commonly attributed to Walter Mapes*, Camden Society, o.s., xvi (London, 1841).

these latter, Wright explained his basic premise: chronicles 'furnish the materials for the substance of history, but we must seek other materials in order to throw life and colour into this dry substance, and show the feelings and motives which set it to work'. And, again, 'A single passage of the satirist or poet will sometimes throw more light over the character of historical events than whole pages of research and discussion.'[2] This, then, was the motivation which inspired the great collection of political songs of which the present volume was but the first instalment.

However, strictly speaking, 'political songs' is a misnomer. Many of them are not really songs at all, and are most unlikely ever to have been sung. There are, of course, exceptions, the robust *Song against the King of Almaigne* for one. *Vulneratur Karitas* has a line of musical notation associated with it in the manuscript, although it is later than the text, while the songs on the death of Piers Gaveston were parodies of known hymns and hence could certainly be sung.[3] Moreover, the poems do not represent a single genre. Broadly speaking, we can divide the great majority of the

[2] Thomas Wright (ed.), *The Anglo-Latin Satirical Poets and Epigrammatists of the Twelfth Century*, 2 vols. (Rolls Series, London, 1872), i, p. x.

[3] See below notes 24, 45, 48 and 54.

items Wright collected into three categories. There
are the political verses in the true, or at least the
narrow, sense of the term, celebrating or be-
moaning particular current events. There are the
venality satires attacking either specific vices or
the vices of various social classes and groups, a
long tradition in West European culture going
back to the late eleventh century.[4] And, finally,
there are the verses of social protest which draw
heavily upon the latter but which are more histor-
ically specific in that they are responses to particular and topical grievances. Nevertheless, Wright's
volume has a clear validity. Despite the differences
in form and genre, there are strong interconnec-
tions. The literature of social protest arose essentially out of venality satire whilst the political
poems in the narrow sense most often contain a
subtext of moral opprobrium in one guise or
another. Thus a unifying feature across the three is
the pervading undercurrent of moral condemnation. Wright's material, however, though it has
often been utilised to good effect, has rarely been
studied as a whole. The basic reason for this lies
within the development of modern academic disci-

---

[4] The classic exposition is by John A. Yunck, *The Lineage of Lady Meed: The Development of Mediaeval Venality Satire* (Notre Dame, Indiana, 1963). See also Jill Mann, *Chaucer and Medieval Estates Satire* (Cambridge, 1973).

plines. It has been used as a ready quarry for illustrative material by historians interested in the reigns of specific kings or in particular aspects of social or institutional life. It has been compartmentalised by scholars working in either Middle English or Anglo-Norman language and literature. The Middle English peoms, for example, have been studied by scholars interested in the development of English lyrics. Six of the items were included by Rossell Hope Robbins in his collection of *Historical Poems of the Fourteenth and Fifteenth Centuries*, where they are re-edited with extensive notes.[5] Others have studied the political songs in search of the antecedents of the great literary works of the late fourteenth century. Particular attention has been focused, for example, upon the *Simonie* or *Poem on the Evil Times of Edward II*.[6] Or, they have been used to provide commentary on Chaucer, as

[5] Rossell Hope Robbins (ed.), *Historical Poems of the Fourteenth and Fifteenth Centuries* (New York, 1959), nos. 2–7. The six are: *Song on the Flemish Insurrection, Song on the Execution of Sir Simon Fraser, Song on the Death of Edward I, Song of the Husbandman, Satire on the Consistory Courts* and *Song against the Retinues of the Great People*. Robbins noted all previous editions and these have not, therefore, been included here. The last three have recently been re-edited in Thorlac Turville-Petre, *Alliterative Poetry of the Later Middle Ages: An Anthology* (London, 1989).

[6] Elizabeth Salter, '*Piers Plowman* and *The Simonie*', *Archiv*, 203 (1967), 241–54, repr. in Elizabeth Salter (ed. D. Pearsall and N. Zeeman), *English and International: Studies in the Literature, Art and Patronage of Medieval England* (Cambridge, 1988), pp. 158–69.

for example the *Satire on the Consistory Courts* to illustrate the historicity of the Summoner.[7] The Anglo-Norman poems have also excited interest, especially from the language point of view, and most have been re-edited by Isabel Aspin for the Anglo-Norman Text Society.[8] Strangely, though, given its contemporary vitality throughout the twelfth and thirteenth centuries, it is the Latin literature produced in England which has been the most neglected over the years. Here again, it is demarcation within academe which has been largely to blame. Recently A.G. Rigg has set out to remedy this situation in a full-scale survey of what he calls Anglo-Latin literature.[9]

Assessment of the vernacular poems in terms of their literary quality has tended to be harsh. Some, as Aspin says of the laments for Simon de Montfort and Edward I, are 'heartbreakingly pedestrian'.

[7] See, in particular, L.A. Haselmayer, 'The Apparitor and Chaucer's Summoner', *Speculum*, 12 (1937), 43–57.

[8] Isabel S.T. Aspin (ed.), *Anglo-Norman Political Songs*, Anglo-Norman Text Society, no. XI (Oxford, 1953). The reader may wish to turn to this for further textual criticism and the elucidation of obscurities. It should also be noted that Aspin includes several items that are not found in Wright's volume. They are: *The Prisoner's Prayer, Thomas Turberville, The Lament of Edward II, Sur les états du monde, Lettre du prince des envieux*, and *The Ingratitude of the Great*. To these Mary Dominica Legge added *La Piere d'Escoce*, a poem written soon after the death of Edward I and telling the history of the Scottish Stone of Destiny ('La Piere d'Escoce', *Scottish Historical Review*, 38 (1959), 109–13). See also M.D. Legge, *Anglo-Norman Literature and its Background* (Oxford, 1963), pp. 351–7.

[9] A.G. Rigg, *A History of Anglo-Latin Literature 1066–1422* (Cambridge, 1992).

Interest in the 'songs' is always likely to be historical rather than aesthetic. Nevertheless, they cannot be denied a certain appeal, whether in terms of their craftsmanship, their rather racy quality, or indeed both. On the whole the Latin pieces tend to be of higher quality; the *Song of Lewes* for example is of real literary merit. To some extent, however, the division of these pieces according to language is also artificial. Genre cuts across language. Moreover, as Wright himself pointed out, a number of them employ more than one language and one of them, the *Proverbia Trifaria* or *Song on the Times*, is an amalgam of Anglo-Norman, Latin and English.

A growing interest among historians in the social context of this type of literature as well as recent shifts within literary scholarship have led to the realisation that the time is ripe for a deeper analysis of this material; hence the reissue of this volume.[10] J.R. Maddicott has recently led the way with an incisive discussion of the poems of social protest, in particular, and has called for further

---

[10] For a discussion of the similar material from the later fourteenth century, see Janet Coleman, *English Literature in History, 1350–1400: Medieval Readers and Writers* (London, 1981), esp. pp. 58–156. See also John Taylor, *English Historical Literature in the Fourteenth Century* (Oxford, 1987), and Richard W. Kaeuper, *War, Justice and Public Order: England and France in the Later Middle Ages* (Oxford, 1988).

work. He suggests that the protest literature which survives from the turn of the thirteenth and fourteenth centuries onwards – and which is qualitatively different from the more general satire which went before – represents a genuine new development.[11] Admittedly, material of this nature tended to be ephemeral and we know that much has been lost.[12] However, as Maddicott stresses, there was now much more to protest about, particularly in terms of increased demands being made by the state and in terms of the onset of economic distress. 'On to the stem provided by the sermon and the satire – part homily, part artifice, part exercise – there is apparently grafted a newer type of complaint, rooted in genuine grievances, which moves the literature of protest from the general to the particular.'[13]

It is hardly surprising that scholars should have refined the dating of some of these poems since the publication of Wright's volume, and that he is sometimes found to be seriously in error. He had a tendency to assume that the date of a poem corre-

[11] J.R. Maddicott, 'Poems of Social Protest in Early Fourteenth-Century England', in W.M. Ormrod (ed.), *England in the Fourteenth Century: Proceedings of the 1985 Harlaxton Symposium* (Woodbridge, 1986), pp. 140–3.

[12] See R.M. Wilson, *The Lost Literature of Medieval England* (2nd edn., London, 1970), pp. 188,196.

[13] Maddicott, 'Poems of Social Protest', p. 142.

sponded to its appearance in manuscript. Some of the Latin pieces belong, in fact, to the late twelfth century. On the other hand, two of the vernacular ones date from around 1340. As a result, the volume has a slightly broader chronological span than Wright gave it. Equally, we have a better understanding of the context of some of these poems than was available in Wright's day, although that is not invariably true. He was sometimes led into error, and his titles can be misleading. Moreover, as far as content is concerned, an editor today would undoubtedly make different decisions. There are some omissions and a few dubious inclusions.

Most of the poems have been re-edited over the years (many more than once), either individually or in various combinations. Nevertheless, the integrity of Wright's volume has been maintained here and it is being reissued in its entirety.[14] The breadth of his approach should be a stimulus to research, cutting across old boundaries. But, equally, the political poems should not be studied

[14] A revised edition was produced by Edmund Goldsmid under the title *Thomas Wright, Bibliotheca Curiosa: The Political Songs of England from the Reign of John to that of Edward II*, 4 vols. (Edinburgh, 1884). The longer Latin texts (and most of the Appendix) were omitted, leaving Wright's translations to stand alone, while his notes were severely pruned and brought to the foot of the text. A very few corrections were made, but little was added.

as a single corpus, in isolation. To have re-edited
the volume, quite apart from the size of the task,
would have risked fossilising Wright's choices,
discouraging newer approaches and combinations.
Furthermore, his work is of historical interest in its
own right. For various reasons, then, it was
thought better to reissue Wright's volume intact
whilst bringing the reader up to date with work
undertaken in the meantime. The remainder of this
introduction is divided into two parts. Section II is
designed to update the reader on the individual
items and their specific importance, noting refine-
ments in dating, for example, and the existence of
more recent editions. In this section the three sub-
categories of political poems in the strict sense, the
venality satires and the poems of social protest and
complaint, are dealt with in turn. Section III
moves to more general considerations affecting
their interpretation and hence to the broader
significance of the material.

II

Among the earliest political songs, in the narrow
sense of the term, are the topical *sirventes* of the
troubadours, a number of which concerned the
activities (or supposed inactivity) of John and

Henry III in defence of their interests in southern
France. The poem in which Bertran de Born the
younger attempted to persuade his fellow poet,
Savaric de Mauléon, to desert John's cause is especially famous and has helped to determine views
both of the king's character and of his pertinacity,
at least until very recently.[15] 'No man may ever
trust him', wrote Bertran, 'for his heart is soft and
cowardly.' Less justly perhaps, he tells us that
John loved hunting, fishing and repose – his
hounds and his hawks – better than he loved attention to war, and that he lost the hearts of his people
through his failure to succour them, near and far.[16]
The poem on the battle of Lincoln of May 1217
contains another judgement on John. The anger of
the avenging God no longer allowed this furious
king to reign. But his death was a glorious one, for
in it he confounded his enemies, allowing the
loyalist barons to defeat the rebels in the name of
his young son. Henry III was also the subject of

[15] For a more recent edition, with commentary, see M. de Riquer, *Los
Trovadores*, 3 vols. (Barcelona, 1975), ii. 952–4, and for a discussion of Bertran de
Born *lo fils*, W.D. Paden, Jr., T. Sankovitch and P.H. Stäblein, *The Poems of
Bertran de Born* (Berkeley and London, 1986). For Savaric see H.J. Chaytor,
Savaric de Mauléon, Baron and Troubadour (Cambridge, 1939); his *Song on the
Siege of Thouars* is discussed on p. 18. For a recent, wide-ranging discussion of the
society which produced the *sirventes* see Linda M. Paterson, *The World of the
Troubadours: Medieval Occitan Society, c.1100–c.1300* (Cambridge, 1993).

[16] For a more judicious assessment see J.C. Holt, *The Northerners* (2nd edn.,
Oxford, 1992), pp. 147,159.

sirventes. His Brittany campaign of 1230 had been urged on by an unknown troubadour who had called upon Henry to spurn the easy life and to show martial valour; that way he would win back his possessions in France.[17] Wright was surely mistaken, however, in connecting the first of his two *sirventes* by Bernart de Rovenac with this campaign. Aimed at James I of Aragon and Raymond VII of Toulouse as well as Henry III, it is closer in spirit to the time of Henry's Gascon campaign of 1242–3 which excited much interest among the troubadours.[18] It belongs, most probably, to 1241–2. The second Rovenac *sirventes*, aimed again at Henry and at James of Aragon, urges action at the time when Louis of France is on crusade. Given that it makes reference to King Alfonso (X, of Castile), it can be narrowed down to 1252–4.

[17] A. Jeanroy, 'Un sirventes politique de 1230', in *Mélanges d'histoire du moyen âge offerts à M. Ferdinand Lot* (Paris, 1925), pp. 275–83; F.M. Powicke, *Henry III and the Lord Edward*, 2 vols. (Oxford, 1947), i. 181.

[18] A. Jeanroy, 'Le soulèvement de 1242 dans la poésie des troubadours', *Annales du Midi*, 16 (1904), 311–29. There is a critical edition of the poems of Bernart de Rovenac by Gunther Bosdorff in *Romanische Forschungen*, 22 (1908), 761–827. For some recent comment on Bernart see E.M. Ghil, *L'Age de Parage: Essais sur le poétique et le politique en Occitanie au XIIIe siècle* (New York, Bern and Frankfurt, 1989), pp. 19, 259–69, 292. For Henry III's campaigns see Powicke, *Henry III and the Lord Edward*, ch. v, the same author's *The Thirteenth Century* (Oxford, 1953), ch. iii, and Robert Stacey, *Politics, Policy and Finance under Henry III 1216–45* (Oxford, 1987), ch. 5.

As regards political songs in the narrow sense, however, the high water mark was of course the time of Simon de Montfort and the baronial reform. Never before had they contained such exhilaration and commitment. It would be difficult to overstate their value in recapturing the mood of the time.[19] They are, however, decidedly *parti pris*. As C.L. Kingsford, who re-edited the *Song of Lewes*, put it, 'All the songs on the Barons' War which have survived favour the constitutional cause.'[20]

Among the literary products of the mid-thirteenth-century struggle, however, the *Song of Lewes* has pride of place. It is clearly written by a partisan, shortly after the battle of Lewes on 14 May 1264. Kingsford believed that it was written by a Franciscan friar, perhaps educated at Oxford under the influence of Adam Marsh and Bishop

[19] The poetry arising from the political struggle of mid thirteenth-century England has been cited by its major historians, although none of them subjected it to a systematic analysis. Among those who notice these works are: W.H. Blauuw, *The Barons' War*, (2nd edn., London, 1871); G.W. Prothero, *The Life of Simon de Montfort, Earl of Leicester* (London, 1877); C. Bémont, *Simon de Montfort* (Paris, 1884), and the translation of its second edition by E.F. Jacob, *Simon de Montfort, Earl of Leicester* (Oxford, 1930); Powicke, *Henry III and the Lord Edward*.

[20] C.L. Kingsford (ed.), *The Song of Lewes* (Oxford, 1890), p. vii. This is a full critical edition, with an introduction, emended text, translation and copious notes. There is a more accessible translation in H. Rothwell (ed.), *English Historical Documents*, iii (London, 1975), no.232, which incorporates some revisions made by Sir Maurice Powicke.

Grosseteste and personally associated with either Simon himself or his close supporter, Bishop Stephen Berksted, or indeed both. There is no direct evidence for any of this, but none of it is inherently improbable given what is known of the contours of the Montfortian 'party'. Essentially a lengthy 'exposition for the benefit of educated men of the principles of opposition to Henry III',[21] it is by any standards a polished piece of work. Heavy with biblical allusion, it is nevertheless imbued with contemporary tension and strife, and not only in its partisanship for Simon and his followers. Among its most prominent concerns is the question of the right relationship of the king to the law. It also shows that the full contours of Continental chivalric knighthood had by this time invaded English thought. At the same time it is fervently anti-alien. Its most remarkable feature, however, is that it not only states the essence of the baronial cause but it fully engages with (and, of course, refutes) the arguments of the royalist side.[22]

[21] Rothwell, *English Historical Documents*, iii. 899.

[22] For further comment, in addition to Kingsford, see Powicke. *Henry III and the Lord Edward*. II, ch. xi. For the latest discussion of the battle of Lewes itself see David Carpenter. *The Battles of Lewes and Evesham 1264/5* (Keele, 1987), and for the issues in contention between the parties before and after the battle see also J.R. Maddicott, 'The Mise of Lewes, 1264', *English Historical Review*, 98 (1983), 588–603. For national identity at this period see M.T. Clanchy. *England and its Rulers, 1066–1272* (Glasgow. 1983) ch. x. For knighthood at this period see P.R. Coss. *The Knight in Medieval England* (Stroud. 1993), chs. 2–3.

Another product of the battle of Lewes is the *Song against the King of Almaigne*. Vastly different in tone, it nevertheless exhibits the same mood of triumphalism. The target is the king's brother, Richard of Cornwall, elected king of the Romans in January 1257, and the poet makes great play with the fact that Richard had been forced to take refuge in a windmill when the battle turned ugly for the royalists.[23] The song is justly famous for its wonderful refrain which seems to encapsulate a contemporary view of Richard as well as the prevailing mood of the time:

> Richard, thah thou be ever trichard,   [deceiver]
> trichen shalt thou never more[24]   [deceive]

The same pun is alluded to in the *Song of the Peace with England*, a French poem which satirises, in a rather coarse fashion, both Henry III's delusions about his capacity to restore his lands in France and the empty bravado of his magnates. Wright inexplicably linked this poem with Louis IX's

[23] For a wide-ranging discussion of his career and activities, see N. Denholm-Young, *Richard of Cornwall* (New York, 1947). Richard's personality and character are summarised on pp. 153–5.

[24] The song was edited by Carleton Brown in *English Lyrics of the Thirteenth Century* (Oxford, 1932), no. 72, pp. 131–2, 222–4, where previous editions are cited. It is given the confusing title *A Song of Lewes*. It is printed again, with notes, in R.T. Davies, *Medieval English Lyrics: A Critical Anthology* (London, 1963). pp. 55–6, under the title *Against the Barons' Enemies*.

'arbitration' between the English king and his barons in the Mise of Amiens of January 1264. In fact, as George Prothero pointed out, 'nothing in the song agrees with this hypothesis'. The song is about conquest not mediation, and it would have been totally out of place after the kings had come to terms in the Treaty of Paris, published on 4 December 1259. On the other hand, Prothero's attempt to link it with Henry III's campaign of 1242 is also unconvincing in that it involves treating its reference to the king's son, Edward 'of the flaxen hair', three years old in 1242, as 'chivaler, hardouin et honest', as a 'satirical exaggeration of his father's pride in him'.[25] Edward was knighted in Gascony in October 1254, and it may be that the poem was composed about that time. However, it is probable that the poem does not reflect any specific debate at the English court but is a more general satire on the pretensions of the English. It is interesting to note that Simon de Montfort is shown as out of step with the king's other advisers, explicitly in not denigrating the military capacity of the French.

Two other songs reflect the course of the reform movement. The joyous and highly partisan *Song of the Barons*, which is unfortunately incomplete,

---

[25] Prothero, *The Life of Simon de Montfort*, pp. 55–6.

belongs to 1263, almost certainly to the summer, after the return of Simon de Montfort to England in April and the plundering of the properties of the enemies of reform, to which the song refers.[26] The plaintive *Song upon the Division among the Barons*, on the other hand, with its particular castigation of the earls of Gloucester and of Norfolk, for their desertion of the cause and its continued, defiant, belief in Simon de Montfort and his dwindling number of supporters, belongs to the months before Simon's death at the battle of Evesham on 4 August 1265.[27]

Nor were these the only political poems produced during these years. A badly burned Cottonian manuscript, not noticed by Wright, contains, in addition to a chronicle written at Ramsey Abbey dealing with the barons' wars, a series of contemporary verses. They include a poem on the events of 1258 which speaks both of the famine and of the Provisions of Oxford, an attack on Louis IX for his verdict in favour of the king in the Mise of Amiens, and an account of the causes of the conflict. A longer but incomplete poem deals with the battles of Lewes and Evesham

[26] It is re-edited in Aspin, *Anglo-Norman Political Songs*, pp. 12–23.

[27] The poem is contained in Rishanger's chronicle (J.O. Halliwell, *The Chronicle of William de Rishanger of the Barons' Wars*, Camden Society Old Series, no. 15 (1840), pp. 18–20).

Meanwhile, the poems celebrating Edward's victories had introduced a note of strident patriotism, an extension perhaps of the anti-alien feeling which had figured so strongly during the Montfortian era.[37] It is present in the short poem on the deposition of the Scottish king, John Balliol, in 1296. The author of the rather prolix and ponderous *Song on the Scottish Wars*, writing after Edward's victory at Falkirk in 1298, first of all calls upon God to repress the power of the French, Scots and Welsh and to give victory to the English against their enemies and then proceeds to chronicle the iniquities of the Scots, those 'kilted people, numerous and savage', that 'barbarous, brutal and foolish race'.[38] The same triumphal spirit and the same anti-Scottish (and for that matter anti-Welsh) feeling are present in the contemporary chronicle of Pierre de Langtoft. They are present in the author's expressed views and style of narration but also, quite strikingly, in those songs – purporting to be soldiers' songs – which he skilfully integrates into his text.[39] As the

[37] For national sentiment at this time see Thorlac Turville-Petre, 'The "Nation" in English Writings of the Early Fourteenth Century', in Nicholas Rogers (ed.), *England in the Fourteenth Century* (Stamford, 1993), pp. 128–39, and the same author's forthcoming book, *Ingland the Nacion*.

[38] For these poems see Rigg, *Anglo-Latin Literature*, pp. 228–9, 374. The poem on the Scottish wars is of different lengths in different manuscripts, and one version seems to have been adapted to Edward III.

author of the *Song on the Scottish Wars* puts it, with
a king like Edward, 'flower of the world', the
enemies of the English had reason indeed to fear.
The same sentiment is expressed in the triumphant
poem on the execution of the traitor, Sir Simon
Fraser, in 1306, although perhaps with somewhat
less conviction.[40] To the Scot the poet offers the
following resounding advice:

> 'hang up thyn hachet and thi knyf
> Whil him lasteth the lyf
> with the long shonkes' ...

Not all opinion on Edward I, however, had been so
adulatory. Langtoft himself, for example, came to
see the king's failings more clearly as his reign
drew to a close, comparing him adversely in many
important respects with the model of kingship,

---

[39] In fact, it seems that 'Langtoft wrote these taunts in tail-rhyme stanzas in
order to distinguish them from the dignified alexandrines of the body of the
chronicle, and he composed some lines in English in order to lend the songs an air
of authenticity' (Thorlac Turville-Petre, 'Politics and Poetry in the Early
Fourteenth Century: The Case of Robert Manning's *Chronicle*', *Review of English
Studies*, n.s., 39 (1988), 8–9). For a critical edition of the text see Jean Claude
Thiolier (ed.), *Pierre de Langtoft: le règne d'Edouard I* (Créteil, 1989).

[40] The poem is re-edited by Robbins in *Historical Poems*, no. 4, pp. 14–21,
252–6, together with the *Song on the Flemish Insurrection* and the *Elegy on the
Death of Edward I* (nos. 3–5, pp. 9–24, 250–8). The latter is also no. 26 (pp. 91–4)
in R.T. Davies (ed.), *Medieval English Lyrics: A Critical Anthology* (London,
1963). Edward's hanging of the supporters of the newly crowned Robert Bruce is
also celebrated in a biblical parody entitled *Lectio actuum Scotorum*. See Rigg,
Anglo-Latin Literature, p. 229.

Arthur. Wykes was critical of his extravagance and, for financial reasons, of his expulsion of the Jews.[41] As we shall see, the poems of social protest give a rather different picture of Edwardian England. Moreover, the poem which Wright entitles *On the King's Breaking his Confirmation of Magna Carta* undoubtedly belongs to Edward's last years, at least in its original form.[42] The version printed by Wright from the Auchinleck manuscript is an amalgamation of this poem with a Middle English rendering of the Latin *Sayings of the Four Philosophers*.[43] But this version omits the second half of the second and third stanzas and makes significant alterations to three other lines. There are then four lines which are only found in the Auchinleck version. They provide a link with the sayings of the wise men which follow and may not, therefore, have formed part of the original. The consequence of the alterations, and no doubt the intention, was to remove the topical allusions

[41] For contemporary views of Edward see Michael Prestwich, *Edward I* (London, 1988), pp. 3, 559–60.

[42] For what follows see Aspin, *Anglo-Norman Political Songs*, pp. 56–66, where the earlier version is edited together with the relevant portion of the Auchinleck text. The former is found in Cambridge, St. John's College MS 112, a manuscript which belonged in the fourteenth century to Durham Priory.

[43] For the mechanics of how this was done see V.J. Scattergood, 'Political Context, Date and Composition of *The Sayings of the Four Philosophers*,' *Medium Aevum*, 37 (1968), 157–65, which also lists editions, and S. Wenzel, *Preachers, Poets and the Early English Lyric* (Princeton, 1986), pp. 185–9.

which would have been of less interest to a later
audience. It is precisely these allusions, of course,
which give us the political context of the poem.
The original opening referred to papal inconstancy
and to 'Merewale', vicar of God, who agreed to the
specific act of undoing alluded to in the poem. The
latter has been taken to be Henry Woodlock of
Marwell, who became bishop of Winchester in
January 1305, although why he should have been
singled out is not at all clear. On 29 December 1305
the pope absolved Edward I from his political
concessions of 1297–1301, an absolution which was
published at St Paul's in June 1306. In May 1306
the king issued his Forest Ordinance which went
back on his undertaking of 1297. This was symptomatic of the king's attitude in these years and a
matter of considerable current concern.[44] The original poem, then, belongs to the years 1305–6. In
the Auchinleck version it becomes a more general
statement on the condition of the land, albeit a
well-crafted one. Although this could well belong
to the reign of Edward II, the grounds for

---

[44] See H. Rothwell, 'Edward I and the Struggle for the Charters, 1297–1305',
in R.W. Hunt, W.A. Pantin and R.W. Southern (eds.), *Studies in Medieval History
presented to F.M. Powicke* (Oxford, 1948), pp. 319–32, and Prestwich, *Edward I*, ch.
19. Another complication is that the original poem is entitled *De Provisione
Oxonie*, a reference to the Provisions of Oxford of the baronial reform programme
of 1258–9.

connecting it as Wright did with the king's specific failure to abide by the Ordinances in 1311 are not particularly strong.

The political poems from the reign of Edward II are, in fact, concentrated on the events of a few years. There are two poems of exaltation (in fact, parodies of hymns) on the execution of the king's favourite Piers Gaveston in 1312,[45] and a sombre poem on the battle of Bannockburn (23–4 June 1314).[46] In reality, the latter is largely a lament on the death of the earl of Gloucester, and the poet makes his death, and the supposed treachery which caused it, symptomatic of the state of the realm.[47] Complaint about the contemporary level

---

[45] The hymns are by Venantius Fortunatus. There is another parody of Venantius in the *Office of Thomas of Lancaster*. See Rigg, *Anglo-Latin Literature*, pp. 243–4, 376. For the latest accounts of Gaveston's career in England, see J.S. Hamilton, *Piers Gaveston, Earl of Cornwall 1307–1312: Politics and Patronage in the Reign of Edward II* (Detroit, 1988) and Pierre Chaplais, *Piers Gaveston: Edward II's Adoptive Brother* (Oxford, 1994).

[46] Not, of course, 1313 as given by Wright (below, p. 261). The Scottish victory was also celebrated in verse by Robert Baston, the Carmelite friar whom Edward II took with him in anticipation of victory and whom Bruce pressed into service, and by an anonymous Scots poet. See Rigg, *Anglo-Latin Literature*, pp. 244–5, 376. The texts of the poems are in W. Goodall (ed.), *Joannis de Fordun Scotichronicon cum supplementis et continuatione Walteri Boweri*, 2 vols. (Edinburgh, 1759), ii. 250–1, 262–7, and in N.F. Shead, Wendy B. Stevenson and D.E.R. Watt (eds.), *Scotichronicon by Walter Bower* (Aberdeen, 1991), vi. 367–76. Baston's poem was originally longer. Forty-three missing lines supplied from an additional fragment are printed in W.D. Macray, 'Rober Baston's Poem on the Battle of Bannockburn', *English Historical Review*, 19 (1904), 507–8.

[47] For an account of the battle of Bannockburn, see G.W.S. Barrow, *Robert Bruce* (London, 1965), pp. 290–332. The Bartholomew who is said to have deserted Gloucester on the battlefield seems to have been Sir Bartholomew de Badlesmere. See M. Prestwich, *The Three Edwards* (London, 1981), pp. 54–5.

of morality is, indeed, an undercurrent throughout these poems. It is present, even, in the one piece from the reign of Edward II which is out of line with the rest, both subject-wise and chronologically: the *Office of St Thomas of Lancaster*, which seeks his veneration as a martyr and as a champion of right. He 'fought for the law of England's liberty'.[48] His career, in some respects, paralleled that of Simon de Montfort, and if the comparison seems to us to be unjustified there can be no doubt that many contemporaries felt otherwise. Thomas appeared to stand by the Ordinances in the same steadfast manner as Simon had stood by the Provisions of Oxford.[49] The cult of Thomas of Lancaster was spontaneous, and it proved remarkably enduring, encouraged by high aristocratic, and later royal, patronage.[50] His death had been

[48] For a discussion of the *Office* see C. Page, 'The Rhymed Office for St. Thomas of Lancaster: Poetry, Politics and Liturgy in Fourteenth-Century England', *Leeds Studies in English*, 14 (1983), 135–6. Although the poems are without music in the manuscript, their melodies are recoverable in most cases. The incipits refer the singer to chants already known. As Page points out, their use may not have been solely liturgical. They could conceivably have been used quite literally as political songs. Similarly, the poems on the death of Gaveston were doubtless intended to share the melodies of the hymns by Fortunatus which they parodied.

[49] For his career see J.R. Maddicott, *Thomas of Lancaster* (Oxford, 1970). His contemporary reputation and the comparison with Simon de Montfort are discussed on pages 318–34.

[50] For a comparison between the cults of Simon de Montfort and Thomas of Lancaster see Simon Walker's wide-ranging discussion of political saints in England (above, note 34), where detailed references to the respective geography and chronology of the cults may be found.

brought about, in part at least, by an act of treachery. The treachery of Sir Robert Holland, which helped to bring about the earl's defeat at the battle of Boroughbridge, is more certain and better documented than the circumstances surrounding the death of the gallant but incautious Gloucester at Bannockburn.[51]

This undercurrent of moral condemnation links the political songs with the venality satire which was so characteristic of the age. Some of these satires were of a general nature, others attacked more specific institutions, social groups or vices. Wright included seven items of the former type under the title *Song on the Times*, or in one case *Poem on the Evil Times*. The three earliest of these are in Latin. By their very nature, being generalised complaint about the moral state of the world, they are difficult to date with any precision. The first, which Wright calls *Invectio contra avaritiam*, is an attack upon Rome and the pecuniary nature of its activities. The line of opposition is the

---

[51] J.R. Maddicott, 'Thomas of Lancaster and Sir Robert Holland: A Study in Noble Patronage', *English Historical Review*, 86 (1971). It should be noted that Robbins edits a song, *Summer Sunday*, which he considers, following Carleton Brown, to be a lament on the death of Edward II, composed when 'the memory of his misdeeds had receded'. (*Historical Poems*, no. 38, pp. 98–102, 301–3). Sadly, there is little to support this view. It is re-edited in Turville-Petre, *Alliterative Poetry of the Later Middle Ages*, pp. 140–7, where critical notices will be found. The poem is in Laud 108.

traditional one, and Wright himself seems sceptical
of the view that this was written during the
Interdict and that King John is alluded to in two
different guises in the text. The other two are more
general satires on the prevalence of vice, although
the second, known as *Contra avaros*, speaks of
'Rome lying in the depths of turpitude'. The third
is more secular in tone. After laying into the rich,
it revolves around the activities of four brothers,
the play on whose names sums up the vices of this
world. They belong to the school of the twelfth-
century scholar and poet, Walter de Chatillon, and
are therefore earlier than Wright suggests.[52] By
contrast, Wright's *Song against the Bishops*,
supposedly in the time of Henry III, is actually a
satire on the morals of the upper clergy by Walter
de Chatillon himself.[53]

Moving forward in time, the song on the times

[52] Walter de Chatillon spent some time at the court of Henry II before
returning to France after the murder of Becket. See F.J.E. Raby, *A History of
Secular Latin Poetry*, 2 vols. (2nd. edn, Oxford, 1957), ii. 190–214. For *Contra
averos*, also known from its opening line as *Quam sit lata scelerum et quam longa
tela*, see also Jill Mann, *Chaucer and Medieval Estates Satire*, p. 304, and references
given there. For the poem on the four brothers see Rigg, *Anglo-Latin Literature*,
pp. 234, 374. All three come from the same thirteenth-century manuscript,
Harley MS 978, which also contains the light-hearted and rather delightful *Song
upon the Tailors* as well as the *Song of Lewes*.

[53] It is edited by K. Strecker, *Die Lieder Walters von Chatillon im der
Handschrift 351 von St Omer* (Berlin, 1925), p. 46, and by F.J.E. Raby, *The Oxford
Book of Medieval Verse* (Oxford, 1959), no. 17.

known also, from its opening words, as *Vulneratur karitas* (Charity is Wounded) is found in a collection of legal texts, probably compiled before the Statute of Westminster of 1285. It consists of alternate stanzas of Latin and French. Aspin points out in her edition that the Latin work may have been anterior and the work of a different poet. The rather bitter tone leads her to suggest that it was written during the disturbed years of 1265–7, after the defeat of the Montfortians.[54] Kingsford, similarly, thought it the work of 'some old follower of Simon'.[55] Though not inherently improbable, this is of course pure conjecture.

The English poem which Wright calls a *Song on the Times of Edward I* is, most probably, somewhat later. A date of around *c.* 1308 has been assigned,[56] but the reference to the hobelars (*hoblurs*), the lightly armed horsemen who, the author says, rob the husbandman, points to the 1320s or 1330s, while the manuscript (Harley 913) seems to date from shortly after 1329.[57] This is a subject the

---

[54] Aspin, *Anglo-Norman Political Songs*, pp. 149–56.

[55] Kingsford, *The Song of Lewes*, p. xx.

[56] Kaeuper, *War, Justice and Public Order* pp. 331–2, gives the date as *c.* 1308.

[57] For the ways in which military conscription added to the burdens of the peasantry in this period see J.R. Maddicott, *The English Peasantry and the Demands of the Crown*, Past and Present Supplement No. 1 (Oxford, 1975), pp. 34–45. For the hobelars see also A.E. Prince, 'The Army and Navy', in W.A. Morris, J.R. Strayer and W.H.Dunham (eds.), *The English Government at Work*,

author clearly feels particularly strongly about. The hobelars, he says, should not be buried in church, but thrown out as you would a hound. Essentially a venality satire of the traditional type, the poem contains within it the illustrative fable of the Lion, the Fox and the Ass, rather as the Middle English version of the *Sayings of the Four Philosophers* is appended to the poem *On the King's Breaking of his Confirmation of Magna Carta*.

Contained in the same manuscript is the Latin *Song on the Venality of the Judges* which in fact brings a wide variety of corrupt officials into its purview.[58] An interesting sidelight is provided by the *Song against the Scholastic Studies*.[59] Why study logic, the author asks, with all its tribulations,

---

1327–1336, 3 vols. (Cambridge, Mass., 1940–50), i (1940), 338–40, and Philip Morgan, *War and Society in Medieval Cheshire 1277–1403* (Manchester, 1987), pp. 38–48. For the manuscript see below, note 94.

[58] It is also contained, as Wright points out in his notes, in BL Royal 12 C. xii. This poem may be compared to the Latin *Passio iusticiariorum Anglie* which tells of Edward I's purging of his judges and other officials on his return from Gascony in 1289. See Rigg, *Anglo-Latin Literature*, pp. 235–6, and for the full text P. Lehmann, *Die Parodie im Mittelalter* (2nd edn, Stuttgart, 1963), no. 8, pp. 199–202.

[59] It is edited by K. Strecker in *Studi Medievale*, n.s. 1 (1928), p. 386. See also Raby, *A History of Secular Latin Poetry*, II, p. 208. The latter part of the poem deals, in fact, with the corruption of sheriffs and their clerks. It is translated, as the *Song against Sheriffs*, by Helen Cam in *The Hundreds and the Hundred Rolls* (London, 1930), p. 106. She believed it to be contemporary with the Hundred Rolls of 1274–5.

when one could study the law. The lawyers abound in riches: 'now he goes on horseback who once went on foot'. Let the rich men study the arts. If they get themselves into trouble through being unworldly, they can always turn to the lawyers. A wealthy logician, by contrast, is a rare bird, like a black swan!

Venality satire began with attacks upon the church, generally from the inside, and this long remained a prominent strain. Walter de Chatillon's poem, which Wright called *Song against the Bishops*, is a typical product. Everything in the church, it seems, is for sale. It is from the same manuscript as the *Song of the Church*, which seems to have misled Wright as to its date. This attacks the clerical tenth for which Henry III gained papal agreement following his taking of the cross in 1250 but which was diverted in 1255 to help finance his ambition to put his second son, Edmund, upon the throne of Sicily.[60] The tax, which began to be collected in 1256, caused considerable opposition within the church in England. The manuscript rubric tells us that the song was made in that year 'upon the desolation of the English church'.[61] The

[60] See Powicke, *Henry III and the Lord Edward*, ch. ix.

[61] An updated version of the poem, in Douce MS 137, was produced during the reign of Edward I (in 1291 or just possibly 1276) which speaks of the king's intention to go to Syria. Both are edited in Aspin, *Anglo-Normal Political Songs*, pp. 36–41.

king and the pope, we are told, think of nothing
else but how they can take silver and gold from the
church. The *Song on the Bishops* of the reign of
John similarly attacks the three worldly bishops
who sided with the king in his quarrel with the
pope over the presentation to the see of Canterbury, the quarrel which led to the imposition of the
Interdict. These last are, on one level, political
songs in the narrow sense, but the perennial back-
drop is the worldliness of the church: 'thus lucre
conquers Luke'. *L'Ordre de Bel Ayse*, by contrast, is
a satire specifically on the religious orders. Its
provenance is revealed early on in that the first
order to be mentioned is the peculiarly English
order of the Gilbertines of Sempringham. The
organisation of this order, where men and women
lived in close proximity, allows the author to intro-
duce an emphasis on sexual licence which runs
throughout the poem. Aspin argues for a date
around 1300, although not on particularly strong
grounds. The failure to mention the Templars may
indicate a date after the suppression of that order
in 1312.[62] Ecclesiastical courts are singled out for
criticism in the early fourteenth-century *Satire on
the Consistory Courts* for their overbearing behav-

---

[62] Aspin, *Anglo-Norman Political Songs*, pp. 130–42, where it is re-edited.

iour, graft and hypocrisy in the guardianship of public morals.[63]

One of Wright's songs on the times is patently misnamed. Known in one of its manuscripts as *Proverbia Trifaria*, it is in fact a series of proverbs in couplets. Latin, French and English are mixed throughout. It belongs to the first half of the fourteenth century, before 1340.[64]

And so we came to the last of Wright's seven, the *Poem on the Evil Times of Edward II*, better known as the *Simonie*. This, in the tradition of estates satire, is a comprehensive indictment of society, more so even than *Contra avaros*.[65] It begins and ends with the clergy, since they are held responsible ultimately for the prevalence of sin in others, as well as their own. In this case there can be no doubt of the date. Having painted a depressing picture of the ubiquity of evil in his society, the author looks back across the calamities of recent years as God's action and a warning to mankind. Cold weather and famine were followed by cattle

[63] It is re-edited in Robbins, *Historical Poems*, no. 6, pp. 24–7, 258–9, and in Turville-Petre, *Alliterative Poetry of the Later Middle Ages*, pp. 28–31.

[64] Aspin, *Anglo-Norman Political Songs*, pp. 157–68. The complete text is found in two other manuscripts besides BL Royal 12 C. xii. These are Bodleian Rawlinson A. 273 and Trinity College, Oxford MS 7. For BL Royal 12 C. xii see below, note 107.

[65] Mann, *Chaucer and Medieval Estates Satire*, pp. 3–4, 304, 310. See also Ruth Mohl, *The Three Estates in Medieval and Renaissance Literature* (New York, 1933).

murrain, then by further dearth and by inter-
necine strife. The best blood of the land, he says,
has been shamefully brought to ground. The last
reference is clearly to the battle of Boroughbridge
and to the deaths of Thomas of Lancaster and his
fellows, while the famine recalls the years 1315–17
and the manifold distress of the years immediately
following.[66] Had the king already been overthrown, this too would surely have figured. The
poem was written, therefore, after the battle of
Boroughbridge but whilst Edward II was still on
the throne. Wright published the poem from the
text in the great Auchinleck manuscript.[67] It is
contained in two other manuscripts, *viz.* Peterhouse MS 104, a late fourteenth-century manuscript which also contains the sermons of Master
Ralph Acton, a famous Oxford preacher of the
early fourteenth century, and Bodley MS 48, a religious and literary miscellany of *c.* 1425.[68] The text

---

[66] See, especially, Ian Kershaw, 'The Great Famine and Agrarian Crisis in
England 1315–1322', *Past and Present*, 59 (May 1973); repr. in R.H. Hilton (ed.),
Peasants, Knights and Heretics (Oxford, 1976), pp. 85–132.

[67] See below, note 97.

[68] The Peterhouse version, however, differs considerably from the Auchinleck
text. See J. Wells, *A Manual of the Writings in Middle English, 1050–1400* (New
Haven, 1916; repr. 1930), pp. 231–2. It was published by C. Hardwick in 1849 as
A Poem on the Evil Times of Edward II (Publications of the Percy Society, no. 28,
pp. 1–36). The incomplete text of Bodley 48 is printed by T.W. Ross, 'On the Evil
Times of Edward II: A New Version from MS Bodley 48', *Anglia*, 75 (1957),
177–93. Ross has also edited a composite edition in *Colorado College Studies*, 8

was clearly well known in the fourteenth century, and very probably by both Langland and Chaucer. The poem's importance in terms of literary history is considerable. In its skilful alliteration and its fulsome critique of contemporary social values it points forward to *Piers Plowman*, some forty years later. With its bitter topicality and its sympathy for the poor and oppressed, it is a significant early example of the literature of social protest which grew out of venality satire and which, beginning in this period, became a characteristic feature of the fourteenth-century social and literary scene.[69] Its specificity is sometimes striking. The *Simonie* gives us the price of corn during the great famine as 40s or more per quarter. It tells us also that the situation eased only to worsen once again as it became clear to God that people would not mend their ways.

The *Simonie* has much in common with the more specific poems of social protest of the early to mid

---

(1966). The most recent edition is D. Embree and E. Urquhart (eds.), *þe Simonie*, Middle English Texts, vol. 24 (Heidelberg, 1991). For commentary see, in addition to Ross, Salter, '*Piers Plowman* and *The Simonie*', Turville-Petre, 'The "Nation" in English Writings', and Ordelle G. Hill, *The Manor, the Plowman, and the Shepherd: Agrarian Themes and Imagery in Late Medieval and Early Renaissance English Literature* (Cranbury, New Jersey, 1993), pp. 28–32. See also Maddicott, 'Poems of Social Protest in Early Fourteenth-Century England', pp. 138–40.

[69] See, in particular, Janet Coleman, *English Literature in History 1350–1400: Medieval Readers and Writers*, ch. 3, 'The Literature of Social Protest'.

fourteenth century. One of the most famous of these is the *Outlaw's Song of Trailbaston*.[70] It is a frontal attack, although perhaps a little tongue in cheek, against the operation of the criminal law. The poet claims to have been falsely accused under the articles of trailbaston. He will take himself, he says, to the wood of Belregard, where the jay flies, the nightingale sings and the sparrowhawk hovers, and where there is no falseness and no bad law, and he invites others to do likewise. Two of the justices, we are told, are pious men, but the other two – Spigurnel and Belflour (*recte* Beaufoy) – are men of cruelty. Woe betide them, or indeed the wicked jurors, if they were to fall into his power. He would teach them the game of trailbaston! He has served his king, he says, in Flanders, Scotland and Gascony, and this is his reward. If God does not intervene he believes an insurrection may occur.

The poem has an immediate context. The commissions of trailbaston were a response to the growing problem of disorder in Edwardian England. The word itself was derived from the gangs who 'trailed' around the countryside with 'bastons' or clubs committing felonies and gener-

---

[70] The poem is re-edited, with notes and commentary, by Aspin, *Anglo-Norman Political Songs*, pp. 67–78. There is also translation and a brief but perceptive discussion in R.B. Dobson and J. Taylor (eds.), *Rymes of Robyn Hood: An Introduction to the English Outlaw* (London, 1976), pp. 250–4.

ally subverting justice. The commissions of oyer
and terminer, established under the Ordinance of
Trailbaston which was promulgated in parliament
in the spring of 1305, carried the same name.[71]
Four of the five judges for the ten counties of the
western circuit were those named by the poet.[72]
Since one of these four – Henry Spigurnel – was not
appointed to the renewed commission in February
1307, the poem was clearly written before then but
after April 1305.

From the social historian's point of view the
poem is especially interesting in terms of the development of outlaw literature. It has many features
in common with the mid fourteenth-century *Tale
of Gamelyn* and with the earliest surviving tales of
Robin Hood, those incorporated into the *Gest*
which dates from the end of the fourteenth
century.[73] These common features go beyond a

[71] See Alan Harding, *The Law Courts of Medieval England* (London, 1973), pp.
88–90, and Prestwich, *Edward I*, pp. 284–7. For a more detailed discussion of the
context see A. Harding, 'Early Trailbaston Proceedings from the Lincoln Roll of
1305', in R.F. Hunnisett and J.B. Post (eds.), *Medieval Legal Records* (London,
1978), pp. 144–68.

[72] For some records of the western circuit see R.B. Pugh, *Wiltshire Gaol Delivery
and Trailbaston Trials, 1275–1306*, Wiltshire Record Society, 33 (1978).

[73] For the outlaw literature see, in particular, Maurice Keen, *The Outlaws of
Medieval England* (London, 1961; revised edn. 1977); J.C. Holt, *Robin Hood*
(London, 1982; revised edn. 1989); Dobson and Taylor, *Rymes of Robyn Hood*. The
subject continues to attract scholarly interest. The foreword to the second edition
of Dobson and Taylor, *Rymes of Robyn Hood* (Gloucester, 1989), brings the discussion virtually up to date. For the *Tale of Gamelyn* see Richard Kaeuper, 'An
Historian's Reading of *The Tale of Gamelyn*', *Medium Aevum*, 52 (1983), 51–62.

shared attitude towards outlawry and towards the
greenwood; they include scepticism over the workings of the law itself and a reliance upon, often
violent, self-help. The poem is also important in
terms of contemporary reaction to the trailbaston
commissions themselves. The author is clearly very
informed about legal procedures, and he under-
stands well the combination of individual oral
complaints (*querele*) with the jury of presentment
which characterised the proceedings. As he points
out, the whole process was prone to malicious
accusation. He also echoes the traditional complaint about profiteering by those who administered the law and, especially, about the rapacity of
the judges coming from Westminster.

However, we must be careful not to take the
poet's arguments at face value. That the author
tells us he was a soldier returning from the wars is
significant. As Alan Harding succinctly puts it,
Edward I 'had brought the atmosphere of war into
English society'.[74] Moreover, there is a further
dimension. It is significant that the two justices
whom the author praises – William Martin and
Gilbert de Knovill – were those drawn from the
south-west, while the two he condemns – Spigurnel
and Beaufoy – were those who came from

[74] Harding, *The Law Courts of Medieval England*, p. 90.

outside.[75] Amongst the gentry there was a firm
view that justice in the localities was best administered by local men. There seems every reason to
suppose that the author, who was probably a man
of some local significance – a 'well-informed and
remarkably self-confident member of local
society'[76] – reflects this view. Whether that would
have meant that justice was less partial, given the
gentry's own predilection for violent crime, must
be a matter of considerable doubt. The relationship between central government and local society
on the question of law and order was no simple
matter.

One of the problems in contemporary perception
of royal justice was that it was perceived as a
means of mulcting the provinces. Financial oppression by the central government features in a
number of the poems of protest of the early fourteenth century. The *Song of the Husbandman* is a
harrowing account of the oppressions suffered by
the peasantry.[77] This poet has, in fact, three
sources of complaint: the weather, the lord of the
manor and the extortions of his officials, and the
demands of the Crown and of royal agents. The

---

[75] Aspin, *Anglo-Norman Political Songs*, pp. 68, 77.

[76] Dobson and Taylor, *Rymes of Robyn Hood*, p. 251.

[77] The poem is re-edited by Robbins, *Historical Poems of the Fourteenth and Fifteenth Centuries*, no. 2, pp. 7–9, 49–50.

good years and corn have gone, he tells us, and the
rye rots 'for wickede wederes by brok ant by
brynke'.[78] The lords, he perceives, live well off the
peasants' backs: 'And al is piked of the pore, the
prikyares prude' (and all the pride of the rider is
picked from the poor). He is harried, moreover, by
a whole set of manorial officials, who rob him
mercilessly.[79] Over and above this, however, he is
taxed by the Crown. Every fourth penny must go
to the king. Beadles come with the summons of the
green wax, the means by which the Exchequer
called in its debts. He claims he has to pay ten
times over, presumably because of the extortion
practised by officials. They hunt us, he says, as the
hound does the hare ('me us honteth ase hound
doth the hare'). As a result he has to spend what
little he has saved. But, worse than that, he has to
sell the corn while it lies in the field; even his seed-
corn is sold for the king's silver. As a result his land
lies fallow. Meanwhile his plough oxen have been

---

[78] For the effects of the weather upon living standards in this period see
Christopher Dyer, *Standards of Living in the Later Middle Ages: Social Change in
England c. 1200–1520* (Cambridge. 1989), ch. 10.

[79] The *Song of the Husbandman* may be compared with a Latin poem written
by a canon of Leicester satirising the complaints of the abbey's villeins at
Stoughton and their failed attempt to pursue their claims to freedom in the royal
courts early in the reign of Edward I (R.H. Hilton, 'A Thirteenth-Century Poem
on Disputed Villein Services', in his *Class Conflict and the Crisis of Feudalism*
(London, 1985), pp. 108–13; repr. from *English Historical Review*, 56 (1941), 90–7).

taken. The situation has bred many bold beggars. When he thinks of this condition he could nearly weep ('when y thenk o mi weole wel neh y wepe').

The effects of royal taxation upon the peasantry during this period have been subjected to thorough investigation by J.R. Maddicott.[80] There can be no doubt that the burden of central taxation, coming on top of the peasants' other burdens and problems, could cause considerable distress. Since Edward I had placed the economy on a war footing during the 1290s the burden of taxation had increased dramatically. It was not only a question of the subsidies on moveable goods. Among the other problems was purveyance, the king's prerogative right to purchase compulsorily for his household, which was open to considerable abuse. It was probably for this reason that our poet's cattle were seized, although they could also have been seized as distraint for debt. As regards the consequences of taxation, it may be that the poet was exaggerating for effect. However, instances of all of the evils he mentioned are easily found, more so during the years 1336–41 when the government, financing the early stages of the Hundred Years' War,

---

[80] Maddicott, *The English Peasantry and the Demands of the Crown*. I have drawn liberally upon this work in the discussion. No précis, however, can do justice to either its subtlety or its thoroughness.

reached the peak of its oppression. The state of the
economy during the first half of the fourteenth
century is a matter of contention, but there can be
no doubt that the burden of taxation had a
depressing effect and that this effect was more
strongly felt during the time of Edward III.[81]

The poem has traditionally been dated to
around 1300. However, it is probably later. The
combination of heavy taxation, appalling weather
and general distress suggests the years 1315–17 as
a likely time of composition. There was, in fact,
widespread resistance to royal levies during these
famine years. However, a date of 1340 has been
suggested and this would fit even better with the
level of peasant distress to which the poem refers.[82]
As to the poet, it should not be assumed that he
was a humble man. He portrays himself as a relatively well-to-do tenant, at least before the disaster
which apparently overtook him. I say apparently
because, just as with the outlaw above, we cannot
necessarily assume that the writer is in precisely

[81] For the latest work on the state of the economy see the essays in Bruce M.S.
Campbell (ed.), *Before the Black Death: Studies in the 'Crisis' of the Early Fourteenth
Century* (Manchester, 1989). For the effects of the Crown's actions upon the
economy see especially the essay by W.M. Ormrod, 'The Crown and the English
Economy, *c.* 1290–*c.* 1340'.

[82] T. Stemmler, *Die Englischen Liebesgedichte des MS. Harley 2253* (Bonn, 1962),
pp. 30–4. This date has been accepted by Maddicott ('Poems of Social Protest in
Early Fourteenth-Century England', p. 132).

the situation he describes. He may be there through an intuitive and imaginative leap. Equally, the poem shows some skill in versification and is by no means an uncontrolled outpouring of bitterness. 'Concatenation links the stanzas, and waves of emotion unify the poem, opening in gloom, rising to excited bitterness, receding into general lamentation, and closing in despair.'[83] It was patently not written by an 'unlettered rustic'.[84]

The *Song of the Husbandman* has some themes in common with the contemporary *Song against the King's Taxes*. A learned poem, written in a mixture of French and Latin, this complains that the king's taxes burden the poor not the rich. The subsidy of one-fifteenth is collected year after year so that people need to sell their goods in order to pay it. In the case of both subsidy and wool tax, much of the money collected never reaches the king but remains with the collectors.[85] Like the author of the *Song of Trailbaston* before him, the poet thinks there could be a rising, if only the people had a

[83] Thomas L. Kinney, 'The Temper of Fourteenth-Century English Verse of Complaint', *Annuale Mediaevale*, 7 (1967), 79. See the discussion in Hill, *The Manor, the Plowman, and the Shepherd*, ch. 1.

[84] See Arthur K. Moore, *The Secular Lyric in Middle English* (Lexington, 1951), p. 87.

[85] The same point is made in the *Simonie*.

leader. One of the most interesting features of the poem is its statement that the internal market is depressed through the shortage of money, a phenomenon for which taxation was undoubtedly part cause. Wright thought the poem belonged to the reign of Edward I. Aspin, however, has argued convincingly for the years 1337–40.[86] The reference to the king as a *jeovene bachiler* suggests the young Edward III and tends to rule out the 1290s. The regular collection of a fifteenth fits well with the opening years of the Hundred Years' War. An interesting feature is the argument that the king should not go outside of his kingdom to make war, at least not without the consent of his people, an echo of the Ordinances of 1311 and yet another pointer to the date.

III

Turning now from the specific contexts of individual pieces to general considerations, the first point to note is the recent work on the social history of the languages in use in twelfth- to four-

[86] Aspin, *Anglo-Normal Political Songs*, where the poem is re-edited, pp. 105–15. E.B. Fryde has argued for an even narrower date of 1338–9, in 'Parliament and the French War, 1336–40', in T.A. Sandquist and M.R. Powicke (eds.), *Essays in Medieval History presented to Bertie Wilkinson* (Toronto, 1969), p. 263 n. 71. See also Maddicott, *English Peasantry and the Demands of the Crown*, p. 49.

teenth-century England. Research has shown, in fact, just how complex was the relationship between them. No longer can we talk glibly, as Wright himself could, of 'the clerk (or scholar) with his Latin, the courtier with his Anglo-Norman, and the people with their good old English' (p.63). Latin, the international language of scholarship and learning, was more widely known and used in society across this period, especially in its practical manifestations, than has sometimes been supposed.[87] On the other hand, it is now recognised that by the closing decades of the twelfth century English was already the first language of the descendants of the French-speaking invaders of the eleventh century and that French itself was an acquired language.[88] It continued to be acquired

[87] On this issue see M.B. Parkes, 'The Literacy of the Laity', in D. Daiches and A. Thorlby (eds.), *Literature and Civilization: The Middle Ages* (London, 1973), p. 557; R.V. Turner, 'The Miles Literatus in the Twelfth and Thirteenth Centuries: How Rare a Phenomenon?', *American Historical Review*, 83 (1978), 928–45; and more comprehensively M.T. Clanchy, *From Memory to Written Record: England 1066–1307* (2nd edn, Oxford, 1993), especially ch. 7.

[88] See Ian Short, 'Patrons and Polyglots: French Literature in Twelfth-Century England', in M. Chibnall (ed.), *Anglo-Norman Studies XIV: Proceedings of the Battle Conference 1991* (Woodbridge, 1992), esp. pp. 245–9; the same author's 'On Bilingualism in Anglo-Norman England', *Romance Philology*, 33 (1979–80), 467–79; Clanchy, *From Memory to Written Record*, ch. 6; W. Rothwell, 'The Role of French in Thirteenth-Century England', *Bulletin of the John Rylands Library*, 58 (1976), 445–66. For a more sociolinguistic discussion see R.A. Lodge, 'Language Attitudes and Linguistic Norms in France and England in the Thirteenth Century', in P.R. Coss and S.D. Lloyd (eds.), *Thirteenth Century England IV* (Woodbridge, 1992).

throughout the period covered by this volume and
beyond, not only for reasons of social exclusion –
'For unless a man knows French he is thought of
little account', wrote Robert of Gloucester[89] – but
also because it was used, increasingly from the
middle of the thirteenth century, as a language of
administration. Literature in French verse had
flourished, of course, in the twelfth century and
continued to do so during the thirteenth. At the
end of the twelfth century English was being
employed successfully as a literary medium and its
use was by no means confined to the lower orders.
A century later it was steadily gaining ground as a
literary language. The employment of written
languages was determined by a variety of factors,
including tradition and political and practical
considerations as well as social status.[90] There is
certainly no simple relationship between spoken
and written language. One might write in Latin
but think in French, or compose in French but
think in English. It is true, of course, that there
was a widespread ignorance of French among the
lower orders and there never was a time when the
population as a whole was bilingual. But in the

[89] 'Vor bote a man conne frenss. me telth of him lute': *The Metrical Chronicle of
Robert of Gloucester*, ed. W.A. Wright, 2 vols., Rolls Series, LXXVI (London,
1887), ii. 544, line 742.
[90] Clanchy, *From Memory to Written Record*, p. 223.

sense that all three languages flourished and inter-penetrated, England during this period can prop-erly be said to have been a polyglot society.

What, then, does this mean for our under-standing of the 'political songs'? Literary scholars have often looked for specific audiences for literary works under consideration. Arguably, however, audiences have been imagined too discretely. This was already a fairly sophisticated society and it would seem more profitable to seek to understand the means of dissemination of political songs rather than to try to define their readership too closely. To be sure, some were more learned than others, presupposing a more restricted readership. This is certainly true of the material from Harley 978. This manuscript contains an important collec-tion of Latin goliardic poems, most of which Wright published elsewhere.[91] For the present volume he took three *Songs on the Times*, together with the *Song of Lewes* and the *Song upon the Tailors*.[92] The inclusion of a Calendar which gives the obits of various early thirteenth-century

---

[91] T. Wright (ed.), *The Latin Poems of Walter Mapes*, Camden Society, o.s., XVI (1841).

[92] The manuscript is described by Kingsford, *The Song of Lewes*, pp. vii–xviii. Kingsford also published a further item from the manuscript for the first time, a comic poem entitled *La Besturme* (Appendix III). See also Rigg, *Anglo-Latin Literature*, p. 238.

abbots of Reading suggests that the manuscript was once held in that house.[93] However, it does not follow that a manuscript emanating from a religious house would contain only matter of high moral seriousness. Harley 978, in addition to the above items, a collection of antiphons, moral percepts and letters, contained also medical recipes, the delightful song *Sumer is i-cumen in*, and the *Fables* and the *Lays* of Marie de France. There is also a poem on the keeping of hawks. The relationship between monasteries and lay society was often close and there can be no doubt that monastic libraries were used as a repository and a source for the borrowing of books. Nevertheless, their role can be exaggerated. There used to be a widely held presumption in favour of monastic ownership and production of manuscripts containing literary works, at least as far as the thirteenth and early fourteenth centuries are concerned. Those that could not be assigned to the monks were consigned to the friars, the so-called 'friars' miscellanies'. In fact, no known thirteenth-century manuscripts with vernacular texts can be shown to be of mendicant origin.[94] Moreover, lay

---

[93] Kingsford, *The Song of Lewes*, pp. viii–ix.

[94] See John Frankis, 'The Social Context of Vernacular Writing in Thirteenth-Century England: The Evidence of the Manuscripts', in P.R. Coss and S.D. Lloyd (eds.), *Thirteenth-Century England I* (Woodbridge, 1986), pp. 179–84. By contrast,

involvement in the production and circulation of manuscripts is now known to have been more direct than used to be supposed.

Wright drew no less than twelve of the items contained in this volume from Harley 2253. This great trilingual miscellany contains *inter alia* religious pieces in verse and prose, saints' lives and fabliaux as well as the political songs and the lyrics for which it is especially famous.[95] It is now known to have been written by a scribe with strong contacts in and around Ludlow rather than specifically in the household of the bishop of Hereford as was once thought.[96] It was compiled (or at least completed) during the early 1340s, as the redating of both the *Song of the Husbandman* and the *Song*

Harley 913, from which Wright took the *Song on the Venality of the Judges*, the *Song of Nego* and a *Song on the Times of Edward I*, appears to have been a genuine Franciscan miscellany from the early 1330s. It was put together, at least in its final form, at the Franciscan house at Waterford. For a description of Harley 913, and a discussion of its provenance, see Angela M. and Peter J. Lucas, 'Reconstructing a Disarranged Manuscript: The Case of MS Harley 913, a Medieval Hiberno-English Miscellany', *Scriptorium*, 44 (1990), 286–99. See also M. Benskin, 'The Hands of the Kildare Poems Manuscript', *Irish University Review*, 20 (1990), 163–93, and Rigg, *Anglo-Latin Literature*, p. 307.

[95] For the complete contents see the introduction to the facsimile edition by N.R. Ker (*Facsimile of British Museum MS. Harley 2253*, Early English Text Society, o.s., no. 255, 1965), where editions are noted. Most of the English poems are to be found in K. Böddeker (ed.), *Altenglische Dichtungen des MS. Harley 2253* (Berlin, 1878). G.L. Brook (ed.), *The Harley Lyrics: The Middle English Lyrics of MS Harley 2253* (Manchester, 1956) does not contain political songs.

[96] See Carter Revard, 'Richard Hurd and MS. Harley 2253', *Notes and Queries*, 224 (1979), 199–202.

against the King's Taxes makes clear. The contents
of Harley 2253 are an indication in themselves that
in terms of audience and transmission the political
songs cannot be studied in isolation. By contrast,
only two pieces – the *Simonie* and the poem *On the
King's Breaking his Confirmation of Magna Carta* –
come from the other great trilingual literary
manuscript of this period, the Auchinleck. Equally
varied in content, the Auchinleck is particularly
famous for its collection of romances and for its
provenance. It was produced by a London 'bookshop' of some description, although probably not
in a single workshop, during the early years of
Edward III.[97] Some of the works were certainly in
circulation prior to the manuscript and, no doubt,
prior to the activities of the bookshop. Not all of
them originated in London, any more than all of
the contents of Harley 2253 originated in the West

---

[97] For the detailed discussion of the contents see the facsimile edition: D.
Pearsall and I. Cunningham (eds.), *The Auchinleck Manuscript* (London, 1977).
The precise nature of this bookshop, first identified by L.H. Loomis ('The
Auchinleck Manuscript and a Possible London Bookshop of 1330–40',
Publications of the Modern Language Association of America, 57 (1942)) is still a
matter of scholarly debate. See A.I. Doyle and M.B. Parkes, 'The Production of
Copies of the *Canterbury Tales* and the *Confessio Amantis* in the Early Fifteenth
Century', in M.B. Parkes and Andrew G. Watson (eds.), *Medieval Scribes,
Manuscripts and Libraries: Essays Presented to N.R. Ker* (London, 1978), pp.
163–210, esp. pp. 192–203, and T.A. Shonk, 'A Study of the Auchinleck
Manuscript: Bookmen and Bookmaking in the Early Fourteenth Century',
Speculum, 60 (1985), 71–91.

of England. Another manuscript which has a bearing on the issues raised here is Bodleian Library Digby 86. Another trilingual manuscript with a wide variety of content, religious and secular, it was one of those manuscripts which used to be thought of as friars' miscellanies. In fact, it was produced in or shortly before 1282 in the diocese of Worcester. It was owned successively by two local gentry families whose names appear in its marginalia and it was almost certainly produced for the earlier of them. It has items in common with Harley 2253 and Auchinleck, although not, in fact, any of the political songs.[98] It is another indication of the circulation of the content of these manuscripts. It also points to the role of the gentry in the transmission of such material; families loaned manuscripts and copied items from one another.[99] In other words, whilst religious houses undoubtedly played an important role in copying and preserving texts, much of the transmission of literature took place directly within secular society; we can say this even more emphatically if we understand by it both the laity and the secular clergy.

[98] B.D.H. Miller, 'The Early History of Bodleian MS Digby 86', *Annuale Medievale*, 2 (1961), 23–55.

[99] On this issue see P.R. Coss, 'Aspects of Cultural Diffusion in Medieval England: The Early Romances, Local Society and Robin Hood', *Past and Present*, 108 (August 1985), 35–79.

Without close interrogation, surviving manuscripts can sometimes give a distorted picture of the circulation of texts. Harley 2253 and Auchinleck were very probably unusual products in their own day. Moreover, manuscripts as we have them now are not necessarily in their original form. A medieval reader could assemble or rearrange 'booklets' into a composite volume. These booklets could circulate independently and may well have been produced commercially in some instances.[100] Books were expensive to produce and to own, and relatively few lay persons could have afforded them.[101] Songs and similar material must have circulated for the most part in less robust and enduring forms. One of these was loose parchment rolls. On Easter Day 1282 two rolls of songs, valued at 6d and 2d respectively, were stolen from a woman on the king's highway near her home at Wereham, Norfolk, together with a missal worth 20s and a manual worth 6s 8d, as she claimed.[102] Another clue is provided by the author of the

[100] See, in particular, P.R. Robinson, 'The "Booklet": A Self-Contained Unit in Composite Manuscripts', in A. Gruys and J.P. Gambert (eds.), *Codicologia 3, Essais typologiques* (Leiden, 1980), pp. 46–69. Harley 913, for example, was constructed from five booklets. See above, note 94.

[101] This question is reviewed by R. Malcom Hogg in 'Some Thirteenth-Century English Book Prices', in P.R. Coss and S.D. Lloyd (eds.), *Thirteenth Century England V* (Woodbridge, 1995), pp. 179–94.

[102] Cam, *The Hundreds and the Hundred Rolls*, p. 182.

Outlaw's Song of Trailbaston who claims, in his final
stanza, to have written his poem on a piece of
parchment and to have thrown it onto the highway
for others to find it. Of course, we should not take
this literally. The point is that such things will
have circulated singly. The unique, and incomplete,
copy of the *Song of the Barons* is on a parchment
roll from the late thirteenth or early fourteenth
century.[103] In this way they might come to be
copied onto the fly-leaves of manuscripts, as for
example was a Latin poem on the death of Simon
de Montfort.[104] This also helps to explain how such
items came to appear in so-called commonplace
books, essentially collections of pieces which particularly interested a compiler. The *Song against
the King's Taxes* from Harley 2253, for example, is
also found in a commonplace book which comes
from the minor Cistercian monastery of Whalley in
Lancashire. The book is largely designed to preserve items of a practical nature, such as deeds,

---

[103] BL Add. MS 23986. On the dorse is a Middle English poem entitled
Interludium de clerico et puella. The manuscript has been missing, however, since
October 1971. The hand of the *Song* has been dated to the late thirteenth century
and that of the *Interludium* to the early fourteenth. The dialect of the latter is
apparently that of northern Yorkshire or south Lincolnshire. As the manuscript
belonged to a Lincolnshire family in Wright's day, it 'may not have strayed very
far from its point of origin' (Andrew Taylor, 'The Myth of the Minstrel
Manuscript', *Speculum*, 66 (1991), 68–9). See also Aspin, *Anglo-Norman Political
Songs*, pp. 12–13, and Clanchy, *From Memory to Written Record*, p. 143.

[104] See above p. xxv.

writs to the local sheriff, tables of weights and
measures as well as extracts from statutes and plea
rolls, most of which date from the 1330s or early
1340s.[105] Similarly, two of the three manuscripts
which contain the trilingual *Proverbia Trifaria*
have been described as 'scrapbooks',[106] although
the term may be a little misleading. One of them
contains the romance *Fouke Fitz Warin* and the
Short English Metrical Chronicle.[107] There can be
little doubt, then, that some of these items circulated widely. As we have seen, the *Song against the
King's Taxes* is found in two very different manuscripts from different areas of the country very
shortly after its production. The compiler of a
great compendium manuscript like Harley 2253
probably drew his material from a range of
sources. By the early fourteenth century some
items were already being disseminated from
London. The poem *On the King's Breaking his
Confirmation of Magna Carta*, which found its way
into the Auchinleck Manuscript, is also found in its
original version dating from 1305–6 in a manu-

---

[105] Maddicott, 'Poems of Social Protest in Early Fourteenth-Century England',
pp. 137–8.

[106] By Aspin, *Anglo-Norman Political Songs*, p. 157.

[107] This is BL Royal 12 C. xii, which was written in part by the same scribe as
Harley 2253. See Carter Revard, 'Three More Holographs in the Hand of the
Scribe of MS Harley 2253 in Shrewsbury', *Notes and Queries*, n.s., 28 (1981),
199–200. It also contains the *Office of Thomas of Lancaster*.

script which belonged in the fourteenth century to Durham Priory.[108] Linguistic evidence suggests that the poem originated in the south.

There is every reason to suppose, therefore, that many of these pieces circulated widely and that they reached a fairly wide audience. Whether that means they should be regarded as popular, in any real sense of the term, however, seems doubtful. The *Song against the King of Almaigne*, which was clearly intended to be sung, may have been exceptional and reached an unusually wide audience. For the most part, however, the political songs as we have them are for a literate and quite sophisticated audience. Thus, Aspin's analogy with the popular press of today is somewhat misleading, or if it is to be sustained would presuppose the *Guardian* rather than the tabloid press. Perhaps we should call them middle brow. They were appreciated, no doubt, by a broad spectrum of society, encompassing members of the gentry, clerics and the varieties of *hommes d'affaires*, those who could be expected to comprehend French, English and at least some Latin.

This is not to deny that the relationship of these works to popular, and indeed to oral, culture is a complex one. They seem to draw upon a whole

[108] See above note 42.

vocabulary of saws, proverbs and the like which is largely irrecoverable by us and which helps to explain some of their elusive quality. These, together with contemporary perceptions and topical allusions, add to the obscurities of language which sometimes make the poems difficult for the modern reader to understand fully.

What, then, of the authors? As has universally been supposed, most of them were very probably clerics of one sort or another. Having said that, there is no good reason why any of them should not have been a layman; a literate knight, for example, like Walter de Bibbesworth the mid thirteenth-century author of the *Tretiz de Langage*, designed to improve a lady's French, or a lay lawyer, or indeed any other sort of non-clerical *gentil homme*. Such men, clerics or laymen, exhibited not only a versatility but also, one supposes, a sheer enjoyment in their use of the available languages; they were indeed 'lords of language' in Michael Clanchy's happy phrase.[109]

There is another medium, however, through which this material may have reached a wider audience, and that is by means of the sermon. Owst, years ago, pointed to the parallel between the protest songs and both the content and

---

[109] Clanchy, *From Memory to Written Record*, p. 223.

metrical form of many fourteenth-century sermons, an argument which has been taken up
recently by John Maddicott.[110] Indeed, he makes
the very plausible suggestion that preachers may
themselves have been among the authors of early
fourteenth-century poems of social protest.[111] It
was probably more by this means than any other
that some of this material retained a presence in
oral culture. If the reissue of Thomas Wright's
Political Songs helps to stimulate further discussion
of problems such as these, then it will have served
its purpose.

PETER COSS

---

[110] G.R. Owst, *Literature and Pulpit in Medieval England* (2nd edn, Oxford,
1961), pp. 213–16; Maddicott, 'Poems of Social Protest in Early Fourteenth-
Century England', pp. 134–6.

[111] Maddicott, 'Poems of Social Protest in Early Fourteenth-Century
England', pp. 134–6. Indeed, he has two names to suggest. One is Master Ralph
Acton, a famous Oxford preacher whose sermons are found in a manuscript which
also contains the *Simonie*, and William of Pagula, the known author who wrote
the *Speculum Regis Edwardii Tertii*, a tract condemning the evils of royal
purveyance, around 1331.

THOMAS WRIGHT'S
PREFACE TO
1839 EDITION

Few historical documents are more interesting or important than the contemporary songs in which the political partizan satirised his opponents and stirred up the courage of his friends, or in which the people exulted over victories gained abroad against their enemies or at home against their oppressors, or lamented over evil counsels and national calamities. Yet, though a few specimens have been published from time to time in collections of miscellaneous poetry, such as those of Percy and Ritson, and have never failed to attract attention, no book specially devoted to ancient Political Songs has yet appeared.

The quantity of such productions has generally varied with the character of the age. They were frequent from a very early period in other countries of Europe, as well as England. It would be easy to produce proofs that in our island they were very numerous in Saxon times, – a few specimens, indeed, have escaped that destruction which visits the monuments of popular and temporary feeling before all others; and for years after the Norman conquest the oppressed people continued to sing the songs of former days at their rustic festivals or amid their everyday labours. As the feelings which caused them to be remembered died away gradually before the weight of a new political system, a new class of songs also arose. From the Conquest to the end of the twelfth century, the political songs of the Anglo-Normans were in a great measure confined, as far as we can judge from the few specimens that are left, to laudatory poems in Latin, or to funereal elegies on princes and great people. Yet we can hardly doubt that, with the turbulent barons of these troublous times, the harp of the minstrel must have resounded frequently to subjects of greater present excitement.

With the beginning of the thirteenth century opened a new scene of political contention. It is amid the civil commotions of the reign of John, that our manuscripts first present traces of the songs in which popular opinion sought and found a vent, at the same time that the commons of England began to assume a more active part on the stage of history. The following reign was a period of constant excitement. The weak government of Henry the Third permitted every party to give free utterance to their opinions and intentions, and the songs of this period are remarkably bold and pointed. These effusions are interesting in other points of view besides their connexion with historical events; they illustrate in a remarkable manner the history of our language; they show us how Latin, Anglo-Norman, and English were successively the favourite instruments by which the thoughts of our ancestors were expressed; and collaterally they show us how the clerk (or scholar) with his Latin, the courtier with his Anglo-Norman, and the people with their good old English, came forward in turns upon the scene. In our Songs we see that, during the earlier part of the reign of the third Henry, the satirical pieces which inveighed against the corruptions of the state and demanded so loudly their amendment, are all in Latin, which is as much as to say that they came from the scholastic part of the people, or those who had been bred in the universities, then no small or unimportant part of the community. They seem to have led the way as bold reformers; and the refectory of the monastery not less than the baronial hall rang frequently with the outbursts of popular feeling. The remarkable and highly interesting declaration of the objects and sentiments of the Barons, which was published after the battle of Lewes, is written in Latin. Amid the Barons' wars was composed the first political song in English

that has yet been found. It is remarkable that all
the songs of this period which we know, whether in
Latin, Anglo-Norman, or English, are on the
popular side of the dispute – all with one accord
agree in their praise and support of the great
Simon de Montfort.

The circumstance of our finding no songs in
English of an earlier date does not, however, prove
that they did not exist. On the contrary, it is prob-
able that they were equally abundant with the
others; but the Latin songs belonged to that
particular party who were most in the habit of
committing their productions to writing, and
whose manuscripts also were longest preserved. It
is probable that a very small portion of the earlier
English popular poetry was ever entered in books –
it was preserved in people's memory until, gradually forgotten, it ceased entirely to exist except in
a few instances, where, years after the period at
which it was first composed, it was committed to
writing by those who heard it recited. The English
song on the battle of Lewes is found in a manuscript written in the reign of Edward II.; when,
perhaps, the similar character of the time led
people to give retrospective looks to the doings of
Earl Simon and his confederate barons. They were
sometimes written on small rolls of parchment, for

the convenience of the minstrel, who thus carried them about with him from house to house, and chanted them at the will of his entertainers. From these rolls and loose scraps they were occasionally copied into books, long after they had ceased to possess any popular interest, by some "clerk" who loved to collect antiquities; for in those days, too, there were antiquaries. One of the Anglo-Norman songs printed in this collection is taken from the original roll; and the Latin songs on the death of Peter de Gaveston were found in a manuscript written in the fifteenth century.

The constant wars of the reign of Edward I. – the patriotic hatred of Frenchman and Scot, which then ran at the highest – furnished the ground-work of many a national song during the latter years of the thirteenth century and the first years of the fourteenth. The English song becomes at this period much more frequent, though many were still written in Latin. Popular discontent continued to be expressed equally in Latin, Anglo-Norman (a language the influence of which was now fast declining), and English. In the "Song against the King's Taxes," composed towards the end of the thirteenth century, we have the first specimen of that kind of song wherein each line began in one language and ended in another; and

which, generally written in hexameters, seems to
have been extremely popular during the two
centuries following. One song, in the reign of
Edward II. presents in alternate succession all the
three languages which were then in use. The political songs during this last-mentioned reign are not
very numerous, but they are by no means devoid of
interest.

It was the Editor's original intention to continue
the series of songs in the present volume to the
deposition of Richard II. But, having adopted the
suggestion of giving a translation, with the hope of
making them more popular, and finding that in
consequence the volume was likely to extend to a
much greater length than was at first calculated
upon, it has been thought advisable to close the
present collection with another convenient historical period, the deposition of his grandfather
Edward II.; and it is his intention at some future
period to form a second volume, which will be
continued to the fall of the house of York in the
person of the crook-backed Richard III.

The wars of Edward III. produced many songs,
both in Latin and in English, as did also the troubles which disturbed the reign of his successor.
With the end of the reign of Edward II. however,
we begin to lose sight of the Anglo-Norman

language, which we shall not again meet with in these popular effusions. During the fifteenth century political songs are less numerous and also less spirited. With it we are introduced to a dark period of literature and science. It was the interval between the breaking up of the old system, and the formation of the new one which was to be built upon its ruins. When we come to the wars of the Roses, so fatal to the English nobility and gentry, the page even of history becomes less interesting, because it is less intellectual: – the great mental workings which had influenced so much the political movements of the thirteenth and fourteenth centuries, were replaced by the reckless and short-sighted bitterness of personal hatred, and the demoralizing agency of mere animal force. As it had required a long age of barbarism and ignorance to sweep away even the latest remnants of ancient pagan splendour, before the site was fit to build up the beautiful edifice of Christian civilization; so it seemed as though another, though a shorter and comparatively less profound, age of barbarism was required to turn men's minds from the defective learning of the schools, and the imperfect literature to which they had been habituated, and to break down old prejudices and privileges, which were but impediments in the way of

the new system that came in with the Reformation.

The nature of the following collection of Songs
requires little explanation. They have been
brought together from scattered sources. It was
the Editor's desire to make it as complete as
possible; but further research will probably bring
to light other songs of no less interest, and these, if
they become sufficiently numerous, he hopes will
be collected together as a supplement to the
present volume. He has also omitted a few Anglo-
Irish songs, because he expects they will, ere long,
receive more justice than he is capable of doing
them, at the hands of Mr. Crofton Croker. It is
hoped that the texts will be found as correct as the
manuscripts would allow. The translation is offered
with diffidence, and requires many excuses; the
variety of languages and dialects in which they are
written, their dissimilarity in style of composition,
the cramped constructions which were rendered
necessary in the Latin Songs to allow the multi-
plicity of rhymes, the allusions which cannot now
be easily explained, and above all, the numerous
corruptions which have been introduced by the
scribes from whose hands the different manuscripts came (for the greater part of these songs
have been printed from unique copies), are the

cause of so many difficulties, that in some instances little more has been done than to guess at the writer's meaning. The translation is in general as literal as possible – the Anglo-Norman, French, and English Songs are rendered line for line; but the Editor is almost inclined to regret that he did not give a freer version.

The Appendix consists of extracts from the in-edited metrical chronicle of Peter Langtoft, which are here introduced, because they contain frag-ments in what was then termed *"ryme cowée,"* or tailed rhyme, which are apparently taken from songs of the time. The text is printed from a tran-script made by the Editor several years ago; and it contains many lines of the English songs which are not found in the manuscripts preserved at the British Museum. The Editor introduces these extracts the more willingly, as it is not very prob-able that the Chronicle itself will be published at present. As a monument of the Anglo-Norman language, it is far inferior to many others that remain still inedited; and, as a historical docu-ment, it is already well known through the English version of Robert de Brunne, which was printed by Thomas Hearne. The collations have been made chiefly with a philological view; the comparison of the different manuscripts shows us how entirely the grammatical forms of the Anglo-Norman language were at this time neglected. To these extracts, the Editor has been enabled to add a very curious English poem from the Auchinleck MS. at Edinburgh, by the extreme kindness of David Laing, Esq., to whom the Camden Society owes the transcript and collation of the proofs of this poem.

It only remains for the Editor to fulfil the agreeable task of expressing his gratitude for the assistance which, in the course of the work, he has derived from the kindness of his friends: to Mons. d'Avezac, of Paris, so well known by his valuable contributions to geographical science, to whom he has had recourse in some of the greater difficulties in the French and Anglo-Norman songs, and who collated with the originals those which were taken from foreign manuscripts before they were sent to press; to Sir Frederick Madden, from whom he has derived much assistance in the English songs, and whose superior knowledge in everything connected with early literature and manuscripts has been of the greatest use to him; to James Orchard Halliwell, Esq., for many services, and for collating with the originals the songs taken from Cambridge Manuscripts; and to John Gough Nichols, Esq., for the great attention which he has paid to the proofs, and for various suggestions, which have freed this volume from very many errors that would otherwise have been overlooked.

THOMAS WRIGHT

POLITICAL SONGS.

KING JOHN. 1199—1216.

THE thirteenth century opens amid the violence of party feelings, and the few political songs which we find during the reign of King John are full of keenness. Early in his reign the English Monarch suffered himself to be robbed of his possessions in Normandy, and the poetry of the Troubadours contains many expressions of regret at their separation from England, and bitter reflections on the King's cowardice and weakness. The following song seems to have been written when Thouars was in danger, during Philippe Auguste's incursions into Poitou, in 1206. Savary of Mauleon is famous in contemporary history, and was himself a poet of no small renown. He was a firm adherent to the English party.

SONG ON THE SIEGE OF THOUARS.

[Royal Library at Paris, MS. du fonds de St. Germain, No. 1989, fol. 111, vº.
13th cent.]

Mors est li siècles briemant,
Se li rois Touwairs sormonte ;
De ceu li vait malement
Ke li faillent li troi conte,

TRANSLATION.—The world will shortly come to nought,—if the king overcome Thouars.—On this account it fares ill with it,—that the three earls

Et li vieillairs de Bouaing
I averait grant honte,
C'après la mort à vifconte
Morrait à si mauté.

Savaris de Maliéon,
Boens chiveliers à cintainne,
Se vos fals à ces besons,
Perdue avons nostre poinne ;
Et vos, xanexals
Asi d'Anjow et dou Mainne,
Xanexal ont an Torainne
Atre ke vos mist.

Et vos, sire xanexals,
Vos et Dan Jehan dou Mainne,
Et Ugues, antre vos trois
Mandeis à roi d'Alemaigne,
Ke cist rois et cil Fransois
C'ameir ne nos d[a]ignent,
Cant por .j. mulet d'Espaigne
Laxait Bordelois.

desert it,—and the old man of Bouaing—would have there great shame,—that
after the death of the viscount—he should die in such evil case.

Savary of Mauleon,—a good knight at the quintain,—if you fail us in this
need,—we have lost our labour ;—and you, Seneschal,—both of Anjou and of
Maine,—they have placed a seneschal in Touraine—other than you.

And you, Sir Seneschal,—you and Sir John of Maine,—and Hugh, between
you three,—send word to the King of Almain,—that this king and him of
France,—deign not to love us,—when for a mule of Spain—he left the
Bordelois.

Et vos, signors bacheleirs,
   Ki ameis lois et proeses,
   Cant vos souliez garreir
Touwairs iert vos forteresce.
   Jà Deus ne vos doust porteir
   Ne mainche ne treses,
   Se Touwairt au teil tristesce
   Laixiez oblieir.

And you, Sir bachelors,—who love praise and prowess,—when you were wont to war—Thouars was your fortress.—Now God hinder you from bearing—sleeves or tresses,—if Thouars in such distress—you allow to be forgotten.

John's own friends, disgusted with his weakness, began to desert him ; and the following bitter song was addressed by the younger Bertrand de Born, to Savary de Mauleon, to persuade him to follow their example.

A SIRVENTE ON KING JOHN.
[Raynouard, Choix, tom. iv. p. 201.]

QUANT vei lo temps renovellar,
   E pareis la fueill' e la flors,
   Mi dona ardimen amors
E cor e saber de chantar ;
E doncs, pois res no m' en sofraing,
   Farai un Sirvent escozen,
   Que trametrai lai par presen
   Al rei Joan que s n'a vergoing.

TRANSLATION.—When I see the fair weather return,—and leaf and flower appear,—love gives me hardiesse—and heart and skill to sing ;—then, since I do not want matter,—I will make a stinging sirvente,—which I will send yonder for a present,—to King John, to make him ashamed.

E deuria s' be'n vergoignar,
    Si l' membres de sos ancessors,
    Com laissa sai Peitieus e Tors
Al rei Felip ses demandar ;
Per que tota Guiana plaing
    Lo rei Richard, qu' en deffenden
    En mes mant aur e mant argen ;
Mas acest no m' par 'n aia soing.

Mais ama l' bordir e l' cassar,
    E bracs e lebriers et austors,
    E sojorn ; per que il faill honors,
E s' laissa vius deseretar ;
Mal sembla d'ardimen Galvaing,
    Que sai lo viram plus soven ;
    E pois autre cosseil non pren,
Lais sa terra al seignor del Groign.

Miels saup Lozoics desliurar
    Guillelme, e l' fes ric secors
    Ad Aurenga, quan l'Almassors
A Tibaut l'ac fait asetjar :

And well he ought to be ashamed,—if he remember his ancestors,—how he
has left here Poitou and Touraine—to King Philip, without asking for them.—
Wherefore all Guienne laments—King Richard, who in its defence—would
have laid out much gold and much silver ;—but this man does not appear to
me to care much for it.

He loves better fishing and hunting,—pointers, greyhounds, and hawks,—
and repose, wherefore he loses his property,—and his fief escapes out of his
hands ;—Galvaing seems ill-furnished with courage,—so that we beat him here
most frequently ;—and since he takes no other counsel,—let him leave his land
to the lord of the Groing.

Louis knew better how to deliver—William, and gives him rich succour—at
Orange, when the Almassor—had caused Tiebald to besiege him ;—glory and

Pretz et honor 'n ac ab gazaing ;
  Jeu o dic per chastiamen
  Al rei Joan que pert sa gen,
Que non lor secor pres ni loing.

Baron, sai vir mon chastiar
  A vos, cui blasme las follors
  Que us vei far, e pren m'en dolors,
Car m' aven de vos a parlar,
Que pretz avetz tombat e' l' faing,
  Et avetz apres un fol sen,
  Que non doptas chastiamen,
Mas qui us ditz mal, aquel vos oing.

Domna, cui dezir e tenc car
  E dopt e blan part las meillors,
  Tant es vera vostra lauzors
Qu'ieu non la sai dir ni comtar ;
C'aissi com aurs val mais d'estaing,
  Valetz mais part las meillors cen,
  Et ez plus leials vas joven
Non son a Dieu cill de Cadoing.

honour he had with profit ;—I say it for a lesson—to King John who loses his people,—because he succours them not near or far off.

Barons, on this side my lesson of correction aims—at you, whose delinquencies it blames—that I have seen you do, and I am grieved thereat,—for it falls to me to speak of you,—who have let your credit fall into the mud,—and afterwards have a foolish sentiment,—that you do not fear correction,—but he who told you ill, it is he who disgraces you.

Lady, whom I desire and hold dear,—and fear and flatter above the best,—so true is your praise,—that I know not how to say it or to relate it ;—that, as gold is more worth than tin,—you are worth more than the best hundred,—and you are better worth to a young man,—than are they (the monks) of Caen to God.

Savarics, reis cui cors sofraing
Greu fara bon envasimen,
E pois a flac cor recrezen,
Jamais nuls hom en el non poing.

Savary, a king without a heart,—will hardly make a successful invasion,—
and since he has a heart soft and cowardly,—let no man put his trust in him.

The dishonours which John suffered abroad, were, however, soon forgotten in the troubles which broke out at home. The following virulent libel on the three bishops of Norwich, Bath, and Winchester, who adhered to the King in his quarrel with the Pope about the presentation to the see of Canterbury, was no doubt the work of one of his ecclesiastical opponents.

SONG ON THE BISHOPS.

[Flacius Illyricus, p. 161.]

Planctus super Episcopis.

COMPLANGE tui, Anglia,
Melos suspendens organi;
Et maxime tu, Cantia,
De mora tui Stephani.
Thomam habes sed alterum,
Secundum habes iterum

TRANSLATION.—Complain, O England! and suspend the melody of thine organ, and more especially thou, Kent, for the delay of thy Stephen. But thou hast another Thomas; thou hast again a second Stephen, who putting

Stephanum, qui trans hominem
Induens fortitudinem
    Signa facit in populo.
Dolos dolens metropolis
    Quos subdoli parturiunt,
Orbata tuis incolis,
    Dolose quos ejiciunt,
Largos emittis gemitus,
Patre privata penitus.
Sed cum habebis Stephanum,
Assumes tibi tympanum,
    Chelym tangens sub modulo.

Ubi es, quæso, Moyses,
    Per quem cedat confractio ?
Ubi legem zelans Phinees,
    Per quem cesset quassatio ?
Quis natum David arguens ?
Quis Thaü signum statuens
In limine et postibus,
Ut sic confusis hostibus
    Liberetur Israel ?

on a fortitude beyond that of man, performs signs among the people. O metropolis ! who grievest over the plots which the cunning people bring forth,
bereaved of thine inhabitants, whom they treacherously have ejected, thou
givest vent to heavy groans, being utterly deprived of thy father. But when
thou shalt have Stephen, thou wilt take up the timbrel, and touch the harp to
measure.

    Where art thou, I ask, O Moses ! through whom may the rupture cease ?
Where Phineas, zealous for the law, through whom the scourging may have an
end ? Who is there to accuse the son of David ? Who is there that may set the
sign of Thau on the threshold and the door-posts, that thus, her enemies being
confused, Israel may be liberated ? Abraham, father of many people, arise,

Abraham, pater gentium
  Multarum, surge, domine,
Agar expelle filium,
  Saræ ancillæ dominæ ;
Nam post subducet aliam.
Jam adversus ecclesiam
Prævalent portæ Tartari :
Jam ludo ludunt impari
      Isaac et Ismael.

Balthasar bibit iterum
  De vasis templi Domini :
Vasa rapit vas scelerum
  Dei dicata nomini.
Scribentem cerno digitum,
Et literis implicitum
Scriptis, " Mane, Tecchel, Phares ;"
Quid sibi velit ea res,
      Rei probabit exitus.
Jam patet in prætorio,
  Et infimis et arduis,
Quod regni jam divisio
  Et finis est in januis.

lord, expel the son of Agar, the waiting-maid of her mistress Sarah ; for after she shall deceive the other. Now the gates of Tartarus prevail against the Church : now Isaac and Ismael play at an unequal game.

Balthasar drinks again out of the vessels of the Lord's temple : the vessel of iniquities carries away the vessels dedicated to God's name. I perceive the hand, writing, and involved in the written letters, " Mane, Techel, Phares ;" what this thing may mean, the event of the thing will prove. Now it appears in the court, both to the low and the high, that at present the division and end

Crescit malorum cumulus,
Est sacerdos ut populus,
Currunt ad illicitum,
Uterque juxta libitum
  Audax et imperterritus.

Plebs in Ægypti cophino
 Servit, et sudat anxia
Sub Pharaone domino :
 Edicta currunt varia :
Exactor opus exigit,
Israel lutum colligit.
Non est qui eum eruat,
Vel Pharaonis subruat
  Equos cum ascensoribus.
Spargit Assur ac dejicit
 Lapides Sanctuarii.
Quare ? quia non objicit
 Se lapis adjutorii.
Imo qui se objicere
Deberent, et effundere
Sanguinem pro justitia,
Tractant de avaritia,
  Quos his noto apicibus.

of the kingdom is at the gate. The mass of evils increases ; the priest is as the people ; they, bold and fearless, hasten to that which is unlawful, each according to his will.

The people serves in the coffer of Egypt, and anxiously sweats under the rule of Pharaoh : various edicts fly about : the collector exacts the work, Israel collects clay. There is no one who may rescue him, or who may overwhelm the horses of Pharaoh with their riders. Assur scatters and overthrows the stones of the Sanctuary. Why ? because the Stone of Help does not oppose itself. Nay, they who ought to oppose, and to shed their blood for justice's sake, are occupied with avarice, whom I signalise by these marks.

Si præsuli Bathoniæ
   Fiat quandoque quæstio,
Quot marcæ bursæ regiæ
   Accedant in scaccario :
Respondet voce libera,
Mille, centum, et cætera,
Ad bursam regis colligo,
Doctus in hoc decalogo,
     Cæcus in forma canonis.
Tu, Norwicensis bestia,
   Audi quid dicat veritas :
Qui non intrat per ostia
   Fur est. An de hoc dubitas ?
Heu ! cecidisti gravius
Quam Cato quondam tertius :
Cum præsumpta electio
Justo ruat judicio,
     Empta per dolum Simonis.

Wintoniensis armiger
   Præsidet ad Scaccarium,
Ad computandum impiger,
   Piger ad Evangelium,
   Regis revolvens rotulum ;

If the question were perchance asked of the bishop of Bath, " How many marks come in to the King's purse in the Exchequer ? " he would answer readily, " A thousand, a hundred, and so on, I collect into the King's purse," learned as he is in this decalogue, blind in the form of the canon. Thou, beast of Norwich ! hear what the Truth saith : " He who enters not by the door is a thief." Dost thou doubt of this ? Alas ! thou hast fallen more heavily than once the third Cato, since thy presumed election falls by just judgment, having been bought by the craft of Simon.

The arm-bearer of Winchester presides at the Exchequer, diligent in computing, sluggish at the Gospel, turning over the King's roll ; thus lucre over-

Sic lucrum Lucam superat,
Marco marcam præponderat,
    Et libræ librum subjicit.
Hi Belphegor prænunciant,
    Et sedem Baal subjiciunt;
Ut melius proficiant,
    Baal sibi præficiunt,
Complectuntur pro niveis
Nigra, stercus pro croceis.
Hi tres insatiabiles,
Sanguisugis persimiles,
    "Affer," dicunt, "non sufficit."

Tres tribus his appositi
    Sunt, sed longe dissimiles,
Virtutum flore præditi,
    Morum vigore nobiles,
Noe, David, et Daniel,
Quos depingit Ezechiel.
Justitiam hi sitiunt,
Ob hæc sese objiciunt
    Murum pro domo Domini.

comes Luke; he makes a marc weigh heavier than Mark, and subjects the bible to the scales. These are they who fore-show Belphegor; they subject the seat to Baal; that they may profit better, they make Baal their lord; they embrace black for white, dung instead of saffron. These three are insatiable—very like unto leeches; they cry, "Give! there is not enough!"

There are three opposed to these, but very unlike them, endowed with the flower of virtues, noble in the vigour of good-breeding—Noah, David, and Daniel, whom Ezechiel paints. These thirst after justice: for this they

Joannes nostri temporis
  Surgit Decanus Angliæ,
Canus mente, vi roboris
  Stratam vadit justiciæ,
Canit laudum præconia
Qui jure de Ecclesia
Mariæ nomen accipit,
Dum conflictum hunc suscipit
  Sacræ devotus Virgini.

Heliensis progreditur,
  Huïc datur discrimini,
Heli ut *ensis* dicitur,
  Parcens paucis, vel nemini.
Helia, ensem exere,
Et impios tres contere,
Ac Babylonis principem
Hujus doli participem
  Ictu prosterne simplici.
Tu, Wolstani subambule,
  Es in conflictu tertius,
Robustus insta sedule
  Triumphi veri conscius.

oppose themselves as a wall for God's house. John arises the dean of England of our time, hoary in mind : with the might of oak, he proceeds on the way of justice ; he sings the proclamations of praises, who rightly takes his name from the church of Mary, while he undertakes this conflict in devotion to the Holy Virgin.

He of Ely advances ; he is given to this battle, as he is called the Sword of Hely, sparing few or none. Helias, draw forth the sword, and bruise the three impious ones, and lay prostrate the prince of Babylon, the participater in this plot, with a single blow. Thou, who walkest in the place of Wolstan, art the third in the conflict : robust as thou art, press on sedulously, certain of a true

Hæres Wolstani diceris,
Si vere sit, tu videris:
Prius resigna baculum,
Et ephod et annulum,
    Quam Baal velis subjici.

De Roffensi episcopo
    Nil scio mali dicere.
Mentior et rem syncopo:
    Hic est, et hic a latere
Est pauper Sarisburiæ,
Qui dormit usque hodie,
Ignem et aquam bajulat,
Nec causatur, nec ejulat
    Pro desolata vinea.
I Romam, liber parvule,
    Nec remeare differas,
Saluta quosque sedule,
    Et Papæ salve differas.
Dic quid de tribus sentiam.
Ipse promat sententiam,
Utrum suo judicio
Sint liberi a vitio;
    Et michi detur venia.

triumph. Thou art called the heir of Wolstan; if thou be truly so, thou art seen : sooner resign the staff, and the ephod, and the ring, than be willing to bow to Baal.

I know nothing ill to say of the bishop of Rochester. I lie, and cut the matter short; he is here, and here by his side the poor man of Salisbury also, who sleeps till to-day; he carries about fire and water, nor pleads for, nor bewails, the desolated vineyard. Go to Rome, little book, nor delay thy return ; salute them all diligently ; and carry a salutation to the Pope : tell what I think of the three : let him give judgment, whether in his opinion they be free from vice ; and let pardon be granted to me.

It was during these religious dissensions that arose up, or at least became strong, that powerful spirit of opposition to the papal tyranny, which produced during the whole of this century so much satirical poetry; much of it attributed, perhaps with little reason, to Walter Mapes. The following song is supposed to have been written during the interdict. In the fourth line the lion is said to designate King John, and the asses the Bishops, and at the end the King is represented by Jupiter, whilst the Pope receives the contemptuous designation of Pluto.

SONG ON THE TIMES.

[MS. Harl. 978, fol. 108, rº. Reign of Hen. III.]

Invectio contra avaritiam.

UTAR contra vitia carmine rebelli;
Mel proponunt alii, fel supponunt melli,
Pectus subest ferreum deauratæ pelli,
Et leonis spolium induunt aselli.

Disputat cum animo facies rebellis,
Mel ab ore defluit, mens est plena fellis;
Non est totum melleum quod est instar mellis;
Facies est alia pectoris quam pellis.

Vitium est in opere, virtus est in ore,
˙Picem tegunt animi niveo colore:

TRANSLATION.—I will use against vices rebelling song; others put forward honey, while under the honey they lay on gall; the iron breast is concealed under the gilt skin, and asses put on the lion's spoil.—The rebelling face disputes with the soul within; honey flows from the mouth, the mind is full of gall; it is not all sweet that looks like honey; the breast has a different countenance from the skin.—While vice is in the work, virtue is in the face;

Membra dolent singula capitis dolore,
Et radici consonat pomum in sapore.

    Roma mundi caput est, sed nil capit mundum :
Quod pendet a capite totum est inmundum ;
Transit enim vitium primum in secundum,
Et de fundo redolet quod est juxta fundum.

    Roma capit singulos et res singulorum ;
Romanorum curia non est nisi forum.
Ibi sunt venalia jura senatorum,
Et solvit contraria copia nummorum.

    Hic in consistorio si quis causam regat
Suam, vel alterius, hoc in primis legat,—
Nisi det pecuniam Roma totum negat,
Qui plus dat pecuniæ melius allegat.

    Romani capitulum habent in decretis,
Ut petentes audiant manibus repletis :
Dabis, aut non dabitur, petunt quia petis ;
Qua mensura seminas, et eadem metis.

they cover the pitchy blackness of the mind with a white colour; each of the members suffers by the pain of the head, and the flavour of the apple depends upon the root from whence it springs.—Rome is the head of the world ; but it receives nothing clean ; all that depends from the head is unclean ; for the first vice passes on into the second, and that which is near the bottom smells of the bottom.—Rome receives all, and the goods of all ; the court of the Romans is but a market. There are offered for sale the rights of the senators, and abundance of money dissolves all differences of opinion.—Here, in the consistory, if any body plead a cause, be it his own or another's, let him first read this,—" Unless he give money, Rome denies every thing; he who gives most money will come off the best."—The Romans have a chapter in the decretals, that they should listen to petitions from those who come with their hands full ; thou shalt give, or nothing shall be granted thee ; they ask because thou askest ; by the same measure as you sow, you shall reap.—A bribe

Munus et petitio currunt passu pari,
Opereris munere si vis operari :
Tullium ne timeas si velit causari,
Nummus eloquentia gaudet singulari.

Nummis in hac curia non est qui non vacet ;
Crux placet, rotunditas, et albedo placet,
Et cum totum placeat, et Romanis placet,
Ubi nummus loquitur, et lex omnis tacet.

Si quo grandi munere bene pascas manum,
Frustra quis objiciet vel Justinianum,
Vel sanctorum canones, quia tanquam vanum
Transferunt has paleas, et inbursant granum.

Solam avaritiam Roma novit parca,
Parcit danti munera, parco non est parca :
Nummus est pro numine, et pro Marco marca,
Et est minus celebris ara, quam sit arca.

Cum ad papam veneris, habe pro constanti,
Non est locus pauperi, soli favet danti ;

and a petition go side by side, and it is with a bribe that you must work if you wish to succeed : then you need have no fear, even of Tully, were he pleading against you ; for money possesses a singular eloquence.—There is nobody in this court who does not look after money : the cross on the coin pleases them ; the roundness of it, and the whiteness thereof, pleases them ; and since every part of it pleases, and it is the Romans whom it pleases, where money speaks, there all law is silent.—If you only feed the hand well with some goodly bribe, it will be in vain even to quote Justinian against you, or the canons of the saints, because they would throw them away as vanity and chaff, and pocket the grain.—Penurious Rome claims acquaintance with nothing but avarice ; she spares to him who brings gifts, but she spares not to him who is penurious : money stands in the place of God, and a marc for Mark, and the altar is less attended than the coffer.—When you come to the Pope, take it as a rule, that there is no place for the poor, he favours only

Vel si munus præstitum non est aliquanti,
Respondet hic tibi sic, Non est michi tanti.

    Papa, si rem tangimus, nomen habet a re,
Quicquid habent alii, solus vult papare ;
Vel si verbum Gallicum vis apocopare,—
Paez, Paez, dit li mot, si vis impetrare.

    Papa quærit, chartula quærit, bulla quærit,
Porta quærit, cardinalis quærit, cursor quærit,
Omnes quærunt : et si quod des uni deerit,
Totum jus falsum est, tota causa perit.

    Das istis, das aliis, addis dona datis,
Et cum satis dederis, quærunt ultra satis.
O vos bursæ turgidæ, Romam veniatis ;
Romæ viget physica bursis constipatis.

    Prædantur marsupium singuli paulatim ;
Magna, major, maxima, præda fit gradatim.
Quid irem per singula ? colligam summatim,—
Omnes bursam strangulant, et expirat statim.

the giver ; or if there is not a bribe of some value or another forthcoming, he answers you, " I am not able."—The Pope, if we come to the truth of the matter, has his name from the fact, that, whatever others have, he alone will suck the pap ; or if you like to apocopate a French word, " pay, pay," saith the word, if you wish to obtain anything.—The Pope begs, the brief begs, the bull begs, the gate begs, the cardinal begs, the cursor begs,—all beg ! and if you have not wherewith to bribe them all, your right is wrong, and the whole cause comes to nothing.—You give to these, you give to the others, you add gifts to those already given, and when you should have given enough, they seek as much more. O, you full purses, come to Rome ! at Rome there is choice medicine for costive pockets.—They all prey upon the purse by little and little ; great, greater, or greatest, gradually becomes a prey to them. Why should I go through all the particulars ? I will put it in a few words ; they all choke the purse, and it expires immediately.—Yet the purse imitates

Bursa tamen Tityi jecur imitatur,
Fugit res, ut redeat, perit, ut nascatur,
Et hoc pacto loculum Roma deprædatur,
Ut cum totum dederit, totus impleatur.

Redeunt a curia capite cornuto :
Ima tenet Jupiter, cœlum tenet Pluto,
Et accedit dignitas animali bruto,
Tanquam gemma stercori et pictura luto.

Divites divitibus dant, ut sumant ibi,
Et occurrunt munera relative sibi :
Lex est ista celebris, quam fecerunt scribi,
Si tu michi dederis, ego dabo tibi.   *Finit.*

the liver of Tityus ; the substance flies in order to return ; dies that it may be
born : and on this condition Rome preys upon the pocket, that when it has
given all, it may all be filled again.—They return from the court with mitred
heads ; Jupiter is placed in the Infernal Regions, Pluto holds Heaven, and dignity is given to a brute animal, as a jewel to the dung and a picture to the mud.
—The rich give to the rich, that they may receive again, and gifts mutually
meet one another : that law is most in use, which they have caused to be
written, " If you give to me, I will give to you."

KING HENRY III. 1216—1272.

The death of King John offered an opportunity of putting an end to the distractions that had become so universal during the latter years of his reign, which most of the belligerents were glad to embrace. The following short, but highly spirited poem, was probably written immediately after the pacification which followed the taking of Lincoln, apparently by a church-man, and certainly a partizan of King Henry. Some of the expressions in it, such as " the iron-girt bees of war," and the like, remind us of the lofty metaphors of Saxon verse.

THE TAKING OF LINCOLN.

[From MS. Cotton. Vespas. B. xiii. fol. 130. v°. in a hand of the beginning of the 14th Cent.]

¶ *Incipiunt versus de Guerra Regis Johannis.*

Serpserat Angligenam rabies quadrangula gentem.
In proprium jurata jugum, motuque minaci
Gens sibi degenerans, ut libera serviat, alta
Corruat, incolumis ægrotet, tuta pavescat,
Vendicat antiquas inimico consule leges;
Non legis libra, non juris luce, nec igne
Sacri consilii, sed nec lima rationis,
Fulgurat in vetitum spreta ratione voluntas.

Translation.—A four-fold rage had crept upon the English nation. Con-spiring against its own government, and threatening rebellion, the degenerate nation,—that it may change freedom for slavery,—that it may fall from its high position, from health to sickness, from safety to danger,—lays claim to ancient laws under a hostile governor ; not governed by the balance of the law, not by the light of justice, nor by the fire of holy counsel, nor yet by the file of reason, the

¶ Prima fuit rabies proprio concepta tumore ;
Altera belligeras Francorum traxerat alas ;
Conduxit nigras Scottorum tertia turmas ;
Flexit quarta leves tenui sub veste Galenses.

¶ Fœdera rumpuntur pacis, tonitrusque minaces ;
Serpsit in attonitas corrupta licentia turres,
In quibus ægra fides latuit, medicumque salutis
Expectata diu, tandem de munere Christi
Convaluit, traxitque suas in bella cohortes.

¶ Hæc rabies patiente Deo permissa parumper
Non concessa fuit, ut molles fulmina mentes
Comburant, nec ut ira Dei confundat inermes.
Sed cordis scrutator oves deserta petentes
Errantesque diu proprio revocavit amore,
Vapulet ut meritas medicato verbere culpas,
Divinasque minas clementia patris amicans
Ubere materno lenivit verbera patris.

¶ Anglorum nutabat honor, regnique venustas,
Inclinata caput divini judicis iram

will, in despite of reason, darts like lightning into what is forbidden. ¶ The first rage was conceived by its own pride ; the second drew hither the warlike legions of the French ; the third conducted the black troops of the Scots ; the fourth bent the inconstant Welsh under their light garment. ¶ The leagues of peace are broken, and the threatening thunders follow ; corrupt licence has crept into the astonished towers, in which Faith lay hid and sick, and long waiting a physician of health, at length by the generosity of Christ she recovered, and drew out her bands to the wars. ¶ This rage, by the sufferance of God, was permitted for a while, but not allowed that the lightnings should burn the effeminate minds, or that the anger of God should confound the defenceless. But the Searcher of hearts recalled by his own love the sheep which sought the desert and were long wandering, that he might correct the deserving faults with a healing lash, and reconciling his divine threats with paternal mercy, softened the corrections of a father with the love of a mother. ¶ The honour of the English bowed, and the comeliness of the Kingdom ; its bending head

Senserat, et tumido timuit servire tyranno.

Pendula palma, diu dubio protracta favore,

Nunc risit Gallis, nunc risum contulit Anglis,

Verius applaudens istis, fallacius illis.

¶ Non tulit ulterius regem regnare furentem

Vindicis ira Dei ; cecidit percussus ab illo

Cujus templa, domos, combusserat igne minaci.

A face fax oritur fati, flammæque furorem

Dum furit in regem febris vindicta fugavit.

Summus honos mors illa fuit, culmenque decoris

Attulit, in nullo quod erat superatus ab hoste,

Et tot erant hostes ; victus victore superno,

Invictusque suos hostes moriendo momordit.

¶ Desinat ira tumens ; discat servire potestas

Curvarique Deo, cui subdens colla resurget ;

In surgendo cadet : brevis est humana potestas,

Et brevibus discat finem properare diebus.

¶ Planxerat extinctum regio viduata Johannem,

Degenerique timens sua subdere colla marito

had felt the anger of the divine judge, and feared to serve the proud tyrant.
The balanced palm, long held out with dubious favour, now smiled on the
French, now turned its smile to the English, applauding with more truth these
latter, more deceitful to the others.   ¶ The anger of an avenging God allowed
no longer the furious king to reign ; he fell, struck by him whose temples and
houses he had burnt with threatening fire.   From this torch arises the torch of
fate, and the avenging fever, while it raged against the king, drove away the rage
of the flame.   That death was the highest honour, and was accompanied with
the highest glory, that he was in nothing overcome by the enemy, amidst so
many enemies ; vanquished by the conqueror who is above, and unconquered,
he bit his own enemies even in his death.   ¶ Let proud anger cease ; let power
learn to serve and to bow to God, in submitting the neck to whom she elevates
herself ; in rising she falls : short is the power of man ; and let it learn that the
end approaches in a few days.   ¶ The widowed state had mourned the death of
John, and, fearing to bow the neck to a degenerate husband, the tear of the

Invocat Angligenas Anglorum lacrima vires ;
Quo gravior dolor est, propior medicina doloris.
¶ Fulserat interea minimæ scintillula formæ,
Regia progenies, laceri spes unica regni,
Stella quasi succensa Deo, nubemque paternam
Exuit, irradians nova lux, stellasque fugatas
Fulmine de patrio pueri candela vocavit.
¶ O Pietas preciosa Dei ! qui magna magistrat,
Fortia confundit, infirma levat, feritates
Fulminat, inflatos frangit, qui virginis alvo
Parvulus egressus, parvum suscepit alendum,
Ecclesiæque dedit gremio, quem matris in ulnas
Blanda parens recipit, nato blandita parentis
Obsequio, teneram capiti positura coronam.
Consilium cœleste fuit, quod consona sacri
Unio consilii regi parere puello
Non timuit, timuitque magis servire tyranno.
¶ Unio sacra novum maturat ad ardua regem ;
Utilitas, pietasque, fides, concurrere fatis

English calls up the strength of England ; the heavier the grief, the nearer is
its cure.   ¶ Meanwhile had shone forth the minute spark of most small beauty,
the royal offspring, sole hope of the torn Kingdom, a star, as it were, lit by
God, it had divested itself of the cloud that obscured its father, shining forth a
new light, and the candle of the child called back the stars which had been
scared by the father's thunder.   ¶ O precious piety of God ! who masters
things that are great, confounds those that are strong, raises such as are
infirm, strikes ferocity with lightning, breaks the haughty, who himself having
come a child out of the virgin's womb, thus took a child to nourish, gave it to
the bosom of the Church, which the gentle parent receives in a mother's arms,
rendered gentle by the obedience now newly born, and about to place on its
head a tender crown.   It was heavenly ordinance, that the consonant union of
holy counsel feared not to obey a boy king, and feared more to serve a tyrant.
¶ Sacred union matures the new king to lofty things ; utility, and piety, and
faith, swear together to concur with the fates, and to sign them all with

Conjurant, cunctos[que] crucis signare sigillo ;
Constiterant vexilla crucis, regemque novellum
Ambierant, bajulosque crucis crux alba decorans
Instabiles statuit fidei fundamine turmas.
¶ O famosa viri legatio, lima beati
Consilii, sidus recti, speculum rationis,
Gala dei cultor, curæ cristata galero !
Anglia victrices strinxit divinitus enses,
In commune bonum fundunt castella catervas
Signiferas, belloque truces, hostique minaces.
¶ Tempus erat quo terra novo pubescere partu
Cœperat, et teneras in crines solverat herbas,
Vellera pratorum redolens infantia florum
Pinxerat, et, renovas crispans coma primula silvas,
Innumeras avium revocavit ad organa linguas,
Gallica tum rabies aquilonis adhæserat Anglis,
Conjurata manus medios transire per Anglos,
Londoniis egressa suis, longasque latebras

the seal of the Cross ; they had raised together the standard of the Cross and
had ranged themselves round the new King, and the white cross decorating
the bearers of the Cross fixed the unstable troops in the foundation of faith.
¶ O famous legation of a man ! file of blessed council ! star of right ! mirror
of reason ! helmet of the worship of God ! crested with the plume of care !
England hath grasped her conquering swords by impulse of God ; her castles
pour forth for the common good the standard-bearing troops, fierce in war, and
threatening the enemy.   ¶ What time the Earth had begun to bloom with new
fruitfulness, and had spread out her fresh grass in locks, redolent of flowers
had painted the young fleece of the fields, and, whilst the new verdure curled
the renascent woods, recalled innumerable tongues of birds to the song ; then
the Gallic fury had resolved to join the English of the north, the band having
conspired to pass through the midst of the English, having issued from their
London, the army of Louis deserted the long shades, and the proud earls

Deseruit Lodovica cohors, comitesque superbos
Concessa pudet ire via, Montique Sorello
Subsidium ferale ferunt, nam quo magis illum
Major palma colit, graviorem ferre ruinam
Præcavet ira Dei ; sed cautior inde recessit
Nobilitas comitum, fidei flos, regia virtus,
Cestrensis clipeus, donec frendente tumultu
Transierat rabies notum super ardua castrum,
Trigintæque latus, longique superbia belli
Fluxit ad obsessam matronæ nobilis arcem.
¶ Huc ubi fata feras fremitu flexere phalangas,
Fama volat, comitesque vocat, comitumque sodales
Cestrenses, crescitque seges clipeata virorum.
Regia signa micant, et conjurata sequuntur
Agmina, clara fides cum denique protrahit ora,
Candida signa crucis juvenum præstantia pingunt
Pectora, consolidat communis corda voluntas ;
Vincendi spes una fuit, victoria cunctas
In facies præmissa patet, plausuque secundo

have the shame of going the way that is open to them, and they carry fierce aid
to Mountsorrel; for as a greater victory attends it, so has the anger of God
ordained that it should not undergo a greater ruin. But with more caution
retires thence the nobility of earls, the flower of the faith, the royal strength, the
shield of Chester, until with roaring tumult the rage of the others had passed the
famous castle on the heights (Nottingham), and the bank of Trent, and the pride
of long war had flown to the besieged citadel of the noble matron (Lincoln).
¶ Hither when the fates have turned the fierce troops with a murmuring noise,
Fame flies, and calls the earls, and the Cestrensian companions of the earls, and
the shielded harvest of men increases. The royal standards glitter, and the con-
spiring bands follow, when clear faith at last draws out their faces, the bright signs
of the Cross paint the excelling breasts of the youth, a common will strengthens
their hearts ; there was one sole hope of conquering ; victory was already
stamped on all their faces ; and with a shout, ominous of good, they put forth their

Permittunt socias in consona prælia dextras.

¶ Instabat sabbatum quo festa peracta superni
Flaminis, et trinum celebrat deitatis honorem
Vespera ; sol prima lambebat lampade terras,
Cum tuba terribili dederat præludia cantu ;
Bella movent ferrata duces, tot signa videres
Nutantes tremulo galeas superare volatu,
Tot clipeos vario mutantes signa colore.
Fulsit in armatas solaris gratia turmas,
Febricitabat iners, validabant corda feroces.
Venit ut attonitam constantia Martis ad urbem,
Terribili juvenes muros cinxere corona,
Rimanturque novos aditus ; nec protinus urbem
Invasere duces; legatio mittitur intus
Sacrilegos revocare viros ad fœdera pacis.
Nec placuit pax ulla feris, convitia fundunt,
Legatos spernunt, adduntque minacia verba.

¶ Irrita legati postquam mandata reportant,

associated hands to the accordant battle. ¶ The sabbath was at hand in which
the festival of the high God is performed, and the eve celebrates the triune
honour of the deity ; the sun was touching the earth with his first light, when
the trumpet with its terrible song had given the flourish ; the leaders move iron
war ; many were the standards you might see with tremulous flight above the
nodding helms, many the shields changing their ensigns with various colours.
The beauty of the sun shone upon the armed troops ; the coward became
feverish ; the brave strengthened their hearts. When the constancy of war
came to the astonished town, the youth encircled the walls with a fearful
wreath, and seek new approaches ; nor do the leaders immediately attack the
city ; a legation is sent in to summon the sacrilegious men to the league of
peace. Yet no peace satisfied these fierce men ; they utter insults, despise the
messengers, and add threatening words. ¶ When the messengers bring back

Magnanimos monet ire duces; tum bellicus horror
Infremuit, tonuere tubæ, mugitus in auras
Horridus insurgit, et, constrepitante tumultu,
Mirari poterant terrena tonitrua nubes.
Transiliunt fossas, transcendunt mœnia, portas
Confringunt, aditus rumpunt, et prælia miscent.
Et gladiis fecere viam; confusio digna
Sacrilegos sternit, fundunt examina Christi
Ferrigeras Mavortis apes, stimulisque timendis
Hostiles penetrant tunicas, squamosaque ferri
Texta secant, Saulosque trahunt ad vincula Pauli,
Reddidit et lepores conversio sacra leones.
¶ Hic Moyses in Monte stetit, Josue stationem
Fixerat hic solis, magnum premit inde Goliam
Funda lapisque David; vidit venerabile mirum
Lincolniensis honor, vidit maris ira trophæum
Imperiale Dei, vidit quadrangula pestis
In se victrici vexilla resurgere palma.
Vidit, et obstupuit, sensitque superbia belli

the angry message, the leaders order their bold followers to the attack; then
the horror of war roared, the trumpets thundered, a fearful noise rose into the
air, and in the resounding tumult the clouds might wonder at earthly thunders.
They leap over the fosses, mount over the walls, break the gates, force the
passages, and join battle. And they made way with their swords; a merited
confusion strikes the sacrilegious men; the hives of Christ send forth the iron-
girt bees of war, and with fearful stings they penetrate the hostile shirts, and
cut the scaly textures of iron, and draw Sauls to the chains of Paul, and the
holy conversion turned hares into lions. ¶ Here stood Moses in the Mount;
here Josua had fixed the station of the sun; there the sling and stone of David
overcome the great Golias; the honour of Lincoln sees the venerable wonder;
the rage of the sea sees the imperial trophy of God; the four-fold plague sees
the standards rise again against it with conquering palm. It saw, and was

Pro puero pugnare Deum; nec sponte quievit,
Sed crepuit, pacisque pedes in colla recepit.
¶ O famosa dies, nostrum veneranda per ævum !
Bellica qua rabies latuit, qua pacifer ensis
Pestiferas domuit partes, qua gratia Christi
Dedecus extersit natum, fideique lavacro
Proluit inscriptum versa de fronte pudorem.

Expliciunt versus de Guerra regis Johannis.

astonished ; and the pride of war felt that God fought for the boy ; nor was it quiet by its own will, but it burst, and received the feet of peace on its neck. ¶ O famous day, to be venerated through our age ! in which the rage of war hid itself,—in which the peace-bringing sword subdued our pestiferous divisions,—in which the grace of Christ washed out the dishonour that had been brought forth, and, with the font of faith, cleansed from the averted brow the disgrace which had been inscribed on it.

All authorities agree in describing the great pride and avarice and luxury of the nobles in general, but particularly of the Romish prelates, at the beginning of the thirteenth century. The following song is a fair specimen of the unsparing satire which was universally directed against them by their contemporaries.

SONG ON THE CORRUPTIONS OF THE TIME.

[MS. Harl. No. 978. fol. 105, vº. reign of Hen. III.]

Contra avaros.

QUAM sit lata scelerum et quam longa tela
Sub qua latent pectora vitiis anhela,

TRANSLATION.— How wide and how long is the web of crimes with which our breasts, choked with vices, are enveloped, tell, and reveal,

Musa vultu lugubri refer et revela,
Si curas cor spectantis tetigisse querela.

Pensant vota miseræ gentis et prophanæ
Non virtutis pretium, set lini vel lanæ ;
Vespere quod agitur est infectum mane,
O curas hominum, o quantum est [in] rebus inane!

Est ad jura quilibet oculus obtusus ;
Omnis ad injurias animus diffusus ;
Ad fortunæ prodeunt aleas et usus
Mille hominum spes et rerum discolor usus.

Cum Sabinæ conferant saltum meretrici,
Pauperizent Arabes sub toga mendici,
Suo neget Tydeus fidem Polynici,
Spectatum admissi, risum teneatis, amici ?

Singulos per singula si nosse labores,
Qui cultores otii, qui doli structores,
Qui ministri Mammonæ, qui Dei spretores,
Ætatis cujusque notandi sunt mores.

O muse, with a mournful countenance, if you care to touch the heart of the spectator with your lament.—The wretched and profane people seem to form their wishes in consideration, not of the price of virtue, but of flax or wool : what is done in the evening is unwrought in the morning. O cares of men ! O how much emptiness there is in things !—Every eye is blind to justice ; every mind is large to injustice ; a thousand hopes of men and the differing aspects of things depend on the dice and uses of fortune.—When chaste maidens join in dance with the strumpet, when the Arabs play the pauper under the robe of a beggar, when Tydeus denies his faith to his Polynices, then, if you are admitted to the spectacle, my friends, can you restrain your laughter ?—If you are anxious to know all men by their several failings, who practise sloth, who are the plotters of treason, who the servants of Mammon, who the despisers of God, we must observe the manners of every age of life.—The boy, as he learns

Puer pede certior, odit fores, foras
Fugit, minus minimis colit res, honoras,
Et iram post gaudia, breves rumpens moras,
Colligit et ponit, temere mutatur in horas.

A custode juvenis evolat et seris,
Gaudet equis, canibus, aleis, et meris,
Venator libidinis, auceps mulieris,
Utilium tardus provisor, prodigus æris.

Vir ut præsit civibus, imperet prætori,
Ut extendat prædia fune longiori,
Et impregnet scrinia censu pleniori ;
Quærit opes et amicitias, inservit honori.

Multa circumveniunt senem casus duri,
Vel quod eget, abstinens, census perituri,
Vel quod tractat gelide res, ut prosint furi,
Dilator, spe longus, iners, avidusque futuri.

Sic ætates variat temporum respectus,
Transit ætas tenera cordis in affectus,
Vir in alta, sed ei quem torquet senectus,
Fervet avaritia miseraque cupidine pectus.

the use of feet, hates the doors, flies abroad ; he respects things and honours less than the least ; anger and joy succeed each other with short intervals, for his changes are sudden.—The youth flies from his tutor and confinement ; he delights in horses, dogs, dice, and wine, a hunter of his pleasures, whose occupation is with women, a slow provider of useful things, prodigal of money.—When arrived at manhood, that he may rule the citizens and dictate to the prætor, that he may extend his possessions with a longer cable, and fill his bags with greater treasure, he seeks riches and friendships, and is a slave to honours.—Many serious troubles surround the old man, either that, from stinginess, he spares his perishing wealth, or that he handles his riches with fear, lest they should fall to the thief ; he is one who delays long, depending on hope, inactive, and greedy of the future.—Thus difference of time causes variety of ages ; the tender age is occupied on the affections of the heart, the man on lofty things, but he whom old age bends, his breast glows with avarice and

Omnis ad hoc hominum animus senescit,
Qui dum quærit extra se res, quærens se nescit,
Non rebus crescentibus ambitus quiescit ;
Crescit amor nummi quantum ipsa pecunia crescit.

　Sed hoc uno veniam vitium meretur,
Quod cum rerum dominis semper dominetur ;
Tanto mens conspectius quæ nil reveretur
Crimen habet, quanto qui peccat major habetur.

　Roma, turpitudinis jacens in profundis,
Virtutes præposterat opibus inmundis,
Vacillantis animi fluctuans sub undis,
Diruit, ædificat, mutat quadrata rotundis.

　Vultus blandos asperat, quibus nunc arrisit ;
Sinu fovet placido quos prius elisit ;
Dum monetam recipit, tractat, et revisit ;
Quod petiit, spernit, repetit quod nuper omisit.

　Si non recte percipit quocumque modo rem,
Et quem primo didicit non oblita morem,

miserable cupidity.—In this respect the whole mind of men grows old, which,
while it seeks things external, is ignorant of itself in the pursuit ; ambition is
not quieted by success : the love of money increases as fast as the money itself
increases.—But in this point alone may vice claim some credit, that it is always
prevalent among the great ; yet that disposition which respects no control is the
more conspicuously criminal, in proportion as the sinner occupies a higher station.—Rome, lying in the depths of turpitude, ranks virtues beneath filthy lucre ;
fluctuating under the waves of a vacillating mind, she overthrows, builds, and
changes square things for round.—She despises the bland countenances at which
but now she smiled ; she cherishes in her placid breast those whom before she
rolled down ; while she receives money, she treats and revises : what she sought
she despises, and seeks again what lately she let go.—If she does not perceive
rightly a thing in any manner whatever, and has not forgotten the custom which

Morem testæ redolet, quæ diutiorem
Quo semel est inbuta recens servabit odorem.

  Coram cardinalibus, coram patriarcha,
Libra libros, reos res, Marcum vincit marca,
Tantumque dat gratiæ lex non parco parca,
Quantum quisque sua nummorum servat in arca.

  Si stateram judicum quæris, quæras ære,
Cum ab ære pendeat gratia stateræ ;
Non quæras inducias, sed quod quærunt quære,
Unde habeas quærit nemo, sed oportet habere.

  Commissus notario munera suffunde ;
Statim causæ subtrahet, quando, cur, et unde,
Et formæ subjiciet canones rotundæ,
Quem res plus nimio delectavere secundæ.

  Roma cunctos erudit ut ad opus transvolent,
Plus quam Deo Mammonæ cor et manus inmolent,
Sic nimirum palmites mala stirpe redolent,
Cui caput infirmum cetera membra dolent.

she first learnt, she smells of the custom of the cask, which will keep very
long the odour with which it was once endued while fresh.—Before the cardinals and before the patriarch, a pound overcomes the Bible, money the accused, and a marc Mark, the law sparing to him who is not sparing, gives only
as much grace as each has money in his purse.—If you seek the balance of
the judges, you should seek it with copper, since the favour of the balance
hangs from copper ; you should not ask respite, but ask what they ask ;
whence you obtain it nobody will inquire, but you needs must have it.—When
you are turned over to the notary, pour out your bribes ; he will at once ex-
tricate you from your cause, when, why, or whence it may arise, and will
subject the canons to the form that is round (i. e. the coin), whom prosperity
delights not a little.—Rome teaches all that they should fly over to expediency,
that they should offer heart and hand to Mammon rather than to God ; thus it
happens that the branches smell of a bad root ; where the head is infirm, the other

Calcant archipræsules colla cleri prona,
Et extorquent lacrimas ut emungant dona ;
Nec, si ferunt miseri pauca, vel non bona,
Æquis accipient animis, donantve corona.

Si de contumelia cæperit quis conqueri,
Statim causæ porrigunt aurem, manum muneri ;
Si semel acceperint rem pluralis numeri,
Cras poterunt fieri turpia sicut heri.

Diligit episcopus hilarem datorem,
Fas et nefas ausus post muneris odorem,
Nescius resumere, post lapsum pudorem,
Ejectum semel attrita de fronte ruborem.

Nec archidiacono minor turpitudo,
Quem semel arripuit serio vel ludo
Tenet, nec misertus est inopi vel nudo;
Non missura cutem nisi plena cruoris hirudo.

Decanus insidias natus ad æternas,
Ut exploret symbolum et res subalternas,

members are in pain.—The archbishops tread under foot the necks of the
clergy, and extort tears in order that they may be dried by gifts ; nor, if the
poor wretches bring few or not good ones, do they take them in good part, or
acknowledge them with favour.—If any one begins to complain of an injury,
they immediately stretch their ear to the cause, their hand to the gift; if
they once receive a thing of the plural number, to-morrow the same basenesses
may be done as yesterday.—The bishop loves a cheerful giver, and dares either
right or wrong after the smell of a bribe, unable to resume, after he has
thrown shame aside, the blush once rejected from his worn brow.—Nor is there
less baseness in the archdeacon ; whom he has once taken up, whether in
earnest or in joke, he holds ; nor has he mercy for the needy or the naked ;
the leech which will not let go the skin till he is filled with blood.—The dean,
born to everlasting wiles, that he may explore the creed (symbolum) and the
things which succeed, changing the tune of his tongue and yesterday's gar-

Mutans linguæ modulum et vestes hesternas,
Migrat in obscuras humili sermone tabernas.

Presbiter quæ mortui quæ dant vivi, quæque
Refert ad focariam, cui dat sua seque;
Ille sacri nominis, ille mentis æquæ,
Legem qui Domini meditatur nocte dieque.

Fulti verbis laici cleri delinquentis,
Non tam verbis inhiant quam famæ docentis :
Nec sensus sic flectere minis aut tormentis
Humanos edicta valent, quam vita regentis.

Regna movent principes statusque lascivi,
Ut ducant exercitus, pœnam donativi
Infligentes rustico miseroque civi ;
Quicquid delirant reges plectuntur Achivi.

Qui regni vel curiæ curis accinguntur,
Dum arrident detrahunt, et dum blandiuntur
Jacturam vel dedecus semper moliuntur ;
Nulla fides pietasve viris qui castra sequuntur.

Si te civis percipit, demollit ut urat,
Si dena contuleris mutuum futurat,

ments, migrates with humble speech to the obscure taverns.—The priest, whatever either the dead or the living give, carries all to his fireside-woman, to whom he gives himself and what he has; he of the holy name and the equal mind, who meditates the law of the Lord by day and by night.—The laymen resting on the words of the clergy who depart from them, pay less attention to the words than to the character of the teacher : nor can laws subdue the senses of men by threats and torments, so much as the example of the ruler.—The luxurious princes stir kingdoms and states, that they may lead armies, inflicting the punishment of a tax on the rustic and the miserable citizen ; for whenever the kings run wild, the Greeks pay the piper.—They who are occupied with the cares of the kingdom or of the court, detract while they smile, and when they flatter they are plotting damage or disgrace ; there is neither faith nor honesty in those who follow camps.—If a citizen perceive you, he caresses

Te de tuo submovet, percipe, dum durat ;
Pone merum et talos pereat, qui crastina curat.
   Si quis ad forensium domos devolutus
Censum palam deferat, et minus astutus,
Nam cum cubans dormiet fessus et imbutus,
Vivitur ex rapto, non hospes ab hospite tutus.
   Sic raptus, insidiæ, dolus, et simultas
Reddunt gentes devias, miseras, et stultas ;
Sic inescant omnium mentes inconsultas
Ambitus, et luxus, et opum metuenda facultas.
   Sed quid confert miseris luxus aut potestas
Qui spretis virtutibus colunt res funestas,
Aurum, gemmas, purpuram, et opes congestas ?
Cum labor in dampno est, crescit mortalis egestas.
   Quid ad rem, de purpura, gemmis, auro, rure ?
Assunt cum divitiis odia, jacturæ,
Placita, jejunia, metus, et de jure
Insompnes longo veniunt ex agmine curæ.
   Regnat pauper tutius quam rerum collator,
Qui, dum rapit domini gratiam delator,

that he may burn you ; if you lay down ten, he puts the payment of his stake to
another time ; he cheats you out of your own ; look to it, while it lasts ; he may
perish behind the wine and the dice, who leaves care till to-morrow.—If any
one going to the houses of the lawyers, carries his money openly, he also is a
simpleton ; for when he sleeps in his bed weary and full, people live by rapine,
the guest is not safe from his host.—Thus rapine, snares, treachery, and strife,
lead people into error, misery, and folly ; thus ambition and luxury, and the
revered possession of riches, allure the foolish minds of all men.—But what
availeth luxury and power to those miserable people who, despising virtues,
esteem only things that produce evil, such as gold, gems, and heaps of wealth ?
when our labour is expended on what is injurious to us, the misery of mortals
is on the increase.—What avails it to talk of purple, gems, gold, land ? With
riches we have feuds, losses, pleas, fastings, fears, and justly sleepless cares
come in a long train.—The poor man reigns more safely than he that amasses

Vel onustum spoliat prudens spoliator;
Cantabit vacuus coram latrone viator.

 Sæpe vivunt gratius rebus destituti,
Sub exili tegete lateris aut luti,
Quam in regum domibus mollibus induti;
Serviet æternum qui parvo nesciet uti.

 Sed si quæris copiam veræ facultatis,
Rejice superflua, cole quod est satis,
Exue divitias, nudus cede fatis;
Tolle moram, nocuit semper differre paratis.

 Si dum iter arripis ad utiliora,
Spem metus dissuadeat, vel successus mora,
Animum ne revoces, nec reflectas lora,
Grata superveniet quæ non sperabitur hora.

 Thesaurizes illud quo non potes abuti,
Curam gerens inopis, cæci, claudi, muti;
Animæ, non animo servias vel cuti,
Pauca voluptati debentur, plura saluti.

 Nemo regis solio tutus, vel asylo,
Cum nec lingua nequeat exprimi vel stilo

wealth, who, while the informer deprives the lord of his favour, or the lurking spoiler spoils him who is laden, he, an empty traveller, will sing before the thief.—They who are destitute often live more pleasantly under a slight hut of brick or mud, than those who are delicately clothed in the palaces of kings; he will be ever a slave who knows not how to use moderation.—But if you seek abundance of true property, reject superfluity, seek what is enough, strip yourself of riches, and die naked; delay not this, for those who are prepared are ever injured by delay.—If while you are on your road to what is more useful, fear dissuade hope, or delay endanger success; change not your mind, nor slacken your reins; the grateful hour will arrive when least expected.— Treasure up that which you cannot abuse, having a care of the needy, the blind, the lame, and the dumb; serve your soul, and not your mind or your skin; you owe little to pleasure, but more to your salvation.—No one is safe on a king's throne, or in a sanctuary, since it can be expressed neither by tongue nor pen

Quam sub fato pendulo vicinoque pilo,
Omina sunt hominum tenui pendentia filo.
  Prospere dum navigas æquoris extremum,
Pensa non præsentia, sed futura demum,
Et puppim considerans, non proram vel remum,
Omnem crede diem tibi diluxisse supremum.

by how slender a thread the destinies of men hang under the imminent approach
of death.—While you navigate prosperously the far side of the sea, weigh not
the present but the future, and considering the poop more than the prow or the
oar, act as though you thought every day your last.

The foreign policy of Henry III. was even less manly
than that of his father. Among the many songs of the Normans and Poitevins, reclaiming the assistance of their ancient
sovereign, we may give as an example the Sirvente of Bernard
de Rovenac, addressed to Henry and his contemporary James I.
King of Aragon, from whom Louis IX. had taken Languedoc
to give it as a portion to his brother Alphonsus. There is
internal evidence that it was written about 1229, the year in
which Henry III. made his ill-conducted expedition into
Brittany.

A SIRVENTE AGAINST KING HENRY.

[Raynouard, Choix, tom. iv. p. 203.]

JA no vuelh do ni esmenda
    Ni grat retener
    Dels ricx ab lur falz saber,
Qu'en cor ay que los reprenda

TRANSLATION.—I wish neither for the gifts and favours—nor to obtain the
good-will—of the rich, with their false wisdom;—but I have in my heart the

Dels vils fatz mal yssernitz ;
E no vuelh sia grazitz
Mos sirventes entr' els flacx nualhos,
Paupres de cor et d' aver poderos.

Rey Engles prec que entenda,
      Quar fa dechazar
      Son pauc pretz per trop temer,
Quar no'l play qu' els sieus defenda,
      Qu'ans es tan flacx e marritz
      Que par sia adurmitz,
Qu'el reys frances li tolh en plas perdos
Tors et Angieus e Normans e Bretos.

Rey d'Arago, ses contenda,
      Deu ben nom aver
      Jacme, quar trop vol jazer ;
E qui que sa terra s prenda,
      El es tan flacx e chausitz
      Que sol res no y contraditz ;
E car ven lay als Sarrazis fellos
L'anta e'l dan que pren say vas Lymos.

intention to reproach them—with their vile deeds ill-conceived ;—and I don't
wish to be agreable—my Sirventes among the cowardly idlers,—poor in heart
and heavy in riches.

The English King, I pray him to hear it,—for he causes to fall—his little
glory by too much timidity,—for it does not please him to defend his own people,
—and thus he is so cowardly and so vile,—that he seems to be asleep,—while
the French King takes from him with impunity—Tours, and Angiers, and Normans, and Bretons.

The King of Aragon, without any doubt,—ought really to have the name—
of James ; for he is too willing to lie down ;—and whoever it be that takes his
land,—he is so cowardly and caitiff,—that he does not even contradict it ;—and
he revenges on that side against the felon Saracens——the shame and damage
which he receives on this side towards Limoux.

Ja tró son payre car venda
　　No pot trop valer,
　　Ni s cug qu' ieu li diga plazer,
Tró foc n'abraz e n'essenda
　　E n' sian grans colps feritz ;
　　Pueys er de bon pretz complitz,
S'al rey frances merma sos tenezos,
Quar el sieu fieu vol heretar N Anfos.

Coms de Toloza, la renda
　　Que soletz tener
　　De Belcaire us deu dolar,
S'al deman faitz lonj' atenda
　　Vos e 'l reys que us es plevitz ;
　　L'enprendemen n'er aunitz,
S'ar no vezem tendas e pabalhos,
E murs fondre, e cazer autas tors.

　　Ricx homes, mal yssernitz,
　　En vey hom vostres malz ditz,
E laissera us, s'ie us vis arditz ni pros,
Mas no us tem tan que ja m'en lays per vos.

Until he have revenged his father,—he cannot have much esteem,—nor let him imagine that I will speak to please him,—unless he ravage and put in flames,—and unless great blows be struck.—For there will have been accomplished great honour,—if he narrows the domains of the French King,—for Don Alfonse desires to inherit his fief.

Earl of Toulouse, the rent—which you used to hold—from Beaucaire, you ought to regret,—if you make long delay to demand it,—you, and that King, because you are in league ;—that undertaking will not be disgraced,—if we now see tents and pavilions,—and walls fall and high towers break.

Rich men, ill-advised,—one sees your evil sayings,—I would let you alone, if I saw you hardy and courageous,—but I do not fear you so much as to leave it on your account.

―――――

The following Sirvente, by the same author, is also directed against Henry and James, and was written about the year 1250. It repeats the same articles of accusation, and its object was to persuade those kings to invade the dominions of Louis, while he was himself absent on his crusade.

A SIRVENTE AGAINST KING HENRY.

[Raynouard, tom. iv. p. 205.]

D'un sirventes m'es grans volontatz preza,
Ricx homes flacx, e non sai que us disses,
Quar ja lauzor no y auria ben meza,
Ni us aus blasmar, e val pauc sirventes
Que laza quan blasmar deuria;
Pero si tot vos par follia,
A me platz mais que us blasme dizen ver,
Que si menten vos dizia plazer.

Amdos los reys an una cauz' empressa,
Selh d'Arago et aisselh dels Engles,
Que no sia per elbs terra defeza
Ni fasson mal ad home qu'el lur fes,
E fan merces e cortezia,

TRANSLATION.—I am seized by a great desire of writing a sirvente,—O rich yet cowardly men! and I know not what I shall say to you,—for there will be little room for praise ;—nor dare I blame you, and a sirvente is worth little—which praises when it ought to blame :—but though it may seem all folly to you,—yet it pleases me more to blame you by telling the truth,—than if I spoke falsehood to please you.

Both the kings have resolved on one thing,—he of Aragon and he of the English,—that by them the land shall not be defended,— and that they will do ill to no one who does ill to them ;—they are merciful and courteous ;—for they

Quar al rey que conquer Suria
Laisson en patz lur fieus del tot tener;
Nostre Senher lur en deu grat saber.

Vergonha m pren, quant una gens conqueza
Nos ten aissi totz vencutz e conques,
   E degr' esser aitals vergonha prezza,
Quom a me pren, al rey Aragones
   E al rey que pert Normandia,
   Mas prez an aital companhia
Que ja nulh temps no fasson lur dever,
Et anc non vitz autre tan ben tener.

E pus no pren en la leuda torneza
Qu'a Monpeslier li tollon siey borzes,
   Ni no y s venja de l'anta que y a preza,
Ja no 'lh sia mais retragz Carcasses,
   Pos als sieus eys no s defendria,
   Assatz fa sol qu'en patz estia;
Patz non a ges senher ab gran poder,
Quan sas antas torna a non chaler.

let the King who is conquering Syria—retain their fiefs altogether in peace;—
our Lord ought to be very thankful to them for it.

Shame seizes on me, when a vanquished people—holds us thus all subdued
and conquered,—and such shame ought to seize—the King of Aragon, as
seizes me,—and the King who loses Normandy,—but they take such company—
that now they never perform their duty,—and I never saw another hold so
well.

And afterwards he does not receive the tax,—which at Montpellier his
burgesses take from him,—neither does he revenge himself of the disgrace he
received there,—now Carcasson may no more be recovered by him;—for he
would not defend his own eyes,—his only endeavour is that he may be in
peace;—a noble lord with great power has no peace,—when he turns his ways
to nonchalance.

Ges trop lauzar, quan valors es mal meza,
Non apel patz, quar mala guerra es;
  Ni ja per me non er per patz enteza,
Mielhs deuria aver nom gauch de pages,
    E dels ricx que perdon tot dia
    Pretz, e ja fort greu no lur sia,
Quar pauc perdon e pauc lur deu doler,
Quar ges de pauc non pot hom trop mover.

  Lo reys N Anfos a laissat cobezeza
Als autres reys, qu'a sos ops non vol ges,
  Et a sa part elh a preza largueza,
Mal a partit qui reptar l'en volgues;
    E dic vos que m par vilania
    Qui partis e qui 'l mielhs s' atria ,
Mas ges pertant non a fag non dever,
Quar a pres so qu'elhs no volon aver.

  Ricx malastrucx, s'ieu vos sabia
  Lauzor, volontiers la us diria;
Mas no us pessetz menten mi alezer,
Que vostre grat no vuelh ni vostr' aver.

To praise people too much, when valour is ill esteemed,—I do not call it peace, for it is bad war;—nor shall it now be understood by me for peace,—it ought rather to have the name of pages' play,—and of the rich who lose every day—honour, and yet it grieves them not much,—for they lose little and need not grieve much,—for we cannot be moved much by a little thing.

The king Don Alfonso has left covetousness—to the other kings, because he will not make use of it,—and he has taken for his share largess,—he has an ill share who wishes to recover this from him ;—and I tell you that it appears to me villany,—when one shares and takes the best to himself ;—yet no one has done otherwise than right,—when he has taken that which others will not have.

Rich men ill-advised, if I knew any thing in you—worthy of praise, I would willingly tell you of it ;—but think not to take up my leisure,—for I desire neither your thanks nor your goods.

Henry's embarrassments at home were now becoming every day more numerous and more complicated. Scarcely any part of the nation, clergy, barons, or people, were any longer his friends. The following song (made in 1256) was evidently written by one belonging to the former of these classes, indignant at the taxes which the King, with the consent of the Pope, had levied on the clergy, in the vain hope of placing one of his sons on the throne of Sicily, and afterwards to pay the debt which he had contracted towards the supreme pontiff. The King of France, quoted as an example, was the saintly Louis IX.

THE SONG OF THE CHURCH.

[MS. Cotton. Jul. D. vii. fol. 133, v°. of 13th century.]

Istud canticum factum fuit anno gratiæ m°cc°lvi° supra
desolatione Ecclesiæ Anglicanæ.

Or est acumpli à men acient
La pleinte Jeremie, ke oï avez suvent ;
   ke dit cument set sule
   cité pleine de fule
Plurant amerement,
   ore est sanz mariage
   e mis en tailage,
La dame de la gent.
Cest est seint eglise trestut apertement,
Ke est ja hunie e tut mis a vent :

TRANSLATION.—Now is accomplished as I conceive—the plaint of Jeremiah, which you have often heard,—who tells how this sole—city full of people—bewailing bitterly,—is now without marriage—and put in contribution,—the Lady of the people.—That is holy church very evidently,—who is now dis-

E si est maumise, nus veum cument.
 Ele gent e plure,
 n'a ad nul ke sucure
De sun marement.

Jà fu cleregie
 franche e à desus,
Amée e cherie,
 nule ren pot plus.
Ore est enservie,
E trop envilie,
 e abatu jus ;
Par iceus est hunie,
Dunt dut aver aïe ;
 jo n'os dire plus.

Li rois ne l'apostoile ne pensent altrement,
Mès coment au clers tolent lur or e lur argent.
 Co est tute la summe,
 ke la pape de Rume
Al rei trop consent,
 pur aider sa curune
 la dime de clers li dune,
De ço en fet sun talent.

graced and all put to sale ;—and truly is she in ill case, we see how.—She
laments and weeps,—there is none who helps her—out of her desolation.

Formerly clergy was—free and uppermost,—loved and cherished,—nothing
could be more so.—Now it is enslaved,—and too much debased,—and trodden
down.—By those is it disgraced,—from whom it ought to have help ;—I dare
not say more.

The king and the pope think of nothing else,—but how they may take from
the clergy their gold and their silver.—This is the whole affair,—that the pope
of Rome—yields too much to the king,—to help his crown,—the tenth of the
clergy's goods he gives him,—and with that he does his will.

Jo ne quid pas ke li rois face sagement,
Ke il vit de roberie ke il de la clergie prent.
 Jà ne fra bone prise,
  pur rober seinte eglise ;
Il la say verament.
 Ke vot aver semblance,
  regarde le rois de France
E sun achevement.

I do not think that the King acts wisely,—that he lives of robbery which he commits upon the clergy.—He will never be a gainer,—by robbing holy church ;—he knows it truly.—He who seeks an example,—let him regard the King of France—and his achievement.

The next Song, directed against the avarice of the Bishops, appears to be of about the same date. In the manuscript it is written, like the foregoing, as prose.

A SONG AGAINST THE BISHOPS.

[From the same folio of the same MS.]

Licet æger cum ægrotis,
Et ignotus cum ignotis,
Fungar tamen vice totis,
Jus usurpans sacerdotis ;
 flete, Syon filiæ,
  præsides ecclesiæ
  imitantur hodie
Christum a remotis.

Translation.—Although sick with those who are sick, and unknown with those who are unknown, yet I will assume all characters in turn, usurping the right of the priest : weep. ye daughters of Sion, the bishops of the church at the present day are but remote imitators of Christ !

Jacet ordo clericalis
In respectu laicalis,
Sponsa Christi fit venalis,
Generosa generalis ;
    veneunt altaria,
    venit eucharistia,
    cum sit nugatoria
Gratia venalis.

Donum Dei non donatur
Nisi gratis conferatur ;
Quod qui vendit vel mercatur,
Lepra Syri vulneratur ;
    quem sic ambit ambitus,
    ydolorum servitus
    templo sancti spiritus
Non compaginatur.

In diebus juventutis
Timent annos senectutis,
Ne fortuna destitutis

The clerical order is debased in respect of the laity ; the spouse of Christ is made venal,—she that is noble, common ; the altars are for sale ; the eucharist is for sale, although venal grace is vain and frivolous.

God's gift is not given if it be not conferred gratis ; and he who sells and makes merchandise of it, is, in so doing, struck with the leprosy of Syrus ; the service of idols, at which his ambition thus aims, may not be engrafted on the temple of the Holy Spirit.

In their days of youth, they look forwards to old age with fear, lest, deserted by fortune, they possess no longer their sleek skin. But while they

Desit eis splendor cutis.
 Sed dum quærunt medium,
 vertunt in contrarium,
 fallit enim vitium
Specie virtutis.

Tu qui tenes hunc tenorem,
Frustra dicis te pastorem ;
Nec te regis ut rectorem,
Rerum mersus in ardorem :
 Hæc est alia
 sanguisugæ filia,
 quam venalis curia
Duxit in uxorem.

seek the mean, they turn into the contrary extreme ; for vice deceives them
in the guise of virtue.

 Thou who holdest this course, vainly thou callest thyself a pastor ; neither
doest thou govern thyself like a ruler, immersed in the heat of temporary affairs ;
she is another—daughter of the leech, whom the venal court has taken to wife.

The following is another bitter satire on the vices of the
great, during the reign of Henry III. Who were the four
brothers against whom the song is more particularly directed,
would not be easily ascertained without other particulars besides
those here furnished.

A SONG ON THE TIMES.

[MS. Harl. No. 978. fol. 123, vº. of the 13th cent.]

MUNDI libet vitia cunctis exarare ;
Nam in mundo video multos nunc errare,

TRANSLATION.—Everybody has a right to satirize the world's vices ; for
now I see many in the world err, despise what is good, love what is bad, and

Spernere quod bonum est, quod malum est amare,
Et ad mala sæpius sponte declinare.

Mundus quia malus est, male scit nocere;
Mala novit facere, nescit pœnitere;
Caro quicquid appetit pro posse vult habere,
Sed quod Deus præcipit nequit adimplere.

Jam nil valet aliquis ni sciat litigare,
Nisi sciat cautius causis cavillare,
Nisi sciat simplices dolis impugnare,
Nisi sciat plenius nummos adunare.

Mundi status hodie multum variatur,
Semper in deterius misere mutatur;
Nam qui parcit nemini, quique plus lucratur,
Ille plus dilectus est et plus commendatur.

Rex et regni proceres satis sunt amari;
Omnes fere divites nimis sunt avari;
Pauper pauca possidens debet depilari,
Et ut ditet divitem rebus spoliari,

Bona per superflua dives excæcatur;
Circa temporalia tota mens versatur:

most frequently turning off spontaneously to evil.—Because the world is depraved, it knows how to do injury; it knows how to act ill, but not how to repent; the flesh will do all it can to possess whatever it desires, but is unable to fulfill God's commandments.—Now nobody is esteemed unless he knows how to litigate; unless he can cavil cunningly in law-suits; unless he can overreach the simple; unless he know how to amass abundance of money.—The state of the world is at the present day constantly changing; it is always becoming miserably worse; for he who spares nobody, and who is bent most on gain, is most beloved and most commended.—The King and his nobles are sufficiently 'bitter; almost all the rich men are too avaricious; the poor man, who possesses little, must be robbed and spoiled of his property to enrich the wealthy.— The rich man is blinded by superfluous wealth; his whole mind is occupied with temporal matters; and, since he is too much pleased with vanities, he

Et in vanis quoniam nimis delectatur,
Bona differt facere, malum non vitatur.

   Ex prælatis plurimum Deum non timentes
Sunt sub boni specie mala facientes,
Hiique plus quam laici sæpe sunt nocentes,
Bene curant corpora, male pascunt mentes,

   Regnat nunc impietas, pietas fugatur,
Nobilisque largitas procul relegatur ;
Stricta nam tenacitas multos comitatur,
Et in multis caritas sic refrigeratur.

   Fas et nefas ambulant pene casu pari,
Vix est jam quem pudeat nefas operari ;
Carus hic acceptus est qui scit adulari,
Hicque privilegio gaudet singulari.

   Quod ad lucrum pertinet nimis affectatur ;
Lucra quisquis prospicit, cautus judicatur ;
Res qui servat strictius, sapiens vocatur ;
Sua qui dat largius, stultus reputatur.

   Dolus avaritiæ comes copulatur ;
Fidei perfidia jam parificatur ;

puts off the doing of good, but avoids not the evil.—Of the prelates, there are
very many who, having no fear of God, do evil under the mask of good, and
they often do more injury than the laymen ; they take great care of the body, but
feed ill the mind.—Now impiety reigns, piety is driven away, and noble libe-
rality is sent into far exile ; for narrow stinginess is the companion of many,
and thus in many charity is become cold.—Right and wrong march nearly on
an equal footing ; there is now scarcely one who is ashamed of doing what is
unlawful ; the man is held dear who knows how to flatter, and he enjoys a
singular privilege.—Lucre is a thing too much sought after ; whoever has an eye
to it, is considered prudent ; he who keeps very close what he has, is called a wise
man ; he who gives liberally, is set down for a fool.—Treachery accompanies
avarice ; perfidy is now put on equality with honesty ; for he who knows how

Nam qui scit decipere, prudens prædicatur;
Qui plus mali perpetrat plus appretiatur.

Quatuor sunt maxime qui sic operantur,
Et cum malefecerint pejus meditantur,
Quorum infra scelera satis declarantur,
Et eorum nomina sic intitulantur.

Hii sunt fratres quatuor, Robertus, et Ricardus,
Gilebertus postea, vir valde Wandelardus,
Quartus inter alios frater est bastardus,
Galfridus, qui piger est, et ad bona tardus.

Cuique satis proprie nomen adaptatur,
Per quod quæ proprietas cujusque sit notatur;
Nam qui recte nominum vim interpretatur,
Scire potest certius quid significatur.

Competenter per *Robert, robbur* designatur;
Et per *Richard, riche hard* congrue notatur;
Gilebert non sine re *gilur* appellatur;
Gefrei, si rem tangimus, in *jo frai* commutatur.

Per istorum nomina, quæ sic figurantur,
Modus, fraus, et opera multorum denotantur;

to deceive, is proclaimed a prudent man; and he who does most ill is most prized.—There are four persons in particular who work thus; who, even while doing ill, are meditating to do worse, whose crimes are sufficiently declared below, and whose names are as follows:—They are four brothers, Robert, and Richard; next Gilbert, a true Wandelard; the fourth is a bastard brother, Geoffrey, who is a sluggard, and slow to do anything good.—Each of them has a very appropriate name, by which his own character is described; for if any one interpret rightly the names, he may know most accurately what each signifies.—By *Robert*, is very sufficiently indicated *a robber;* and by *Richard*, with much fitness, a *rich hard* man; *Gilbert* is not without reason called a *guiler;* and *Geoffrey* is, if we come to the point, changed into *jo frai* (i. e. I will do it). —By these people's names, which are thus described, are denoted the habit, and fraud, and works, of many men; and in order that these may be made more mani-

Et ut cunctis clarius hæc aperiantur,
Melius et plenius hic notificantur.

   Robertus excoriat, extorquet, et minatur;
Et Ricardus retinet totum quod lucratur;
Gilebertus decipit, et inde gloriatur;
Galfridus se procrastinat, et nil operatur.

   Veritatem prosequar ore nunc aperto :
Vir quicunque rabidus consors est Roberto;
Vir fallax et cupidus par fit Gileberto ;
Vir piger et tepidus Galfridus est pro certo.

   Tempus piger protrahit omni tardus hora ;
Operari negligit quæ sunt meliora ;
Bona nimis differens ruit in pejora ;
Et ut bene faciat semper est in mora.

   Hic promittit quodlibet, sed nil vult implere ;
Semper dicit "faciam," nunquam facit vere ;
Sed cum mors est proxima, tunc incipit dolere ;
Magnum est periculum tam sero pœnitere.

   Quisque sibi caveat ne decipiatur ;
Pœnitere studeat antequam labatur ;

fest to all, they are here published better and more fully —Robert fleeces, extorts,
and threatens ; and Richard keeps all he gains ; Gilbert deceives, and afterwards boasts of it ; Geoffrey procrastinates, and does nothing.—I will follow
up the truth now in full cry : every ravenous man is the companion of Robert ;
a false and miserly man is similar to Gilbert ; a slow and listless man is, without doubt, a Geoffrey.— The latter idly protracts the time, behindhand at whatever hour is appointed, he neglects to do what is good, and by putting off the good
he falls into that which is evil, and he is always backward in acting well :—
he promises anything, but will perform nothing ; he always says, " I will do,"
but never does ; but when death is at hand, he begins to lament : there is great
danger in repenting so late.—Let every one take care that he is not himself
deceived ; let him try to repent before his end, that he may merit well while he

Dum est compos corporis bene mereatur,
Ne dum differt interim forte moriatur.

　　Fons et auctor, Dominus, summæ pietatis
Nobis hic sic annuat flere pro peccatis,
Et dum sumus validi pœnitere gratis,
　Ut possimus alibi gaudere cum beatis !　AMEN.

is in health, lest by putting it off, he chance to die before it is done.—The Lord,
who is the fountain and author of the highest degree of piety, give us here the
inclination so to mourn for our faults, and to be penitent spontaneously while
we are in health, that in the next world we may be in joy with the saints !

A perpetual subject of popular outcry against the great, during
this and the following centuries, was afforded by the foreign
and extravagant fashions in dress, which were prevalent. A
glance at the illuminations in contemporary manuscripts will
show us that these complaints were not without foundation. We,
even at the present day, can with difficulty conceive the immense sums which were in former days expended on the toilet.
This profusion was frequently and severely commented upon in
the prose writings of the clergy, and was not uncommonly the
subject of popular satire. The following song upon the tailors
is very playful.

SONG UPON THE TAILORS.

[MS. Harl. 978. fol. 99. vº. reign of Hen. III.]

In nova fert animus mutatas dicere formas
Corpora, Dii cœptis, nam vos mutastis et illas,
Aspirate meis.

　　Ego dixi, dii estis ;
　　Quæ dicenda sunt in festis
　　　Quare prætermitterem ?

TRANSLATION.—I have said, ye are gods ; why should I omit the service

Dii, revera, qui potestis
In figuram novæ vestis
    Transmutare veterem.

Pannus recens et novellus
Fit vel capa vel mantellus,
    Sed secundum tempora
Primum capa, post pusillum
Transmutatur hæc in illum ;
    Sic mutatis corpora.

Antiquata decollatur,
Decollata mantellatur,
    Sic in modum Proteos
Demutantur vestimenta ;
Nec recenter est inventa
    Lex metamorphoseos.

Cum figura sexum mutant ;
Prius ruptam clam reclutant
    Primates ecclesiæ ;
Nec donatur, res est certa,
Nisi prius sit experta
    Fortunam Tiresiæ.

which should be said on festival days ? Gods certainly ye are, who can trans-
form an old garment into the shape of a new one.—The cloth, while fresh and
new, is made either a cape or mantle ; but, in order of time, first it is a cape,
after a little space this is transformed into the other ; thus ye " change
bodies."—When it becomes old, the collar is cut off ; when deprived of the
collar, it is made a mantle : thus, in the manner of Proteus, are garments
changed ; nor is the law of metamorphosis a new discovery.—With their shape
they change their sex ; the primates of the church privately close up again what
was before torn ; nor is it given, assuredly, till it has first undergone the

Bruma tandem revertente,
Tost unt sur la chape enté
    Plerique capucium;
Alioquin dequadratur,
De quadrato retundatur,
    Transit in almucium.

Si quid restat de morsellis
Cæsi panni sive pellis,
    Non vacat officio:
Ex hiis fiunt manuthecæ,
Manutheca quidem Græcè
    Manuum positio.

Sic ex veste vestem formant,
Engleis, Tyeis, Franceis, Normant,
    Omnes generaliter;
Ut vix nullus excludatur.
Ita capa declinatur,
    Sed mantellus aliter.

Adhuc primo recens anno,
Nova pelle, novo panno,
    In arca reconditur;

fortune of Tiresias.—When, at length, winter returns, many engraft immediately upon the cape a capuce ; then it is squared ; after being squared it is rounded ; and so it becomes an aumuce.—If there remain any morsels of the cloth or skin which is cut, it does not want a use : of these are made gloves ; a glove is called in Greek " the placing of the hands."—This is the general manner they all make one robe out of another, English, Germans, French, and Normans, with scarcely an exception. Thus *cape* is declined ; but *mantle* otherwise.— In the first year, while it is still fresh, the skin and the cloth being both new,

Recedente tandem pilo,
Juncturarum rupto filo,
    Pellis circumciditur.

Sic mantellus fit apella ;
Ci git li drap, e la pel là,
    Post primum divortium ;
A priore separata
Cum secundo reparata
    Transit in consortium.

Quod delictum dices majus ?
Istud palam est contra jus :
    Nam si nupsit alteri,
Conjugium est violatum,
Dum fit novo copulatum
    Reclamante veteri.

N'est de concille, ne de sene,
Deus dras espuser à une pene,
    E si nus le juggium ;
Permittunt hoc decreta ? non :
Sed reclamat omnis canon
    Non esse conjugium.

it is laid up in a box; when, however, the fur begins to be worn off, and the thread of the seams broken, the skin is circumcised.—Thus the mantle is made a Jew; here lays the cloth, there the skin, after the first divorce : being separated from its former husband, after separation it passes in reparation to marriage with a second husband.—But what will you say is a greater crime? this is clearly against right; for if she have married a second, the marriage is broken, when a new conjunction is made in spite of the reclamations of the old partner.—It is neither canonic nor wise to marry two cloths to one fur, and so we judge it. Do the decretals permit this? No: on the contrary, every canon declares, that it is no marriage.—The cloth having been first circum-

Pannus primum circumcisus,
Viduatus et divisus
    A sua pellicula,
Jam expertus Judaismum,
Emundatur per baptismum
    A quacumque macula.

Circumcisus mundatusque,
Est adeptus utriusque
    Legis testimonium;
Quem baptismus emundavit,
Cum secunda secundavit
    Pelle matrimonium.

Pilis expers, usu fractus,
Ex Esaü Jacob factus,
    Quant li peil en est chaü,
Inversatur vice versa,
Rursus idem ex conversa
    Ex Jacob fit Esaü.

Pars pilosa foris paret,
Sed introrsus pilis caret
    Vetustas abscondita;

cised, then widowed and separated from its skin, now having experienced
Judaism, is cleansed by baptism, from every stain (*i. e.* it is dyed).— Being
circumcised and cleaned, and having obtained the testimony of both laws, he
whom baptism has cleansed, contracts a new marriage with a second skin.—
Being devoid of hair, and worn by use, from Esau having become Jacob, when
the hair is fallen from it, the process is inverted, and again conversely from
Jacob it becomes Esau.—The hairy part is turned out, but the old part, con-

Datur tamen, k'il n'i eit perte,
Servienti, pur deserte,
Mantellus hypocrita.

cealed inwardly, is bare of hairs. Now the hypocritical mantle, in order that
there may be nothing lost, is given to the servant for his wages.

We are now approaching the eventful period of the Barons'
wars. The turbulent Welshmen were ever ready to seize an
opportunity of invading the Marches; and the following song,
whether it were composed by one of them, or be the work
of one of the English who took the opportunity of satirising
them, gives us a fair picture of the spirit in which they interfered.

THE SONG OF THE WELSH.

[From the Public Library of Leyden, MS. Vossius, No. 104, fol. 144, r°.
of the 13th cent.]

TRUCIDARE Saxones soliti Cambrenses
Ad cognatos Britones et Cornubienses ;
Requirunt ut veniant per acutos enses,
Ad debellandos inimicos Saxonienses.
    Venite jam strenue loricis armati ;
Sunt pars magna Saxonum mutuo necati,
Erit pars residua per nos trucidati :—
Nunc documenta date qua sitis origine nati.

TRANSLATION.—The Cambrians, who are used to slay the Saxons, salute
their relations the Britons and Cornish-men: they require them to come with their
sharp swords to conquer their Saxon enemies.—Come now, vigorously, armed
with coats of mail ; a great part of the Saxons are fallen in mutual slaughter,
the remainder shall be slain by us : now is the time for you to show of what blood

Mellinus veredicus nunquam dixit vanum ;
Expellendum populum prædixit vexanum.
Et vos hoc consilium non servatis sanum ;
Cernite fallaces quorum genus omne profanum.

    Prædecessor validus rex noster Arturus
Si vixisset hodie, fuissem securus
Nullus ei Saxonum restitisset murus ;
Esset ei[s] sicut meruerunt in prece durus.

    Procuret omnipotens sibi successorem
Saltem sibi similem, nollem meliorem,
Qui tollat Britonibus antiquum dolorem,
Et sibi restituat patriam patriæque decorem.

    Hoc Arturi patruus velit impetrare,
Sanctus [qui]dam maximus, Anglum ultra mare ;
Scimus festum Martis kalendis instare,—
Ad natale solum Britones studeat revocare.

    Virtuosos filii patres imitantur ;
Sic Arturum Britones virtute sequantur :
Quam probo, quam strenuo monstrant procreantur ;
Ut fuit Arturus sic victores habeantur !

you are sprung.—The soothsayer Merlin never said a thing that was vain ; he foretold that the mad people should be expelled. And you do not keep this wise counsel; observe deceitful people of whom the whole race is accursed.—If our valiant predecessor, King Arthur, had been now alive, I am sure not one of the Saxon walls would have resisted him ; he would have been hard to them, spite of their prayers, as they have deserved.—May the Omnipotent procure him a successor only similar to him, I would not desire a better, who may deliver the Britons from their old grievance, and restore to them their country and their country's glory.—May it please the uncle of Arthur to obtain this for us, a certain very great saint, [to send] the Englishman over the sea ; we know that his festival is approaching on the kalends of March (St. David's day), may he make it his study to recall the Britons to their native land.—Sons imitate their virtuous fathers, so let the Britons take Arthur for their example in valour ;

Regnabat Parisius potestas Romana,
Frollo gygas strenuus, cujus mens ursana ;
Hunc Arthurus perimit, credit fides sana,
Testis tentorium sit et insula Parisiana.

Insanit qui Britones necat generosos ;
Videtur quod habeat sic eos exosos,
Namque per invidiam clamat odiosos
Semper et assidue, quos audit victoriosos.

Ex hac gente iiij°ʳ sunt imperatores,
Arthurus, Broinsius, fortes bellatores,
Constantinus, Brennius, fere fortiores.
Hii monarchiam tenuerunt ut probiores.

Solum suum Karolum Francia præjectat ;
Et Ricardum Anglia probitate jactat ;
Paucitatem numerus major labefactat,
Virtutem regis quia quadrupla gloria mactat.

Istis suis finibus contigit regnare ;
Illis duces, præsides, reges triumphare,
Quibus nullo merito se possint æquare ;
Est quam regnare longe plus induperare.

they show from what a good and brave man they are descended; as Arthur
was, so let them be, conquerors !—The Roman power reigned at Paris, the
bold giant Frollo, with the bearish mind ; him Arthur slew : every person of
good faith believes it : witness the tent and the Parisian island.—He is a madman who kills the noble Britons : it seems that he holds them thus hated ; for
he invidiously proclaims them hateful always and incessantly, who he hears are
victorious.—Of this nation there have been four great commanders, Arthur
and Broinsius, powerful warriors ; Constantine and Brennius, more powerful,
if it were possible ; these held the monarchy by reason of their being the
best.—France can only boast of her Charlemaine ; and England glories in the
valour of King Richard ; a larger number overcomes a smaller, because a four-
fold glory increases the valour of the King.—To these latter it was granted to
reign within their own bounds ; to the others, to triumph, over commanders,
governors, and kings, with whom they can in no respect claim equality : it is a
far greater thing to command, than to reign.

The following fragment of what appears once to have been a long ballad, made to be sung in the halls of the Barons, seems to have been written soon after the disturbances in London in 1263, though there is not enough preserved to enable us to determine the precise occasion on which it was composed. Several nobles are here joined together, who afterwards took different sides.

THE SONG OF THE BARONS.

[A roll of parchment, of the 13th cent. in a private library.]

*   *   *   *

Mès de Warenne ly bon quens,
Que tant ad richesses et biens,
Si ad apris de guere,
En Norfolk en cel pens[is]
Vint conquerrant ses enemis,
Mès ore ne ad que fere.

Sire Jon Giffard deit bien nomé,
Que n'out gueres un pem . . é
En cele chivauchée ;
E si fu touz jors à devant,
Prus e sages et pernant,
E de grant renomée.

TRANSLATION.—But the good Earl of Warenne,—who has so much riches and property,—and has skill in war,—in Norfolk in this thought—he came conquering his enemies,—but now he has nothing to do.

Sir John Gifford ought well to be named,—who had scarcely a . . . —in this riding-bout;—and he was always forward,—valiant and wise, and active,—and of great renown.

Et Sire Jon D'Ayvile,
Que onques ni aima treyson ne gile,
    Fu en lur conpanie ;
Et sire Peres de Montfort,
Si tint bien à lur acord,
    Si out grant seignurie.

Et de Cliffort ly bon Roger
Se contint cum noble ber,
    Si fu de grant justice ;
Ne suffri pas petit ne grant,
Ne arère ne par devant,
    Fere nul mesprise.

Et Sire Roger de Leyburne,
Que sà et là sovent se torne,
    Mout ala conquerrant ;
Assez mist paine de gainer,
Pur ses pertes restorer,
    Que Sire Edward le fist avant.

Mout furent bons les barons ;
Mès touz ne sai nomer lur nons,
    Tant est grant la some :

And Sir John Dayville,—who never loved treason or guile,—was in their company ;—and Sir Peter de Montfort,—he held firm to their agreement,—and had great seignory.

And the good Roger de Clifford—behaved like a noble baron,—and exercised great justice ;—he suffered neither little nor great,—neither behind or before,—to do any wrong.

And Sir Roger de Leyburne,—who often turns him on this side and on that,—made great progress conquering ;—he laboured much to gain,—to restore his losses,—which Sir Edward had caused him before.

Right good men were the barons ;—but I cannot tell all their names,—the

Pur ce revenk al quens Simon,
Pur dire interpretison,
   Coment hom le nome.

Il est apelé de Monfort,
Il est el mond et si est fort,
   Si ad grant chevalerie ;
Ce voir, et je m'acort,
Il eime dreit, et het le tort,
   Si avera la mestrie.

El mond est veréement ;
Là ou la comun à ly concent,
   De la terre loée ;
C'est ly quens de Leycestre,
Que baut et joius se puet estre
   De cele renomée.

Ly eveske de Herefort
Sout bien que ly quens fu fort,
   Kant il prist l'affère :
Devant ce esteit mult fer,
Les Engleis quida touz manger,
   Mès ore ne set que fere.

number is so great :—therefore I return to Earl Simon,—to give the interpretation,—what is his name.

He is called de Montfort ;—he is in the world *(monde)*, and he is strong
(fort) ;—and he has great chivalry :—this is true, and I agree to it,—he loves
right and hates wrong,—and he shall have the mastery.

He is truly in the world,—there where the commons are in accord with him—
which are praised of the land ; —it is the Count of Leicester,—who may be glad
and joyous—of this renown.

The Bishop of Hereford—knew well that the Earl was strong,—when he
took the matter in hand ;—before that he (the bishop) was very fierce ;—he
thought to eat up all the English ;—but now he does not know what to do.

Et ly pastors de Norwis,
Qui devoure ses berbis,
    Assez sout de ce conte;
Mout en perdi de ses biens,
Mal ert que ly lessa riens,
    Ke trop en saveit de honte.

Et Sire Jon de Langelé,
Soune chose fu gainé,
    Deheiz eit que l'en pleine !
Tot le soen en fist porter
De Cliffort mi Sire Roger,
    Ne vout que rien remeine.

Ne à Sire Mathi de Besile
Ne lesserent une bile,
    En champ u en vile.
Tot le soen fu besilé,
E cointement fu detrussé
    Par un treget sanz gile.

Mès mi Sire Jon de Gray
Vint à Lundres, si ne sai quoi,
    Que must une destance

And the pastor of Norwich,—who devours his own sheep,—knows enough of this story ;—he lost much of his goods ;—it is pity they left him anything,—who was too much acquainted with shame.

And Sir John de Langley,—his property was gained,—cursed be he who complains of it ;—all he had my lord Roger de Clifford—caused to be carried away ;—he would let nothing remain.

Neither to Sir Matthew de Besile—did they leave one farthing,—in country or in town.—All his property was ravaged,—and neatly was he stripped—by a 'treget' without guile.

But Sir John de Gray—came to London, and some thing or other—made a

Par entre Lundres et ly,
Que tot son hernois en perdi,
   Ce fu sa meschance.

Et Sire Willem le Latimer
Vint à Lundres pur juer,
   *   *   *   *

quarrel—between London and him,—that he lost all his harness ;—that was his mischance.

And Sir William le Latimer—came to London to play, * * •

The following satyrical song seems to have been written on the occasion of the intermediation of Louis IX. of France, between the contending parties in England, in the beginning of the year 1264. Much of its point consists in a rather gross play upon words which cannot always be translated; it is written in a very broad dialect; and the numerous instances of bad French, which are observed in it, were, no doubt, committed intentionally, to increase the hilarity of the listeners, at the expense of the English and their King.

SONG OF THE PEACE WITH ENGLAND.

[From a MS. of the thirteenth century, in the Bibl. du Roi, at Paris, No. 7218, fol. 220, v°.]

Or vint la tens de May, que ce ros panirra,
Que ce tens serra beles, roxinol chanterra,
Ces prez il serra verdes, ces gardons florrirra ;
J'ai trova à ma cul .j. chos que je dirra.

Translation.—Now comes the time of May, when the rose will open,—when the seasons will be fair, and the nightingale sing,—the fields will be green, and the gardens will bloom ;—I have found behind me a thing which I will relate.

De ma ray d'Ingleters qui fu à bon naviaus,
Chivaler vaelant, hardouin, et léaus,
Et d'Adouart sa filz qui fi blont sa chaviaus,
Mai covint que je faites .j. dit troute noviaus.

Et de ce rai de Frans, cestui longue baron,
Qui tenez Normandi à tort par mal choison;
Lonc tens fout-il croupier sor Parris son maison,
Qu'il onc for por .i. gaire ne chauça d'asperon.

Sinor, tendez à mai; ne devez pas rier:
Ce navel que je port doit tout le mont crier.
L'autr'ier je fi à Londres une grosse concier;
Là ne movra baron la meilleur ne la pier,

Que tout ne fout venez à ce grand plaidement.
Là arra fet tel chos, je craie vraiement,
Qu'i farra rois François .i. grant poentement
De ce terres qu'il tient contre le Glaise gent.

Sinor, lonc tens fout-il que Mellins profita
Que Philippes de Frans, .i. sinor qui fi jà,

Of my King of England, who is in a good ship,—a valiant knight, hardy, and loyal,—and of Edward his son, who hath flaxen hair,—it pleases me to make a saying which is quite new.

And of that King of France, that long baron,—who held Normandy wrongfully by ill event;—long time did he settle his house upon Paris,—that he never but for a war alone put on his spur.

Lords, attend to me; you must not laugh:—all the world ought to cry this news which I bring.—The other day there was at London a great assembly;—there no baron, from the best to the worst, would move,

But they would all come to this great debating.—There would have been done such a thing, I believe truly,—that it would have caused the French King a great fright—concerning the lands which he holds against the English people.

Lords, it is a long time since Merlin prophecied—that Philip of France, a

Conquerra tout ce ters quanqu'il fout par deçà,
Mès toute vois, dit je l', qu'encore Glais l'arra.

Or sont-il vint le tans que Glais voura vauchier;
S'il trovez la François qui la voura groncier,
Qui parra si froirrous d'espé ou de levrier,
Qu'il n'arra talant por gondre Glais grondier.

Le bon rai d'Ingleter se traina à .i. part,
Li et Trichart sa frer irrous comme lipart.
Il suspire de cul, si se claima à l'art,—
" Hui Diex ! com puis-je voir de Normandi ma part ?"

" Ne vous maie mi ," dit la conte à Clocestre,
" Vous porra bien encors ; tel chos poistron bien estre,
Se Diex salva ma cul, ma pié, et ma poing destre,
Tu sarra sus Parris encore troute mestre."

La cont Vincestre dit au buer rai d'Ingletiere,
" Rai, rai, veus-tu sivier ? Festes mouvoir ton guere,
Et je te conduira trestout ton gent à foire :
Tu porras Normandi à ce pointes conquerre."

lord who was formerly,—should conquer all the land, such as it is, on this side ;—
but, at all events, I say it, the English will still have it.

Now is come the time that the English would make an inroad,—if he should
find the French inclined to grumble,—who would appear frightened by swords and
by greyhounds(?),—that he would have no courage to grumble against the English.

The good King of England drew himself on one side,—he and Richard his
brother, as angry as leopards.—He sighs from behind, and so cries with
alacrity,—" O God ! how may I have my part of Normandy ?"

" Do not disturb yourself at all," said the Earl of Gloucester,—" you may
still do it; such things may still easily be,—if God preserve my backside, my
foot, and my right fist,—thou shalt still be entire master over Paris."

The Earl of Winchester said to the noble King of England,—" King, King,
wilt thou follow ? Set agoing the war,—and I will conduct thee all thy people
in abundance :—at this juncture thou wilt be able to conquer Normandy.

"Se je pois rai François à bataille contrier,
Et je porrai mon lance desus son cul poier,
Je crai que je ferra si dourrement chier
Qu'il se brisa son test, ou ma cul fu rompier.

Je prendrez bien droitur, se je puis, à Diex poise,
Quant j'arra en mon main Normandi et Pontoise ;
Je ferra soz Parris achier mon gent Gloise,
Puis vondrai prender Frans, maugré conte d'Angoise.

Par la .v. plais à Diex, François maubali sont ;
Si g'i la puis grapier, certes il chateront.
Quant Inglais irront là, mult bahot i serront ;
Par la mort Dieu ! je crai que toutes s'enfuiront."

Sir Symon à Montfort atendi ce navel,
Doncques sailli à piez ; il ne fout mie bel.
A dit à rai Inglais, "Par le cors saint Anel !
Lessiez or cesti chos :—François n'est mi anel.

Se vous aler seur leus, il se voudra dafandre :
Toute ta paveillons metra feu à la cendre.

"If I can constrain the King of France to a battle,—and I can strike him
with my lance behind,—I think that I shall make him fall so hard—that he will
break his head, or my tail will be broken.

"I will take good right, if I can, with God's will,—when I shall have in my
hand Normandy and Poitou,—I will make my English people approach to
Paris,—and then I will go to take France in spite of the Earl of Anjou.

"By the five wounds of God ! the French are in bad case ;—if I can lay hold
upon them, truly they shall be punished.—When the English go there, there
will be a great disturbance ;—God's death ! I think they will all fly away."

Sir Simon de Montfort heard this speech,—then he leaped on his feet ; he
did not look very handsome.—Says he to the English King, "By the body of
the holy Lamb !—now let this thing alone ; the Frenchman is not a lamb.

"If you attack them, they will defend themselves :—he will burn all thy tents

Il n'a si vaelant qui l'ose mi atendre ;
Mult sarra maubali qui le François puet prendre."

" Qoi dites-vous, Symon ?" pona Rogier Bigot ;
" Bien tenez-vous la rai por binart et por sot ?
Fout insi hardouin que vous sone plus mot,
Ne te pot besoner por vostre mileur cot !"

" Sir Rogier," dit la rai, " por Dieu, ne vous chaele !
Ne sai mi si irrous contre ce merdaele.
Je ne dout mi Françoys tout qui sont une mele ;
Je farra ma talent comment la chos aele.

Je pandra bien Parris, je suis toute certaine ;
Je bouterra le fu en cele eve qui [fu] Saine ;
La moulins arderra ; ce fi chos mult gravaine
Se n'i menja de pain de troute la semaine.

[P]ar la .v. plais à Diex, Parris fout vil mult grant
Il i a .i. chapel dont je fi coetant ;
Je le ferra portier, à .i. charrier rollant,
A Saint Amont à Londres toute droit en estant.

to ashes.—There is no man so valiant who dare wait for him ;—they will be in ill case whom the Frenchman can catch."

" What is that you say, Simon ?" replied Roger Bigot ;—" do you take the King for a simpleton and a fool ?—if you are so bold as to say another word,— you will not serve yourself with your best coat."

" Sir Roger," said the King, " for God's sake ! dont be in a heat ;—I am not so angry against this scamp.—I dont care half a farthing for all the French that are ;—I will do as I like, let the matter go as it will.

" I will easily take Paris, I am quite certain ;—I will set fire to the river which is called Seine ;—I will burn the mill ; this will be a very grievous thing,—if they eat no bread all the week.

" By the five wounds of God ! Paris is a very great city !—There is a chapel, of which I am desirous ;—I will cause it to be carried in a rolling cart,— straight to Saint Amont in London, just as it stands.

Quant j'arra soz Parris mené tout me naviaus,
Je ferra le moustier Saint Dinis la Chanciaus
Corronier d'Adouart soz sa blonde chaviaus.
La voudra vous toer de vaches à porciaus.

Je crai que vous verra là endret grosse fest,
Quant d'Adouart arra corroné France test.
Il l'a bien asservi, ma fil; il n'est pas best;
Il fout buen chivaler, hardouin, et honest."

"Sir rai," ce dit Rogier, "por Dieu à mai entent;
Tu m'as percé la cul, tel la pitié m'a prent.
Or doint Godelamit, par son culmandement,
Que tu fais cestui chos bien gloriousement!"

Explicit la pais aus Englois.

" When I have led all my ships to Paris,—I will cause the Chancellor in the monastery of St. Denis—to crown Edward on his flaxen hair.—There I will kill for you cows and pigs.

" I believe that you will see there a great feast,—when France shall have crowned Edward's head. He has well deserved it, my son; he is no fool;—he is a good knight, brave, and courteous."

" Sir King," said Roger, "for God's sake, listen to me;—thou hast pierced me behind, so much has pity overcome me;—Now may God Almighty ordain, by his commandment,—that thou perform this thing very gloriously!"

The decisive battle of Lewes, in 1264, was the subject of great exultation amongst the adherents of Simon de Montfort. The following song, in English, is directed against the king's brother, Richard Earl of Cornwall, who had become very unpopular by his foreign schemes of ambition. He took shelter at a windmill, after he saw the king's party defeated.

SONG AGAINST THE KING OF ALMAIGNE.

[MS. Harl. No. 2253, fol. 58 v°, of the reign of Edw. II.]

Sitteth alle stille ant herkneth to me :
The Kyn of Alemaigne, bi mi leauté,
Thritti thousent pound askede he
For te make the pees in the countré,
  ant so he dude more.
 Richard, thah thou be ever trichard,
  trichen shalt thou never more.

Richard of Alemaigne, whil that he wes kyng,
He spende al is tresour opon swyvyng ;
Haveth he nout of Walingford o ferlyng :—
Let him habbe, ase he brew, bale to dryng,
  maugre Wyndesore.
 Richard, thah thou be ever, etc.

The Kyng of Alemaigne wende do ful wel,
He saisede the mulne for a castel,
With hare sharpe swerdes he grounde the stel,
He wende that the sayles were mangonel
  to helpe Wyndesore.
 Richard, etc.

TRANSLATION.—Sit all still and listen to me :—the King of Almaigne, by my loyalty,—thirty thousand pound he asked—to make peace in the country,—and so he did more.—Richard, though thou art ever a traitor,—thou shalt never more deceive.

Richard of Almaigne, while he was king,—he spent all his treasure upon luxury ;—have he not of Wallingford one furlong :—let him have, as he brews, evil to drink,—in spite of Windsor.

The King of Almaigne thought to do full well,—they seized the mill for a castle ;—with their sharp swords they ground the steel,—they thought the sails had been mangonels—to help Windsor.

The Kyng of Alemaigne gederede ys host,
Makede him a castel of a mulne post,
Wende with is prude ant is muchele bost,
Brohte from Alemayne mony sori gost
                    to store Wyndesore.
        Richard, etc.

By God, that is aboven ous, he dude muche synne,
That lette passen over see the Erl of Warynne:
He hath robbed Engelond, the mores, ant th[e] fenne,
The gold, ant the selver, ant y-boren henne,
                    for love of Wyndesore.
        Richard, etc.

Sire Simond de Mountfort hath swore bi ys chyn,
Hevede he nou here the Erl of Waryn,
Shulde he never more come to is yn,
Ne with sheld, ne with spere, ne with other gyn,
                    to help of Wyndesore.
        Richard, etc.

Sire Simond de Montfort hath suore bi ys cop,
Hevede he nou here Sire Hue de Bigot,

The King of Almaigne gathered his host,—he made him a castle of a mill-post,—he went with his pride and his great boast,—brought from Almaigne many a wretched soul—to garrison Windsor.

By God, that is above us, he did great sin,—who let the Earl of Warenne pass over sea :—he hath robbed England both the moor and the fen,—of the gold and the silver, and carried them hence,—for love of Windsor.

Sir Simon de Montfort hath sworn by his chin,—had he now here the Earl of Warenne,—he should never more come to his lodging,—neither with shield, nor with spear, nor with other contrivance,—to help Windsor.

Sir Simon de Montfort hath sworn by his head,—had he now here Sir Hugh

Al he shulde quite here twelfmoneth scot,
Shulde he never more with his fot pot
   to helpe Wyndesore.
  Richard, etc.

Be the luef, be the loht, sire Edward,
Thou shalt ride sporeles o thy lyard
Al the ryhte way to Dovere ward;
Shalt thou never more breke fore-ward,
   ant that reweth sore:
  Edward, thou dudest ase a shreward,
   forsoke thyn emes lore.
  Richard, etc.

de Bigot,—he should pay here a twelvemonth's scot,—he should never more
tramp on his feet,—to help Windsor.

 Be it agreeable to thee, or disagreeable, Sir Edward,—thou shalt ride spurless
on thy hack—all the straight road towards Dover;—thou shalt never more
break covenant;—and that sore rueth thee;—Edward, thou didst like a shrew,—
forsookest thine uncle's teaching.

The following long, but singularly interesting, poem may be
considered as the popular declaration of the principles with
which the barons entered into the war, and the objects which
they had in view. It bears internal proofs of having been written
immediately after the decisive battle of Lewes; and the moderate and deeply moral and religious feeling which the reforming
party here shows, even in the moment of triumph, is extremely
remarkable, and is closely connected with the complaints against
the licentiousness of the other party in the satyrical songs which
precede. We might almost suppose ourselves transported to
the days of Wickliffe or Cromwell.

THE BATTLE OF LEWES.

[MS. Harl. 978. fol. 128, r°. of the middle of the 13th cent.]

CALAMUS velociter scribe sic scribentis,
Lingua laudabiliter te benedicentis,
Dei patris dextera, domine virtutum,
Qui das tuis prospera quando vis ad nutum;
In te jam confidere discant universi,
Quos volebant perdere qui nunc sunt dispersi.
Quorum caput capitur, membra captivantur;
Gens elata labitur, fideles lætantur.
Jam respirat Anglia, sperans libertatem;
10 Cuï Dei gratia det prosperitatem!
Comparati canibus Angli viluerunt,
Sed nunc victis hostibus caput extulerunt.

Gratiæ millesimo ducentesimoque
Anno sexagesimo quarto, quarta quoque
Feria Pancratii post sollempnitatem,
Valde gravis prelii tulit tempestatem
Anglorum turbatio, castroque Lewensi;
Nam furori ratio, vita cessit ensi.

TRANSLATION.—Write quickly, O pen of one who, writing such things as follow, blesses and praises with his tongue, thee, O right hand of God the Father, Lord of virtues, who givest prosperity at thy nod to thine own, whenever it is thy will; let all those people now learn to put their trust in thee, whom they, who are now scattered, wished to destroy—they of whom the head is now taken, and the members are in captivity; the proud people is fallen; the faithful are filled with joy. Now England breathes in the hope of liberty; [10] to which (England) may the grace of God give prosperity! The English were despised like dogs; but now they have raised their head over their vanquished enemies.

In the year of grace one thousand two hundred and sixty-four, and on the Wednesday after the festival of St. Pancras, the army of the English bore the brunt of a great battle at the castle of Lewes: for reasoning yielded to rage,

Pridie qui Maii Idus confluxerunt,
20 Horrendi discidii bellum commiserunt;
Quod fuit Susexiæ factum comitatu,
Fuit et Cicestriæ in episcopatu.
Gladius invaluit, multi ceciderunt,
Veritas prævaluit, falsique fugerunt.
Nam perjuris restitit dominus virtutum,
Atque puris præstitit veritatis scutum.
Hos vastavit gladius foris, intus pavor;
Confortavit plenius istos cœli favor.
Victoris sollempnia sanctæque coronæ
30 Reddunt testimonia super hoc agone;
Cum dictos ecclesia sanctos honoravit,
Milites victoria veros coronavit.
Dei sapientia, regens totum mundum,
Fecit mirabilia bellumque jocundum;
Fortes fecit fugere, virosque virtutis
In claustro se claudere, locis quoque tutis.
Non armis sed gratia christianitatis,
Id est in ecclesia, excommunicatis

and life to the sword. They met on the fourteenth of May, [20] and began the battle of this terrible strife; which was fought in the county of Sussex, and in the bishopric of Chichester. The sword was powerful; many fell; truth prevailed; and the false men fled. For the Lord of valour resisted the perjured men, and defended those who were pure with the shield of truth. The sword without, and fear within, routed the former; the favour of heaven comforted very fully the latter. The solemnities of the victor, and the sacred crowns, [30] give testimony on this contest; since the Church honoured the said persons as saints, and victory crowned the true soldiers. The wisdom of God, which rules the whole world, performed miracles and made a joyful war; caused the strong to fly, and the valorous men to shut themselves up in a cloister, and in places of safety. Not in arms, but in the grace of Christianity, that is in the Church, remained the only refuge for those who were excommunicated; after

Unicum refugium restabat, relictis
40 Equis, hoc consilium occurrebat victis.
Et quam non timuerant prius prophanare,
Quam more debuerant matris honorare,
Ad ipsam refugiunt, licet minus digni,
Amplexus se muniunt salutaris ligni.
Quos matrem contempnere prospera fecerunt,
Vulnera cognoscere matrem compulerunt.
Apud Northamptoniam dolo prosperati,
Spreverunt ecclesiam infideles nati;
Sanctæ matris viscera ferro turbaverunt,
50 Prosperis non prospera bella meruerunt.
Mater tunc injuriam tulit patienter,
Quasi per incuriam, sed nec affluenter:
Punit hanc et alias quas post addiderunt,
Nam multas ecclesias insani læserunt;
Namque monasterium, quod Bellum vocatur,
Turba sævientium, quæ nunc conturbatur,
Inmisericorditer bonis spoliavit,
Atque sibi taliter bellum præparavit.

deserting their horses [40] this counsel alone occurred to the vanquished.
And her whom previously they had not hesitated to profane, her whom they
ought to have honoured in the place of a mother—in her they seek refuge,
though little worthy of it, and seek their defence in embracing the wood of
salvation.   Those whom prosperity caused to despise their mother, their
wounds compelled to know their mother.   When at Northampton they succeeded by treachery, the faithless children despised the church; with the sword
they disturbed the bowels of the holy mother, and in their prosperity [50] did
not merit a successful war.   The mother then bore the injury patiently, as
though heedless of it, but not letting it pass unmarked: she punishes this and
other injuries which were afterwards added, for the madmen ravaged many
churches; and the band of enraged men, which has now been thrown into confusion, mercilessly spoiled the monastry which is called Battle, of its goods, and

Monachi Cystercii de Ponte-Roberti
60 A furore gladii non fuissent certi,
   Si quingentas principi marcas non dedissent.
   Quas Edwardus accipi jussit, vel perissent.
   Hiis atque similibus factis meruerunt
   Quod cesserunt hostibus et succubuerunt.
   Benedicat dominus .S. de Monte-Forti!
   Suis nichilominus natis et cohorti!
   Qui se magnanimiter exponentes morti,
   Pugnaverunt fortiter, condolentes sorti
   Anglicorum flebili, qui subpeditati
70 Modo vix narrabili, peneque privati
   Cunctis libertatibus, immo sua vita,
   Sub duris principibus langüerunt ita,
   Ut Israelitica plebs sub Pharaone,
   Gemens sub tyrannica devastatione.
   Sed hanc videns populi Deus agoniam,
   Dat in fine seculi novum Mathathiam,
   Et cum suis filiis zelans zelum legis,
   Nec cedit injuriis nec furori regis.

thus they prepared a *battle* for themselves. The Cistercian monks of Robertsbridge [60] would not have been safe from the fury of the sword, unless they had given five hundred marks to the prince, which Edward ordered to be received, or they had perished. By these, and similar deeds, they merited to give way and succumb before their enemies. May the Lord bless Simon de Montfort! and also his sons and his army! who, exposing themselves magnanimously to death, fought valiantly, condoling the lamentable lot of the English who, trodden under foot in a manner scarcely to be described, [70] and almost deprived of all their liberties, nay, of their lives, had languished under hard rulers, like the people of Israel under Pharaoh, groaning under a tyrannical devastation. But God, seeing this suffering of the people, gives at last a new Matathias, and he with his sons, zealous after the zeal of the law, yields neither to the insults nor to the fury of the king.

Seductorem nominant .S. atque fallacem ;
80 Facta sed examinant probantque veracem.
Dolosi deficiunt in necessitate ;
Qui mortem non fugiunt, sunt in veritate.
Sed nunc dicit æmulus, et insidiator,
Cujus nequam oculus pacis perturbator :
" Si laudas constantiam, si fidelitatem,
Quæ mortis instantiam vel pœnalitatem
Non fugit, æqualiter dicentur constantes
Qui concurrunt pariter invicem pugnantes,
Pariter discrimini semet exponentes,
90 Duroque cognomini se subjicientes."
Sed in nostro prelio cuï nunc instamus,
Qualis sit discretio rei videamus.

   Comes paucos habuit armorum expertos
Pars regis intumuit, bellatores certos
Et majores Angliæ habens congregatos,
Floremque militiæ regni nominatos ;
Qui Londoniensibus armis comparati,
Essent multis milibus trecenti prælati ;

They call Simon a seductor and a traitor ; [80] but his deeds lay him open
and prove him to be a true man.   Traitors fall off in time of need ; they who do
not fly death, are those who stand for the truth.   But says his insidious enemy
now, whose evil eye is the disturber of peace, " If you praise the constancy
and the fidelity, which does not fly the approach of death or punishment, they shall
equally be called constant who, in the same manner, go to the combat fighting on
the opposite side, in the same manner exposing themselves to the chance
of war, [90] and subjecting themselves to a hard appellation." But in our war in
which we are now engaged, let us see what is the state of the case.

   The earl had few men used to arms ; the royal party was numerous, having
assembled the disciplined and greatest warriors in England, such as were called
the flower of the army of the kingdom ; those who were prepared with arms from
among the Londoners, were three hundred set before several thousands ; whence

Unde contemptibiles illis extiterunt,
100 Et abhominabiles expertis fuerunt.
Comitis militia plurima tenella;
In armis novitia, parum novit bella.
Nunc accinctus gladio tener adolescens
Mane stat in prelio armis assuescens;
Quid mirum si timeat tyro tam novellus,
Et si lupum caveat impotens agnellus?
Sic ergo militia sunt inferiores
Qui pugnant pro Anglia, sunt et pauciores
Multo viris fortibus, de sua virtute
110 Satis gloriantibus, ut putarent tute,
Et sine periculo, velut absorbere
Quotquot adminiculo Comiti fuere.
Nam et quos adduxerat Comes ad certamen,
De quibus speraverat non parvum juvamen,
Plurimi perterriti mox se subtraxerunt,
Et velut attoniti fugæ se dederunt;
Et de tribus partibus tertia recessit.
Comes cum fidelibus paucis nunquam cessit.

they were contemptible to those, [100] and were detested by those who were experienced. Much of the earl's army was raw; fresh in arms, they knew little of war. The tender youth, only now girt with a sword, stands in the morning in battle accustoming himself to arms; what wonder if such an unpractised tyro fear, and if the powerless lamb dread the wolf? Thus those who fight for England are inferior in military discipline, and they are much fewer than the strong men, who boasted in their own valour, [110] because they thought safely, and without danger, to swallow up, as it were, all whom the earl had to help him. Moreover, of those whom the earl had brought to the battle, and from whom he hoped for no little help, many soon withdrew from fear, and took to flight as though they were amazed; and of three parts, one deserted. The earl with a few faithful men never yielded. We may compare our battle

Gedeonis prelium nostro comparemus,
120 In quibus fidelium vincere videmus
    Paucos multos numero fidem non habentes,
    Similes Lucifero de se confidentes.
    " Si darem victoriam," dicit Deus, " multis,
    Stulti michi gloriam non darent, sed stultis."
    Sic si Deus fortibus vincere dedisset,
    Vulgus laudem talibus non Deo dedisset.

      Ex hiis potest elici quod non timuerunt
    Deum viri bellici, unde nil fecerunt
    Quod suam constantiam vel fidelitatem
130 Probet, sed superbiam et crudelitatem ;
    Volentes confundere partem quam spreverunt,
    Exeuntes temere cito corruerunt.
    Cordis exaltatio præparat ruinam,
    Et humiliatio meretur divinam
    Dari sibi gratiam ; nam qui non confidit
    De Deo, superbiam Deus hanc elidit.
    Aman introducimus atque Mardocheum ;
    Hunc superbum legimus, hunc verum Judæum ;

with that of Gideon; [120] in both of which we see a few of the faithful conquer
a great number who have no faith, and who trust in themselves like Lucifer did.
God said, " If I should give the victory to the many, the fools will not give the
glory to me, but to fools." So if God had made the strong to conquer, the
common people would have given the credit of it to the men, and not to God.

From these considerations it may be concluded that the warlike men did not
fear God, wherefore they did nothing to prove their constancy or fidelity,
[130] but they showed on the contrary their pride and and cruelty ; and wishing
to confound those whom they despised, issuing forth boldly, they perished
quickly. Exaltation of the heart brings on ruin, and humility merits to
receive the divine grace ; for he who does not trust in God, God overthrows his
pride. We may bring forward as examples Aman and Mardocheus ; we read
that the former was arrogant, the latter a true Israelite ; the gallows which

Lignum quod paraverat Aman Mardocheo,
140 Mane miser tollerat suspensus in eo.
Reginæ convivium Aman excœcavit,
Quod ut privilegium magnum reputavit;
Sed spes vana vertitur in confusionem,
Cum post mensam trahitur ad suspensionem.
Sic extrema gaudii luctus occupavit,
Cum finem convivii morti sociavit.
Longe dissimiliter accidit Judæo,
Honorat sublimiter quem rex, dante Deo.
Golias prosternitur projectu lapilli;
150 Quem Deus persequitur, nichil prodest illi.
Ad prædictas varias adde rationes,
Quod tot fornicarias fætidi lenones
Ad se convocaverant, usque septingentas,
Quas scire debuerant esse fraudulentas,
Sathanæ discipulas ad decipiendas
Animas, et faculas ad has incendendas,
Dolosas novaculas ad crines Samsonis
Radendos, et maculas turpis actionis

Aman had prepared for Mardocheus, [140] in the morning the wretch bore it himself in order to be hanged upon it. The queen's banquet blinded Aman, which he reputed as an extraordinary privilege; but his vain expectation is turned into confusion, when after the feast he is dragged to the gallows. Thus sorrow followed close upon joy, when it coupled death with the end of the feast. Very differently, it happens, to the Israelite, whom, by God's will, the king honours. Golias is overthrown by the stroke of a little stone; [150] nothing profits him whom God pursues. Add to the various reasons already mentioned, that the stinking bawds collected with them so many strumpets, amounting to seven hundred, which they ought to have known to be fraudulent persons, disciples of Satan to deceive men's souls, and matches to set them on fire, treacherous scissars to cut the hairs of Samson, inflicting the stains of base action on the

Inferentes miseris qui ncn sunt cordati,
160 Nec divini muneris gratia firmati,
Carnis desideriis animales dati,
Cujus immunditiis, brutis comparati,
Esse ne victoria digni debuerunt,
Qui carnis luxuria fœda sorduerunt :
Factis lupanaribus robur minuerunt,
Unde militaribus indigni fuerunt.
Accingitur gladio super femur miles,
Absit dissolutio, absint actus viles ;
Corpus novi militis solet balneari,
170 Ut a factis vetitis discat emundari.
Qui de novo duxerant uxores legales,
Domini non fuerant apti bello tales,
Gedeonis prelio teste, multo minus
Quos luxus incendio læserat caminus.
Igitur adulteros cur Deus juvaret,
Et non magis pueros mundos roboraret ?
Mundentur qui cupiunt vincere pugnando ;
Qui culpas subjiciunt sunt in triumphando ;

wretches who are not strong in heart, [160] nor made firm by the grace of the divine gift, but animals dedicated to the lust of the flesh, by the uncleanness of which, reduced to the level of brutes, they ought not to be worthy of victory, who grovelled in the foul luxury of the flesh ; they diminish their strength in the stews which they had made, therefore they were unworthy of the attributes of knights. A knight is girt on the thigh with a sword, that it may not be ungirt, and that vile deeds should be eschewed ; the body of a new knight is accustomed to be bathed, [170] in order that he may learn to be clean from unlawful deeds. They who had newly married lawful wives, were not fit for the Lord's warfare, as the battle of Gideon witnesseth, much less those whom the furnace of luxury hath injured with its fire. Why then should God help adulterers, and not rather strengthen clean children? Let them be clean who desire to conquer in fighting ; they who vanquish their faults are in the way to triumph ; first let them

Primo vincant vitia, qui volunt victores
180 Esse cum justitia super peccatores.
Si justus ab impio quandoque videtur
Victus, e contrario victor reputetur ;
Nam nec justus poterit vinci, nec iniquus
Vincere dum fuerit juris inimicus.
Æquitatem comitis Symonis audite :
Cum pars regis capitis ipsius et vitæ
Solam pœnam quæreret, nec redemptionem
Capitis admitteret, sed abscisionem,
Quo confuso plurima plebs confunderetur,
190 Et pars regni maxima periclitaretur,
Ruina gravissima statim sequeretur ;
Quæ mora longissima non repareretur !
.S. divina gratia præsul Cycestrensis,
Alta dans suspiria pro malis immensis
Jam tunc imminentibus, sine fictione,
Persüasis partibus de formatione
Pacis, hoc a Comite responsum audivit :
" Optimos eligite, quorum fides vivit,

conquer their vices, [180] who wish with justice to have the victory over sinners. If the just man seems sometimes to be vanquished by the impious man, on the contrary he should be reputed the conqueror; for neither can the just man be vanquished, nor the unjust man conquer while he is the enemy of the law.

Listen to the equity of Earl Simon : when the royal party would be satisfied only with his head and his life, nor would allow his head to be redeemed, but would have it cut off, by whose confusion they hoped the body of the people should be confounded, [190] and the greatest part of the state brought into danger, so that the most grievous ruin would immediately follow ;—may it be very long before this happen !—Stephen, by divine grace, bishop of Chichester, groaning deeply for the immense evils which were then impending, (without exaggeration,) the two parties being persuaded to treat of a peace, received this answer from the

Qui decreta legerint, vel theologiam
200 Decenter docuerint sacramque sophiam,
Et qui sciant regere fidem Christianam ;
Quicquidque consulere per doctrinam sanam
Quicquidve discernere tales non timebunt,
Quod dicent, suscipere promptos nos habebunt ;
Ita quod perjurii notam nesciamus,
Sed ut Dei filii fidem teneamus."
Hinc possunt perpendere facile jurantes,
Et quod jurant spernere parum dubitantes,
Quamvis jurent licita, cito recedentes,
210 Deoque pollicita sana non reddentes,
Quanta cura debeant suum juramentum
Servare, cum videant virum nec tormentum
Neque mortem fugere propter jusjurandum,
Præstitum non temere, sed ad reformandum
Statum qui deciderat Anglicanæ gentis,
Quem fraus violaverat hostis invidentis.
En Symon obediens spernit dampna rerum,
Pœnis se subjiciens, ne dimittat verum,

Earl: "Choose the best men, who have a lively faith, [200] who have read the decretals, or who have taught, in a becoming manner, theology and sacred wisdom, and who know how to rule the Christian faith, whatever they may resolve by sound doctrine, or whatever they may have the courage to decree, they shall find us ready to agree to what they shall dictate, in such a manner as that we may escape the stigma of perjury, and keep the league as children of God." Hence it may easily be understood by those who swear, and show little reluctance to despise what they swear, receding quickly from it although they swear to what is right, [210] and not rendering whole what they have promised to God, with how much care they ought to keep their oath, when they see a man neither avoiding torment nor death on account of his oath, which was made not inconsiderately, but for the reformation of the fallen state of the English nation, which the fraud of an inveterate enemy had violated. Behold Simon, obedient,

Cunctis palam prædicans factis plus quam dictis,
220 Quod non est communicans veritas cum fictis.
Væ perjuris miseris, qui non timent Deum !
Spe terreni muneris abnegantes eum,
Vel timore carceris, sive pœnæ levis ;
Novus dux itineris docet ferre quævis
Quæ mundus intulerit propter veritatem,
Quæ perfectam poterit dare libertatem.
Nam Comes præstiterat prius juramentum,
Quod quicquid providerat zelus sapientum
Ad honoris regii reformationem,
230 Et erroris devii declinationem,
Partibus Oxoniæ, firmiter servaret,
Hujusque sententiæ legem non mutaret ;
Sciens tam canonicas constitutiones
Atque tam catholicas ordinationes
Ad regni pacificam conservationem,
Propter quas non modicam persecutionem
Prius sustinuerat, non esse spernandas ;
Et quia juraverat fortiter tenendas,

despises the loss of property, submitting himself to punishment, rather than
desert the truth, proclaiming to all men openly by his deeds more than by his
words, [220] that truth has nothing in common with falsehood. Woe to the
perjured wretches who fear not God ! denying him for the prospect of an earthly
reward, or for fear of imprisonment or light punishment ; the new leader of the
journey teaches to bear all that the world may inflict on account of truth, for it
is this which can give perfect liberty. For the Earl had first pledged his oath
that whatever the zeal of the wise had provided for the reformation of the King's
honour, [230] and for the repression of wandering error, at Oxford, he would
steadfastly keep it, and would not change the law then ordained, knowing that
such canonical constitutions, and such catholic ordinances for the pacific con-
servation of the kingdom, on account of which he had before sustained no slight
persecution, were not to be despised ; and because he had sworn to hold them

Nisi perfectissimi fidei doctores
240 Dicerent, quod eximi possent juratores,
 Qui tale præstiterant prius jusjurandum,
 Et id quod juraverant non esse curandum.
 Quod cum dictus pontifex regi recitaret,
 Atque fraudis artifex forsitan astaret,
 Vox in altum tollitur turbæ tumidorum,
 " En jam miles subitur dictis clericorum !
 Viluit militia clericis subjecta !"
 Sic est sapientia Comitis despecta ;
 Edwardusque dicitur ita respondisse,
250 " Pax illis præcluditur, nisi laqueis se
 Collis omnes alligent, et ad suspendendum
 Semet nobis obligent, vel ad detrahendum."
 Quid mirum si Comitis cor tunc moveretur,
 Cum non nisi stipitis pœna pareretur ?
 Optulit quod debuit, sed non est auditus ;
 Rex mensuram respuit, salutis oblitus.
 Sed ut rei docuit crastinus eventus,
 Modus quem tunc noluit post non est inventus.

firmly, unless the most perfect doctors of the faith should say, [240] that the jurators might be absolved, who had before taken such oath, and that no further account was to be made of what they had sworn. Which, when the said bishop recited to the king, and perhaps the artificer of fraud was standing by, the voice of the crowd of arrogant courtiers was raised high, " See now the soldier is to give way to the sayings of clerks ! The military order subjected to clerks is debased !" Thus the wisdom of the Earl was despised ; and Edward is said to have answered thus : [250] " They shall have no peace unless they all put halters about their necks, and deliver themselves up to us to be hanged, or to be drawn." What wonder if the Earl's heart was then moved, when nothing but the pain of the stake was prepared for him ? He offered what he ought to do, but he was not listened to ; the king rejected measure, forgetting what was good for him. But, as the event of the matter next day taught him,

Comitis devotio sero deridetur,
260 Cujus cras congressio victrix sentietur.
Lapis hic ab hostibus diu reprobatus,
Post est parietibus duobus aptatus.
Angliæ divisio desolationis
Fuit in confinio, sed divisionis
Affuit præsidio lapis angularis,
Symonis religio sane singularis.
Fides et fidelitas Symonis solius
Fit pacis integritas Angliæ totius;
Rebelles humiliat, levat desperatos,
270 Regnum reconsilians, reprimens elatos.
Quos quo modo reprimit? certe non laudendo,
Sed rubrum jus exprimit dure confligendo;
Ipsum nam confligere veritas coegit,
Vel verum deserere, sed prudens elegit
Magis dare dexteram suam veritati,
Viamque per asperam junctam probitati,
Per grave compendium tumidis ingratum,
Optinere bravium violentis datum,

the measure which he then refused, afterwards was not to be had. In the
evening was derided the Earl's devotion, [260] the shock of which, next day, was
found to be victorious. This stone, long rejected from the doorway, was afterwards fitted to the two walls. The division of England was on the verge of
desolation, but the corner-stone was there as a help to the division, the truly
singular religion of Simon. The faith and fidelity of Simon alone becomes
the security of the peace of all England; he humbles the rebellious, raises those
who were in despair, [270] reconciling the kingdom, repressing the proud.
And how does he repress them? certainly not by praising them; but he
presses out the red juice in the hard conflict; for truth obliges him to fight,
or to desert the truth, and prudently he chooses rather to devote his right hand
to the truth, and by the rough way, which is joined to probity, by the harder and
shorter way which is unpleasant to the proud, to obtain the reward which is given

Quam per subterfugium Deo displicere,
280 Pravorumque studium fuga promovere.
Nam quidam studuerant Anglorum delere
Nomen, quos jam cæperant exosos habere,
Contra quos opposuit Deus medicinam,
Ipsorum cum noluit subitam ruinam.
Hinc alienigenas discant advocare
Angli, si per advenas volunt exulare.
Nam qui suam gloriam volunt ampliare,
Suamque memoriam vellent semper stare,
Suæ gentis plurimos sibi sociari,
290 Et mox inter maximos student collocare;
Itaque confusio crescit incolarum,
Crescit indignatio, crescit cor amarum,
Cum se premi sentiunt regni principales
Ab hiis qui se faciunt sibi coæquales,
Quæ sua debuerant esse subtrahentes,
Quibus consüeverant crescere, crescentes.
Eschaetis et gardiis suos honorare
Debet rex, qui variis modis se juvare

to those who use force, than to displease God by shrinking, [280] and to promote the designs of bad men by flight. For some men had studied to erase the name of the English, whom they had already begun to regard with hatred, against whom God opposed a medicine, since he did not desire their sudden ruin,

Hence let the English learn to call in strangers, if they wish to be exiled by strangers. For these when they wish to enlarge their own glory, and wish their own memory to stand always, study to associate with themselves very many of their own nation, [290] and by degrees to make them the principal nobles; and thus grows the confusion of the natives, with indignation and bitterness of heart, when the chief men of the kingdom feel themselves to be beaten down by those who make themselves their equals, taking from them the things which ought to appertain to them, growing by the things by which they used to grow. The King ought to honour with escheats and wards his own people, who can

Possunt, qui quo viribus sunt valentiores,
300 Eo cunctis casibus sunt securiores.
　Sed qui nil attulerant, si suis ditantur,
　Qui nullius fuerant, si magnificantur,
　Crescere cum ceperint, semper scandunt tales
　Donec supplantaverint viros naturales ;
　Principis avertere cor a suis student,
　Ut quos volunt cadere gloria denudent.
　Et quis posset talia ferre patienter ?
　Ergo discat Anglia cavere prudenter,
　Ne talis perplexitas amplius contingat,
310 Ne talis adversitas Anglicos inpingat.
　Hüic malo studuit comes obviare,
　Quod nimis invaluit quasi magnum mare,
　Quod parvo conamine nequibat siccari,
　Sed magno juvamine Dei transvadari.
　Veniant extranei cito recessuri,
　Quasi momentanei, sed non permansuri.
　Una juvat aliam manuum duarum,
　Neutra tollens gratiam verius earum ;

help him in various ways, who, by as much as they are more powerful by their own strength, [300] are so much the more secure in all cases. But those who have brought nothing, if they are enriched by his goods, if they are made great who were of no account, such men, when they begin to grow, always go on climbing till they have supplanted the natives ; they study to avert the prince's heart from his own people, that they may strip of glory those whose ruin they are seeking. And who could bear such things patiently? Therefore let England learn prudently to have a care, lest such a perplexity should happen any more, [310] lest such an adversity should fall upon the English. The Earl studied to obviate this, because it had gained too much head, like a great sea, that could not be dried by a small effort, but must be forded by a great assistance from God. Let strangers come to return quickly, like men of a moment, but not to remain. One of the two hands aids the other, neither of them bearing more really the grace which belongs to both ; let it help, and not injure, by retaining its

Juvet et non noceat locum retinendo.

320 Quæque suum valeat ita veniendo;
Gallicus ad Anglicum benefaciendo,
Et non per sophisticum vultum seducendo,
Nec alter alterius bona subtrahendo;
Immo suum potius onus sustinendo.
Commodum si proprium comitem movisset,
Nec haberet alium zelum, nec quæsisset
Toto suo studio reformationi
Regni, sed intentio dominationi,
Solam suam quæreret, et promotionem

330 Suorum proponerat, ad ditationem
Filiorum tenderet, et communitatis
Salutem negligeret, ac duplicitatis
Palli[o] supponeret virus falsitatis;
Sic fidem relinqueret Christianitatis,
Et horrendæ subderet se pœnalitatis
Legi, nec effugeret pondus tempestatis.
Et quis potest credere quod se morti daret,
Suos vellet perdere, ut sic exaltaret?

place. [320] Each thing would avail its own possessor if they come so; the Frenchman by doing good to the Englishman, and not seducing by a flattering face, nor the one withdrawing the goods of the other; but rather by sustaining his own portion of the burden. If his own interest had moved the Earl, he would neither have had any other zeal, nor would he have sought with all his power for the reformation of the kingdom, but he would have aimed at power, he would have sought his own promotion only, and made his first object the promotion of his friends, [330] and would have aimed at enriching his children, and would have neglected the weal of the community, and would have covered the poison of falsehood with the cloak of duplicity, and would thus have deserted the faith of christianity, and would have subjected himself to the retribution of fearful punishment, nor would he have escaped the weight of the tempest, And who can believe that he would give himself to death, that he would sacrifice his friends, in order that he might thus raise himself high? If those

Callide si palliant honorem venantes;

340 Et quod mortem fugiant semper meditantes;

Nulli magis diligunt vitam temporalem,

Nulli magis eligunt statum non mortalem.

Honores qui sitiunt simulate tendunt,

Caute sibi faciunt nomen quod intendunt;

Non sic venerabilis .S. de Monte-forti,

Qui se Christo similis dat pro multis morti;

Ysaac non moritur cum sit promptus mori;

Vervex morti traditur, Ysaac honori.

Nec fraus nec fallacia Comitem promovit,

250 Sed divina gratia, quæ quos juvet novit.

Horam si vocaveris locumque conflictus,

Invenire poteris quod ut esset victus

Potius quam vinceret illi conferebat;

Sed ut non succumberet Deus providebat.

Non de nocte subito surripit latenter;

Immo die redito pugnat evidenter.

Sic et locus hostibus fuit oportunus,

Ut hinc constet omnibus esse Dei munus,

who hunt after honour cover their object cunningly; [340] always meditating at the same time how they may avoid death; none love more the present life, none choose more eagerly a position devoid of danger. They who thirst after honours dissimulate their aim, they make themselves cautiously the reputation which they seek. Not so the venerable Simon de Montfort, who, like Christ, offers himself a sacrifice for many; Isaac does not die, although he is ready for death; it is the ram which is given to death, and Isaac receives honour. Neither fraud nor falsehood promoted the Earl, [350] but the Divine grace which knew those whom it would help. If you consider the time and the place of the conflict, you will find that they promised him a defeat rather than victory; but God provided that he should not succumb. He does not take them on a sudden by creeping stealthily by night; but he fights openly when day is come. So also the place was favourable to his enemies, that thus it might

Quod cessit victoria de se confidenti.

360 Hinc discat militia, quæ torneamenti
Laudat exercitium, ut sic expedita
Reddatur ad prælium, qualiter contrita
Fuit hic pars fortium exercitatorum,
Armis imbecillium et inexpertorum :
Ut confundet fortia, promovet infirmos,
Confortat debilia Deus, sternit firmos.
Sic nemo confidere de se jam præsumat;
Sed in Deum ponere spem si sciat, sumat
Arma cum constantia, nichil dubitando,

370 Cum sit pro justitia Deus adjuvando.
Sicque Deum decuit Comitem juvare,
Sine quo non potuit hostem superare.
Cujus hostem dixerim ? Comitis solius ?
Vel Anglorum sciverim regnique totius ?
Forsan et ecclesiæ, igitur et Dei ?
Quod si sic, quid gratiæ conveniret ei ?
Gratiam demeruit in se confidendo,
Nec juvari debuit Deum non timendo.

appear plainly to all to be the gift of God, that victory departed from him
who put his trust in himself. [360] Hence let the military order, which praises
the practice of the tournament, that so it may be made expert at fighting, learn
how the party of the strong and skilful was here bruised by the arms of those
who were feeble and unpractised : that he may confound the strong, God pro-
motes the weak, comforts the feeble, lays prostrate the firm. Thus let no one
now presume to trust in himself; but if he know how to place his hope in God,
he may take up arms with constancy, nothing doubting, [370] since God is a
help for those who are on the side of justice. Thus it was right that God should
help the Earl, for without God he could not overcome the enemy. Of whom
should I call him the enemy ?—of the Earl alone ? or should I recognise him as
the enemy of the English and of the whole kingdom ?—perhaps also of the
Church, and therefore of God ? And if so, how much grace ought he to have ?
He failed to deserve grace who trusted in himself, and he did not merit to be

Cadit ergo gloria propriæ virtutis ;
380 Et sic in memoria, qui dat destitutis
Viribus auxilium, paucis contra multos,
Virtute fidelium conterendo stultos,
Benedictus dominus Deus ultionum !
Qui in cœlis eminus sedet super thronum,
Et virtute propria colla superborum
Calcat, subdens grandia pedibus minorum.
Duos reges subdidit et hæredes regum,
Quos captivos reddidit transgressores legum,
Pompamque militiæ cum magna sequela
390 Dedit ignominiæ ; nam barones tela
Quæ zelo justitiæ pro regno sumpserunt,
Filiis superbiæ communicaverunt,
Usque dum victoria de cœlo dabatur,
Cum ingenti gloria quæ non sperabatur,
Arcus namque fortium tunc est superatus,
Cœtus inbecillium robore firmatus ;
Et de cœlo diximus, ne quis glorietur ;
Sed Christo quem credimus omnis honor detur !

helped who did not fear God. Thus falls the boast of personal valour,
[380] and so for evermore praised be the Lord God of vengeance ! who gives
aid to those who are destitute of force, to a few against many, crushing fools
by the valour of the faithful ; who sits on a throne in heaven above, and
by his own strength treads upon the necks of the proud, bowing the great
under the feet of the less. He has subdued two kings and the heirs of kings,
whom he has made captives, because they were transgressors of the laws ; and
he has turned to shame the pomp of knighthood with its numerous retinue ;
[390] for the barons employed on the sons of pride the arms, which, in
their zeal for justice, they had taken up in the cause of the kingdom, until
victory was given them from heaven, with a great glory that was not expected. For the bow of the strong was then overcome, and the troop of the weak
was established with strength ; and we have said that it was done by heaven,
lest any one should boast of it ; let all the honour, on the contrary, be given to

Christus enim imperat, vincit, regnat idem ;
400 Christus suos liberat, quibus dedit fidem.
   Ne victorum animus manus osculetur
   Suas, Deum petimus quod illis præstetur ;
   Et quod Paulus suggerit ab ipsis servetur,
" Qui lætatus fuerit, in Deo lætetur."
   Si quis nostrum gaudeat vane gloriatus,
   Dominus indulgeat, et non sit iratus !
   Et cautos efficiat nostros in futurum ;
   Ne factum deficiat, faciant se murum !
   Quod cæpit perficiat vis omnipotentis,
410 Regnumque reficiat Anglicanæ gentis !
   Ut sit sibi gloria, suis pax electis,
   Donec sint in patria se duce provectis.
   Hæc Angli de prælio legite Lewensi,
   Cujus patrocinio vivitis defensi ;
   Quia si victoria jam victis cessisset,
   Anglorum memoria victa viluisset.

Christ, in whom we believe ! For Christ at once commands, conquers, reigns !
[400] Christ delivers his own, to whom he has given his promise. We
pray God to grant that the minds of the conquerors may not attribute their
success to themselves, and let what Paul says be observed by them, "He
who would be joyful, let him be joyful in God." If any one of us indulge in vain
glory, may God be indulgent to him, and not angry ! and may he make our party
cautious in future ; lest deeds be wanting, may they make themselves a wall !
May the power of the Almighty perfect what it has begun, [410] and restore
to its vigour the kingdom of the English people ! that glory may be to himself,
and peace to his elect, until they be in the country where he shall lead them.   O
Englishmen ! read this concerning the battle of Lewes ! by the influence of
which you are saved from destruction : for if victory had gone over to those
who are now vanquished, the memory of the English would have lain in
.disgrace.

Cuï comparabitur nobilis Edwardus?
Forte nominabitur recte leopardus.
Si nomen dividimus, leo fit et pardus:
420 Leo, quia vidimus quod non fuit tardus
Aggredi fortissima, nullius occursum
Timens, audacissima virtute discursum
Inter castra faciens, et velut ad votum
Ubi et proficiens, ac si mundum totum
Alexandro similis cito subjugaret
Si fortunæ mobilis rota semper staret;
In qua summus protinus sciat se casurum,
Qui regnat ut dominus parum regnaturum.
Quod Edwardo nobili liquet accidisse,
430 Quem gradu non stabili constat cecidisse.
Leo per superbiam, per ferocitatem;
Est per inconstantiam et varietatem
Pardus, verbum varians et promissionem,
Per placentem pallians se locutionem.
Cum in arcto fuerit quicquid vis promittit;
Sed mox ut evaserit, promissum dimittit.

To whom shall the noble Edward be compared? Perhaps he will be rightly
called a leopard. If we divide the name, it becomes a lion and a pard :—
[420] a lion, for we have seen that he was not slow to meet the strongest ;
fearing the attack of none ; making a charge in the thick of the battle with the
most unflinching bravery, and as though at his will, and wherever he went, as
if, like Alexander, he would soon subdue the whole world, if the mutable
wheel of Fortune would but stand still; in which, although he stand at
the top, let him know that his fall is near at hand, and that he who reigns like
a lord will not reign long. Which, in fact, has happened to the noble Edward,
[430] who has manifestly fallen from his unstable position. He is a lion by
his pride and by his ferocity ; by his inconstancy and changeableness he is a
pard, not holding steadily his word or his promise, and excusing himself with
fair words. When he is in a difficulty, he promises just what you will ; but as

Testis sit Glovernia, ubi quod juravit
Liber ab angustia statim revocavit.
Dolum seu fallaciam quibus expeditur
440 Nominat prudentiam ; via qua venitur
Quo vult quamvis devia recta reputatur ;
Nefas det placentia, fasque nominatur ;
Quicquid libet licitum dicit, et a lege
Se putat explicitum, quasi major rege.
Nam rex omnis regitur legibus quas legit ;
Rex Saül repellitur, quia leges fregit ;
Et punitus legitur David mox ut egit
Contra legem ; igitur hinc sciat qui legit,
Quod non potest regere qui non servat legem ;
450 Nec hunc debent facere ad quos spectat regem.
O Edwarde ! fieri vis rex, sine lege ;
Vere forent miseri recti tali rege !
Nam quid lege rectius qua cuncta reguntur,
Et quid jure verius quo res discernuntur ?

soon as he has escaped the danger, he forgets his promise. Witness Gloucester,
where, as soon as he was out of the difficulty, he revoked immediately what he
had sworn. The treachery or falseness by which he gains his ends [440] he calls
prudence ; the way by which he arrives at his object, be it ever so crooked, is
reputed to be straight ; when wrong serves his purpose, it is called right ; he calls
lawful whatever he wills, and thinks himself absolved from the law, as though
he were greater than a king : for every king is ruled by the laws which he enacts.
King Saul was deposed, because he brake the laws ; and we read that David
was punished, as soon as he did contrary to the law ; hence, therefore, let
him who reads know, that he cannot reign who does not keep the law ;
[450] nor ought they, whose province it is to do so, to elect such a man for
their king. O Edward ! thou desirest to be made a king without law ; they
would be truly miserable who were ruled by such a king ! For what is more
just than law, by which all things are ruled ? and what more true than justice,
by which all things are administered ? If thou wouldest have a kingdom,

Si regnum desideras, leges venerare ;
Vias dabit asperas leges impugnare,
Asperas et invias quæ te non perducent;
Leges si custodias ut lucerna lucent.
Ergo dolum caveas et abomineris ;
460 Veritati studeas, falsum detesteris.
Quamvis dolus floreat, fructus nequit ferre ;
Hoc te psalmus doceat ; ad fideles terræ
Dicit Deus, " Oculi mei sunt, sedere
Quos in fine seculi mecum volo vere."
Dolus Northamptoniæ vide quid nunc valet;
Nec fervor fallaciæ velut ignis calet.
Si dolum volueris igni comparare,
Paleas studueris igni tali dare,
Quæ mox, ut exarserint, desistunt ardere,
470 Et cum vix inceperint terminum tenere.
Ita transit vanitas non habens radices ;
Radicata veritas non mutat per vices.
Ergo tibi libeat id solum quod licet,
Et non tibi placeat quod vir duplex dicet.

reverence the laws ; they are but rough roads, which are opposed to law, rough
and crooked roads which will not lead thee to thy journey's end ; but if thou
keepest the laws, they shine like a lamp. Therefore avoid and detest treachery ;
[460] labour after truth and hate falsehood. Although treachery may flourish, it
cannot bear fruit ; the Psalm may teach thee this ; God says to the faithful of the
earth, " They are my eyes, and it is my will that they shall sit with me at the end
of time." Observe how little thou hast gained by thy treachery at Northampton ;
the heat of deceit does not warm like fire. If you will compare treachery to
fire, feed studiously such fire with straw, which ceases to glow as soon as it is
burnt up, [470] and is consumed almost as soon as kindled. So passeth
away vanity which hath no roots ; rooted truth is not subject to vicissitudes :
therefore let that alone be permitted thee which is lawful, and let not what the
double man shall say please thee. A prince shall project things which are

Princeps quæ sunt principe digna cogitabit :
Ergo legem suscipe, quæ te dignum dabit
Multorum regimine, dignum principatu,
Multorum juvamine, multo comitatu.
Et quare non diligis quorum rex vis esse ?
480 Prodesse non eligis, sed tantum præesse.
Qui nullius gloriam nisi suam quærit,
Ejus per superbiam quicquid regit, perit.
Ita totum periit nuper quod regebas ;
Gloria præteriit quam solam quærebas ;
En radicem tangimus perturbationis
Regni de quo scribimus, et dissentionis
Partium quæ prælium dictum commiserunt.
Ad diversa studium suum converterunt.
Rex cum suis voluit ita liber esse ;
490 Et sic esse debuit, fuitque necesse
Aut esse desineret rex, privatus jure
Regis, nisi faceret quicquid vellet ; curæ
Non esse magnatibus regni, quos præferret
Suis comitatibus, vel quibus conferret

worthy of a prince : therefore take the law under thy protection, which will
make thee worthy to govern many, worthy of the principality, of the aid of many,
and of a numerous retinue.   And why lovest thou not those of whom thou
desirest to be king?   [480] Thou choosest not to profit them, but only to
govern.   He who seeks only his own glory, every thing that he governs is ruined
by his pride.   Thus recently the whole which thou governest has been ruined ;
the glory which alone thou soughtest is past.

Lo! we are touching the root of the perturbation of the kingdom of which
we are speaking, and of the dissension of the parties who fought the said battle.
The objects at which these two parties aimed were different.   The king, with
his, wished thus to be free :   [490] and so [it was urged on his side] he ought
to be ; and he must cease to be king, deprived of the rights of a king, unless he
could do whatever he pleased ; it was no part of the duty of the magnates of the

Castrorum custodiam, vel quem exhibere
Populo justitiam vellet, et habere
Regni cancellarium thesaurariumque.
Suum ad arbitrium voluit quemcumque,
Et consiliarios de quacumque gente,
500 Et ministros varios se præcipiente,
Non intromittentibus se de factis regis
Angliæ baronibus, vim habente legis
Principis imperio, et quod imperaret
Suomet arbitrio singulos ligaret.
Nam et comes quilibet sic est compos sui,
Dans suorum quidlibet quantum vult et cuï
Castra, terras, redditus, cuï vult committit,
Et quamvis sit subditus, rex totum permittit.
Quod si bene fecerit, prodest facienti ;
510 Si non, ipse viderit, sibimet nocenti
Rex non adversabitur.   Cur conditionis
Pejoris efficitur princeps, si baronis,

kingdom to determine whom he should prefer to his earldoms, or on whom he should confer the custody of castles, or whom he would have to administer justice to the people, and to be chancellor and treasurer of the kingdom.   He would have every one at his own will, and counsellors from whatever nation he chose, [500] and all ministers at his own discretion ; while the barons of England are not to interfere with the king's actions, the command of the prince having the force of law, and what he may dictate binding upon every body at his pleasure.   For every earl also is thus his own master, giving to every one of his own men both as much as he will, and to whom he will ; he commits castles, lands, revenues, to whom he will ; and although he be a subject, the king permits it all.   Which, if he do well, is profitable to the doer ; [510] if not, he must himself see to it ; the king will not hinder him from injuring himself. Why is the prince worse in condition, when the affairs of the baron, the knight,

Militis, et liberi res ita tractantur?

Quare regem fieri servum machinantur,

Qui suam minuere volunt potestatem,

Principis adimere suam dignitatem,

Volunt in custodiam et subjectionem

Regiam potentiam per seditionem

Captivam retrudere, et exhæredare

520 Regem, ne tam ubere valeat regnare

Sicut reges hactenus qui se præcesserunt,

Qui suis nullatenus subjecti fuerunt,

Sed suas ad libitum res distribuerunt,

Et ad suum placitum sua contulerunt.

Hæc est regis ratio, quæ vera videtur,

Et hæc allegatio jus regni tuetur.

    Sed nunc ad oppositum calamus vertatur :—

Baronum propositum dictis subjungatur;

Et auditis partibus dicta conferantur,

530 Atque certis finibus collata claudantur,

Ut quæ pars sit verior valeat liquere.

Veriori pronior populus parere.

and the freeman, are thus managed? Therefore they aim at making the king a slave, who wish to diminish his power, to take away his dignity of prince ; they wish by sedition to reduce captive into guardianship and subjection the royal power, and to disinherit the king, [520] that he shall be unable to reign so fully as hitherto have done the kings who preceded him, who were in no respect subjected to their people, but administered their own affairs at their will, and conferred what they had to confer according to their own pleasure. This is the King's argument, which has an appearance of fairness, and this is alleged in defence of the right of the kingdom.

    But now let my pen turn to the other side :—let me describe the object at which the barons aim ; and when both sides have been heard, let the arguments be compared, [530] and then let us come to a final judgment, so that it may be clear which side is the truest. The people is more prone to obey the truer

Baronum pars igitur jam pro se loquatur,
Et quo zelo ducitur rite prosequatur.
Quæ pars in principio palam protestatur,
Quod honori regio nichil machinatur ;
Vel quærit contrarium, immo reformare
Studet statum regium et magnificare ;
Sicut si ab hostibus regnum vastaretur,
540 Non sine baronibus tunc reformaretur,
Quibus hoc competeret atque conveniret ;
Et qui tunc se fingeret, ipsum lex puniret
Ut reum perjurii, regis proditorem,
Qui quicquid auxilii regis ad honorem
Potest, debet domino cum periclitatur,
Cum velut in termino regnum deformatur.
  Regis adversarii sunt hostes bellantes,
Et consiliarii regi adulantes,
Qui verbis fallacibus principem seducunt,
550 Linguisque duplicibus in errorem ducunt :
Hii sunt adversarii perversis pejores ;
Hii se bonos faciunt cum sint seductores,

party. Let therefore the party of the barons speak for itself, and proclaim in
order by what zeal it is led. Which party in the first place protests openly, that
it has no designs against the kingly honour ; nay, it seeks the contrary, and
studies to reform and magnify the kingly condition ; just as if the kingdom were
ravaged by enemies, [540] then it would not be reformed without the barons,
who would be the capable and proper persons for this purpose ; and should any
one then hang back, the law would punish him as one guilty of perjury, a
traitor to the king, who owes to his lord, when he is in danger, all the aid he
can give to support the king's honour, when the kingdom is as it were nigh
its end by devastation.

  The adversaries of the king are enemies who make war upon him, and
counsellors who flatter the king, who seduce their prince with deceitful words,
[550] and who lead him into error by their double tongues : these are adversaries
worse than those who are perverse ; it is these who pretend to be good whilst they

Et honoris proprii sunt procuratores ;
Incautos decipiunt, quos securiores
Reddunt per placentia, unde non caventur,
Sed velut utilia dicentes censentur.
Hii possunt decipere plusquam manifesti,
Qui se sciunt fingere velut non infesti.
Quid si tales miseri, talesque mendaces,
560 Adhærerent lateri principis, capaces
Totius malitiæ, fraudis, falsitatis,
Stimulis invidiæ puncti, pravitatis
Facinus exquirerent, per quod regni jura
Ad suas inflecterent pompas, quæque dura
Argumenta fingerent, quæ communitatem
Paulatim confunderent, universitatem
Populi contererent et depauperarent,
Regnumque subverterent et infatuarent,
Quod nullus justitiam posset optinere,
570 Nisi qui superbiam talium fovere
Vellet, per pecuniam largiter collatam ;
Quis tantam injuriam sustineret ratam ?

are seducers, and procurers of their own advancement ; they deceive the incautious, whom they render less on their guard by means of things that please them,
whereby they are not provided against, but are considered as prudent advisers.
Such men can deceive more than those who act openly, as they are able to make
an outward appearance of being not hostile. What if such wretches, and such
liars, [560] should haunt the prince, capable of all malice, of fraud, of falsehood,
excited by the spurs of envy, should seek to do that extreme wickedness, by
which they should sacrifice the privileges of the kingdom to their own ostentation,
that they should contrive all kinds of hard reasons, which by degrees should
confound the commonalty, should bruise and impoverish the mass of the people,
and should subvert and infatuate the kingdom, so that no one could obtain
justice, [570] except he who would encourage the pride of such men as these
by large supplies of money ; who could submit to the establishment of such an

Et si tales studiis suis immutarent
Regnum, ut injuriis jura supplantarent;
Calcatis indigenis advenas vocarent;
Et alienigenis regnum subjugarent:
Magnates et nobiles terræ non curarent,
Atque contemptibiles in summo locarent;
Et magnos dejicerent et humiliarent;
580 Ordinem perverterent et præposterarent;
Optima relinquerent, pessimis instarent;
Nonne qui sic facerent regnum devastarent?
Quamvis armis bellicis foris non pugnarent,
Tamen diabolicis armis dimicarent,
Et regni flebiliter statum violarent;
Quamvis dissimiliter, non minus dampnarent.
Sive rex consentiens per seductionem,
Talem non percipiens circumventionem,
Approbaret talia regni destructiva;
590 Seu rex ex malitia faceret nociva,
Proponendo legibus suam potestatem,

injury? And if such, by their conduct, should change the state of the kingdom;
if they should banish justice to put injustice in its place; if they should call in
strangers and trample upon the natives; and if they should subdue the kingdom
to foreigners; if they should not care for the magnates and nobles of the land,
and should place contemptible persons over them; and if they should over-
throw and humiliate the great; [580] if they should pervert and turn upside-down
the order of things; if they should leave the measures that are best, to advance
those which are worst;—do not those who act thus devastate the kingdom?
although they do not make war upon it with arms from abroad, yet they fight
with diabolical arms, and they violate, in a lamentable manner, the constitution
of the kingdom; although not in the same manner [as a foreign enemy], yet
they do no less damage. Whether the king, seduced to give his consent, not
perceiving the design, should approve measures so destructive to the kingdom;
[590] or whether the king should follow such an injurious course with an ill

Abutendo viribus propter facultatem ;
Sive sic vel aliter regnum vastaretur,
Aut regnum finaliter destitueretur,
Tunc regni magnatibus cura deberetur,
Ut cunctis erroribus terra purgaretur.
Quibus si purgatio convenit errorum,
Convenit provisio gubernatrix morum,
Qualiter prospicere sibi non liceret,
600 Ne malum contingere posset quod noceret?
Quod postquam contigerit debent amovere,
Subitum ne faciat incautos dolere.
Sic quod non eveniat quicquam prædictorum,
Quod pacis impediat vel bonorum morum
Formam, sed inveniat zelus peritorum
Quod magis expediat commodo multorum ;
Cur melioratio non admitteretur,
Cuï vitiatio nulla commiscetur?
Nam regis clementia regis et majestas
610 Approbare studia debet, quæ molestas

design of setting his own power above the laws, abusing his strength to please
his own will ; if thus or otherwise the kingdom be wasted, or the kingdom be
finally left destitute, then the magnates of the kingdom are bound to look to it,
that the land be purged of all errors. To whom if such a purgation of errors belongs, if such a provision belongs to them to regulate customs, how can it otherwise than appertain to them [600] to look out that no evil may happen which
would be injurious ?   Which, after it has happened, they ought to remove, lest
by a sudden occurrence it give those who do not provide against it cause to
grieve.   Thus, in order that no one of the aforesaid things may happen, which
may hinder the form of peace and good customs, but that the zeal of the
experienced men may find what is most expedient for the utility of the many,
why is a reform not admitted, with which no corruption shall be mixed ?
For the king's clemency and the king's majesty [610] ought to approve the
endeavours, which so amend grievous laws that they be milder, and that

Leges ita temperant quod sunt mitiores,

Et dum minus onerant Deo gratiores.

Non enim oppressio plebis Deo placet,

Immo miseratio qua plebs Deo vacet.

Phara[o] qui populum Dei sic afflixit,

Quod vix ad oraculum Moysi quod dixit

Poterant attendere, post est sic punitus,

Israel dimittere cogitur invitus;

Et qui comprehendere credidit dimissum,

620 Mersus est dum currere putat per abyssum.

Salomon conterere Israel nolebat,

Nec ullum de genere servire cogebat;

Quia Dei populum scivit quem regebat,

Et Dei signaculum lædere timebat;

Et plusquam judicium laudat misereri,

Et plusquam supplicium pacem patri[s] veri.

Cum constat baronibus hæc cuncta licere,

Restat rationibus regis respondere.

Amotis custodibus vult rex liber esse,

630 Subdique minoribus non vult sed præesse;

they be, while less onerous, more pleasing to God. For the oppression of the commons pleaseth not God, but rather the commiseration whereby the commons may have time to think upon God. Pharaoh, who so afflicted the people of God, that they could with difficulty repair to the oracle which he had appointed to Moses, was afterwards so punished, that he was obliged to dismiss Israel against his will; and when he thought to catch them after they were dismissed, [620] he was drowned whilst he thought to run through the deep. Solomon was unwilling to bruise Israel, nor would he reduce to servitude any one of the race; because he knew that it was God's people over whom he reigned; and he feared to hurt the imprint of God; and he praises mercy more than judgment, and the peace of a true father more than execution.

Since it is clear that the barons have a right of doing all this, it remains to answer the king's arguments. The king wishes to be free by the removal of his guardians, [630] and he will not be subject to his inferiors, but be placed over

Imperare subditis et non imperari ;
Sibi nec præpositis vult humiliari.
Non enim præpositi regi præponuntur ;
Immo magis incliti qui jus supponuntur.
Unius rex aliter unicus non esset,
Sed regnarent pariter quibus rex subesset.
Et hoc inconveniens quod tantum videtur,
Sit Deus subveniens, facile solvetur.
Deum namque credimus velle veritatem,
640 Per quem sic dissolvimus hanc dubietatem.
Unus solus dicitur et est rex revera,
Per quem mundus regitur majestate mera ;
Non egens auxilio quo possit regnare,
Sed neque consilio qui nequit errare.
Ergo potens omnia sciensque præcedit
Infinita gloria omnes quibus dedit
Sub se suos regere quasique regnare,
Qui possunt deficere, possunt et errare,
Et qui suis viribus nequeunt præstare,
650 Suisque virtutibus hostes expugnare,

them ; he will command his subjects and not be commanded ; he will be humiliated neither to himself nor to those who are his officers. For the officers are not set over the king ; but on the contrary they are rather the noble men who support the law. Otherwise there would not be one king of one state, (?) but they would reign equally to whom the king was subject. Yet this inconvenience also, though it seem so great, with the assistance of God, is easily solved : for we believe that God wills truth, [640] through whom we dissolve this doubt as follows. He is said to be, and is in truth, one king alone, by whom the universe is ruled in pure majesty ; who neither wants help whereby he may reign, nor even counsel, in as much as he cannot err. Therefore, all-powerful and all-knowing, he excels in infinite glory all those to whom he has given to rule and, as it were, to reign under him over his people, who may fail, and who may err, and who cannot avail by their own independent strength, [650] and vanquish their enemies by their own valour, nor govern kingdoms by

Neque sensu proprio regna gubernare,
Sed erroris invio male deviare.
Indigent auxilio sibi suffragante,
Necnon et consilio se rectificante.
Dicit rex : " Consentio tuæ rationi ;
Sed horum electio subsit optioni
Meæ ; quos voluero michi sociabo,
Quorum patrocinio cuncta gubernabo ;
Et si mei fuerint insufficientes,
660 Sensum non habuerint, aut non sint potentes,
Aut si sint malevoli, et non sint fideles,
Sed sint forte subdoli, volo quod reveles
Cur ad certas debeam personas arctari,
A quibus prævaleam melius juvari ?"
Cujus rei ratio cito declaratur,
Si quæ sit arctatio regis attendatur ;
Non omnis arctatio privat libertatem,
Nec omnis districtio tollit potestatem.
Potestatem liberam volunt principantes,
670 Servitutem miseram nolunt dominantes.

their own wisdom, but in an evil manner wander in the track of error. They
want help which should assist them, and counsel which should set them right.
Says the king, " I agree to thy reasoning ; but the choice of these must be left
to my option ; I will associate with myself whom I will, by whose support I will
govern all things ; and if my ministers should be insufficient, [660] if they want
sense or power, or if they harbour evil designs, or are not faithful, but are
perhaps traitors, I desire that you will explain, why I ought to be confined to
certain persons, when I might succeed in obtaining better assistance ?" The
reason of this is quickly declared, if it be considered what the constraint of the
king is : all constraint does not deprive of liberty, nor does every restriction
take away power. Princes desire free power ; [670] those who reign decline

Ad quid vult libera lex reges arctari ?

Ne possint adultera lege maculari.

Et hæc coarctatio non est servitutis,

Sed est ampliatio regiæ virtutis.

Sic servatur parvulus regis ne lædatur ;

Non fit tamen servulus quando sic arctatur.

Sed et sic angelici spiritus arctantur.

Qui quod apostatici non sint confirmantur.

Nam quod Auctor omnium non potest errare,

680 Omnium principium non potest peccare,

Non est inpotentia, sed summa potestas,

Magna Dei gloria magnaque majestas.

Sic qui potest cadere, si custodiatur

Ne cadat, quod libere vivat, adjuvatur

A tali custodia, nec est servitutis

Talis sustinentia, sed tutrix virtutis.

Ergo regi libeat omne quod est bonum,

Sed malum non audeat ; hoc est Dei donum.

Qui regem custodiunt ne peccet temptatus,

690 Ipsi regi serviunt, quibus esse gratus

miserable servitude. To what will a free law bind kings ?—to prevent them from being stained by an adulterated law. And this constraint is not one of slavery, but is rather an enlarging of the kingly faculty. Thus the king's child is kept from being hurt; yet he is not made a slave when he is thus restricted. Nay, the very angels are restricted in this manner, who are confirmed from becoming apostates. For, that the Author of all things cannot err, [680] that He who is the beginning of all things cannot sin, is not impotence, but it is the highest degree of power, the great glory of God and his great majesty. Thus, he who may fall, if he be kept from falling, so that he may live free from danger, he reaps advantage from such keeping, nor is such a support slavery, but it is the safeguard of virtue. Therefore that there be permitted to a king all that is good, but that he dare not do evil,—this is God's gift. They who keep the king from sinning when he is tempted, [690] they serve the king, to whom he

Sit, quod ipsum liberant ne sit servus factus,
Quod ipsum non superant a quibus est tractus.
Sed quis vere fuerit rex, est liber vere
Si se recte rexerit regnumque; licere
Sibi sciat omnia quæ regno regendo
Sunt convenientia, sed non destruendo.
Aliud est regere quod incumbit regi;
Aliud destruere resistendo legi.
A ligando dicitur lex, quæ libertatis
700 Tam perfecte legitur qua servitur gratis.
    Omnis rex intelligat quod est servus Dei;
Illud tantum diligat quod est placens ei;
Et illius gloriam quærat in regendo,
Non suam superbiam pares contempnendo.
Rex qui regnum subditum sibi vult parere,
Reddat Deo debitum alioquin vere;
Sciat quod obsequium sibi non debetur,
Qui negat servitium quo Deo tenetur.
Rursum sciat populum non suum sed Dei,

should be grateful, that they deliver him from being made a slave; so that those by whom he is led do not overcome him. But he who should be in truth a king, he is truly free if he rule rightly himself and the kingdom; let him know that all things are permitted him which are in ruling convenient to the kingdom, but not such as destroy it. It is one thing to rule according to a king's duty, and another to destroy by resisting the law. The law receives its name from binding *(a ligando)*, [700] which is so perfectly said of liberty, whereby it is served gratefully. (?)

Let every king bear in mind that he is a servant of God; let him love that only which is pleasing to Him; and let him seek His glory in reigning, not his own pride in despising his peers. A king who wishes his subject kingdom to yield obedience to him, let him render his duty to God in other things truly; let him know that obedience is not owing to him who denies the service in which he is bound to God. Again, let him know that the people is not his

710 Et ut adminiculum suum prosit ei :
    Et qui parvo tempore populo præfertur,
    Cito clausus marmore terræ subinfertur.
    In illos se faciat ut unum ex illis ;
    Saltantem respiciat David cum ancillis.
    Regi David similis utinam succedat,
    Vir prudens et humilis qui suos non lædat;
    Certe qui non læderet populum subjectum,
    Sed illis impenderet amoris affectum,
    Et ipsius quæreret salutis profectum,
720 Ipsum non permitteret plebs pati defectum.
    Durum est diligere se non diligentem;
    Durum non despicere se despicientem;
    Durum non resistere se destituenti;
    Convenit applaudere se suscipienti.
    Principis conterere non est, sed tueri ;
    Principis obprimere non est, sed mereri
    Multis beneficiis suorum favorem,
    Sicut Christus gratiis omnium amorem.

but God's ; [710] and that it is profitable to him as his help : and that he who
for a short period is placed over the people, soon, closed in marble, will be
buried in the earth. Towards them let him make himself as one of them ;
let him regard David joining the dance of the maids. I wish one similar to
David may succeed the king—a prudent and humble man, who would not injure
his people ; in truth, who would not hurt the people which is subjected to him,
but would exhibit towards them a loving regard, and would aim at their prosperity ; [720] the commons would not allow him to suffer wrong. It is hard to
love one who does not love us; it is hard not to despise one who despises
us; it is hard not to resist one who ruins us ; we naturally applaud him
who favours us. It is not the part of a prince to bruise, but to protect;
neither is it the part of a prince to oppress, but rather to deserve the favour of
his people by numerous benefits conferred upon them, as Christ by his grace
has deserved the love of all. If a prince love his subjects, he will necessarily

Si princeps amaverit, debet reamari;
730 Si recte regnaverit, debet honorari;
Si princeps erraverit, debet revocari
Ab hiis quos gravaverit injuste negari,
Nisi velit corrigi; si vult emendari,
Debet ab hiis erigi simul et juvari.
Istam princeps teneat regulam regnandi,
Ut opus non habeat non suos vocandi :
Qui confundunt subditos principes ignari,
Sentient indomitos sic nolle domari.
Si princeps putaverit universitate
740 Quod solus habuerit plus de veritate,
Et plus de scientia, plus cognitionis,
Plus abundet gratia, plusque Dei donis :
Si non sit præsumptio, immo sit revera,
Sua tunc instructio suorum sincera
Subditorum lumine corda perlustrabit;
Et cum moderamine suos informabit.
Moysen proponimus, David, Samuelem,
Quorum quemque novimus principem fidelem;

be repaid with love ; [730] if he reign justly, he will of a necessity be honoured ; if the prince err, he ought to be recalled by those whom his unjust denial may have grieved, unless he be willing to be corrected ; if he is willing to make amends, he ought to be both raised up and aided by these same persons. Let a prince maintain such a rule of reigning, that it may never be necessary for him to avoid depending on his own people. The ignorant princes who confound their subjects, will find that those who are unconquered will not thus be tamed. If a prince should think [740] that he alone has more truth, more knowledge, and more intelligence than the whole people, that he abounds more in grace and the gifts of God, if it be not presumption, but it be truly so, then his instruction will visit the true hearts of his subjects with light, and will instruct his people with moderation.

We instance Moses, David, Samuel—each of whom we know to have

Qui a suis subditis multa pertulerunt,
750 Nec tamen pro meritis illos abjecerunt,
Nec illis extraneos superposuerunt,
Sed rexerunt per eos qui sui fuerunt.
"Ego te præficiam populo majori,
Et hunc interficiam ;" dicit Deus.—" Mori
Malo, quam hic pereat populus," benignus
Moyses respondeat, principatu dignus.
Sicque princeps sapiens nunquam reprobabit
Suos, sed insipiens regnum conturbabit.
Unde si rex sapiat minus quam deberet;
760 Quid regno conveniat regendo? num quæret
Suo sensu proprio quibus fulciatur,
Quibus diminutio sua suppleatur?
Si solus elegerit, facile falletur,
Utilis qui fuerit a quo nescietur.
Igitur communitas regni consulatur ;
Et quid universitas sentiat, sciatur,
Cuï leges propriæ maxime sunt notæ.
Nec cuncti provinciæ sic sunt idiotæ,

been a faithful prince ; who suffered many things from their subjects, [750] and
yet for their deserts they did not cast them off, nor set strangers over them, but
governed by means of those who were their own people. " I will place thee
over a greater people ; and I will slay this people ;" saith God. " I had rather
die, than this people should perish," answered kind Moses, who was worthy to
govern. And thus a wise prince will never reject his people, but an unwise one
will disturb the kingdom. Wherefore, if a king is less wise than he ought to be,
[760] what advantage will the kingdom gain by his reign? Is he to seek by
his own opinion on whom he should depend to have his failing supplied? If he
alone choose, he will be easily deceived, who is not capable of knowing who will
be useful. Therefore let the community of the kingdom advise ; and let it be
known what the generality thinks, to whom their own laws are best known.
Nor are all those of the country so uninstructed, as not to know better than

Quin sciant plus cæteris regni sui mores,
770 Quos relinquunt posteris hii qui sunt priores.
Qui reguntur legibus magis ipsas sciunt;
Quorum sunt in usibus plus periti fiunt;
Et quia res agitur sua, plus curabunt,
Et quo pax adquiritur sibi procurabunt.
Pauca scire poterunt qui non sunt experti;
Parum regno proderunt, nisi qui sunt certi.
Ex hiis potest colligi quod communitatem
Tangit quales eligi ad utilitatem
Regni recte debeant; qui velint et sciant
780 Et prodesse valeant, tales regis fiant
Et consiliarii et coadjutores;
Quibus noti varii patriæ sunt mores;
Qui se lædi sentiunt, si regnum lædatur;
Regnumque custodiunt, ne, si noceatur
Toti, partes doleant simul patientes;
Gaudenti congaudeant, si sint diligentes.
Nobile juditium regis Salomonis

strangers the customs of their own kingdom, [770] which have been bequeathed from father to son. They who are ruled by the laws, know those laws best; they who experience them are best acquainted with them; and since it is their own affairs which are at stake, they will take more care, and will act with an eye to their own peace. They who want experience can know little; they will profit little the kingdom who are not stedfast. Hence it may be collected, that it concerns the community to see what sort of men ought justly to be chosen for the utility of the kingdom; they who are willing and know how, [780] and are able to profit it, such should be made the councillors and coadjutors of the king; to whom are known the various customs of their country; who feel that they suffer themselves when the kingdom suffers; and who guard the kingdom, lest, if hurt be done to the whole, the parts have reason to grieve while they suffer along with it; which rejoice, when it has cause to rejoice, if they love it. Let us call attention to the noble judgment of King Solomon: she who did not feel

Ponamus in medium ; quæ divisionis
Parvuli non horruit inhumanitatem,
790 Quia non condoluit atque pietatem
Maternam non habuit, quod mater non erat
Teste rege docuit; ergo tales quærat
Princeps, qui condoleant universitati,
Qui materne timeant regnum dura pati.
Sed si quem non moveat ruina multorum ;
Si solus optineat quæ vult placitorum ;
Multorum regimini non est coaptatus,
Suo cum sit omnium soli totus datus.
Communis conveniens est communitati ;
800 Sed vir incompatiens cordis indurati
Non curat si veniant multis casus duri ;
Casibus non obviant tales modo muri.
Igitur eligere si rex per se nescit
Qui sibi consulere sciant, hinc patescit
Quid tunc debet fieri.   Nam communitatis
Est ne fiant miseri duces dignitatis

horror at the cruelty of dividing the infant, [790] because she did not feel for it,
and wanted maternal love, shewed, as the king testified, that she was not its
mother : therefore let a prince seek such [councillors] as may condole with the
community, who have a motherly fear lest the kingdom should undergo any
sufferings.   But if any one be not moved by the ruin of the many—if he alone
obtain what pleas he will—he is not fitted to rule over the many, since he is
entirely devoted to his own interest, and to none other.   A man who feels
for others, is agreeable to the community ; [800] but a man who does not feel
for others, who possesses a hard heart, cares not if misfortunes fall upon the
many—such walls are no defence against misfortunes.   Therefore, if the king
has not wisdom to choose by himself those who are capable of advising him, it
is clear, from what has been said, what ought then to be done.   For it is a thing
which concerns the community to see that miserable wretches be not made the

Regiæ, sed optimi et electi viri,
Atque probatissimi qui possint inquiri.
Nam cum gubernatio regni sit cunctorum
810 Salus vel perditio, multum refert quorum
Sit regni custodia; sicut est in navi;
Confunduntur omnia si præsint ignavi;
Si quis transfretantium positus in navi
Ad se pertinentium abutatur clavi,
Non refert si prospere navis gubernetur.
Sic qui regnum regere debent, cura detur
Si de regno quispiam non recte se regit;
Viam vadit inviam quam forsan elegit.
Optime res agitur universitatis,
820 Si regnum dirigitur via veritatis.
Et tamen si subditi sua dissipare
Studeant, præpositi possunt refrenare
Suorum stultitiam et temeritatem,
Ne per insolentiam vel fatuitatem

leaders of the royal dignity, but the best and chosen men, and the most approved that can be found. For since the governance of the kingdom is either the safety or perdition of all, [810] it is of great consequence who they are that have the custody of the kingdom; just as it is in a ship; all things are thrown into confusion if unskilful people guide it; if any one of the passengers belonging to it who is placed in the ship abuse the rudder, it matters not whether the ship be governed prosperously or not. So those who ought to rule the kingdom, let the care be given to them, if any one of the kingdom does not govern himself rightly; he goes on a wrong path which perhaps he has himself chosen. The affairs of the generality are best managed [820] if the kingdom is directed in the way of truth. And, moreover, if the subjects labour to dissipate their property, those who are set over them may restrain their folly and temerity, lest by the presumption and imbecility of fools, the power of the kingdom be weakened,

Stultorum potentia regni subnervetur,
Hostibus audacia contra regnum detur.
Nam quocumque corporis membro violato,
Fit minoris roboris corpus.   Ita dato
Quod vel viri liceat propriis abuti,
830 Quamvis regno noceat; plures mox secuti
Et libertatem noxiam, sic multiplicabunt
Erroris insaniam, quod totum dampnabunt.
Nec libertas proprie debet nominari,
Quæ permittit inscie stultos dominari ;
Sed libertas finibus juris limitetur,
Spretisque limitibus error reputetur.
Alioquin liberum dices furiosum,
Quamvis omne prosperum illi sit exosum.
Ergo regis ratio de suis subjectis,
840 Suomet arbitrio quorum volunt vectis,
Per hoc satis solvitur, satis infirmatur ;
Dum quivis qui subditur majore domatur.
Quia nulli hominum dicemus licere
Quicquid vult, sed dominum quemlibet habere

and courage be given to enemies against the kingdom.   For whatever member of
the body be destroyed, the strength of the body is diminished thereby. So if it be
allowed even that men may abuse what belongs to themselves, [830] when it be
injurious to the kingdom, many immediately after following also the injurious
liberty, will so multiply the wildness of error, that they will ruin the whole. Nor
ought it properly to be named liberty, which permits fools to govern unwisely ;
but liberty is limited by the bounds of the law ; and when those bounds are despised, it should be reputed as error. Otherwise you will call a raving madman free,
although he be at enmity with everything like prosperity. Therefore the king's
argument concerning his subjects, [840] who are ruled at their own choice by whom
they will, is by this sufficiently answered and overthrown ; since every one who is
subject, is ruled by one who is greater. Because we say that no man is permitted

Qui errantem corrigat, benefacientem
Adjuvat, et erigit quandoque cadentem.
Præmio præferimus universitatem;
Legem quoque dicimus regis dignitatem
Regere; nam credimus esse legem lucem,
850 Sine qua concludimus deviare ducem.
Lex qua mundus regitur atque regna mundi
Ignea describitur; quod sensus profundi
Continet mysterium, lucet, urit, calet;
Lucens vetat devium, contra frigus valet,
Purgat et incinerat quædam, dura mollit,
Et quod crudum fuerat ignis coquit, tollit
Torporem, et alia multa facit bona.
Sancta lex similia p'rat (?) regi dona.
Istam sapientiam Salomon petivit;
860 Ejus amicitiam tota vi quæsivit.
Si rex hac caruerit lege, deviabit;
Si hanc non tenuerit, turpiter errabit;
Istius præsentia recte dat regnare,

all that he will, but that every one has a lord who may correct him when erring, and aid him when doing well, and sometimes raises him up when he is falling. We give the first place to the community: we say also that the law rules over the king's dignity; for we believe that the law is the light, [850] without which we conclude that he who rules will wander from the right path. The law whereby is ruled the world and the kingdoms of the world, is described as being of fire; which contains a mystery of deep meaning: it shines, burns, warms; shining, it hinders the wanderer from quitting his right path; it avails against the cold; it purges and burns to cinders some things; it softens what is hard, and what had been raw the fire cooks; it takes away numbness, and it does many other good things. The sacred law is equally serviceable to the king. Solomon asked for this wisdom; [860] its friendship he sought with all his might. If the king want this law, he will wander from the right track; if he does not hold it, he will err foully; its presence gives the power of reigning rightly, and its absence

Et ejus absentia regnum perturbare.

Ista lex sic loquitur, " per me regnant reges ;

Per me jus ostenditur hiis qui condunt leges."

Istam legem stabilem nullus rex mutabit ;

Sed se variabilem per istam firmabit.

Si conformis fuerit huïc legi, stabit ;

870 Et si disconvenerit isti, vacillabit.

Dicitur vulgariter, " ut rex vult, lex vadit :"

Veritas vult aliter, nam lex stat, rex cadit.

Veritas et caritas zelusque salutis

Legis est integritas, regimen virtutis ;

Veritas, lux, caritas, calor, urit zelus ;

Hæc legis varietas tollit omne scelus.

Quicquid rex statuerit, consonum sit istis ;

Nam si secus fecerit, plebs reddetur tristis ;

Confundetur populus, si vel veritate

880 Caret regis oculus, sive caritate

Principis cor careat, vel severitate

Zelum non adimpleat semper moderate.

---

overturns the kingdom.   This law speaks thus, " Kings reign through me ;
through me justice is shown to those who make laws." No king shall alter
this firm law ; but by it he shall make himself stable when he is variable.   If
he conform to this law, he will stand ; [870] and if he disagree with it, he will
waver.   It is said commonly, " As the king wills, so goes the law : " but the
truth is otherwise, for the law stands, but the king falls.   Truth and charity
and the zeal of salvation, this is the integrity of the law, the regimen of virtue ;
truth, light, charity, warmth, zeal burns ; (?) this variety of the law takes
away all crime.   Whatever the king may ordain, let it be consonant to these ;
for if it be otherwise, the commonalty will be made sorrowful ; the people will
be confounded, if either the king's eye want truth, [880] or the prince's heart
want charity, or he do not always moderately fulfil his zeal with severity.

Hiis tribus suppositis, quicquid placet regi
Fiat; sed oppositis, rex resistit legi.
Sed recalcitratio stimulo non nocet;
Pauli sic instructio de cœlo nos docet.
Sic exhæredatio nulla fiet regi,
Si fiat provisio concors justæ legi.
Nam dissimulatio legem non mutabit,
890 Cujus firma ratio sine fine stabit.
Unde si quid utile diu est dilatum,
Irreprehensibile sit sero perlatum.
Et rex nihil proprium præferat communi;
Quia salus omnium sibi cessit uni.
Non enim præponitur sibimet victurus;
Sed ut hic qui subditur populus securus.
Reges esse noveris nomen relativum;
Nomen quoque sciveris esse protectivum;
Unde sibi vivere soli non licebat,
900 Qui multos protegere vivendo delebat.
Qui vult sibi vivere, non debet præesse,

These three things being supposed, whatever pleases the king may be done; but by their opposites the king resists the law. However, kicking against it does not hurt the prick; thus the instruction which was sent from heaven to Paul teaches us. Thus the king is deprived of no inherited right, if there be made a provision in concordance with just law. For dissimulation shall not change the law, [890] whose stable reason will stand without end. Wherefore if anything that is useful has been long put off, it is not to be reprehended when adopted late. And let the king never set his private interest before that of the community; as if the salvation of all yields to him alone. For he is not set over them in order to live for himself; but that his people who is subject to him may be in safety. You must know that the name of king is relative; you should know also that the name is protective; wherefore he cannot live for himself alone [900] who ought by his life to protect many. He who will live

Sed seorsum degere, et ut solus esse.
Principis est gloria plurimos salvare ;
Cum sua molestia multos relevare.
Non alleget igitur suimet profectum,
Sed in quibus creditur subditis prospectum.
Si regnum salvaverit, quod est regis fecit ;
Quicquid secus egerit in ipso defecit.
Vera regis ratio ex hiis satis patet ;
910 Quod vacantem proprio status regis latet.
Namque vera caritas est proprietati
Quasi contrarietas, et communitati
Fœdus insolubile, conflans velut ignis
Omne quod est habile, sicut fit in lignis
Quæ dant igni crescere patiens activo,
Subtracta decrescere modo recitivo.
Ergo si fervuerit princeps caritate,
Quantumcumque poterit de communitate,
Si sollicitabitur quod recte regatur,
920 Et nunquam lætabitur si destituatur,

for himself, ought not to be set over others, but to live separately from them
that he may be alone. It is the glory of a prince to save very many ; to inconvenience himself in order to raise many up. Let him not therefore allege his
own profit, but have regard to his subjects in whom he is trusted. (?) If he work
the salvation of the kingdom, he acts the part of a king ; whatever he does contrary to this, he fails in that point. The true province of a king is sufficiently
clear from these arguments ; [910] that he is ignorant of the condition of a king
who is occupied only with his own affairs. For true charity is as it were contrary
to self-interest, and an indissoluble league to the community, melting like fire
everything that is near, as is done with wood which they subject to the active fire
to increase it, and then in return it is taken away to decrease it. Therefore
if the prince will be warm with charity as much as possible towards the
community, if he shall be solicitous to govern it well, [920] and shall

Unde si dilexerit rex regni magnates,
Quamvis solus sciverit, quasi magnus vates,
Quicquid opus fuerit ad regnum regendum,
Quicquid se decuerit, quicquid faciendum,
Quod sane decreverit illis non celabit,
Præter quos non poterit id quod ordinabit
Ad effectum ducere ; igitur tractabit
Cum suis, quæ facere per se [non] putabit.
Cur sua consilia non communicabit,
930 A quibus auxilia supplex postulabit ?
Quicquid suos allicit ad benignitatem,
Et amicos efficit, fovet unitatem,
Regiam prudentiam decet indicare
Hiis qui suam gloriam possunt augmentare.
Dominus discipulis cuncta patefecit,
Dividens a servulis quos amicos fecit ;
Atque quasi nescius a suis quæsivit
Quid sentirent sæpius, quod profecte scivit.
O ! si Dei quærerent principes honorem,

never be rejoiced at its destruction ; wherefore if the king will love the
magnates of the kingdom, although he should know alone, like a great prophet,
whatever is needful for the ruling of the kingdom, whatever is becoming in
him, whatever ought to be done, truly he will not conceal what he will
decree from those without whom he cannot effect that which he will ordain. He will therefore treat with his people about bringing into effect
the things which he will not think of doing by himself. Why will he not com-
municate his councils [930] to those whose aid he will ask supplicatingly ?
Whatever draws his people to benignity, and makes friends and cherishes
unity, it is fit the royal prudence should indicate it to those who can augment
his glory. Our Lord laid open all things to his disciples, dividing from the
servants those whom he made his friends ; and as though he were ignorant, he
often inquired of his people what was their opinion on matters which he knew

940 Regna recte regerent, et præter errorem.
Si Dei notitiam principes haberent,
Omnibus justitiam suam exhiberent.
Ignorantes dominum, velut excæcati,
Quærunt laudes hominum, vanis delectati.
Qui se nescit regere, multos male reget ;
Si quis vult inspicere Psalmos, idem leget.
Joseph ut se debuit principes docere,
Propter quod rex voluit ipsum præminere.
Et in innocentia cordis sui David,
950 Et intelligentia, Israelem pavit.
Ex prædictis omnibus poterit liquere,
Quod regem magnatibus incumbit videre
Quæ regni conveniant gubernationi,
Et pacis expediant conservationi ;
Et quod rex indigenas sibi laterales
Habeat, non advenas, neque speciales,
Vel consiliarios vel regni majores,
Qui supplantant alios atque bonos mores.

perfectly. Oh! if princes sought the honour of God, [940] they would rule their kingdoms rightly, and without error. If princes had the knowledge of God, they would exhibit their justice to all. Ignorant of the Lord, as though they were blind, they seek the praises of men, delighted only with vanity. He who does not know how to rule himself, will be a bad ruler over others ; if any one will look at the Psalms, he will read the same. Joseph as he ought to teach princes, (?) on which account the king willed that he should be set over others. And David in the innocence of his heart [950] and by his intelligence fed Israel. From all that has been said, it may appear evident, that it becomes a king to see together with his nobles what things are convenient for the government of the kingdom, and what are expedient for the preservation of peace ; and that the king have natives for his companions, not foreigners, nor favourites, for his councillors or for the great nobles of the kingdom, who supplant others and

Nam talis discordia paci novercatur,
960 Et inducit prælia, dolos machinatur.
Nam sicut invidia diaboli mortem
Induxit, sic odia separat cohortem.
Incolas in ordine suo rex tenebit,
Et hoc moderamine regnando gaudebit.
Si vero studuerit suos degradare,
Ordinem perverterit, frustra quæret quare
Sibi non obtemperant ita perturbati ;
Immo si sic facerent essent insensati.

abolish good customs. For such discord is a step-mother to peace, [960] and produces battles, and plots treason. For as the envy of the devil introduced death, so hatred separates the troop. The king shall hold the natives in their rank, and by this governance he will have joy in reigning. But if he study to degrade his own people, if he pervert their rank, it is in vain for him to ask why thus deranged they do not obey him ; in fact they would be fools if they did.

The following Song was written when jealousies and dissensions were rife among the barons, and some of them began to desert the popular cause. It is preserved by William de Rishanger, a contemporary, in his history of the barons' wars. The defection of the Earl of Gloucester contributed not a little to the disastrous termination of the career of Simon de Montfort at the battle of Evesham.

SONG UPON THE DIVISIONS AMONG THE BARONS.

[MS. Cotton. Claudius D. vi. fol. 101 v°, latter part of 13th cent.]

Plange plorans, Anglia, plena jam dolore;
Tristis vides tristia, languens cum mærore ;

TRANSLATION.—Lament with weeping, O England, full as thou now art with matter of grief, in sadness thou beholdest sorrowful things, languishing in sor-

Nisi te respiciat Christus suo more,
Eris vile canticum hostium in ore.

Pepigerunt plurimi salvam te salvare,
Sed jam nimis necgligunt pactum procurare :
Nam se quidam retrahunt, qui possunt juvare ;
Quidam subterfugium quærunt ultra mare.

Hinc est quod incipiunt cæteri certare,
Et in partes varias animos mutare ;
Dum quæ sic dissentiunt nolunt concordare,
Sed incepta nequeunt bene terminare.

Sic respublica perit, terra desolatur ;
Invalescit extera gens et sublimatur ;
Vilescit vir incola et subpeditatur :
Sustinet injurias, non est qui loquatur.

Tam miles quam clericus ambo fiunt muti ;
Facti sunt extranei loquaces astuti :
Inter centum Anglicos non sunt duo tuti ;
Planctum et obprobrium jam sunt assecuti.

O Comes Gloverniæ, comple quod cœpisti ;
Nisi claudas congrue, multos decepisti.

row ; unless Christ in his manner have regard to thee, thou wilt be but a vile
song in the mouth of thine enemies.—Very many have pledged themselves to
preserve thee in safety, but now they have too much neglected their promise :
for many desert, who have it in their power to help ; and some slink away over
the sea.—Hence the rest begin to quarrel, and to go over to different sides ;
while things which disagree in this manner will not be reconciled, and what has
been begun is left unfinished.—Thus the state is ruined, and the land is laid
waste ; the stranger is strengthened and raised up ; the native is debased and
trodden under foot : while he sustains injuries, there is no one who will speak
out.—The knight as well as the clergy are both become mute ; the strangers are
become talkative and cunning : among a hundred Englishmen there are not
two who are safe ; the lot which they have obtained is lamentation and disgrace.
—O Earl of Gloucester, complete what thou hast commenced ; unless thou endest

Age nunc viriliter sicut promisisti,
Causam fove fortitur cujus fons fuisti.

Si, quod absit! subtrahas manum et levamen,
Terræ fraudem faciens, inferens gravamen :
Maledictus maneat! fiat! fiat! Amen.

Comes Simon de Muntford, vir potens et fortis,
Pugna nunc pro patria, sisque dux cohortis :
Non te minæ terreant neque timor mortis,
Rem defende publicam resque tuæ sortis.

O tu, Comes le Bygot, pactum serva sanum :
Cum sis miles strenuus, nunc exerce manum.
Totam turbat modica terra[m] turba canum ;
Exeat aut pereat genus tam prophanum.

O vos magni proceres, qui vos obligastis
Observare firmiter illud quod jurastis ;
Terræ si sit utile quod excogitastis,
Juvet illud citius id quod ordinastis.

Si velletis prosequi quod jam inchoastis,
Consequi poteritis quod desiderastis ;

as thou hast begun, thou hast deceived many. Act now courageously as thou
hast promised, cherish steadily the cause of which thou wast the fountain.—If,
from which God preserve us! thou withdrawest thy hand and support, acting
treacherously towards the land, and inflicting a great injury upon it. . . May he
be cursed for ever! be it so! be it so! amen.—Earl Simon de Montfort, a strong
man and a bold, fight now for thy country, and be the leader of the band ;
neither let threats scare thee, nor the fear of death ; defend the state and thy own
fortune.—O thou, Earl Bigot, keep unbroken thine agreement : as thou art a
brave knight, now use thy hand ; a small troop of dogs puts in commotion the
whole land : may such a cursed race depart or perish !—O you, great nobles,
who bound yourselves to observe firmly the oath which you took ; if what you
imagined be profitable to the land, let that which you have ordained aid it immediately.—If you will carry to an end that which you have begun, you may
obtain that which you desired ; unless the thing which you have long had in

Nisi finem capiat quod diu tractastis,
Vere dici poterit vane laborastis.

Honor nobis maximus erit laus et digna,
Si respondet Anglia vestra gerens signa ;
Quam ut cito liberet a peste maligna,
Adjuvet nunc Domini pietas benigna !

hand be perfected, it may be truly said that you have laboured in vain.—It
will be the highest honour to you and a worthy praise, if England answer by
carrying your standards ; which that he may soon deliver from the malignant
plague, may the benignant piety of the Lord now help it !

The triumph of the barons did not last long. In the battle
of Evesham, fought on the fourth of August in the year
after that of Lewes, their great leader fell, with the best of his
followers. The fate of Simon de Montfort was a subject of
general lamentation; and long afterwards he was revered as a
saint and martyr, and was even believed to work miracles. In
MS. Cotton. Vespas. A. VI. will be found a collection of these
miracles, and a form of prayers to be said in his honour, among
which is the following hymn (fol. 189, r⁰).

Salve, Symon Montis-Fortis,
Totius flos militiæ,
Duras pœnas passus mortis,
Protector gentis Angliæ.
Sunt de sanctis inaudita,
Cunctis passis in hac vita,
Quemquam passum talia ;
Manus, pedes amputari,
Caput, corpus vulnerari,
Abscidi virilia.
Sis pro nobis intercessor
Apud Deum, qui defensor
In terris extiteras.

The whole was preceded by a life of Simon de Montfort, occu-
pying two pages of the manuscript, but which some hostile hand
has carefully erased.   The following song was evidently written
immediately after the battle of Evesham.

THE LAMENT OF SIMON DE MONTFORT.

[MS. Harl. 2253, fol. 59 rº, early in 14th cent.]

CHAUNTER m'estoit, mon cuer le voit, en un dure langage,
Tut en ploraunt fust fet le chaunt de nostre duz baronage,
Que pur la pees, si loynz après se lesserent detrere,
Lur cors trencher, e demenbrer, pur salver Engleterre.
  Ore est ocys la flur de pris, qe taunt savoit de guere,
  Ly quens Montfort, sa dure mort molt enplorra la terre.

Si com je qui, par un mardi, firent la bataile,
Tot à cheval, fust le mal, sauntz nulle pedaile;
Tresmalement y ferirent de le espie forbie,
Qe la part sire Edward conquist la mestrie.
  Ore est ocis, etc.

Mès par sa mort, le cuens Mountfort conquist la victorie,
Come ly martyr de Caunterbyr, finist sa vie;

TRANSLATION.—I am driven to sing, my heart wills it, in sorrowful language,
—all with tears was made the song concerning our gentle barons,—who for the
peace so long after suffered themselves to be destroyed,—their bodies to be cut
and dismembered, to save England.—Now is slain the precious flower, who knew
so much of war, the Earl Montfort, his hard death the land will deeply lament.

    As I believe, it was on a Tuesday, that they fought the battle,—all on horse,
which was the misfortune, without any foot,—very ill they there struck with
the burnished sword,—that the party of Sir Edward gained the mastery.   Now
is slain, etc.

    But by his death the Earl Montfort gained the victory,—like the martyr of

Ne voleit pas li bon Thomas qe perist seinte Eglise,
Ly cuens auxi se combati, e morust sauntz feyntise.
  Ore est ocys, etc.

Sire Hue le fer, ly Despencer, tresnoble justice,
Ore est à tort lyvré à mort, à trop male guise.
Sire Henri, pur veir le dy, fitz le cuens de Leycestre,
Autres assez, come vus orrez, par le cuens de Gloucestre.
  Ore est ocis, etc.

Qe voleint moryr, e mentenir la pees e la dreyture,
Le seint martir lur fra joyr sa conscience pure,
Qe velt moryr e sustenir les honmes de la terre,
Son bon desir acomplir, quar bien le quidom fere.
  Ore est, etc.

Près de son cors, le bon tresors, une heyre troverent,
Les faus ribaus, tant furent maus, e ceux qe le tuerent;
Molt fust pyr, qe demenbryr firent le prodhonme,
Qe de guerrer e fei tener si bien savoit la sonme.
  Ore est, etc.

Canterbury he finished his life;—the good Thomas would not suffer holy Church to perish,—the Earl fought in a similar cause, and died without flinching.— Now is slain, &c.

Sir Hugh the bold, the Despencer, a very noble justice,—is now wrongfully delivered to death, in too shameful a manner.—Sir Henry, in truth I say it, the son of the Earl of Leicester,—enough of others, as you will hear, by the Earl of Gloucester.—Now is slain, etc.

Because they were willing to die, and to maintain peace and right,—the holy martyr will cause them to enjoy his pure conscience,—who is willing to die and to sustain the men of the land,—to accomplish his good desire, for we think he does well.—Now is, etc.

Near his body, the good treasure, an heir they found,—the false ribalds, they were so wicked, and those who slew him;—what was much worse, they caused the worthy man to be dismembered,—who knew so well the art of fighting and of holding faith.—Now is, etc.

Priez touz, mes amis douz, le fitz Seinte Marie
Qe l'enfant, her puissant, meigne en bone vie ;
Ne vueil nomer li escoler, ne vueil qe l'em die,
Mès pur l'amour le salveour, priez pur la clergie.
 Ore est ocys la flur de pris, qe tant savoit de guere,
 Ly quens Montfort, sa dure mort molt enplurra la terre.

Ne say trover rien qu'il firent bien, ne baroun ne counte,
Les chivalers e esquiers touz sunt mys à hounte,
Pur lur lealté e verité, que tut est anentie ;
Le losenger purra reigner, le fol pur sa folie.
 Ore est ocis, etc.

Sire Simoun, ly prodhom, e sa compagnie,
En joie vont en ciel amount, en pardurable vie.
Mès Jhesu Crist, qe en croyz se mist, Dieu en prenge cure,
Qe sunt remis, e detenuz en prisone dure.
 Ore est ocys, etc.

Pray all, my sweet friends, to the Son of St. Mary,—that he lead in good life
the infant, the powerful heir ;—I will not name the scholar, I do not desire any
one to mention him,—but for the love of the Saviour, pray for the clergy.—
Now is slain, etc.

I cannot find any thing that they did well, neither baron nor earl,—the
knights and the esquires are all disgraced,—on account of their loyalty and
truth, which is entirely annihilated ;—the deceitful man may reign, the fool for
bis folly.—Now is slain, etc.

Sir Simon, the worthy man, and his company,—are gone in joy up to
heaven, in everlasting life.—But Jesus Christ, who placed himself on the cross,
and God have care of those,—who are remitted, and detained in hard prison.—
Now is slain, etc.

REIGN OF EDWARD I. 1272—1307.

Henry outlived the defeat of the barons but a very few years.
He died on the sixteenth of November, 1272, while his son
Edward was occupied in warring against the infidels in the East.
Edward was proclaimed king, while absent.   A new monarch
is generally welcomed with songs of praise ; and the following,
evidently the work of a zealous opponent of the popular party,
seems to have been written before his arrival in England.

THE PRAISE OF THE YOUNG EDWARD.

[MS. Cotton. Vespas. B. xiii. fol. 130 v°, 13th cent.]

Eaduuardi regis Anglorum me pepulere
Florida gesta loqui, pudor est famosa tacere.
Hic tener ætate dum vixerat in juvenili,
Conflictus plures superavit corde virili.
Belliger ut pardus, fragrans dulcedine nardus,
Dum viget Eaduuardus, rutilat novus ecce Ricardus.
Sic gemino flore Britones titulantur honore,
Bella per Eaduuardi similis et probitate Ricardi.
Belligeri juvenis laudabat Gallia mores ;
Ampla manus dantis meritos congessit honores.

TRANSLATION.—The flourishing deeds of Edward King of the English oblige
me to talk, for it is shameful to let pass famous actions in silence. He, while
yet in his tender youth, went through many conflicts with a manly heart.
Warlike as a pard, fragrant with sweetness like spikenard, whilst Edward is
in his vigour, behold he shines like a new Richard. Thus the Britons have a
double claim to honour, by the wars of Edward equally and by the valour of
Richard. France praised the manners of the warlike youth ; the ample hand
of the giver amassed merited honours. The envious people desiring to extin-

Invida gens cupiens meritas extinguere laudes,
Excogitando novas cœpit contexere fraudes :
Anglorum proceres legem fingendo novellam,
Ubere de regno terram fecere misellam.
Rex pater et patruus cum bina prole reguntur
Per sibi subjectos, ex quo mala multa sequuntur.
Degener Anglorum gens, quæ servire solebat,
Ordine mutato regem cum prole regebat.
Conjurat populus fruiturus lege novella;
Fædere mox rupto consurgunt horrida bella.
Dum Leycestrensem comitem sibi plebs sociavit,
Intestina sibi dispendia concumulavit.
In regem proprium gens irruit impia, natum
Cum patre et patruo captivat, mox dominatum
Consequitur, gaudent victores, corda tumescunt.
Effugit Eaduardus, statim nova prælia crescunt.
Convocat auxilium, solidantur fædera, crevit
Turma ducis, delusa cohors sua crimina flevit.
Concurrunt partes, quatiuntur tela, vigore

guish his merited praise, began to weave new plots in their mind : the English nobles, by inventing a new law, made a wretched land of a rich kingdom. The king his father, and his uncle, with their two children, are governed by their subjects, out of which many evils follow. The degenerate race of the English, which used to serve, inverting the order of things, ruled over the king and his children. The people conspires, in order to enjoy a new law ; soon after, the league being broken, horrid wars arise. While the populace associated with itself the Earl of Leicester, it accumulated for itself internal exhaustion. The impious people attacks its own king, makes captive the son with his father and uncle, next seizes upon the government ; the victors rejoice, their hearts swell. Edward escapes, and immediately new battles follow. He calls together assistance, leagues are established, the army of the leader increased, the deluded troop laments its crimes. The parties meet ; weapons are clashed ;

Militis Eaduuardi madidantur rura cruore.

Occidit ense Comes, proceres mucrone necantur;

Sic vincunt victi, victores exsuperantur.

Regno pene suo spoliatus seditione,

Victrices turmas miro superavit agone.

Ad regimen regni patrem stirps clara revexit,

Nequiter ablatum quod longo tempore rexit.

Plebs devicta fremit, iterumque potentibus unit

Turmas belligeras, dape, telis, oppida munit.

Insula per proceres vastatur mox Eliensis.

Urbs regni nostri capitanea Londoniensis

Per quosdam capitur, quatitur certamine diro;

Sed debellantur hæc omnia robore miro.

Pax optata redit, conduntur tela, nitescunt

Nubila quæ fuerant, Anglorum gaudia crescunt.

Impiger Eaduuardus devitans otia, signum

Mox crucis assumpsit, cupiens exsolvere dignum

Obsequium Christo, qui se liberavit ab isto

---

the fields are moistened with blood by the vigour of the soldier Edward. The Earl is slain by the sword; the barons are put to death with the weapon's point; thus the vanquished conquer, and the conquerors are overcome. Although by sedition almost robbed of his own kingdom, he overcame the conquering legions by a wonderful effort. The noble offspring carried back his father to the government of the kingdom, wickedly wrested from him, which he had long ruled. The conquered populace roars, and again joins its warlike squadrons to the barons; fortifies towns with provisions and weapons. Soon after the isle of Ely is ravaged by the popular leaders. London, the capital city of our kingdom, is occupied by some, and is shaken with fearful strife; but all these difficulties are conquered with wonderful strength. Peace, wished for, returns; the arms are laid by; clouds have given place to sunshine; the joys of the English increase. The active Edward, flying from idleness, next took up the sign of the cross, desirous of performing a worthy service to Christ, who had

Turbine bellorum ; sequitur pia turba virorum.
Francorum regis germanus rex Siculorum
Innumeros populos ad regnum Tuniciorum
Duxerat, ut vetitum potuit rehabere tributum,
Agminibus cunctis dicens iter hoc fore tutum
In terram sanctam ; cruce plebs signata dolebat,
Dum sua vota male jam commutata videbat.
Eaduuardus sequitur credens bellare potenter
Cum Sarracenis ; gentilis rex sapienter
Prælia devitans, solvit quodcunque petebat.
Rex Lodowicus obit cum prima prole, dolebat
Gallia, rex Karolus remeat, turmasque reduxit,
Anglos cum Siculis, Britonum plebs anxia luxit.
Vota crucis Christi Siculorum rex male frangit,
Et sua delusus populus discrimina plangit.
Applicat in portu Trapennæ, mox borialis
Turbo quatit puppes, populus perit innumeralis,
Mergitur æs totum, salvatur et Anglica classis
Munere divino, quod non periit valor assis.

delivered him from this whirlwind of wars ; a pious troop of men follows. The King of Sicily, brother of the King of France, had conducted a vast host to the kingdom of Tunis, that he might recover the tribute which had been refused, saying that this would be a safe way for the whole army to the Holy Land ; the people which was signed with the cross lamented to see its object thus unpropitiously changed. Edward follows in the belief that there will be powerful fighting with the Saracens ; but the Gentile King wisely avoiding battle, paid whatever he asked. King Louis dies with his eldest son ; France lamented ; King Charles returns, and brings back the troops, the English with the Sicilans ; the anxious Britons wept. The King of Sicily wickedly broke his vow of crusading, and the people, deceived, lamented his changing. He arrives at the port of Trapeni ; soon a whirlwind from the north strikes the fleet ; multitudes of people perish ; all the money is sunk ; but the English fleet is providentially

Rex prodire negat, renuens sua solvere vota.
Dux pius Anglorum similis et sua concio tota
Puppes ascendit, mare transmeat, ad loca tendit
Gentibus obsessa, longævo turbine pressa.
Accon respirat de tanto milite gaudens,
Atque sepulta diu psallit nova cantica plaudens.
Soldanus fremuit, procerem cogitando necare,
Quem per carnificem dirum fecit jugulare.
Hic assessinus Veteris de Monte ferebat
Nuncia conficta, quæ falso conficiebat;
Ingreditur thalamos præcludens hostia, cultro
Vulnera vulneribus impressit; strenuus ultro
Restitit Eaduuardus, tortorem robore stravit,
Quem telo proprio condigna morte necavit.
Et quia condignum Christus famulum sibi novit,
Illius plagas sacro medicamine fovit.

Expliciunt versus secundum Thomam de Wyta compositi de domino Eadwardo Angliæ rege illustrissimo.

saved, without losing the value of a farthing. The king refuses to proceed, or to perform his vow. The pious leader of the English and all his company alike embark, pass the sea, and make for the places which were besieged by the Gentiles, pressed under a long lasting storm. Acre takes breath, rejoicing in such a soldier, and rises as it were from the grave to sing new songs of praise. The Soldan was enraged, and thought to slay the noble leader, whom he caused to be stabbed by a detestable butcher. This assassin brought pretended messages from the Old Man of the Mountain, which were but false pretences; he enters the chamber and shuts the door; with a knife he adds wound upon wound; but Edward, on the other hand, resisted strenuously; with his strength he laid prostrate the murderer, whom he slew with a merited death by his own weapon. And because Christ knew that his servant was worthy, he healed his wounds with a sacred medicine.

Popular dissatisfaction may be traced throughout Edward's reign, we may venture to say from the day in which he mounted the throne. The following song seems to have been popular soon after his accession; and it is written in Latin and Anglo-Norman, in order that it might be sung more generally. In the manuscript, each stanza of the Latin is followed by the corresponding stanza in Anglo-Norman. Between the Latin lines of the first stanza is left space apparently for music.

A SONG ON THE TIMES.

[From MS. Harl. 746, fol. 103 vº, of the beginning of the reign of Edw. I.]

Vulneratur karitas, amor ægrotatur :
Regnat et perfidia, livor generatur.
Fraus primatum optinet, pax subpeditatur ;
Fides vincta carcere nimis desolatur.

In præsenti tempore non valet scriptura ;
Sed sopita veluti latent legis jura,

Amur gist en maladie, charité est nafré ;
Ore regne tricherie, hayne est engendré.
Boidie ad seignurie, pes est mise suz pé ;
Fei n'ad ki lui guie, en prisun est lié.

Ne lerray ke ne vus die, ne vaut ore escripture ;
Mès cum fust endormie e tapist dreiture,

TRANSLATION.—Charity is wounded, love is sick; perfidy reigns, and malice is engendered. The fraud of the rulers prevails, peace is trodden under foot; faith fettered in prison is very desolate.—At present, a writing is of no but right and law lie as it were asleep, and the care of the wicked race

Et nephandi generis excæcata cura
Nullo sensu prævio formidat futura.

Resistentes subruunt iniquitatis nati ;
Perit pax ecclesiæ, regnant et elati.
Hoc silendo sustinent improbi prælati,
Mortem pro justitia recusantes pati.

Strata pace penitus, amor refrigescit ;
Tota tellus Angliæ mærore madescit,
Omnisque dilectio dulcis evanescit :
Cuncti consolatium quærunt quo quiescit.

———

De la gent haye avugle est la cure,
Ke el ne dute mie venjance à venir dure.

Les contre-estanz abatent li fiz de felonie ;
Lors perit seinte eglise, quant orgoil la mestrie.
Ceo sustenent li prelaz ki s'i ne peinent mie,
Pur dreiture sustenir nolent perdre vie.

Pes est acravanté e amur refreidie ;
La terre est desconforté e de plur enmoistie,
Amur et amisté tut est anentie :
N'i ad nul ki ne quert confort et aye.

———

is blind, it has not sufficient foresight to fear the future.—The sons of iniquity
crush those who resist; the peace of the church perishes, and the proud
reign. The wicked prelates support this state of things by their supineness,
for they refuse to suffer death for justice.—Peace being altogether overthrown,
love is cooled; all the land of England is moist with weeping, and all friendship
and kindness has disappeared; all seek consolation and quiet.—The little

Patre carent parvuli pupilli plangentes,
Atque matre orphani fame jam deflentes;
Qui in primis penitus fuerunt potentes,
Nunc subcumbunt gladio, plorant et parentes.

Ecce pravi pueri pauperes prædantur;
Ecce donis divites dolose ditantur;
Omnes pene proceres mala machinantur;
Insani satellites livore lætantur.

Ecce viri confluunt undique raptores;
Ecce pacis pereunt legisque latores;

———

Asez i ad des orphanins grant doel demenanz,
Ke lur parenz sunt mis à fins, dunt il en sunt dolenz,
Cil ki en comencent furent mult pussanz,
Sunt suzmis à le espeye, e plorent li parenz.

Li enfanz felons s'en vunt la povere gent preer;
Li riches à tort enrichiz sunt de autri aver;
A peine i ad haute home ki cesse mal penser;
De hayne sunt haitez li felons esquier.

De tote parz venent li bers ravisanz;
Ore perissent de pes e de la ley li sustenanz;

———

orphans lament the loss of their father, and, deprived of their mother, they sorrow in the midst of hunger; they who at first were very powerful, now fall by the sword, and their parents weep.—Lo! wicked children rob the poor; lo! the wealth of the rich is increased by exacting gifts; almost all the nobles spend their time in contriving evil; the mad esquires delight in malice.—Lo! the rapacious men appear on every side; lo! the supporters of peace and

Dogmata despiciunt truces hii tortores,
Et prodesse nequeunt sancti confessores.

Hii converti respuunt virtute sermonum,
Neque curam capiunt de vita vironum ;
Omnes simul rapiunt, ut mos est prædonum.
Hiis vindictam ingere, Deus ultionum !

———

Enseignement refusent ces cruels tormentanz,
Espleyt ne poent fere cil ki vunt prechanz.

Si il se ne volent amender pur dit ne pur fesance,
Mès pur tuer quant ont poer ben ont la voillance ;
Trestuz en funt ravine, de Deu n'en ont dotance.
Cels metez à declin, sire Deu de venjance !

———

justice perish ; these cruel butchers despise doctrine, and the holy preachers
have no effect.—These men will not be amended by the force of sermons ; nor
do they make any account of the lives of men ; they all plunder together,
like robbers. Take vengeance upon them, O God of vengeance.

———

One of the legacies which St. Louis left to Christendom was
the number of new orders of monks which had been created
during his reign and by his encouragement. They soon spread
from France into England ; but they were very far from being
popular in either country, and were the constant butt of the
gibes and jokes of the poets. The following is a bitter satire
upon the different orders of monks in England in the reign of
Edward I. The idea of caricaturing them by feigning one
order which should unite the different characteristic vices of all
the others, was not new.

THE ORDER OF FAIR-EASE.

[MS. Harl. No. 2253, fol. 121 rº. Reign of Ed. II.]

Qui vodra à moi entendre,
Oyr purra e aprendre
L'estoyre de un Ordre novel,
Qe mout est delitous e bel:
Je le vus dirroi come l'ay apris
Des freres de mon pays.
L'Ordre est si foundé à droit,
Qe de tous ordres un point estroit,
N'i ad ordre en cest mound
10 Dont si n'i ad ascun point.
Le noun de l'Ordre vus vueil dyre,
Qe um ne me pust blamer de lire ;
Qy oyr velt si se teyse,
C'est le Ordre de Bel-Eyse.
De l'Ordre vus dirroi la sonme ;
Quar en l'Ordre est meint prodhonme,
E meinte bele e bone dame.
En cel Ordre sunt sanz blame
Esquiers, vadletz, e serjauntz ;

TRANSLATION.—He who will listen to me, may hear and learn the history of a new Order, which is very pleasant and beautiful : I will tell it you as I have learnt it from the brethren of my country. The Order is so cleverly founded, that it takes a point from all the other orders ; there is not an order in this world, of which there is not there some one point. The name of the Order I will tell you, that I may not be blamed for what I read ; he who will hear, let him be silent, it is the Order of Fair-Ease. Of this Order I will tell you the sum ; for in the order is many a worthy fellow, and many a fair and good dame. In this Order there are without blame, esquires, valets, and ser-

20 Mès à ribaldz e à pesauntz
   Est l'Ordre del tot defendu,
   Qe jà nul ne soit rescu.
   Quar il frount à l'Ordre hounte.
   Quant rybaud ou vyleyn mounte
   En hautesse ou baylie,
   Là oû il puet aver mestrie,
   N'i ad plus de mesure en eux
   Qe al le luop qe devoure aigneux.
   De cele gent lerroi ataunt,
30 E de le Ordre dirroi avaunt.

    En cel Ordre dount je vus dy,
   Est primes issi estably,
   Que ceux qe à l'Ordre serrount,
   De Sympringham averount
   Un point, qe bien pleysant serra,
   Come l'abbeie de Sympringham a,
   Freres e sueres ensemble ;
   C'est bon Ordre, come me semble.
   Mès de tant ert changié, pur veyr,
40 Q'à Sympringham doit aver

jeants ; but to ribalds and to peasants the Order is entirely forbidden, so that no one may be received into it. For they would bring disgrace upon the Order. When ribald or vilein mounts to high place or office, there where he can have power, there is no more moderation in them than in the wolf which devours lambs. Of such people I will say no more, but l will go on to talk about the Order.

In this Order of which I tell you, it is first ordained thus, that those who shall belong to the Order, shall have one point of Sempringham, which will be very agreeable, as the Abbey of Sempringham has, brothers and sisters together ; it is a good Order, as it seems to me. But so far, in truth, it is changed, that at Sempringham there must be between the brothers and the sisters (a

Entre les freres e les sorours,
Qe desplest à plusours,
Fossés e murs de haute teyse;
Mès en cet Ordre de Bel-Eyse
Ne doit fossé ne mur aver,
Ne nul autre destourber,
Qe les freres à lur pleysyr
Ne pussent à lor sueres venyr,
E qu'il n'eit point de chalaunge.
50 Jà n'i avera ne lyn ne launge
Entre eux, e si le peil y a,
Jà pur ce ne remeindra.
De yleoque est ensi purveu,
Qe cil q'à l'Ordre serrount rendu,
De l'abbé deyvent bien estre:
E ce comaund nostre mestre,
Pur bien manger e à talent
Treis foiz le jour, e plus sovent.
E s'il le font pur compagnye,
60 Le Ordre pur ce ne remeindra mie.
De Beverleye ont un point treit,

thing which displeases many,) ditches and walls of high measure; but in this Order of Fair-Ease there must be neither ditch nor wall, nor any other impediment, to hinder the brethren at their pleasure from visiting the sisters, nor shall there be any watch-word. Their intimacy shall neither be separated by linen nor wool, or even by their very skins. From thence also it is provided, that they who shall enter the Order, must be well entertained by the abbot: and this our master commands, to eat well and plentifully three times a day, and oftener. And if they do it for company, the Order on that account shall not be the worse.

Of Beverley they have taken a point, which shall be kept well and accu-

Qe serra tenu bien e dreit,
Pur beyvre bien à mangier,
E pus après desqu'à soper ;
E après al collacioun,
Deit chescun aver un copoun
De chandelle long desqu'al coute,
E tant come remeindra goute
De la chandeille à arder
70 Deivent les freres à beyvre ser.
Un point unt tret de Hospitlers,
Qe sunt mult corteis chevalers,
E ount robes bien avenauntz,
Longes desqu'al pié traynantz,
Soudlers e chausés bien séantz,
E gros palefrois bien amblantz ;
Si deyvent en nostre Ordre aver
Les freres e sueres, pur veyr.
De Chanoynes ont un point pris,
80 Qu'en l'Ordre ert bien assis ;
Quar chanoygnes pur grant peyne
Mangent en la symeygne

rately, to drink well at their meat, and then afterwards until supper ; and afterwards at the collation, each must have a piece of candle as long as the arm below the elbow, and as long as there shall remain a morsel of the candle to burn, the brethen must continue their drinking.

A point they have taken from the Hospitallers, who are very courteous knights, and have very becoming robes, so long that they drag at their feet ; shoes and breeches which fit elegantly, and great palfreys that amble well ; so in our Order, in truth, the brethren and sisters must have them.

Of the Canons they have taken a point, which will agree well with the Order ; for the canons, for great pain, eat in the refectory flesh three days in the

Char en le refreitour treis jours;
Auxi deyvent nos sorours
E nos freres chescun jour
Char mangier en refreitour,
Fors le vendredi soulement,
E le samadi ensement.
E si issint avenist
90 Q'al samadi hoste fust,
E l'em ne ust plenté de pesshon,
L'estor qe fust en la mesoun
Purreint il par congié prendre,
Jà l'Ordre ne serra le meindre.
    Un point ont tret de Moyne Neirs,
Que volenters beyvent, pur veyrs,
E sount cheschun jour yvre,
Quar ne sevent autre vivre;
Mès il le fount pur compagnie,
100 E ne mie pur glotonie.
Auxi est il purveu
Que chescun frere soit enbu,
De jour en jour tot adès
Devant manger e après.

week; so must our sisters and our brethren eat flesh in the refectory every day, except only Friday, and likewise Saturday. And if it so happen that there be a fast on the Saturday, and they have not plenty of fish, they may have leave to take what provisions are in the house; the Order will be none the worse for it.

A point they have taken from the Black Monks, that they love drinking, forsooth, and are drunk every day, for they do not know any other way of living. But they do it for the sake of society, and not at all out of gluttony. Also it is provided, that each brother drink before dinner and after. And if it

E si il avenist ensi
Qe à frere venist amy,
Dount se deyvent ensorter
Pur les freres solacer,
Qui savera bien juer le seyr ;
110 Ce vus di-je de veir,
Yl dormira grant matinée,
Desque la male fumée
Seit de la teste issue,
Pur grant peril de la vewe.
    Des Chanoygnes Seculers,
Qe dames servent volenters,
Ont nos mestres un point treit,
E vueillent qe cel point seit
Bien tenuz e bien uséez ;
120 Quar c'est le point, bien sachez,
Que pluz ad en l'Ordre mester,
Pur les freres solacer.
Si est, sur eschumygement,
Comaundé molt estroitement,
Que chescun frere à sa sorour
Deit fere le giw d'amour
Devant matines adescement,

so happen that a friend visit a brother (for such must be at hand to solace the
brethren) who shall know how to play in the evening ; this I tell you for certain,
he shall sleep late in the morning, until the evil fumes are issued from his head,
for great danger of the sight.

Of the Secular Canons, who willingly serve ladies, our masters have taken a
point, and will that this point be well observed and well used ; for know that
this point is more needful than any in the Order, in order to solace the
brethren.   And so it is commanded very straightly, on pain of excommunica-

E après matines ensement ;
E s'il le fet avant son departyr
130 Troiz foiz à soun pleysyr,
   Jà le frere blame ne avera,
   Ne le Ordre enpeyré serra.
      Gris Moignes sunt dure gent,
   E de lur ordre nequedent
   Vueillent nos mestres pur grever
   L'Ordre un des lur poyntz aver ;
   E si n'est geres corteis,—
   Quar à matines vont sanz breys.
   Auxi deyvent nos freres fere,
140 Pur estre prest à lur affere.
   E quant il fount nul oreysoun,
   Si deyvent estre à genulloun,
   Pur aver greindre devocioun
   A fere lur executioun.
   E ou un seyn sonnent santz plus,
   C'est lur ordre e lur us :—
   Mès nos freres pur doubler,
   Ou deus seynz deyvent soner.
   De taunt est nostre Ordre dyvers,

tion, that the brethren be constant companions of the sisters, both before matins and after, so that the brethren be not blamed for neglecting them, nor the Order receive discredit.

The Grey Monks are a hard race; yet, nevertheless, from their order our masters will that the Order have one of their points for mortification ; and in fact it is not over courteous,—for they go to matins without breeches. So ought our brethren to do, to be more at their ease. And when they make no prayer, they must be on their knees, to have greater and more effectual devotion : and they ring with one bell, and no more,—it is their order and usage :—but our brethren, to double it, must sound with two bells. Our Order has such

150 Qe no sueres deyvent envers
     Gysyr e orer countre-mount,
     Par grant devocioun le fount.
        Issi pernent en pacience,
     C'est point de l'Ordre de Cilence ;
     Chaichons est bon ordre, sanz faile,
     N'est nul des autres qe taunt vayle ;—
     Pur ce vueillent ascun point trere
     De cel ordre à nostre affere.
     Chescun est en sa celle enclos,
160 Pur estre soul en repos ;
     Auxi deyvent nos freres estre,
     Si doit chescun à sa fenestre
     Del herber aver pur solas,
     E sa suere entre ces bras,
     E estre enclos privément,
     Pur survenue de la gent.
        Ne devomz pas entreoublier,
     Si nostre ordre deit durer,
     Les Frere Menours à nul suer,
170 Qe Dieu servent de bon cuer ;
     Si devomz ascun point aver

difference, that our sisters must lay down flat and pray on their backs, they do
it out of great devotion.

   Also they take in patience, it is a point from the Order of Silence ; each is a
good order, without doubt, but none of the others is so valuable ;—therefore they
will take one point of this order for our purpose. Each is shut up in his cell,
to repose himself alone ; so our brothers must be, and each at his window must
have some plants to comfort him, and his sister in his arms, and he must be
shut up privately, that nobody may disturb them.

   We must not forget, if our Order is to last, the Friars Minors, in no case ;

De lur ordre, pur mieux valer.
Lur ordre est fondé en poverte,
Pur quei yl vont la voie apierte
En ciel tot plenerement;
Si vus dirroi bien coment
Yl querent poverte tot dis;
Quaunt il vont par le pays,
Al chief baroun ou chivaler
180 Se lerrount il herberger,
Ou à chief persone ou prestre,
Là ou il purrount acese estre;
Mès par Seint Piere de Ronme,
Ne se herbigerount ou povre honme,—
Taunt come plus riches serrount,
Ostiel plustost demanderount.
Ne ne deyvent nos freres fere
Ostiel, ne autre lyu quere,
Fors là ou il sevent plenté,
190 E là deyvent en charité
Char mangier e ce qu'il ount,
Auxi come les Menours fount.

so must we have a point of their order, to be of more account. Their order is founded in poverty, therefore they go the open way to heaven completely; and I will tell you exactly how they seek poverty always; when they travel through the country, they take up their lodgings with the chief baron or knight, or with the chief person or priest, there where they can be satiated; but, by St. Peter of Rome! they will never lodge with a poor man,—so long as there are richer men to be found, they prefer asking a lodging of them. In the same manner our brethren must not take up their lodging, nor seek other place, than where they know there is plenty, and there they ought in charity to eat flesh and whatever they find, as the Friars Minors do.

Pus qe avomz des menours,
Auxi averomz des Prechours ;
Ne vont come les autres nuyz péez
Eynz vont precher tot chaucéez,
E s'il avient ascune feez
Qu'il seient malades as piés,
Yl purrount, s'il ount talent,
200 Chevalcher tot plenerement
Tote la jornée entière.
Mès tot en autre manere
Deyvent nos freres fere,
Quant il prechent par la terre ;
Car il deyvent tot adès
Tot dis chevalcher loinz e près :
E quant il fount nul sermoun,
Si deyvent estre dedenz mesoun.
E tote foiz après manger
210 Deyvent il de dreit precher ;
Quar meint honme est de tiele manere,
Qu'il ad le cuer pluz dur qe piere,
Mès quant il avera ankes bu
Tost avera le Ordre entendu,

As we owe something to the Minors, we will borrow also of the Preachers ; they do not go bare-foot like the others, but they go preaching with shoes on, and if it happen any time that they have sore feet, they may, if they like, ride on horseback at their ease all the day long. But quite in another manner ought our brethren to do, when they preach through the land ; for they must ride thus always both far and near : and when they make any sermon, they must be within doors. And always after dinner they ought rightly to preach ; for many a man is of such a character, that his heart is harder than stone ; but when he shall have once drunk, then as soon as he has heard the Order, and

E les cuers serront enmoistez,
De plus leger serrount oyez,
Qe à l'Ordre se rendrount
Quant le sermon oy averont.
   Ensi est nostre ordre foundé,
220 E si ount nos freres en pensée,
Qe chescun counté doit aver
Un abbé, qe eit poer
A receyvre sueres e freres,
E fere e tenyr ordres pleneres,
E qe les pointz seient tenuz
Qe nos mestres ount purveuz.
Un provyncial en la terre
Doit aler e enquere,
Pur saver qy l'Ordre tendra.
230 E cely qe le enfreindra,
Serra privément chastié,
E de son meffet reprové.
E ceux qe serront trovez
Qe l'Ordre averount bien usez,
Si deyvent pur lur humilité

the hearts shall be moistened, however little they might have heard, they will listen to the Order, when they have heard the sermon.

Thus is our Order founded, and our brothers have deemed right, that each county must have an abbot, who has power to receive sisters and brothers, and make and hold full orders, and that the points shall be held which our masters have provided. A provincial ought to go and inquire in the land, to know who will hold the Order. And he who shall break it, shall be chastised in private, and reproved for his trespass. And those who shall be found to have made good use of the order, must, for their humility, be raised to dignity, and they shall

Estre mis en digneté,
E serrount abbés ou priours
A tenyr l'Ordre en honeurs.
Issi fount les Augustyns,
240 Qe tant sevent de devyns ;
Par tot enquergent pleynement
Qy tienent l'Ordre lealment,
E ceux qe l'Ordre tendrount
Par tot loé serrount.

Atant fine nostre Ordre,
Q'à touz bonz ordres se acorde,
E c'est l'Ordre de Bel-Eyse,
Qe à plusours trobien pleyse !

be abbots or priors to hold the order in honours. Thus do the Augustine Monks, who know so many devices ; every where they give full encouragement to those who hold the Order loyally, and those who will hold the Order shall be praised everywhere.

Now ends our Order, which agrees with all good orders, and it is the Order of Fair-Ease, which to many may it please too well !

————

Edward endeavoured to call off the vigour of his subjects from domestic sedition to foreign wars. But the expenses dependent upon the latter only added to the many burdens under which the English peasantry laboured ; and it is now that we begin to find the complaints of the latter vented in the shape of popular songs.

SONG OF THE HUSBANDMAN.

[MS. Harl. No. 2253, fol. 64, r⁰ ; reign of Edw. II.]

Ich herde men upo mold make muche mon,
Hou he beth i-tened of here tilyynge,
Gode ȝeres and corn bothe beth a-gon,
Ne kepeth here no sawe ne no song syng.
" Now we mote worche, nis ther non other won,
Mai ich no lengore lyve with my lesinge;
ȝet ther is a bitterore bid to the bon,
For ever the furthe peni mot to the kynge.

Thus we carpeth for the kyng, and carieth ful colde,
And weneth for te kevere, and ever buth a-cast ;
Whose hath eny god, hopeth he nout to holde,
Bote ever the levest we leoseth a-last.

Luther is to leosen ther ase lutel ys,
And haveth monie hynen that hopieth therto ;
The hayward heteth us harm to habben of his ;
The bailif bockneth us bale and weneth wel do ;
The wodeward waiteth us wo that loketh under rys ;
Ne mai us ryse no rest rycheis ne ro.

TRANSLATION.—I heard men on the earth make much lamentation,—how they are injured in their tillage,—good years and corn are both gone,—they keep here no saying and sing no song.—Now we must work, there is no other custom,—I can no longer live with my gleaning ;—yet there is a bitterer asking for the boon,—for ever the fourth penny must [go] to the king.

Thus we complain for the king, and care full coldly,—and think to recover, and ever are cast ;—he who hath any goods, expects not to keep them,—but ever the dearest we lose at last.

It is grievous to lose, where there is little,—and we have many fellows who expect it ;—the hayward commandeth us harm to have of his ;—the bailiff causeth us to know evil, and thinks to do well ;—the woodward has woe in keeping for us, who looketh under branches ;—there may not arise to us or remain with us

Thus me pileth the pore that is of lute pris :
  Nede in swot and in swynk swynde mot swo :"

Nede he mot swynde thah he hade swore,
  That nath nout en hod his hed for te hude.
Thus wil walketh in londe, and lawe is for-lore,
  And al is piked of the pore, the prikyares prude.

Thus me pileth the pore and pyketh ful clene,
  The ryche raymeth withouten eny ryht ;
Ar londes and ar leodes liggeth fol lene,
  Thorh b[i]ddyng of baylyfs such harm hem hath hiht.
Meni of religioun me halt hem ful hene,
  Baroun and bonde, the clerc and the knyht.
Thus wil walketh in lond, and wondred ys wene,
  Falsshipe fatteth and marreth wyth myht.

Stont fulle ythe stude, and halt him ful sturne,
  That maketh beggares go with bordon and bagges.
Thus we beth honted from hale to hurne ;
  That er werede robes, nou wereth ragges.

---

riches or repose.—Thus they rob the poor man, who is of little value :—he
must needs in sweat and in labour waste away so.

He must needs pine away, though he had swore (?),—that hath not a hood to
hide his head.—Thus will walketh in the land, and law is destroyed,—and all
the pride of the rider is picked from the poor.

Thus they rob the poor and pick him full clean,—the rich lord it without any
right ;—their lands and their people lay full lean,—through asking of bailifs such
harm has befallen them.—Many of religion hold them full abject,—baron and
bond-man, the clerk and the knight.—Thus will walks in the land, and consternation is frequent,—falsehood fattens and marrs with might.

He stands full in the place, and holds him full sternly,—that makes beggars
go with bordon and bags.—Thus we are hunted from hall to corner ;—they who
once wore robes, now wear rags.

ȝet cometh budeles, with ful muche bost,—
   " Greythe me selver to the grene wax :
Thou art writen y my writ that thou wel wost."
   Mo then ten sithen told y my tax.
Thenne mot ych habbe hennen a-rost,
   Feyr on fyhshe day launprey ant lax ;
Forth to the chepyn geyneth ne chost,
   Thah y sulle mi bil ant my borstax.

Ich mot legge my wed wel ȝef y wolle,
   Other sulle mi corn on gras that is grene.
ȝet I shal be foul cherl, thah he han the fulle,
   That ich alle ȝer spare thenne y mot spene.

Nede y mot spene that y spared ȝore,
   Aȝeyn this cachereles cometh thus y mot care ;
Cometh the maister budel brust ase a bore,
   Seith he wole mi bugging bringe ful bare.
Mede y mot munten a mark other more,
   Thah ich at the set dey sulle mi mare.

Still there come beadles, with very great boast,—" Prepare me silver for the green wax :—thou art entered in my writing, that thou knowest well of."—More than ten times I paid my tax.—Then must I have hens roasted,—fair on the fish day lamprey and salmon ;—forth to the market gains not cost,—though I sell my bill and my borstax.

I must lay my pledge well if I will,—or sell my corn while it is but green grass.—Yet I shall be a foul churl, though they have the whole,—what I have saved all the year, I must spend then.

I must needs spend what I saved formerly,—I must thus take care against the time these catchpoles come ;—the master beadle comes as roughly as a boar,—he says he will make my lodgings full bare ;—I must give him for meed a mark or

Ther the grene wax us greveth under gore,
    That me us honteth ase hound doth the hare.

He us honteth ase hound hare doh on hulle ;
    Seththe y tek to the lond such tene me wes taht.
Nabbeth ner budeles boded ar sulle,
    For he may scape ant we aren ever caht.

Thus y kippe ant cacche cares ful colde,
    Seththe y counte ant cot hade to kepe ;
To seche selver to the kyng y mi seed solde,
    Forthi mi lond leye lith ant leorneth to slepe.
Seththe he mi feire feh fatte y my folde,
    When y thenk o mi weole wel neh y wepe ;
Thus bredeth monie beggares bolde,
    Ant ure ruȝe ys roted ant ruls er we repe.

Ruls ys oure ruȝe ant roted in the stre,
    For wickede wederes by brok ant by brynke.
Ther wakeneth in the world wondred ant wee,
    Ase god is swynden anon as so for te swynke.

more,—though I sell my mare at the day fixed.—There the green wax grieveth us under garment,—so that they hunt us as a hound doth the hare.

They hunt us as a hound doth a hare on the hill ;—since I took to the land such hurt was given me :—the beadles have never asked their . . ,—for they may scape, and we are always caught.

Thus I take and catch cares full cold,—since I reckoning and cot had to keep ;—to seek silver for the king, I sold my seed,—wherefore my land lies fallow and learneth to sleep.—Since they fetched my fair cattle in my fold,—when I think of my weal I very nearly weep ;—thus breed many bold beggars,—and our rye is rotted and . . . . . . before we reap.

. . . . . . is our rye and rotted in the straw,—on account of the bad weather by brook and by brink.—There wakes in the world consternation and woe,—as good is to perish at once as so to labour.

The following song appears to be directed against the gay fashions in Ladies' clothing which became prevalent about this time, and seem even to have been aped by the middle and lower ranks.

AGAINST THE PRIDE OF THE LADIES.

[MS. Harl. 2253, fol. 61, v°; reign of Edw. II.]

Lord that lenest us lyf, ant lokest uch an lede,
For te cocke with knyf nast thou none nede;
Bothe wepmon ant wyf sore mowe drede,
Lest thou be sturne with strif, for bone that thou bede,
    in wunne
        That monku[n]ne
    Shulde shilde hem from sunne.

Nou hath prude the pris in everuche plawe;
By mony wymmon un-wis y sugge mi sawe,
For ʒef a ledy lyne is leid after lawe,
Uch a strumpet that ther is such drahtes wl drawe;
    in prude
        Uch a screwe wol hire shrude
    Thah he nabbe nout a smoke hire foule ers to hude.

TRANSLATION.—Lord, that givest us life, and regardest every people,—to
........with knife thou hast no need;—both man and woman sorely may
dread,—lest thou be stern with wrath, for the boon that thou askedst,—in joy—
that mankind—should shield themselves from sin.

Now pride hath the prize in every play;—of many unwise women I say my
saw,—for if a lady's linen is laid after law,—every strumpet that there is such
draughts will draw;—in pride—every shrew will clothe herself,—though she
have not a smock to hide her dirty tail.

CAMD. SOC. 6.   X

Furmest in boure were boses y-broht,
Levedis to honoure ichot he were wroht ;
Uch gigelot wol loure, bote he hem habbe soht;
Such shrewe fol soure ant duere hit hath a-boht ;
    in helle
  With develes he shule duelle,
  For the clogges that cleveth by here chelle.

Nou ne lacketh hem no lyn boses in to beren ;
He sitteth ase a slat swyn that hongeth is eren.
Such a joustynde gyn uch wrecche wol weren,
Al hit cometh in declyn this gigelotes geren ;
    upo lofte
  The devel may sitte softe,
  Ant holden his halymotes ofte.

ȝef ther lyth a loket by er outher eȝe,
That mot with worse be wet for lat of other leȝe ;
The bout and the barbet wyth frountel shule feȝe ;
Habbe he a fauce filet, he halt hire hed heȝe,

First in bower were bosses brought,—to honour ladies I wot they were wrought ;—every giglot will lour, unless she have them sought ;—such shrew full sourly and dearly hath bought it ;—in hell—with devils they shall dwell,—on account of the clogs which hang by their jowls.

Now they want no linen to bear bosses in ;—they sit like a slit swine which hangs its ears.—Such a justling contrivance every wretch will wear,—that these giglots' gear all comes to nothing ;—on high—the devil may sit softly,—and hold his sabbaths often.

If there lies a locket by ear or eye,—that may with worse be wet, for lack of other lye ; the but and the barbel with frontlet shall quarrel ;—if she have a false fillet, she holds her head high,—to show—that she is famous and well

to shewe
That heo be kud ant knewe
For strompet in rybaudes rewe.

known—for a strumpet in the ribalds' ranks.

Another song, written apparently about the same period, is a satire upon the smaller Ecclesiastical Courts, and the vexation which they caused to the peasantry.

A SATYRE ON THE CONSISTORY COURTS.

[MS. Harl. No. 2253, fol. 70, v°; of reign of Edw. II.]

Ne mai no lewed lued libben in londe,
Be he never in hyrt so haver of honde,
    So lerede us bi-ledes;
ȝef ich on molde mote with a mai,
Y shal falle hem byfore ant lurnen huere lay,
    Ant rewen alle huere redes.
Ah bote y be the furme day on folde hem by-fore,
Ne shal y nout so skere scapen of huere score;
    So grimly he on me gredes,
That y ne mot me lede ther with mi lawe,

TRANSLATION.—No unlearned (lay) person may live in the land,—be he in assembly never so ...... of hand,—the learned (the clergy) so lead us about;—if I chance to go on the earth with a maid,—I shall fall before them and learn their lay,—and rue all their counsels.—But unless I be on the foremost day in the land before them,—I shall not escape so clear of their score,—they cry on me so grimly,—that I may not lead myself there with my law,—on all kinds of

On alle maner othes that heo me wulleth awe,
   Heore boc ase un-bredes.
      Heo wendeth bokes un-brad,
       Ant maketh men a moneth a-mad;
   Of scathe y wol me skere,
   Ant fleo from my fere;
   Ne rohte he whet it were,
      Boten heo hit had.

Furst ther sit an old cherl in a blake hure,
Of all that ther sitteth semeth best syre,
     And leyth ys leg o lonke.
An heme in an herygoud with honginde sleven,
Ant mo then fourti him by-fore my bales to breven,
     In sunnes ȝef y songe:
Heo pynkes with heore penne on heore parchemyn,
Ant sayen y am breved ant y-broht yn
     Of al my weole wlonke.
Alle heo bueth redy myn routhes to rede,
Ther y mot for menske munte sum mede,
     Ant thonkfulliche hem thonke.
       Shal y thonke hem ther er y go?

oaths that they will give me,—their books as · · · ·—They turn over books that
are not broad,—and make men a month mad;—from hurt I will save myself,—
and fly from my companion;—she recked not what it were,—but she had it.
   First, there sit an old churl in a black gown,—of all who sits there he
seems to be most the lord,—and lays his leg along.—A hem in a cloak with
hanging sleeves,—and more than forty before him to write my bales,—in sins
if I sung :—they pink with their pens on their parchment,—and say I am
briefed and brought in—of all my fair wealth.—They are all ready to read my
sorrow—there I must out of respect give some bribe,—and gratefully thank
them.—Shall I thank them there before I go ?—Yea, the master and his men

ʒe, the maister ant ys men bo.
ʒef y am wreint in heore write,
Thenne am y bac-bite,
For moni mon heo maketh wyte
Of wymmene wo.

ʒet ther sitteth somenours syexe other sevene,
Mys motinde men alle by here evene,
Ant recheth forth heore rolle ;
Hyrd-men hem hatieth, ant uch mones hyne,
For everuch a parosshe heo polketh in pyne,
Ant clastreth with heore colle.
Nou wol uch fol clerc that is fayly,
Wende to the bysshop ant bugge bayly ;
Nys no wyt in is nolle.
Come to countene court couren in a cope,
Ant suggen he hath privilegie proud of the pope,
Swart ant al to-swolle.
Aren heo to-swolle for swore ?
ʒe, the hatred of helle beo heore !
For ther heo beodeth a boke,
To sugge ase y folht toke ;

both.—If I am accused in their writing,—then am I back-bitten,—for many men they make to know—woe from women.

Yet there sit somnours six or seven,—misjudging men all alike,—and reach forth their roll;—herdsmen hate them, and each man's servant,—for every parish they put in pain,—and clatter with their collar (?).—Now will each foolish clerk that is . . . ., go to the bishop and buy bailywick ;—there is no sense in his head.—He comes creeping to the county court in a cope,—and saying he hath proud privilege of the pope,—black and all swollen.—Are they swollen for swearing (?) ?—yea, the hatred of hell be theirs !—for there they

Heo shulen in helle on an hoke
Honge therefore.

Ther stont up a ȝeolumon, ȝeȝeth with a ȝerde,
Ant hat out an heh that al the hyrt herde,
Ant cleopeth Magge ant Malle ;
Ant heo cometh by-modered ase a mor-hen,
Ant scrynketh for shome, ant shometh for men,
Un-comely under calle.
Heo biginneth to shryke, ant scremeth anon,
Ant saith, " by my gabbyng ne shal hit so gon,
Ant that beo on ou alle ;
That thou shalt me wedde ant welde to wyf."
Ah me were levere with lawe leose my lyf,
Then so to fote hem falle.
Shal y to fote falle for mi fo ?
ȝe monie by-swyketh heo swo.
Of thralles y am ther thrat,
That sitteth swart ant for-swat,
Ther y mot hente me en hat,
Er ich hom go.

offer a book,—to say as I baptism took ;—they shall in hell on a hook—hang
for it.

There stands up a yellow-man, and jogs with a rod,—and shouts out aloud that
all the assembly heard,—and calls Mag and Mal ;—and she comes be-mothered
as a moor-hen,—and shrinks for shame, and is ashamed on account of the men,
—un-comely under petticoat.—She begins to screech, and screams anon,—and
says, " by my gabbing, it shall not go so,—and that be on you all ;—that thou
shalt wed me and have me to wife."—But I would rather with law lose my
life,—then so fall at their feet.—Shall I fall at the feet of my foes ?—Yea,
many she deceiveth so.—I am there threatened by thralls,—who sit black and
covered with sweat,—there I must take me a command,—before I go home.

Such chaffare y chepe at the chapitre,
That maketh moni thryve-mon un-thenfol to be,
   With thonkes ful thunne:
Ant seththe y go coure at constory,
Ant falle to fote uch a fayly,
   Heore is this worldes wynne,
Seththen y pleide at bisshopes plee.
Ah! me were levere be sonken y the see,
   In sor withouten synne.
At chirche ant thourh cheping ase dogge y am drive,
That me were levere of lyve then so for te lyve,
   To care of al my kynne.
      Atte constorie heo kenneth us care,
      Ant whissheth us evele ant worse to fare;
   A pruest proud ase a po,
   Seththe weddeth us bo,
   Wyde heo worcheth us wo,
     For wymmene ware.

Such merchandise I buy at the chapter,—that makes many thrifty men to be unthankful,—with very thin thanks :—and since I go creeping to the consistory, —and fall at the foot of each . . . .,—theirs is the world's joy,—since I played at the bishop's pleading.—But I had rather be drowned in the sea,— in sorrow without sin.—At church and through the market like a dog I am driven,—that I would rather be dead than so to live,—to have care for all my kindred.—At the consistory they teach us care,—and wish us evil and worse to fare ;—a priest as proud as a peacock—afterwards weds us both,—widely they work us woe,—for women's ware.

In the latter years of the thirteenth century, Edward became involved in the Scottish wars; and the enmity of the two nations was manifested in multitudes of songs, of which the greater part are lost, although a few are preserved, and a fragment or two of others are found in the old historians.   The following song, attributed in the several manuscripts to different writers, was (if we may judge by the number of copies which remain,) very popular.   Different persons seem, from time to time, to have altered it and added to it.   It appears to have been composed in 1298, soon after the sanguinary battle of Falkirk; but the latter stanzas, found only in one manuscript, have apparenty been added at a somewhat later period.

SONG ON THE SCOTTISH WARS.

[MS. Cotton. Claudius, D. vi. fol. 182, v°; of the beginning of the fourteenth cent. (*C.* 1.)—MS. Cotton. Titus, A. xx. fol. 64, v°; of reign of Edw. III. (*C.*2.)—MS. of Clare Hall, Cambridge, of fourteenth cent.(*Cl.*)—MS. Sloan. No. 4934, fol. 103, r°; a modern copy from a MS. not now known. (*Sl.*)— MS. Bodl. Oxfd. Rawl. B. 214, fol. 216, r°; of the fifteenth cent.]

Ludere volentibus ludens paro lyram;
De mundi malitia rem demonstro miram;
Nil quod nocet referam, rem gestam requiram;
Scribo novam satyram, sed sic ne seminet iram.
    Ira movet militum mentes modernorum,
    Dum inermes detrahunt factis fortiorum;

VARIOUS READINGS.—2. *militia,* C. 2. & Cl. *demonstrans,* C. 2.—3. *perquiram,* Cl.—7. *sed vos non commoveant,* C. 1.

TRANSLATION.—I playing prepare a harp for those who desire to play; I set forth a wonderful matter concerning the malice of the world; I will tell nothing that is noxious, but will relate a historical incident; I write a new satire, yet let it not on that account sow anger.—Anger moves the minds of the soldiers of the present day, since the weak detract from the praise of the

Te tamen non terreant dentes detractorum :
Cum recte vivas, ne cures verba malorum.

[Ira si duraverit, transit in livorem ;
Livor non cohibitus agitat furorem ;
Furor dies breviat, ducens in anguorem ;
Ira odium generat, concordia nutrit amorem.

Amor orbis obiit, virus est in villa ;
†10 Prodiit ex odio pestis non pusilla ;
Lator homicidii levavit vexilla :
Acrius invidia nichil est, nil nequius illa.

Invido nil nequius, nullus est qui nescit ;
Nam de bono proximi dolor ejus crescit.
Unde justus proficit, hinc ipse tabescit.
Sincerum nisi vas, quodcumque infundis acescit.

Ut acescant igitur mentes malignorum,
Narrabo quæ noveram de gestis Anglorum.

VARIOUS READINGS.—8. Instead of this second tetrastich, the Sloane and Cambridge MSS. have the four which are here given in brackets.—[†7. *languorem*, Sl.—†9. *abiit*, Sl.—†12. *Nequius....nil est, nil acrius*, Sl.

---

deeds of the strong ; yet let not teeth of the detractors scare thee : if you live well, you need not care for what evil men say.—[If anger last, it turns into malice ; malice if not restrained drives people into rage ; rage shortens our days, by bringing us into anguish ; anger breeds hatred, whilst concord nourishes love.—The love which was in the world is gone, and poison has taken its place ; out of hatred has sprung no small plague ; the homicide has raised his standard ; nothing is sharper than envy, and nothing more wicked.—There is nothing more wicked than an envious man, as every one knows ; for his unhappiness increases with the prosperity of his neighbour ; he pines away by the very cause which brings profit to the just man. Unless the vessel be clean, whatever you pour in becomes soured.—In order, therefore, that the minds of the wicked may be soured, I will relate what I have learnt of the deeds of the

Non verebor a modo voces invidorum.

†20 Cum recte vivas, ne cures verba malorum.]

    Malis inest proprium mala semper fari,

10 Validis detrahere, viles venerari.

    Ex timore talium nolo vos turbari ;

Laus est discretis a pravis vituperari.

    Pravis enim displicet vitæ rectitudo :

Lex in eis læditur, et est lis pro ludo.

    Ribaldorum requies est inquietudo ;

Dum stultos revoco, quasi frigida ferra recudo.

    Ferrum cudit frigidum quisquis obstinato

Consulit ut redeat de suo peccato;

    Dicit enim sapiens sermone sensato,

20 Verba serit vento qui prædicat infatuato.

    Prædicantur undique fraudes infidorum,

VARIOUS READINGS.—†19. *verebor animo,* Sl. *voces malignorum,* Cl.]—
9. *inest spiritum,* C. 2. *proprie,* Cl.—10. *validos,* Sl.—11. *nubari,* Sl.—13.
sanctitudo, C. 1 and 2.—15. *reproborum,* C. 1.—16. *stultum,* C. 2.—18.
suadet ut, C. 1. *præcipit ut,* Sl. *ut fugiat,* Cl. *a suo,* Sl.—19. *serato,* Sl.—21.
malignorum, Cl.

English. Henceforward I will not fear the words of the envious. If you live
well, you need not care for what evil men say.]—It is the property of wicked
men always to say evil, to detract from the able, to respect the vile. I am
unwilling that you should be disturbed by the fear of such men ; it is praiseworthy in the prudent to be abused by the wicked.—For the wicked are dis-
pleased by rectitude of life : the law is injured in them, and they esteem
strife as a joke. The repose of ribalds is inquietude ; to attempt to convert
fools is, as it were, to put cold iron on the anvil.—Every one strikes cold iron,
who counsels the obstinate man to desert his sins ; for the wise man says very
sensibly, " he sows words in the wind who preaches to a madman."—Every
where are preached the fraudulent actions of the faithless men, who molest

Qui molestant Angliam viribus armorum;
Franci, Scoti, Wallici, potestatem quorum
Comprimat omnipotens qui continet alta polorum !
   Polorum dispositor quem clamamus Deum,
Qui per multa populum protexit Hebræum,
Anglicis ex hostibus tribuat trophæum !
Mille viris præbere potest pincerna Lyæum.
   Ut pincerna pluribus dat per velle potum,
30 Ita suis Dominus vires dat ad votum ;
Edwardus rex inclitus istud habet notum ;
Christo devotum studeat se tradere totum.
   Totus Christo traditur rex noster Edwardus;
Velox est ad veniam, ad vindictam tardus ;
Fugat adversarios tanquam leopardus ;
Fama fœtet fatui, justus redolet quasi nardus.

Various Readings.—24. *Destruat ipse Deus qui*, C. 1 and 2. *possidet*, C.
2.—25. *clamavimus*, Sl.—26. *cuncta*, Cl. *produxit*, C. 2.—29. *dare potest pot.*
Cl. *paribus dare possit p.* Sl. *sicut unus pluribus dat pincerna pot.* C. 1.—31.
illud habet, Cl. et Sl.—34. *ad* is omitted in C. 2 and Cl. In Sl. the two lines
(34 and 35) are transposed.—35. *Hostes fugat singulos t.* C. 1. *fugat hostes
undique t.* C. 2.

England by force of arms ; the French, Scotch, and Welsh, whose power
may the Omnipotent who holds the world repress !—May the Governor of the
universe whom we address as God, who protected the Hebrew people through
many difficulties, give the English victory over their enemies ! The butler can
furnish liquor to a thousand men.—As the butler at will gives drink to many, so
the Lord gives strength at his will to those whom he has chosen ; Edward the
noble King knows this ; and he labours to devote himself entirely to Christ.—
Edward our King is entirely devoted to Christ; he is quick to pardon, and
slow to vengeance ; he puts to flight his adversaries like a leopard ; the reputa-

Tanquam nardus redolet laus regis Anglorum,
Qui conatus reprimit hostium suorum;
Ipsum omnes timeant hostes Anglicorum :
40 Sæpe molossus ovem tollit de fauce luporum.

In luporum faucibus Angli sunt hiis annis;
Nam, devictis omnibus Walliæ tyrannis,
Scoti levant lanceas armati sub pannis ;
In paucis annis oriuntur mira Johannis.

Johannes jam Scotiæ clemens rex et castus,
Regni tenens regimen, ut rex erat pastus,
Hunc tandem deposuit gentis suæ fastus.
Exulat ejectus de sede pia protoplastus.
Exulat et merito, quia, sicut legi,

VARIOUS READINGS.—36. C. *virtus redolet*, C. 1. *secet*, by an error, for
fetet, Sl. *istius redolet*, Sl. *fama replens mundum fragrat velut optima n.* C. 2.
—37. *quasi nardus*, Cl. and Sl.—38, 39. *Qui regit rempublicam more Roma-
norum | Innocentes erripit de manu pravorum*, C. 1. *Fama cujus attigit fines
seculorum; | Ipsum tr'imēt Scotici fures jumentorum*, C. 2. *Dum conatus, &c.*
Cl.—41. *faucibus hiis consistunt annis*, Sl.—42. *devinctis*, Sl.—45. *J. rex Sc.
quondam cl. cast.* Cl. *quidem Scotiæ*, Sl.—47. *disposuit*, C. 1 et C. 2.—48. *sede
sua*, C. 1 and Sl.—49. *Hic dum rexit Scotiam prout dudum legi*, C. 1. *Hic
dum sedem tenuit regnum d. l.* Sl. *Hic dum regnum tenuit in scriptis jam l.* Cl.

---

tion of the fool stinks, the just man smells sweet as spikenard.—Like spikenard smells the fame of the King of the English, who represses the attempts
of his enemies ; him let all the enemies of the English fear : often the mastiff
snatches the sheep from the wolves' jaws.—In the wolves' jaws the English
have been of late ; for, when all the turbulent chiefs of Wales were reduced, the
Scotch raise their spears armed in their rags : a few years exhibit the wonderful fortune of John.—John being now King of Scotland, clement and chaste,
governing the kingdom as though he had been bred a king, him at length the pride
of his nation deposed. The first-created was an exile, driven from his pious seat.
—He, however, was deservedly exiled, for, as I have read, he promised homage

50 Spopondit homagium Anglicano regi;
   Declinavit postea frango, frangis, fregi:
   Omnia quæ pepigi prodendo pacta peregi.

   Pactum prætergressus est princeps prænotatus,
   Quando non compescuit pravorum conatus;
   Vox in Rama sonuit, fletus et ploratus;
   Mitis prælatus facit ignavos famulatus.

   Ab ignavis famulis rex inhonoratur;
   Sanctitas subvertitur, lex evacuatur;
   Sæpe fit seditio, pax periclitatur.

60 Sit maledicta domus ubi quisque cliens dominatur!
   Quando cliens imperat, et princeps obedit,
   Tunc ruit respublica, requies recedit.
   O quantos impietas inpunita lædit!
   Inpius impunis semper se vincere credit.
   Credebant duodecim Scotiæ prælati

VARIOUS READINGS.—50. *Quod fecit hom.* Cl. and Sl.—51. *sed declinat,*
C. 2.—55. *resonat,* Cl.—61-68, are omitted in Cl.—64. *Inpius imprimis,* Sl.

---

to the English King; afterwards he declined the verb *frango* (I break); by
breaking all which I had promised, (said he,) I performed my agreement.—The
aforesaid prince broke his promise, when he did not restrain the attempts of the
wicked; a voice was heard in Rama, weeping and lamentation; a remiss master
makes lazy servants.—By slack servants the King is dishonoured; holiness is
overthrown, the law is made of no avail; there is frequent sedition, the peace is
endangered. Cursed be the house, where every dependent is master!—When
the dependant commands, and the prince is a servant, then the state is in danger, and quietness departs. O how many people impiety, when unpunished,
injures! The impious man unpunished always thinks that he conquers.—The
twelve rulers of Scotland thought that they could resist the great valour of the

Anglorum resistere magnæ probitati ;
Ceciderunt igitur plures vulnerati.
Dixit bufo crati, " maledicti tot dominati !"
    Dominantes plurimi sub duce tantillo,
70 Conspirant in Anglicos, rege tunc tranquillo ;
Tandem simul obviant levato vexillo.
Flumina magna trahunt ortum de fonte pusillo.
    De pusillis fontibus magni surgunt rivi ;
Sic de gente Scotiæ conatus lascivi.
Plurimi propterea ducti sunt captivi :
Quicquid delirant reges, plectuntur Achivi.
    Plebs Achiva periit ad Dunbar in bello,
Ubi Scoti cæsi sunt Anglorum flagello.
Videres cadavera, velut in macello
80 Vilia vendentis, tunicato stricta popello.
    Tunicatus populus multus et immanis,

VARIOUS READINGS.—68. *bufo cuncti*, Sl.—69. *sub dicto*, C. 1.—70.
Anglico, Cl.—71. *obviat*, C. 1. *sibi obviant*, Sl. *stulti levant lanceas armato v.*
Cl.—74. *de Scotis miseris*, C. 1. *de plebe Scotiæ*, Sl.—77. *ad Berwik*, C. 2.—
80. *Vilis*, C. 2. *strincta*, C. 2. et Cl. *cincta*, Sl.—81. *inanis*, C. 1. *vilis et*
inanis, Sl.

English; therefore many of them fell by the sword. Said the toad to the har-
row, " cursed be so many rulers !"—Many rulers under such a diminutive
leader conspire against the English, whilst the king was at peace ; at length
they meet with standards raised. Great rivers take their rise from a small
fountain.—From small fountains great rivers arise ; so it is with the wanton
attempts of the people of Scotland. Many thereupon are led captives : whenever the kings run wild, it is the subjects who suffer.—The subject populace
perished in battle at Dunbar, where the Scotch were slain by the flail of the
English. You might see the carcases, as in the shambles of a seller of refuse
meat, cut off from the kilted rabble.—The kilted people, numerous and savage,

Qui solet detrahere viris Anglicanis,
Apud Dunbarre corruit, jam fœtet ut canis :
Sic faciunt stulti, quos gloria vexat inanis.
Vana fecit gloria populum fallacem
Diffiteri dominum Scotiæ veracem ;
Facto tamen prælio veniunt ad pacem.
De fatuo quandoque facit fortuna sagacem.
Sagax est in prælio qui majori cedit ;
90 Sed gens bruta Scotiæ cito fidem lædit.
Nemo potest tollere quod natura dedit :
Osse radicatum raro de carne recedit.
Recessit rex inclitus, parcens plebi tantæ ;
Peragravit Scotiam turba comitante.
Angli castra muniunt, rege sic mandante ;
Nam levius lædit quicquid providimus ante.

VARIOUS READINGS.—83. *cadebant in foveis,* C. 1. *cadebant in prælio,* Sl.—85. *plebem contumacem,* C. 2. *facit...... prophetam fal.* Sl.—86. *Edwardum contempnere dominum v.* C. 2.—88. *quemcunque facit,* Sl.—90. *Scotica,* C. 2.—92. *de carne raro,* C. 1.—93. *recedit,* Sl. *rex igitur,* C. 1.—94. *Scotiam pertransiit,* C. 1.—95. *rege procurante,* C. 1 and Sl.—96. *prævidimus,* C. 1.

---

who are accustomed to detract from the Englishmen, fell at Dunbar, and now stink like a dog : thus do fools, who are tormented by vain glory.—Vain glory made the deceitful people deny the true lord of Scotland ; but after the battle they seek peace. Sometimes fortune makes a wise man of a fool.—He is wise in battle who yields to his superior ; but the wild people of Scotland soon break their faith. No one can take away what nature gave : the disease which is rooted in the bone, can seldom be expelled from the flesh.—The noble king departed, sparing so great a mass of populace ; he traversed Scotland with a crowd of attendants. The English fortify castles, by the king's command ; for that hurts less

Regis providentia bella gubernantur ;
Scoticani proceres Anglis subjugantur :
Statuuntur judices, leges renovantur ;
100 Ipsæ etenim leges cupiunt ut jure regantur.
Rex ad regni regimen dignum deputavit,
Johannem Warenniæ, quem sæpe probavit.
Hic in quantum valuit leges observavit ;
Elatos perdens, humiles in pace locavit.
Rex in pace rediit hiis ita patratis,
Comiti de Flandria succursurus gratis ;
Magnam classem præparat tempestive satis :
Tolle moram, semper nocuit differe paratis.
Nec mora, conveniunt Scotici versuti ;
110 Tactis Evangeliis sacris sunt locuti,

VARIOUS READINGS.—97. *valla*, C. 1.—98. *Scotiani*, C. 1.—99. *revocan-
tur*, Sl. *prænotantur*, C. 1.—100. *ipse rerum*, Sl.—102. *Johan Warenne*, C. 1.
—103. *potuit Scotos registravit*, C. 1. *valuit jura conservavit*, Sl.—104. *pro-
dens*, Sl. *levavit*, C. 1.—105. *in pace rex*, C. 1.—107. *Morari non patitur*,
navibus paratis, C. 1. *Præparat navigia tempestive satis*, Sl.—108. *deferre*,
C. 1.

---

which we have provided against.—The wars are governed by the king's providence ; the Scottish nobles are subdued to the English ; judges are appointed,
the laws are revised ; for the laws themselves require to be regulated
aright.—The king appointed a worthy man to the government of the kingdom,
John de Warenne, whom he had often proved. He to the utmost of his power
observed the laws ; destroying the proud, he placed the humble in peace.—The
king, after these things had been performed, returned in peace, preparing to aid
gratuitously the Count of Flanders ; he prepares a great fleet as quickly as he can ;
banish delay, to those who are prepared it is always injurious to procrastinate.—
Nor was there any delay, for the cunning Scots meet together ; with their hands
on the gospels, they have said that from their station in the south they will not

Quod Trentam non transient austro constituti :
Pauca voluptati debentur, plura saluti.
Scoticani proceres jurant omnes læte,
Et a rege singulis limitantur metæ :
Vide ne perjuri sint, et ruant in rete ;
Nam miranda canunt, sed non credenda, poetæ.
Tunc rex mire credulus mare transfretavit,
Et Francos in Flandria potens expugnavit ;
Senectutis inmemor multos non expavit.
120 Consilio pollet, cui vim natura negavit.
Non negavit Dominus robur et vigorem
Regi, quem constituit fore mundi florem ;
Cujus acta singulos agunt in stuporem ;
Quemvis namque potest animo sufferre laborem.
Labor novus oritur ; Sathan suscitatur ;

VARIOUS READINGS.—111. *Quod trugam non*, C. 2.—112. *P. v. plura debent sal.* Sl.—113. *Per salutem regiam Scoti jurant l.* C. 1 and Sl.—114. *singuli*, Sl.—115. *ac ruant*, C. 1.—119. *sententiæ immemor*, Sl.—120. *vis*, C. 2.—122. *Regem, quem*, Sl.—123. *Ejus bella*, C. 1. *Actus ejus*, Sl.—124. *namque animo potuit*, Sl.

---

pass the Trent : little is owing to pleasure, more to safety.—The Scottish nobles all swear with alacrity, and their boundaries are limited to each by the king ; see that they be not perjured, and fall into the net ; for the poets sing wonderful things that are not to be believed.—Then the king, wonderfully credulous in them, passed the sea, and powerfully warred against the French in Flanders ; unmindful of old age, he was not terrified by numbers. He flourishes by counsel, to whom nature has denied strength.—The Lord has not denied strength and vigour to the king, whom he ordained to be the flower of the world ; whose acts excite everybody's wonder ; for his mind is capable of undergoing every labour.—A new labour arises ; Satan is raised up ; the fidelity

Scotorum fidelitas procul effugatur;

Anglicorum probitas falso depravatur.

Arbitrii nostri non est, quod quisque loquatur.

Loquuntur ad invicem scurræ derelictæ;

130 "Ecce dantur Anglicis triumphales vittæ.

O! Guyllam de Wallia, nos ad ipsos mitte:

Loricam duram possunt penetrare sagittæ.

Omnes sagittarios nostros convocemus;

Ad custodem Scotiæ simul properemus.

Nam pro nostra patria fas est ut pugnemus:

Victorem a victo superari sæpe videmus."

Custos ergo Scotiæ coarctatur nimis;

Et ad Strivelyne convenit gens corde sublimis;

Fraus occidit Anglicos, et ruunt in imis:

140 Non eodem cursu respondent ultima primis.

VARIOUS READINGS.—127. *Et Anglorum*, C. 1 and Sl. *dampnatur*, Sl.—
129. *turbæ de.* C. 2. *derilictæ*, C. 1.—131. *non ad*, Sl.—133. *Viros sag.* C. 1
and Sl. *omnes con.* Sl.—134. *cito prop.* C. 2. This line and the following are
transposed in Sl.—135. *pat. est ut propugnemus*, Sl.—138. *Strivelyn*, C. 1.
Strevelyn, Sl. *properat gens*, C. 2 and Sl.—139. *Defraudantur Anglici*, C. 2.

---

of the Scots disappears entirely; the valour of the English is undeservedly set at
nought. What everybody says, does not rest upon our opinion.—The aban-
doned scoffers hold mutual conversations; "Lo! triumphant garlands are given
to the English. O William de Wallace! send us to them: arrows can penetrate the hard mail.—Let us call together all our archers; let us hasten together against the Guardian of Scotland. For it is right that we should fight for our
country: we often see the conqueror overcome by the vanquished."—Accord-
ingly the Guardian of Scotland is very hard pressed; and the people assemble
at Stirling, proud in spirit; treachery destroys the English, and they are on
the brink of ruin: the end does not correspond with the beginning.—The Earl,

Primus pontem transiit comes dux Anglorum,
Penetrans audaciter cuneos Scotorum;
Sed seductus rediit, non ob vim virorum:
Fraus est materia multorum sæpe malorum.
Fraus effecit Anglicos rubore perfundi,
Dum suorum sanguinem passim vident fundi.
Reus fraudis Levenax est et Ricardus Lundi.
Quam brevis est risus, quam longaque lacrima mundi!
O mundi perfidia! quis te non miratur?
150 Dolus in domesticis latens occultatur;
Versutus pacifico semper adversatur:
Pastor oves minat baculo, lupus ore minatur.
Quid minatur barbara bruta gens et stulta?
Numquid hæc perfidia manebit inulta?

VARIOUS READINGS.—142. *audacter cuneas,* Sl.—144. *mater muliorum,* Sl.—145. *Fraus confecit,* C. 1. *robore,* Sl. *in campo confundi,* C. 2.—146. *bello vident,* C. 1 and Sl.—147. *le faux est et Ricardus secundi,* C. 1. *Letenax et,* C. 2. *Reus fraus L.* Sl.—148. *usus quam,* C. 1. *longa lac.* C. 2 and Sl.—149. *O mundi malitia,* Sl.—151. *admiratur,* C. 1 and C. 2.—152. *bac. minat,* Sl.—153. *miraris,* Sl.—154. *hæc injuria,* Sl. *hæc* is omitted in C. 1.

---

who was leader of the English, first passed the bridge, penetrating boldly into the Scotish columns; but he was driven back by treachery, and not by the force of arms: fraud is often the cause of many evils.—Fraud caused the English to blush, whilst they saw on all sides the blood of their own people flowing; Levenax and Richard Lundi are convicted of fraud. How short is the joy, and how lasting the sorrow, of the world!—O perfidiousness of the world! who is not astonished by thee? Treachery lies hid, concealed among our household; the cunning man is always opposed to the peaceful; the shepherd leads his sheep with a staff, the wolf threatens them with his mouth.—What does the barbarous brutal and foolish race threaten? Will this perfidy remain unavenged?

Veniet rex Angliæ manu non occulta,

Multa super Priamo rogitans, super Hectore multa.

Multa sibi cumulat mala gens superba,

Anglicos ad prælia provocans acerba;

Verbera cum venient, tunc cessabunt verba:

160 Cum totum fecisse putas, latet anguis in herba.

[" Non latebit," inquiunt, " nobis luce Phœbus;

Per nos ruent Anglici simul hiis diebus,

Nullus pervilibus percel speciebus." (?)

Ludit in humanis divina potentia rebus.

O Dei potentia! te pro tuis peto!

Anglis in auxilium veni vultu læto!

Regis causam judicas, gratiam præbeto :

Tu sine principio non vincere falsa jubeto.]

Post hæc dux fallaciæ suum vocat cœtum,

VARIOUS READINGS.—157. *tibi cumulans*, Sl. *magna gens*, C. 2.—158. *Nam fortes*, Sl.—159. *Numquid non intelligit sapientis verba*, C. 1. *Non enim intel. sap. v.* C. 2.—160. The eight lines which follow (included in brackets) are found only in Sl.—161. *Statim dux fallacis*, C. 1. *Falsus d. f. convocavit c.* Sl.

The King of England will come with open force, inquiring much about Priam and much about Hector.—The proud people raise a heap of evils for themselves, provoking the English to the bitter contest; words will cease, when the blows come; though you think you have finished entirely, there is a snake concealed in the grass.—[" The sun," they say, " will not be concealed from us with his light; the time is come when the English will all fall by our hands; no one....
......" The Divine power plays with the prospects of men.—O power of God! I petition thee in favour of thy people! come with a propitious countenance to the aid of the English; judge the king's cause, and give him grace: thou who art without beginning, do not let falseness triumph.]—After this the leader of the

Sciens quod abierit rex noster trans fretum;
Cremare Northumbriam statuit decretum :
" Sæpe videmus," ait, " post gaudia rumpere fletum."
Lugeat Northumbria nimis desolata !
Facta est ut vidua filiis orbata.
Vescy, Morley, Somervile, Bertram sunt in fata :
O quibus, et quantis, et qualibet est viduata !
In hac, cum sit vidua, cunei Scotorum
170 Redigunt in cineres prædia multorum.
Willelmus de Wallia dux est indoctorum ;
Gaudia stultorum cumulant augmenta dolorum.
Ad augmentum sceleris hactenus patrati,
Alnewyke dant ignibus viri scelerati ;
Circumquaque cursitant velut incensati.
Electi pauci sunt, multi vero vocati.

VARIOUS READINGS.—165. *Luge nunc N.*, Sl. *Northumbriæ*, C. 1.—167.
V., Bertram, Sum., Merlaii, C. 1. *Vessy*····*Borthram*, C. 2.—168. *in quantis*,
C. 2. *es viduata*, Sl.—169. *In hanc*, C. 1. *hac, ergo vid.* C. 2. *In te cum sis*,
Sl.—170. *in cinerem*, Sl. *Intrant et dant ignibus prædia proborum*, C. 1.—
172. *cumulat......malorum*, C. 1.—173. *augmenta*, Sl.—174. *Alnewik*, C. 1.
Alnewyk, Sl.

---

plot calls together his party, knowing that our king would be gone over the sea ;
he made an order to ravage Northumberland : " we oft see," says he, " weeping
after joy."—Northumberland, much desolated, may weep ! She is made as a
widow robbed of her children. Vescy, Morley, Somerville, Bertram are dead :
Alas ! of how many, and how great men in every part is she widowed !—In her,
since she is a widow, the troops of the Scots reduce the estates of many to
cinders. William Wallace is the leader of these savages ; the rejoicings of
fools breed increase of griefs.—To increase the wickedness which they had
hitherto perpetrated, these wicked men deliver Alnwick to the flames ; they run
about on every side like madmen. Few are chosen, but many are called.—Many

Multi quærunt mutuo qualiter sit factum,
Quod Newmonasterium non est igne tactum.
Dona spondent monachi, sed non solvunt pactum :
180 Sicut opus fuerat, sic res processit in actum.
Hujus rei gratia captivum ducerunt
Priorem cœnobii, quem tunc repererunt ;
Captis rebus vacuas domos reliquerunt.
Munifici pauci, multi qui munera querunt.
Jam redit in Scotiam populus malignus ;
Et Willelmo datum est militare pignus ;
De prædone fit eques, ut de corvo cignus ;
Accipit indignus sedem, cum non prope dignus.
Digno tandem principi litera præbetur,
190 In qua rei series tota continetur.

VARIOUS READINGS.—177. *sit actum,* Sl.—178. *Nōmonasterium . . . . sit,*
C. 2. *Novummonasterium,* Sl.—179. *non tenent,* C. 2.—180. *ad actum,* C. 2.
—182. *invenerunt,* Sl.—183. *domus,* C. 2.—184. *qui præmia,* C. 1 and Sl.—
185. *suam petit patriam pop.* C. 1. *suam petunt pat. pop.* Sl.—186. *Et Wal-*
lensis accipit m. p. Sl. *Et Wallensem accipit,* C. 1.—188. *quam non,* C. 2. *Si*
non, Sl.—189. *Digno tamen,* C. 1.

---

ask each other how it happened, that the Newminster was not touched by the
fire. The monks promise gifts, but they do not fulfil their promise : as there
was need, so was the thing carried into effect.—On this account they led
away captive the prior of the monastery, whom they then found ; having carried
away the goods, they left the houses empty. Few are munificent, but there are
many who seek after gifts.—Now the malignant people returns to Scotland ;
and the honour of knighthood is given to William ; from a robber he becomes
a knight, just as a swan is made out of a raven ; an unworthy man takes the
seat, when a worthy man is not by.—At length a letter reaches the worthy prince, in which the whole course of events is told. Let nobody be sur-

Si commotus fuerit, nullus admiretur :
Tranquillum nequit esse fretum, dum peste movetur.
Motus, suos milites sic cœpit affari :
" Adhuc vos pro patria decet prœliari,—
Malo semel vincere, quam sæpe turbari :
Bella valent melius quam longa lite gravari."
" Ne graveris," inquiunt, " si Scotorum fures
Propriis capitibus acuant secures ;
Unus Anglus perimet Scoticos quam plures.
200 Non est plaustelo barbati jungere mures."
Vix est mure melior Walays, aut Gilmaurus,
Ad quorum victoriam nunquam crescet laurus ;
Desunt enim robora, deestque thesaurus :
Bella movet citius cui desunt cornua taurus,

VARIOUS READINGS.—191. *Si turbatus,* C. 1 and Sl.—193. *Tunc rex suos,*
C. 1. *affare,* C. 2.—194. *detur prœliari.*—195. *Malo malos perdere, quam sic
molestari,* C. 2. *Malos Scotos perdere, quam sic conturbari,* Sl.—196. *volunt
melius,* C. 1.—199. *perimet totum sicut plures,* C. 2. *Unus nam Anglicus Scotos
valet plures,* Sl.—200. *surgere mures,* C. 2. *mingere m.* C. 1.—201. *Vix est
murus melior mari ait* (?) *Gilm.* C. 1. *melior Scotus Guilm.* Sl,—202. *Ad cujus
vic. crescit,* C. 1 and Sl. *cresset,* C. 2.

---

prized if he was enraged at it : the sea cannot be quiet when the storm rages.—
In his anger he began thus to address his knights : " Again you must prepare to
fight for your country. I would rather conquer once, than be often tormented ;
wars are better than being troubled with lasting strife."—" Do not be troubled," said they, " if the Scottish thieves sharpen axes for their own heads ;
one Englishman will slay very many Scots. It is not the part of a man who
has a beard to join mice to a little cart."—Wallace, or Gilmaurus, is scarcely
better than a mouse, to whose victory the laurel will never grow ; for they want
strength and treasure : a bull who has lost his horns is the more eager for the

Bello cadunt miseri die Magdalenæ;
Fere centum millia subdit rex arenæ;
Cæsorum cadaverum pascuæ sunt plenæ.
Oderunt peccare mali formidine pœnæ.
Pœnæ metu territus tergum dat tyrannus,
210 Cuï quondam placuit decurtatus pannus;
Fallax die prælii fugit ut trutannus.
Sæpe dat una dies quod totus denegat annus.
Una die miseri multi perimuntur;
Et Scotos qui fugerant Angli persequuntur;
Perforantur lanceis, vestesque tolluntur.
Alba ligustra cadunt, vaccinia nigra leguntur.
Cadit, Waleys, tua laus, ut quid arma geris,
Ex quo gentem gladio tuam non tueris,

VARIOUS READINGS.—207. *cæsis cadaveribus*, C. 2 and Sl.—210. *cui quidem*, Sl.—213. *Illa die plurimi Scoti per.* C. 1. *plurimi pravi puniuntur*, Sl.—214. *Fugientes miseros Ang. per.* C. 1. *Fug. mis. Angl. prosequuntur*, Sl.—216. *vaticinia*, Sl.—218. *Ex quo tuum populum tuens non tueris*, C. 1. *Ex quo tuos gladio tutor non t.* Sl.

---

war.—On St. Magdalen's day the wretches fall in battle; the king subdues in the field near a hundred thousand; the meadows are covered with their carcases. The wicked hate sin from the fear of punishment.—Scared by the fear of punishment the tyrant turns his back, whom the short jacket once pleased; faithless in the day of battle he flies like a truant. One day often gives what the whole year denies.—In one day many wretches were slain; and the English pursue the Scots who had fled; they are transfixed with spears, and robbed of their clothes. The white thorns are cut down, while the black bilberries are gathered.—Wallace, thy reputation as a soldier is lost; since thou didst not defend thy people with the sword, it is just thou shouldst now be deprived of thy dominion.

Jus est ut dominio tuo jam priveris.

220 Ast michi qui quondam semper asellus eris.

Eris in proverbium quod non præteribit;

Regnum tuum scissum est, et stare nequibit;

Potum quem paraveras, gens tua jam bibit.

Deridens alios, non inderisus abibit.

O res apta risui, patens hiis diebus!

Fortuna sub variis ludet speciebus.

Profugus de principe, de Juda fit Jebus.

Ludit in humanis divina potentia rebus.

Rebus sic ruentibus rura rex rimatur,

230 Et fures a foveis fugando venatur;

Omnis qui repertus est, gladio mactatur:

Exigit hoc justum, quod culpam pœna sequatur.

VARIOUS READINGS.—219. *Jam tuo dominio jus est ut pri.* C. 1. and Sl.—
220. *acellus,* C. 2. In the Sl. MS. the song ends with this line. In C. 1, it
ends with l. 232, the last twelve lines, however, being written by another and
rather later hand. The rest is found only in C. 2.—221. *scissum quod stare,*
C. 1.—226. *ludis speciebus,* C. 1.—227. *Profugo sub p.* · · · · *Gebus,* C, 1.—
228. *divinis,* C. 1.—230. *a foveis fugat vel ven,* C. 2. *Et suis,* C. 1.

But, in my view, thou wilt always be the ass thou wert formerly.—Thou wilt
pass into a lasting proverb; thy kingdom is divided, and cannot stand; thy
people now drink of the cup which thou hast prepared. He who turns others
into derision, will not escape being derided.—O laughable thing, that has been
manifested in our time! Fortune will play in various ways. The prince has been
turned into an outcast, Judah into Jebus. The Divine power plays with the prospects of men.—Things being brought to this pass, the king searches the country, and hunts the thieves out of their hiding places; every one who is found is
put to the sword: justice requires this, that the punishment come after the

[Consequenter redit rex, ut Francorum florem
Margaretam reginam ducat in uxorem;
Per hanc regna capiunt pacem pleniorem.
Ira cædem generat, concordia nutrit amorem.

    Amor inter principes pullulans præclaros
Exulat a subditis gemitus amaros;
Jamque fit per nuncios firma pax non raros;
240 Hiis etenim rebus conjungit gratia caros.

    Justus est gratiæ Scotis pars pusilla,
Quia non est impiis pax aut mens tranquilla.
Comyn, Karryk, Umfraville erigunt vexilla:
Acrius invidia nichil est, nil nequius illa.

    Nequam sponte natio non vult obedire;
Regem cogit inclitum cum suis redire;
Jam timent qui necligunt ad pacem venire,
Sub gladio diræ mortis languendo perire.

    Deperirent protinus patres et hæredes;
250 Nisi darent citius ad currendum pedes,
Fugientes renuunt villulas et ædes:
Idæos lepores puer exagitat Ganymedes.

fault.—[Next the king returns, that he may marry Queen Margaret, the flower
of the French; through her the kingdoms receive a more complete peace. Anger
begets slaughter, concord nourishes love. — When love buds between great
princes, it drives away bitter sobs from their subjects; and now a firm peace is
negotiated by frequent messengers: for by these things grace makes people
friends.—It is just that the Scots should have a small portion of grace, because the impious people have neither peace nor quiet of mind. Comyn, Carrick,
Umfraville raise their standards: there is nothing more sharp than envy, nor
more wicked.—The nation, voluntarily wicked, will not be obedient; it forces
the illustrious king with his army to return; now they fear who neglect to come
to peace, lest they perish languishingly by the sword of dire death.—Let them
perish utterly both fathers and sons; unless they quickly give their feet to flight,
flying they desert their towns and houses: the child Ganymedes drives about the

Inter hæc rex Franciæ, mittens absque mora,
Regem rogat Angliæ pro treuga decora.
Annuit rex precibus, mox reflectens lora :
Grata superveniet quæ non sperabitur hora
    Horam Scotis optimam fore quis ignorat,
In qua cessat gladius a plebe quæ plorat,
Rexque suos proceres unit et honorat.
260 Dum calor est et pulcra dies, formica laborat.
    Post hos et hujusmodi bellicos labores,
Angli velut angeli semper sunt victores,
Scoticis et Wallicis sunt præstantiores;
Si vitam inspicias hominum sidereus (?) mores.
    Quasi sus insurgeret leonis virtuti,
Sic expugnant Angliam Scotici polluti :
Et rex illos idcirco subdet servituti :
Serviet æterno qui parvo nesciet uti.]

hares on mount Ida.—In the midst of these transactions the King of France, sending without delay, asks an honourable truce of the King of England. The king accedes to his request, soon afterwards turning his reins : the grateful hour will arrive when it is least expected.—Who knows not that that would be the best hour for the Scots, in which the sword ceases from the weeping commonalty, and the king unites and honours the nobles. While it is warm and fair weather, the ant labours.—After all these warlike labours, the English like angels are always conquerors, they are more excellent than the Scotch and Welsh ; you will learn people's manners by contemplating their lives.—As though a swine should resist the valour of the lion, so the filthy Scots attack England ; and the king for that reason reduces them to slavery : he will ever be a slave, who cannot be content with the little which Providence has given him.]

The following verses seem to have been written immediately after John Baliol had retired to Normandy, in 1299. In the manuscript, they are accompanied by a picture representing a ship, full of people, passing the sea.

ON THE DEPOSITION OF BALIOL.

[From MS. Cotton. Julius, A. v. fol. 2, r⁰. of beginning of 14th cent.]

Ecce dies veniunt Scoti sine principe fiunt ;
Regnum Balliolus perdit, transit mare solus.
Defendi bello Scotus mucrone novello
Sperans Gallorum, vires expectat eorum.
De gwerra tuti Gallorum viribus uti
Congaudent Scoti ; currunt ad prælia moti.
Gallia de parvo Scoto profecit in arvo.
Cur in conflictu Scotus ter corruit ictu ?
Conflictu quarto Scoti ponuntur in arto :
    Quales sunt et erunt, carmina plura ferunt.
Carmina qui didicit Trojam per prælia vicit,
    Ovidius docuit quæ sibi causa fuit.
Percussis bellis, sterilis fit Troja puellis ;
Finitis motis, sic fiet Scotia Scotis.

TRANSLATION.—Lo ! the time is come when the Scots are without a prince ; Baliol loses the kingdom, and passes the sea alone. The Scot, hoping to be defended in battle by the new spear of the French, is waiting for their power. The Scots rejoice together in the belief that they will have the better in the war by the aid of the French ; they rebel, and haste to fight. France will profit little the Scot in the field. Why has the Scot been beaten in three battles ? By the fourth battle the Scots are reduced to extremities : such as they are and will ever be, very many songs tell. He who learnt songs conquered Troy in battle ; Ovid has told us what was the cause of it. After the war, Troy was barren of maidens ; when the rebellion is over, so will Scotland be of Scots.

Vastantur gwerra Trojani, de prope terra
Castrorum plena, cum finibus est aliena.
Urbibus et villis proles dominatur Achillis;
Pyrrhus vastat eas, Priamum ploravit Æneas.
Merlinus scribit quod turba superba peribit ;
Latrans exibit canis, et bos profugus ibit.
Tunc nemus Eutherium pennata fronde carebit;
Et genus Albaneum sua regna perire videbit.
Scote miser, plora, tibi flendi jam venit hora;
   Nam regnum patruum desinet esse tuum.
Principe privaris, campo sic subpeditaris,
   Quod meritis miseris semper asellus eris.
Vox de profundis Cambini te vocat undis,
Torquendum clade, quam non novit genus Adæ.
Illuc tende vias, et dæmonis assecla fias !
   Amplius Andreas ducere nescit eas.

Troy is ravaged by war, the land near about being full of camps, it is with its boundaries become the property of another. The son of Achilles rules over the cities and towns; Pyrrhus lays them waste, Æneas has wept for Priam. Merlin writes that the proud crowd shall perish ; the barking dog shall depart, and the ox shall go into exile. Then shall the Eutherian grove be stripped of its feathered branches; and the Albanian race will see their kingdom perish. Wretched Scot, lament, thy hour of weeping is now come ; for the kingdom of thy forefathers ceases to be thine. Thou art deprived of a prince, and art so trodden down in the field, that by thy ill merits thou wilt always be an ass. A voice from the bottom of the Cambine waters calls thee, to be punished with such slaughter as the race of Adam has not yet seen. Hasten thither, and become the companion of the devil! Andrew will no longer be their leader.

The general hatred to the Scots did not hinder the people from feeling grieved by the heavy taxes which were raised to support the war, and more particularly the expeditions into Flanders, (which latter were ill managed, and produced no results,) or from showing their dissatisfaction. The King's measures of ambition were often thwarted by the stern opposition of the barons and the commons. The following song was directed more particularly against the unconstitutional seizure of wool, and generally against all the taxes raised for the Flemish war.

SONG AGAINST THE KING'S TAXES.

[MS. Harl. No. 2253, fol. 137, v°, written in reign of Edw. II.]

Dieu, roy de magesté, ob personas trinas,
Nostre roy e sa meyné ne perire sinas ;
Grantz mals ly fist aver gravesque ruinas,
Celi qe ly fist passer partes transmarinas.
    Rex ut salvetur, falsis maledictio detur !

Roy ne doit à feore de gere extra regnum ire,
For si la commune de sa terre velint consentire :
Par tresoun voit honme sovent quam plures perire ;
A quy en fier seurement nemo potest scire.
    Non eat ex regno rex sine consilio.

TRANSLATION.—O God, king of majesty, for the sake of the Trinity,—do not permit our king and his household to perish ;—great hurt and great ruin he caused him to have,—who made him pass over the sea.—In order that the king may prosper, may his false advisers be accursed.

A king ought not to go out of his kingdom to make war,—unless the commons of his land will consent :—by treason we often see very many perish ;—no one can tell in whom to trust with certainty.—Let not the king go out of his kingdom without counsel.

Ore court en Engletere de anno in annum
Le quinzyme dener, pur fere sic commune dampnum.
E fet avaler que soleyent sedere super scamnum ;
E vendre fet commune gent vaccas, vas, et pannum.
  Non placet ad summum quindenum sic dare nummum.

Une chose est countre foy, unde gens gravatur,
Que la meyté ne vient al roy, in regno quod levatur.
Pur ce qu'il n'ad tot l'enter, prout sibi datur,
Le pueple doit le plus doner, et sic sincopatur.
  Nam quæ taxantur, regi non omnia dantur.

Unquore plus greve à simple gent collectio lanarum,
Que vendre fet communement divitias earum.
Ne puet estre que tiel consail constat Deo carum,
Issi destrure le poverail pondus per amarum,
  Non est lex sana, quod regi sit mea lana.

Uncore est plus outre peis, ut testantur gentes,
En le sac deus pers ou treis per vim retinentes.

Now goes in England from year to year—the fifteenth penny, to do thus a common harm.—And it makes them go down, who used to sit upon a bench ;—and it obliges the common people to sell both cows, vessels, and clothes.—It does not please thus to pay the fifteenth to the last penny.

One thing is against faith, whereby the people is aggrieved,—that the half of what is raised in the kingdom does not come to the king.—Since he has not the whole, as it is given to him,—the people is obliged to give the more, and thus they are cut short.—For the taxes which are raised are not all given to the king.

The collecting of the wool grieves the common people still more,—which drives them commonly to sell their property.—Such counsel cannot be acceptable to God,—thus to destroy the poor people by a bitter burthen.—It is not sound law, which gives my wool to the king.

What is still more contrary to peace, as people witness,— they retain two

A quy remeindra cele leyne ? quidam respondentes,
Que jà n'avera roy ne reygne, sed tantum colligentes.
Pondus lanarum tam falsum constat amarum.

Depus que le roy vodera tam multum cepisse,
Entre les riches si purra satis invenisse;
E plus, à ce que m'est avys, et melius fecisse
Des grantz partie aver pris, et parvis pepercisse.
Qui capit argentum sine causa peccat egentum.

Honme ne doit à roy retter talem pravitatem,
Mès al maveis consiler per ferocitatem.
Le roy est jeovene bachiler, nec habet ætatem,
Nule malice compasser, sed omnem probitatem.
Consilium tale dampnum confert generale.

Rien greve les grantz graunter regi sic tributum ;
Les simples deyvent tot doner, contra Dei nutum.
Cest consail n'est mye bien, sed vitiis pollutum ;
Ceux que grauntent ne paient ren, est male constitutum.
Nam concedentes nil dant regi, sed egentes.

or three parts in the sack.—To whom shall remain this wool ? Some answer,
—that neither king nor queen shall have it, but only the collectors.—Such a
false weight of wool is manifestly a bitter thing.

Since the king is determined to take so much,—he may find enough among
the rich ;—and he would get more and do better, as it appears to me,—to have
taken a part from the great, and to have spared the little.—He sins who takes
the money of the needy without cause.

We ought not to lay such wickedness to the charge of the king,—but to the bad
counsellor, by his rapacity. The king is a young bachelor, and is not of an age—
to compass any malice, but to do all probity.— Such counsel does general harm.

It is no trouble to the great thus to grant to the king a tax ; the simple must
pay it all, which is contrary to God's will.—This counsel is not at all good, but
polluted with vice ;—it is ill ordained, that those who grant should pay nothing.—
For those who make the grant give nothing to the king, it is the needy only who
give.

Coment fra honme bon espleit ex pauperum sudore,
Que les riches esparnyer doit, dono vel favore ?
Des grantz um le dust lever, Dei pro timore ;
Le pueple plus esparnyer, qui vivit in dolore.
Qui satis es dives, non sic ex paupere vives.

Je voy en siècle qu'ore court gentes superbire,
D'autre biens tenir grant court, quod cito vult transire.
Quant vendra le haut juggement, magna dies iræ,
S'il ne facent amendement, tunc debent perire.
Rex dicit reprobis, " ite :"—" venite," probis.

Dieu, que fustes coronée cum acuta spina,
De vostre pueple eiez pitée gratia divina !
Que le siècle soit aleggée de tali ruina !
A dire grosse veritée est quasi rapina.
Res inopum capta, nisi gratis, est quasi rapta.

Tel tribut à nul feor diu nequit durare ;
Devoyde qy puet doner, vel manibus tractare ?

How will they perform good deeds out of the sweat of the poor,—whom the rich ought to spare, by gift or favour ?--they ought to tax the great, for the fear of God ;—and spare more the people, who live in pain.—Thou who art rich enough, live not thus upon the poor.

I see at the present day how people are proud,—with other people's goods they hold great court, which will quickly pass.—When the high judgment comes, the great day of wrath,—unless they make atonement, they must then perish.— The King says to the bad, " Go :" to the good, " Come."

O God, who wast crowned with the sharp thorn,—have pity with divine grace upon thy people !—May the world be comforted of such ruin !—To tell unvarnished truth, it is mere robbery.—The property of the poor taken without their will, is as it were stolen.

Such tribute can in no manner last long ;—out of emptiness who can give,

Gentz sunt à tiel meschief quod nequeunt plus dare ;
Je me doute, s'ils ussent chief, quod vellent levare.
  Sæpe facit stultas gentes vacuata facultas.

Yl y a tant escarceté monetæ inter gentes,
Qe honme puet en marché, quam parci sunt ementes,
Tot eyt honme drap ou blée, porcos vel bidentes,
Rien lever en verité, tam multi sunt egentes.
  Gens non est læta, cum sit tam parca moneta.

Si le roy freyt moun consail, tunc vellem laudare,
D'argent prendre le vessel, monetamque parare ;
Mieu valdreit de fust ma[n]ger, pro victu nummos dare,
Qe d'argent le cors servyr, et lignum pacare.
  Est vitii signum pro victu solvere lignum.

Lur commissiouns sunt trochiers qui sunt ultra mare ;
Ore lur terres n'ount povers eosdem sustentare.

---

or touch anything with his hands.—People are reduced to such ill plight, that
they can give no more ;—I fear, if they had a leader, they would rise in rebellion.—Loss of property often makes people fools.

There is so much scarcity of money among people,—that people can in the
market, there are so few buyers,—although they may have cloth or corn, swine
or sheep,—make nothing of them, in truth, there are so many needy people.—
The people is not joyful, when money is so scarce.

If the king would take my advice, I would praise him then,—to take the
vessels of silver, and make money of them ;—it would be better to eat out of
wood, and to give money for victuals—than to serve the body with silver, and
pay with wood.—It is a sign of vice, to pay for victuals with wood.

The commissions of those who are employed over sea are too dear ;—now the
poor have not their lands to sustain the same.—1 do not know how they can save

Je ne say coment purrount animas salvare,
Que d'autrui vivre voderount, et propria servare.
Non dubitant pœnas cupientes res alienas.

Dieu pur soun seintime noun, confundat errores,
E ceux que pensent fere tresoun, et pacis turbatores !
E vengaunce en facez ad tales vexatores !
E confermez e grantez inter reges amores !
Perdat solamen qui pacem destruit ! AMEN.

their souls,—who would live upon other people's goods, and save their own.—
They cannot doubt but they will be punished, who covet the property of others.
May God, for the sake of his holy name, confound errors,—and those who
meditate treason, and the disturbers of the peace !—and take vengeance on such
tormentors !—and confirm and grant love between the kings !—May he lose
consolation who breaks the peace ! Amen.

Although the English people were grieved by the King's
expensive and ill-conducted foreign wars, yet they were not
wanting in commiseration for the Flemish burghers in their
struggle against France. The song which follows was composed soon after the battle of Courtrai, in which the Comte
d'Artois and his army were defeated and destroyed by the
Flemings in 1302.

SONG ON THE FLEMISH INSURRECTION.

[MS. Harl. No. 2253, fol. 73, v°. of reign of Edw. II.]

Lustneth, lordinges, bothe ȝonge ant olde,
Of the Freynsshe-men that were so proude ant bolde,
Hou the Flemmysshe-men bohten hem ant solde

TRANSLATION.—Listen, Lordings, both young and old,—of the Frenchmen
that were so proud and bold,—how the Flemmish men bought and sold them—

upon a Wednesday.

Betere hem were at home in huere londe,
Then for te seche Flemmysshe by the see stronde,
Wharethourh moni Frenshe wyf wryngeth hire honde,
    ant singeth, weylaway !

The Kyng of Fraunce made statuz newe
In the lond of Flaundres, among false ant trewe,
That the commun of Bruges ful sore con a-rewe,
    ant seiden amonges hem,
" Gedere we us togedere hardilyche at ene,
Take we the bailifs by tuenty ant by tene,
Clappe we of the hevedes an oven o the grene,
    ant caste we y the fen."

The webbes ant the fullaris assembleden hem alle,
Ant makeden huere consail in huere commune halle ;
Token Peter Conyng huere kyng to calle,
    ant beo huere cheventeyn.
Hue nomen huere rouncyns out of the stalle,

---

upon a Wednesday.—Better it had been for them at home in their country,—than to seek Flemings by the sea-strand,—through which many a French woman wrings her hands,—and sings, weladay !

The King of France made new statutes—in the land of Flanders, among false and true,—that the commons of Bruges full sorely began to rue,—and said amongst themselves,—" Let us assemble together boldly in the evening,—let us take the bailiffs by twenties and by tens,—let us clap off their heads above on the green,—and let us cast them in the fen."

The weavers and the fullers assembled them all,—and held their council in their common hall,—they took Peter Conyng to be called their king,—and to be their chieftain.—They took their horses out of the stable,—and closed the

Ant closeden the toun withinne the walle;
Sixti baylies ant ten hue maden a-doun falle,
        ant moni another sweyn.

Tho wolde the baylies, that were come from Fraunce,
Dryve the Flemisshe that made the destaunce;
Hue turnden hem aȝeynes with suerd ant with launce,
        stronge men ant lyht.
Y telle ou for sothe, for al huere bobaunce,
Ne for the avowerie of the Kyng of Fraunce,
Tuenti score ant fyve haden ther meschaunce
        by day ant eke by nyht.

Sire Jakes de Seint Poul y-herde hou hit was;
Sixtene hundred of horsmen asemblede o the gras;
He wende toward Bruges *pas pur pas*,
        with swithe gret mounde.
The Flemmysshe y-herden telle the cas;
A-gynneth to clynken huere basyns of bras,
Ant al hem to-dryven ase ston doth the glas,
        ant fellen hem to grounde.

town within the wall;—seventy bailiffs they made down fall,—and many another man.

Then would the bailiffs that were come from France—drive out the Flemings who made the disturbance;—but they turned against them with sword and with lance,—strong men and nimble.—I tell you for truth, in spite of their vaunting,—and in spite of the patronage of the King of France,—four hundred and five had there mischance—by day and also by night.

Sir Jacques de St. Paul heard how it was:—he assembled sixteen hundred knights on the grass;—they went towards Bruges step by step,—with a very great body of people.—The Flemings heard tell of the case; they begin to clink their basins of brass,—and they break them all to pieces as a stone does glass,—and fell them to the ground.

Sixtene hundred of horsmen hede ther here fyn;
Hue leyȝen y the stretes y-styked ase swyn;
Ther hue loren huere stedes, ant mony rouncyn,
    thourh huere oune prude.
Sire Jakes ascapede by a coynte gyn,
Out at one posterne ther me solde wyn,
Out of the fyhte hom to ys yn,
    in wel muchele drede."

Tho the Kyng of Fraunce y-herde this, anon
Assemblede he is dousse pers everuchon,
The proude Eorl of Artoys ant other mony on,
    to come to Paris.
The barouns of Fraunce thider conne gon,
Into the paleis that paved is with ston,
To jugge the Flemmisshe to bernen ant to slon,
    thourh the flour-de-lis.

Thenne seide the Kyng Philip, " Lustneth nou to me,
Myn eorles ant my barouns gentil ant fre,
Goth, faccheth me the traytours y-bounde to my kne,
    hastifliche ant blyve."

Sixteen hundred knights had there their end ;—they lay in the streets stuck
like swine ;—there they lost their steeds, and many a horse,—through their own
pride ;—Sir Jacques escaped by a cunning contrivance,—out at a postern where
they sold wine,—out of the fight home to his lodging,— in very great fear.

When the King of France heard this, anon—he assembled his douze peers
every one,—the proud Comte d'Artois and others many a one,—to come to
Paris.—The barons of France began to go thither,—into the palace that is paved
with stone,—to judge the Flemings to be burnt and slain,—through the fleur-
de-lis.

Then said King Philip, " Listen now to me,—my earls and my barons gentle
and free,—go, fetch me the traitors in bonds to my knees,—hastily and quickly."

Tho suor the Eorl of Seint Poul, " *Par la goule Dé!*
We shule facche the rybaus wher thi wille be,
Ant drawen hem [with] wilde hors out of the countré,
  by thousendes fyve."

" Sire Rauf Devel," sayth the Eorl of Boloyne,
" *Nus ne lerrum en vie chanoun ne moyne,*
Wende we forth anon ritht withoute eny assoygne,
  ne no lyves man.
We shule flo the Conyng, ant make roste is loyne ;
The word shal springen of him into Coloyne,
So hit shal to Acres ant into Sesoyne,
  ant maken him ful wan."

Sevene eorles ant fourti barouns y-tolde,
Fiftene hundred knyhtes proude ant swythe bolde,
Sixti thousent swyers amonge ȝunge ant olde,
  Flemmisshe to take.
The Flemmisshe hardeliche hem come to-ȝeynes ;
This proude Freinsshe eorles, huere knyhtes, ant huere
sweynes

—Then swore the Comte de Saint Paul, " By the throat of God !—we shall fetch the ribalds wherever it be thy will,—and draw them with wild horses out of the country—by five-thousands."

" Sir Ralf Devel," says the Comte de Bologne,—" we will not leave alive either canon or monk,—let us go forth anon right without any excuse,—nor no man alive (?).—We shall flay the Conyng (rabbit), and cause his loins to be roasted ;—the fame of him shall spring as far as Cologne,—so shall it to Acre and into Saxony,—and make them full pale."

Seven counts and forty barons in number,—fifteen hundred knights proud and very bold,—sixty thousand squires what with young and old,—to take the Flemings.—The Flemings boldly came against them ;—these proud French comtes, their knights, and their men—they killed and slew over the hills and

A-quelleden ant slowen by hulles ant by pleynes,
    al for huere kynges sake.

This Frenshe come to Flaundres so liht so the hare;
Er hit were mydnyht hit fel hem to care;
Hue were laht by the net so bryd is in snare,
    with rouncin ant with stede.
The Flemmisshe hem dabbeth o the het bare;
Hue nolden take for huem raunsoun ne ware;
Hue doddeth of huere hevedes, fare so hit fare,
    ant thareto haveth hue nede.

Thenne seith the Eorl of Artois, " Y ʒelde me to the,
Peter Conyng by thi nome, ʒef thou art hende ant free,
That y ne have no shame ne no vylté,
    that y ne be noud ded."
Thenne swor a bocher, " By my leauté !
Shalt thou ner more the Kyng of Fraunce se,
Ne in the toun of Bruges in prisone be,
    thou woldest spene bred."

the plains,—all for their King's sake.

    These French came to Flanders as light as the hare;—before it was midnight there fell upon them care;—they were caught in the net as a bird is in the snare, —with horse and with steed.—The Flemings dab them on the bare head;—they will take for them neither ransom nor pay;—they dod off their heads, happen what may,—and thereto have they need.

    Then saith the Comte d'Artois, " I yield me to thee,—Peter Conyng by name, if thou art gentle and free,—that I may suffer no shame nor disgrace,—and that I may not be slain."—Then swore a butcher, " By my loyalty !—thou shalt never more see the King of France,—nor be in prison in the town of Bruges,— thou wouldest consume bread."

Ther hy were knulled y the put-falle,
This eorles ant barouns ant huere knyhtes alle ;
Huere ledies huem mowe abide in boure ant in halle
        wel longe.
For hem mot huere kyng other knyhtes calle,
Other stedes taken out of huere stalle :
Ther hi habbeth dronke bittrere then the galle,
        upon the drue londe.

When the Kyng of Fraunce y-herde this tydynge,
He smot doun is heved, is honden gon he wrynge.
Thourhout al Fraunce the word bygon to springe ;
        wo wes huem tho !
Muche wes the sorewe ant the wepinge
That wes in al Fraunce among olde ant ȝynge :
The meste part of the lond bygon for te synge
        " alas ! ant weylawo ! "

Awey thou ȝunge pope ! whet shal the to rede ?
Thou hast lore thin cardinals at thi meste nede ;
Ne keverest thou hem nevere for nones kunnes mede,

There they were heaped into the pit-full,—these counts and barons and all their knights ;—their ladies may wait for them in bower and in hall—very long. —In their place must their king call other knights,—and take other steeds out of their stables :—there they have drunk bitterer than gall,—upon the dry land.

When the King of France heard these tidings,—he cast down his head, his hands he began to wring.—Throughout all France the news began to spread ;—woe was to them all !—Much was the sorrow and the weeping—that was in all France among old and young ;—The greatest part of the land began to sing,—" Alas ! and welaway ! "

Away, thou young pope ! what will be thy counsel ?—Thou hast lost thy cardinals at thy greatest need ;—thou wilt never recover them for any kind of reward,

for sothe y the telle.
Do the forth to Rome to amende thi misdede ;
Bide gode halewen hue lete the betere spede :
Bote thou worche wysloker, thou losest lont ant lede,
          the coroune wel the felle.

Alas ! thou seli Fraunce, for the may thunche shome,
That ane fewe fullaris maketh ou so tome ;
Sixti thousent on a day hue maden fot lome,
          with eorl ant knyht.
Herof habbeth the Flemysshe suithe god game,
Ant suereth bi Seint Omer ant eke bi Seint Jame,
ȝef hy ther more cometh, hit falleth huem to shame,
          with huem for te fyht.

I tell ou for sothe, the bataille thus bigon
Bituene Fraunce ant Flaundres, hou hue weren fon ;
Vor Vrenshe the eorl of Flaundres in prison heden y-don,
          with tresoun untrewe.
ȝe[f] the Prince of Walis his lyf habbe mote,

—for truth I tell thee.—Go forth to Rome to atone for thy misdeeds ;—pray to good saints that they let thee speed better :—unless thou workest more wisely, thou losest land and people,—the crown fell well to the. (?)

Alas ! thou simple France, it may appear a shame for thee,—that a few fullers make thee so tame ;—sixty thousand in a day they made trip quickly, (?)—with count and knight.—Thereof have the Flemings very good game,—and swear by St. Omer and eke by St. James,—if they come there any more, it will fall them to shame,—with them to fight.

I tell you for truth, the battle thus begun,—between France and Flanders, how they were foes ;—for the French had put the Count of Flanders in prison, —with treason faithlessly.—If the Prince of Wales his life might have,—it will

Hit falleth the Kyng of Fraunce bittrore then the sote ;
Bote he the rathere therof welle do bote,
      wel sore hit shal hym rewe.

happen to the King of France more bitter than soot ;—unless he before-hand
do make good amends for it,—very sorely he shall rue it.

———

The following song seems to have been popular about the beginning of the fourteenth century. The wolf and the fox pour-
tray exactly the characters of the two classes of people who then
oppressed and plundered the middle and lower classes.

A SONG ON THE TIMES.

[MS. Harl. No. 913, fol. 44, vᵒ. written about A.D. 1308.]

Whose thenchith up this carful lif,
    Niȝte and dai that we beth inne,
So moch we seeth of sorow and strif,
    And lite ther is of worldis winne,
Hate and wreth ther is wel rive,
    And trew love is ful thinne :
Men that beth in heiiȝist live
    Mest i-charged beth with sinne.

Fals and lither is this lond,
    As al dai we mai i-se :

TRANSLATION.—Whoso reflecteth upon this life which is full of care,—night
and day that we are in,—so much we see of sorrow and strife,—and little there
is of world's joy.—Hate and wrath there is very rife,—and true love is very
rare :—men who are in the highest station of life,—are most laden with sin.
    False and wicked is this land,—as every day we may see :—in it there is both

Therin is bothe hate and onde,—
  Ic wene that ever so wol be.
Coveitise hath the law an honde,
  That the trewthe he ne mai i-se :
Nou is maister pride and onde ;—
  Alas ! Loverde, whi suffrith he ?

Wold holi cherch pilt is miȝte,
  And law of lond pilt him to ;
Than scholde coveitise and un-riȝte
  Ute of lond ben y-do.
Holi cherch schold hold is riȝt
  For no eie no for no love ;
That hi ne schold schow har miȝt
  For lordingen boste that beth above.

To entredite and amonsi
  Al thai, whate hi evir be,
That lafful men doth robbi,
  Whate in lond what in see ;
And thos hoblurs, namelich,
  That husbond benimeth eri of grund ;

hate and contention,—I think it will always be so.—Covetousness hath the law
in hand,—that he may not see the truth :—Now pride is master, and contention ;
—Alas ! Lord ! why suffereth he ?

If holy church would exert its might,—and the law of the land exert it
too ;—then should covetousness and injustice—out of the land be driven.—
Holy church should withhold its right—for no fear nor for no love ;—that they
should not show their might—for the boast of lordings that are above.

To interdict and admonish—all those, whatever they be,—who lawful men
do rob,—whether on the land or on the sea ;—and those hoblers in particular,
—that take from the husbandman the tillage of the ground ;—men ought not

Men ne schold ham biri in non chirch,
 Bot cast ham ute as a hund.

Thos kingis ministris beth i-schend,
 To riȝt and law that ssold tak hede,
And al the lond for t' amend,
 Of thos thevis hi taketh mede.
Be the lafful man to deth i-broȝt,
 And his catel awei y-nom;
Of his deth ne tellith hi noȝt,
 Bot of har prei hi hab som.

Hab hi the silver, and the mede,
 And the catel under-fo,
Of feloni hi ne taketh hede,
 Al thilk trepas is a-go.
Of thos a vorbisen ic herd telle ;
 The Lion is king of all beeste,
And—herknith al to mi spelle—
 In his lond he did an heste.

The Lyon lete cri, as hit was do,
 For he hird lome to telle ;

to bury them in any church,—but to throw them out like a dog.

 Those king's ministers are corrupted,—that should take heed to right and law,
—and all the land for to amend,—of these thieves they take bribe.—If the man
who acts lawfully is brought to death,—and his property taken away;—of his
death they make no account,—but of their prey they have a share.

 If they have the silver and the bribe—and the property received,—they take
no heed of felony,—every trespass is allowed to pass.—Of these a parable I
heard tell ;—the Lion is king of all beasts,—and (hearken all to my tale)—in
his land he made a command.

 The Lion caused to be proclaimed, as it was done,—for he heard frequently

And eke him was i-told also
  That the wolf didde noȝte welle.
And the fox, that lither grome,
  With the wolf, i-wreiid was ;
To-for har lord hi schold come,
  To amend har trepas.

And so men didde that seli asse,
  That trepasid noȝt, no did no gilte,
With ham bothe i-wreiid was,
  And in the ditement was i-pilt.
The voxe hird amang al menne,
  And told the wolf with the brode crune ;
That on him send gees and henne,
  That other geet and motune.

The seli aasse wend was saf,
  For he ne eete noȝt bote grasse ;
None ȝiftes he ne ȝaf,
  No wend that no harm nasse.
Tho hi to har lord com to tune,
  He told to ham law and skille ;

tell ;—and eke it was told him also—that the wolf did not well.—And the fox,
that wicked fellow,—with the wolf was accused ;—before their lord they must
come,—to make amends for their trespass.

 And so men did [accuse] the simple ass,—that trespassed not, nor did any
crime,—with them both he was accused,—and in the indictment was put.—
The fox heard [talk of it] among all men,—and told the wolf with the broad
crown ;—the one sent to him [the Lion] geese and hens,—the other kids and
mutton.

 The simple ass thought he was safe,—for he eat nothing but grass ;—no gifts he
gave,—nor suspected that there was any harm.—When they came in the presence
of their Lord,—he counted out to them law and reason ;—these wicked beasts

Thos wikid bestis luid a-dune,
    " Lord," hi seiid, " what is thi wille ?"

Tho spek the Lion hem to,
    To the fox anone his wille,—
" Tel me, boi, what hast i-do ?
    Men beth aboute the to spille."
Tho spek the fox first anone,
    " Lord King, nou thi wille ;
Thos men me wreiith of the tune,
    And wold me gladlich for to spille.—

Gees no hen nad ic noȝt,
    Sire, for soth ic the sigge,
Bot as ic ham dere boȝt,
    And bere ham up myn owen rigge."
" Godis grame most hi have,
    That in the curte the so pilt !
Whan hit is so, ich vouchsave,
    Ic forȝive the this gilte."

The fals wolf stode behind ;
    He was doggid and ek felle :—

laid themselves down [prostrate],—" Lord," said they, " what is thy will ?"
Then spake the Lion to them,—to the fox in the first place [he declared]
his will,—" Tell me, fellow, what hast thou done ?—Men are about thee to
ruin."—Then spake the fox first,—" Lord King, now thy will ;—these men
accuse me of the town,—and would gladly ruin me.

" Gees nor hen had I not,—Sire, for truth I tell thee,—but as I bought them
dearly,—and bore them upon my own back."—" God's anger may they have,
—that in the court so placed thee !—Since it is so, I vouchsafe,—I forgive
thee this guilt."

The false wolf stood behind ;—he was dogged and eke fell :—" I am come of

" Ic am i-com of grete kind,
   Pes thou graunt me, that miȝt ful welle."
" What hast i-do, bel amy,
   That thou me so oxist pes ? "
" Sire," he seid, " I nel noȝt lie,
   If thou me woldist hire a res.

For ic huntid up the doune,
   To loke, Sire, mi biȝete ;
Ther ic slow a motune,
   ȝe, Sir, and fewe gete.
Ic am i-wreiid, Sire, to the,
   For that ilk gilt ;—
Sire, ichul sker me,
   I ne ȝef ham dint no pilt."

" For soth I sigge the, bel ami,
   Hi nadde no gode munde,
Thai that wreiid the to mei,
   Thou ne diddist noȝt bot thi kund.—
Sei thou me, asse, wat hast i-do ?
   Me thenchith thou cannist no gode.

a great race,—grant thou me peace, who may full well."—" What hast thou
done, fair friend,—that thou so askest me peace ?"—" Sire," he said, " I will
not lie,—if thou wouldst hear me a little while.

" For I hunted up the downs,—to look, Sire, after my gain ;—There I slew
a mutton,—yea, Sire, and a few kids.—I am accused, sire, to thee,—for that
same crime ;—Sire, I shall clear myself,—I gave them neither blow nor hurt."

" For truth I tell thee, fair friend,—they had no good mind,—they who accused thee to me,—thou didst nothing but thy nature.—Tell thou me, ass, what
hast thou done ?—Methinks thou art capable of no good.—Why haddest thou

Whi nadistou, as other mo ?
Thou come of lither stode.

" Sertis, Sire, not ic noȝt ;
Ic ete sage alnil gras,—
More harm ne did ic noȝt ;
Therfor i-wreiid ic was."
" Bel ami, that was mis-do,
That was aȝe thi kund,
For to ete such gras so :—
Hastilich ȝe him bind ;

Al his bonis ȝe to-draw,
Loke that ȝe noȝt lete ;
And that ic ȝive al for lawe,
That his fleis be al i-frette."—
Also hit farith nou in lond,
Whose wol tak therto hede :
Of thai that habbith an hond,
Of thevis hi takith mede.

The lafful man ssal be i-bund,
And i-do in strang pine,

not [done] as others more ?—thou art come of wicked place."
" Certes, Sire, I know not ;—I eat sage and only grass,—more harm did I
not ;—therefore was I accused."—" Fair friend, that was misdone,—that was
against thy nature,—for to eat such grass so :—hastily ye him bind ;
" Draw ye all his bones to pieces,—look that ye do not fail ;—and that I give
all for law,—that his flesh be all torn to pieces."—Thus it fares now in the land,
—whoever will take heed thereto :—of they that have in hand,—of thieves they
take gifts.
The man who acts according to law shall be bound,—and condemned to strong

And i-hold in fast prisund,
  Fort that he mak fine.
And the thef to skap so,
  That doth ever aȝe the riȝt.
God take hede therto,
  That is al ful of miȝt !

Thus farith al the world nuthe,
  As we mai al i-se,
Both est and west, north and suthe ;
  God us help and the Trinité !
Trewth is i-faillid with fremid and sibbe,
  And so wide as al this lond
Ne mai no man therin libbe,
  What throȝ coveitise and throȝ onde.

Thoȝ lafful man wold hold is lif
  In love, in charité, and in pes,
Sone me ssul compas is lif,
  And that in a litil res.
Prude is maister and coveitise,
  The thrid brother men clippith ond ;

pain,—and held in fast prison,—until he pays a fine.—And the thief to escape
so,—that acts ever against the right!—God take heed thereto,—who is all full
of might !

  Thus fares all the world now,—as we may all see,—both east and west, north
and south ;—God and the Trinity help us !—Truth is failed with stranger and
relation,—and as wide as all this land—no man can live therein,—what through
covetousness and through contention.

  Though the man who acts according to law would hold his life—in love, in
charity, and in peace,—soon they will compass his life,—and that in a little space
of time.—Pride is master and covetousness—the third brother is called conten-

Niʒt and dai he fondith i-wisse
Lafful men, to hab har lond.

Whan erth hath erthe i-gette
And of erthe so hath i-nouʒ,
Whan he is therin i-stekke,
Wo is him that was in wouʒ !
What is the gode that man ssal hab,
Ute of this world whan he ssal go ?
A sori wed,—whi ssal ic gab ?—
For he broʒt him no mo.

Riʒt as he com, he ssal wend,
In wo, in pine, in poverté ;—
Takith gode hede, men, to ʒure end,
For as I sigge, so hit wol be.
Y not wharof beth men so prute ;
Of erthe and axen, felle and bone ?
Be the soule enis ute,
A vilir caraing nis ther non.

The caraing is so lolich to see,
That under erth men mot it hide ;

tion ;—night and day they labour certainly—lawful men, to have their land.

When earth has obtained earth,—and thus of earth hast enough,—when he is stuck therein,—woe to him that was in wickedness !—What is the good that man shall have,—when he shall go out of this world ?—A sorry garment,—why shall I joke ?—For he brought him no more.

Just as he came, he shall go,—in woe, in pain, in poverty ;—take good heed, men, to your end,—for as I say, so it will be.—I know not of what men are so proud ;—of earth, and ashes, skin and bone ?—when the soul is once out,—there is no viler carcase.

The carcase is so loathsome to see,—that under earth men must it hide ;—both

Bothe wif and child wol fram him fle,
  Ther nis no frend that wol him bide.
What wol men for the sowle del?
  Corne no mel, wel thou wost;
Bot wel seld at the mele
  A rowȝ bare trenchur, other a crust.

The begger that the crust ssal hab,
  Wel hokerlich he lokith theran:
Soth to sigge, and noȝt to gabbe,
  Riȝt noȝt he is i-paiid a pan.
Than seiith the begger in is mode,
  "The crust is bothe hard and tougth,
The wreche was hard that ow the gode,
  Hard for hard is gode y-nowȝ."

Moch misanter that for him bidde
  Pater noster other crede;
Bot let him hab as he didde,
  For of the ȝift nath he no mede.
Ic red up no mąn thou hab triste,
  No uppon non other;

wife and child will from him fly,—there is no friend that will stay with him.—
What will men for the soul give?—corn nor meal, well thou knowest;—but
very seldom at their meal,—a rough bare trencher, or a crust.
  The beggar that the crust shall have,—right scornfully he looks thereon:—
truth to say, and not to joke,—right not a pan he is paid.—Then saith the beggar in his mood,—"The crust is both hard and tough,—the wretch was hard
that possessed the goods,—hard for hard is good enough."
  May he have much misadventure who for him saith—Pater-noster or creed;
—but let him have as he did,—for of the gift hath he no reward.—I counsel
thee have trust in no man,—nor upon no other;—but share it with your own

Ok del hit with ȝure owen fist,
Trist to soster no brother.

Anurith God and holi chirch,
And ȝiveth the pouir that habbith nede ;
So Godis wille ȝe ssul wirche,
And joi of heven hab to mede.
To whoch joi us bring
Jhesus Crist heven king ! AMEN.

fist,—trust neither to sister nor brother.

Honour God and holy church,—and give to the poor that have need ;—Thus ye shall work God's will,—and have for reward the joy of heaven.—To which joy us bring—Jesus Christ heaven's King. AMEN.

The scholastic philosophy flourished through the thirteenth century, the age of Albertus Magnus, of Grosteste, and of Roger Bacon ; but, towards the close of that period, the importance of the schools and universities was rapidly declining. They had received a shock from the triumph of the monks over the scholars during the reign of St. Louis, which they could never recover. Political events, and the great change which was then operating in the whole political—we may perhaps say social—system, hastened their fall. The nice quibbles of the dialectitian, although they still had their weight in the cloister, began to be sneered at in the world without. The following song, which perhaps belongs to the beginning of the fourteenth century, is directed against the *artistæ*, or those who studied the seven arts, the scholastic *trivium* and *quadrivium*.

SONG AGAINST THE SCHOLASTIC STUDIES.

[From MS. Cotton. Titus A. xx. fol. 66, v°, written in reign of Edw. II.;
and MS. Bodl. Oxford. Rawl. B. 214, fol. 168, v°, of 15th cent.]

Meum est propositum gentis imperitæ
Artes frugi reddere melioris vitæ,
Et ad artes singulas procedatis rite :
Ad mea decepti juvenes documenta venite.
Adversatur legibus omne genus cleri,
Cujus status hodie pejor est quam heri;
Sua sacra presbiter quisque vult tueri.
Ingenium magni livor detraxit Homeri.
Quando contra boream nauta pandit velum,
Et asellus vincere cursu vult camelum,
Non formidat ponere manus os in cœlum :
Vulneror et clausum porto sub pectore telum.
Præferri bidentibus capra vult hirsuta,
Stulta non considerans unde sit induta;
Illi æqua vellera non sunt attributa :
Pennatis avibus quondam testudo locuta.

TRANSLATION.—It is my design to turn the arts of an unskilful race to the
fruit of a better life, and so proceed ye to each of the arts in order : O youth
who have been deceived, come to my lessons.—Every class of the clergy is opposed to the laws, of whom the condition to-day is worse than it was yesterday;
every priest will hold his own rites : envy detracted from the talents of great
Homer.—When the sailor spreads his sail against the north wind, and the ass
thinks to conquer the camel in the race, then the hand fears not to put the
face towards heaven; I am wounded and carry the weapon shut up in my
breast.—The shaggy she-goat wishes to be preferred to the sheep, in her folly
not considering with what she is clothed; so fine a fleece has not been given to
her : as the tortoise once said to the winged birds.—Although the logicians are

Cum sint nuda gloria logici contenti,
Sub egentis propere vivunt indumenti,
Verumtamen invident opulentæ genti.
Summa petit livor, perflant altissima venti.

Modus est invidiæ semper, ut ab imis
Sursum tendant, ultima contradicunt primis :
Invidere negligit infimo sublimis.
Invidus alterius rebus macescit opimis.

Si non cupis vivere pauper et mendicus,
Semper in laboribus sicut servus Stichus,
Igni digna subjici sine fructu ficus,
Dilige sic alios ut sis tibi carus amicus.

Expedit pauperibus abhærere legi ;
Insudare nimium artibus elegi.
Ignoro propterea unde possum regi,
Carmina qui quondam studio florente peregi.

Nonne circa logicam si quis laborabit,
Spinas atque tribulos illi germinabit ?
In sudore nimio panem manducabit;
Vix tamen hoc illi garula lingua dabit.

satisfied with naked glory, and live under the garb of the needy, nevertheless they envy the rich. Envy seeks the summit, the wind blows vehemently on lofty places.—It is always the manner of envy, that they aim from the bottom upwards, the last speak against the first : he who is elevated does not think it worth while to envy him who is most low. The envious man becomes lean by regarding the fatness of another.—If you do not desire to live poor and beggarly, always labouring like the servant Stichus, a fig-tree without fruit worthy to be cast in the fire ; love others so that thou mayest be a dear friend to thyself.— It is good for poor men to adhere to the law ; I have chosen to labour much on the arts. I am ignorant therefore how I may be guided, who once composed verses, while my study flourished.—If any one will expend his labour upon logic, will it not produce him thorns and brambles ? in too much sweat he will eat his bread ; and even that his talkative tongue will hardly give him.—

In arenam logicus frustra semen serit,
Nam metendi tempore fructus nullus erit;
Circa ficum sterilem labor omnis perit.
Arbor qualis erit, talia poma gerit.

Licet sis ad apicem artium provectus,
Fies junioribus in brevi despectus ;
Dicunt de te, " senio desipit affectus."
Æmula quid cessas finem properare senectus ?

Veræ pestilentiæ cathedra tu sedes,
Qui Thebanas lectitas vel Trojanas cædes ;
Affluunt divitiis legistarum sedes,
Et modo vadit equis qui solet ire pedes.

Propter artes vigilans est revera stultus ;
Cur circa Georgicam pateris singultus ?
Ager sic per steriles jaceat incultus,
Telluris si forte velis cognoscere cultus.

Propter leges merito labor est ferendus ;
Ager reddens centuplum non est deferendus.
Est libellus pauperum pauperi legendus ;
Hic tibi præcipue sit pura mente colendus.

The logician in vain sows his seed in the sand, for in harvest time there will be no fruit; upon a barren fig-tree all labour is lost. Such as is the tree, such will be the fruit it bears.—Although you be arrived at the summit of the arts, you will be in a short time despised by the younger aspirants ; they will say of thee, " he doats, affected with old age." Old age, why do you emulous cease to hasten the end?—Thou sittest in the chair of a true pestilence, who readest the tragedy of Thebes or of Troy ; [whilst] the seats of the legists abound in riches, and now he goes on horseback who used to go on foot.—He who sits up at night to study the arts is truly a fool; why do you yawn over the Georgic ? thus the field may lie neglected and barren, while by chance you may be desirous of understanding the culture of the earth.—It is right that we should labour upon the laws ; a field that produces a hundred-fold is not to be set aside. The book of the poor is to be read by the poor man ; this chiefly is the book to be devotedly

Circa dialecticam tempus cur consumis,
Tu qui nullos redditus aliunde sumis ?
Colat qui per patriam natus est e summis,
Dives agro, dives positis in fænore nummis.
Dives in fallaciis discat esse fortis ;
Discat capram facere de persona sortis.
Artes nunquam deserat citra tempus mortis.
Contentus fama lateat Lucanus in hortis.
Si forte deliquerit artibus imbutus,
Ad legistas fugiet si vult esse tutus :
Quia se defendere nescit plus quam mutus,
Græcorum studia nimium diuque sequutus.
Atria nobilium video patere ;
Cum legista venerit dissolvuntur ceræ.
Exclusus ad januam poteris sedere,
Ipse licet venias musis comitatus, Homere.
Logicus araneæ potest comparari,
Quæ subtiles didicit telas operari,
Quæ suis visceribus volunt consummari ;

cultivated by thee.—Why do you consume your time upon dialectics, thou who receivest no income from other sources ? Let him cultivate it who is born of high family in the country, rich in land and rich in money laid out at interest.—Let the rich man learn to be strong in fallacies ; let him learn to make a she-goat of the person of chance. Let him never desert the arts, before the hour of his death. Satisfied with fame, let Lucan lie hid in the gardens.—If imbued in the arts he should chance to fail, he will fly to the legists if he will be safe : because he knows no more how to defend himself than one who is dumb, having pursued too much and too often the study of the Greeks.—I see the halls of the nobles open ; when the legist comes, the bolts are undone ; thou, shut out, mayest sit at the door, although thou thyself, Homer, shouldst come along with the muses. — The logician may be compared to a spider, which learns to spin subtle webs, that are made out of its own bowels ; the reward is a fly, if by

Est pretium musca, si forte queat laqueari.

Si fortuna logico favet in privigno,
Vultu namque logicum respicit benigno ;
Si sit dives logicus hoc sub cœli signo ;
Rara avis in terra nigroque simillima cigno.

Naturæ cognoscere si velis archana,
Stude circa physicam quæ dat membra sana :
Sat quicquid expostulat egestas humana,
Sat Galienus opes et sanctio Justiniana.

chance it can be netted.—If fortune favour a logician in his kindred, for she looks upon the logician with a benignant countenance ; if a logician be rich under this sign of the heavens ; he is a rare bird upon earth, and very like a black swan.—If you wish to know the secrets of nature, study physic which gives health to the limbs ; what man's need requires is enough, Galen and the sanction of Justinian are riches enough.

The following English verses, composed at the same period, seem also intended as a satire upon the studies and arguments of the dialectitians.

THE SONG OF " NEGO."

[From MS. Harl. No. 913, fol. 58, vº. written in 1308.]

Hit nis bot trewth, I wend, an afte
For te sette *nego* in eni crafte ;
Trewth so drawith to heven blisse,
Nego doth noȝt so i-wisse.

TRANSLATION.—It is contrary to truth, I believe, and ....—to set *nego* in any craft ;—truth draweth us to the joy of heaven,—*nego* does not so certainly.

For-sak and save is thef in lore,
Nego is pouer clark in store.
Whan menne horlith ham here and there,
Nego savith ham fram care.
Awei with *nego* ute of place !
Whose wol have Goddis grace;
Whoso wol aȝens the devil fiȝte,
Ther mai *nego* sit a-riȝte.
Ak loke that we never more
Nego sette in trew lore.
For whoso can lite, hath sone i-do,
Anone he drawith to *nego.*
Now o clerk seiith *nego ;*
And that other *dubito ;*
Seiith another *concedo ;*
And another *obligo,*
Verum falsum sette therto;
Than is al the lore i-do.
Thus the fals clerkes of har hevid,
Makith men trewth of ham be revid.

—Forsake and save is a thief in doctrine,—*nego* is a poor clerk in store.—
When men hurl them here and there,—*nego* saves them from care.—Away with
nego out of the place !—whoever will have God's grace ;—he who will against
the devil fight,—there may *nego* sit rightly.—But see that we never more—set
nego in true doctrine.—For he who knows little has soon done,—anon he draws
to *nego.*—Now one clerk says *nego ;*—and the other *dubito ;*—saith another
concedo ;—and another *obligo,*—with *verum falsum* set to it ;—then is all their
learning done.—Thus the false clerks of their head,—make men of truth through
them be bereaved.

The Scottish wars occupied incessantly the remaining years of Edward's reign. The following song was composed probably in the September of the year 1306, soon after the battle of Kirkencliff, and on the immediate occasion of the execution of Sir Simon Fraser, who was taken prisoner there.

SONG ON THE EXECUTION OF SIR SIMON FRASER.

[MS. Harl. 2253, fol. 59, v°. of reign of Edw. II.]

Lystneth, lordynges, a newe song ichulle bigynne,⎤
Of the traytours of Scotlond that take beth wyth gynne ;
Mon that loveth falsnesse and nule never blynne,
Sore may him drede the lyf that he is ynne,
           ich understonde :
        Selde wes he glad
        That never nes a-sad
           of nythe ant of onde.

That y sugge by this Scottes that bueth nou to-drawe,
The hevedes o Londone brugge whose con y-knawe :
He wenden han buen kynges, ant seiden so in sawe ;
Betere hem were han y-be barouns ant libbe in Godes lawe,

TRANSLATION.—Listen, lordings, a new song I will begin,—of the traitors of Scotland who are taken with a trap ;—he who loves falseness, and will never leave it,—sore may he dread the life that he is in,—I believe :—seldom was he glad—that never was sorrowful—for his wickedness and turbulence.

I say that of these Scots who are now drawn,—their heads on London bridge anybody may recognise :—they thought to have been kings, and said so in their talk ;—better was it for them to have been barons and live in God's law,—with

wyth love.

Whose hateth soth ant ryht,

Lutel he douteth Godes myht,

the heye kyng above.

To warny alle the gentilmen that bueth in Scotlonde,

The Waleis wes to-drawe, seththe he was an-honge,

Al quic biheveded, ys bowels y-brend,

The heved to Londone brugge wes send

to abyde.

After Simond Frysel,

That wes traytour ant fykell,

and y-cud ful wyde.

Sire Edward oure kyng, that ful ys of pieté,

The Waleis quarters sende to is oune contré,

On four half to honge, huere myrour to be,

Theropon to thenche, that monie myhten se

ant drede.

Why nolden he be war

Of the bataile of Donbar,

hou evele hem con spede?

love.—He who hateth truth and right,—little he fears God's might,—the high king above.

To be a warning to all the gentlemen who are in Scotland,—the Wallace was drawn, and afterwards was hanged,—beheaded all alive, his bowels burnt,—the head to London Bridge was sent—to remain there.—Afterwards Simon Fraser, who was traitor and fickle,—and known full wide.

Sir Edward our king, who is full of piety,—sent the Wallace's quarters to his own country,—to hang in four parts (of the country), to be their mirror,—thereupon to think, in order that many might see—and dread.—Why would they not take warning—of the battle of Dunbar,—how ill they sped?

Bysshopes and barouns come to the kynges pes,
Ase men that weren fals, fykel, ant les,
Othes hue him sworen in stude ther he wes,
To buen him hold ant trewe for alles cunnes res,
> thrye,
>> That hue ne shulden aʒeyn him go,
>> So hue were temed tho;
>>> weht halt hit to lye?

To the kyng Edward hii fasten huere fay;
Fals wes here foreward so forst is in May,
That sonne from the southward wypeth away:
Moni proud Scot therof mene may
> to ʒere.
>> Nes never Scotlond
>> With dunt of monnes hond
>>> allinge a-boht so duere!

The Bisshop of Glascou ychot he was y-laht;
The Bisshop of Seint André bothe he beth y-caht;
The Abbot of Scon with the Kyng nis nout saht;
Al here purpos y-come hit ys to naht,

Bishops and barons came to the king's peace,—as men that were false, fickle, and lying,—oaths they swore to him in the place where he was,—to be firm and true to him in all kinds of moments,—thrice (?),—that they should not against him go,—so were they tamed then ;—what profits it to lie?

To King Edward they plight their faith ;—false was their covenant as frost is in May,—which the sun from the southward wipes away ;—many a proud Scot thereof may lament—in year.—Was never Scotland—by dint of man's hand—altogether bought so dear.

The Bishop of Glasgow, I wot he was taken ;—the Bishop of St. Andrew, too, he is caught ;—the Abbot of Scone with the King is not .. .. ;—all their purpose

thurh ryhte.
Hii were unwis
When hii thohte pris
aȝeyn huere kyng to fyhte.

Thourh consail of thes bisshopes y-nemned byfore,
Sire Robert the Bruytz furst kyng wes y-core,
He mai everuche day ys fon him se byfore ;
ȝef hee mowen him hente, ichot he bith forlore,
sauntz fayle.
Soht for te sugge,
Duere he shal abugge
that he bigon batayle.

Hii that him crounede proude were ant bolde,
Hii maden kyng of somere, so hii ner ne sholde,
Hii setten on ys heved a croune of rede golde,
Ant token him a kyne-ȝerde so me kyng sholde,
to deme.
Tho he wes set in see,
Lutel god couthe he
kyne-riche to ȝeme.

is come no nothing,—by right.—They were unwise—when they thought it
praiseworthy—against their king to fight.

Through counsel of these bishops named before,—Sir Robert the Bruce first
was chosen king,—he may every day his foes see before him ;—if they may
catch him, I wot he is undone,—without fail.—To say the truth,—dearly he
shall pay—for having begun battle.

They that crowned him were proud and bold,—they made a king of summer,
as they never should,—they set on his head a crown of red gold,—and gave him
a sceptre as one should to a king,—to judge.—When he was set on a throne,
—little good knew he—a kingdom to rule.

Now Kyng Hobbe in the mures ȝongeth,
For te come to toune nout him ne longeth ;
The barouns of Engelond, myhte hue him gripe,
He him wolde techen on Englysshe to pype,
    thourh streynthe :
   Ne be he ner so stout,
   ȝet he bith y-soht out
    o brede and o leynthe.

Sire Edward of Carnarvan, Jhesu him save ant see !
Sire Emer de Valence, gentil knyht ant free,
Habbeth y-suore huere oht that, *par la grace Dée !*
Hee wollith ous delyvren of that false contree,
    ȝef hii conne.
   Much hath Scotlond forlore,
   Whet a-last, whet bifore,
    ant lutel pris wonne.

Nou ichulle fonge ther ich er let,
Ant tellen ou of Frisel, ase ich ou byhet ;
In the batayle of Kyrkenclyf, Frysel was y-take ;
Ys continaunce abated eny bost to make

Now King Hobbe gangeth in the moors,—to come to town he has no desire ;—
the barons of England if they might gripe him,—they would teach him to pipe
in English,—through strength :—be he never so stout,—yet he is sought out—
wide and far.

 Sir Edward of Caernarvon, (Jesus save him and have him in regard !)—and
Sir Aymer de Valence, a gentle knight and liberal,—they have sworn their
oath that, by the grace of God !—they will deliver us from that false country,—
if they can.—Much hath Scotland lost,—what latterly and what before,—and
little praise won.

 Now I shall take up where I left off before,—and tell you of Fraser, as I promised you ;—in the battle of Kirkencliff Fraser was taken ;—his countenance

biside Strivelyn :
Knyhtes ant sweynes,
Fremen ant theynes,
monye with hym.

So hii weren byset on everuche halve,
Somme slaye were, ant somme dreynte hem-selve;
Sire Johan of Lyndeseye nolde nout abyde,
He wod into the water his feren him bysyde
to adrenche.
Whi nolden hii be war ?
Ther nis non aʒeyn stare :—
why nolden hy hem by-thenche ?

This wes byfore Seint Bartholomeus masse,
That Frysel wes y-take, were hit more other lasse :
To Sire Thomas of Multone, gentil baroun ant fre,
Ant to Sire Johan Jose, bytake tho wes he
to honde :
He wes y-fetered weel
Both with yrn ant wyth steel,
to bringen of Scotlonde.

ceased from making any boast—near Stirling :—knights and swains,—freemen
and thanes,—many with him.

They were so beset on every part,—some were slain and some drowned themselves.—Sir John de Lyndsay would not remain,—he waded into the water
with his companions beside him—to drown.—Why would not they beware ?—
There is none looked again (?) :—why would not they reflect ?

It was before St. Bartholemew's mass,—that Fraser was taken, were it more
or less :—To Sir Thomas de Multon, a gentle knight and liberal,—and to Sir
John Jose, he was delivered then—in hand :—he was well fettered—both with
iron and with steel,—to bring out of Scotland.

Sone therafter the tydynge to the kyng com;
He him sende to Londone with mony armed grom;
He com yn at Newegate, y telle yt ou aplyht,
A gerland of leves on ys hed y-dyht
                    of grene;
            For he shulde ben y-knowe
            Bothe of heȝe ant of lowe
                    for treytour, y wene.

Y-fetered were ys legges under his horse wombe;
Bothe with yrn ant with stel mankled were ys honde;
A gerland of peruenke set on ys heved;
Muche wes the poer that him wes byreved
                    in londe:
            So God me amende!
            Lutel he wende
                    so be broht in honde.

Sire Herbert of Morham, feyr knyht ant bold,
For the love of Frysel ys lyf wes y-sold;
A wajour he made, so hit wes y-told,
Ys heved of to smhyte ȝef me him brohte in hold,

Soon afterwards the tidings came to the king;—they sent him to London with many an armed man;—he came in at Newgate, I tell it you faithfully,—a garland of leaves placed on his head—of green;—because he should be known —both by high and by low—as a traitor, I ween.

Fettered were his legs under his horse's belly;—both with iron and with steel manacled were his hands;—a garland of periwinkle set on his head;—much was the power that was taken from him—in land:—As may God amend me!— he little supposed—so to be brought in hand.

Sir Herbert of Morham, a fair knight and bold,—for the love of Fraser his life was sold;—a wager he made, so it was said,—to smite off his head if

wat so bytyde.
Sory wes he thenne,
Tho he myhte him kenne
thourh the toun ryde.

Thenne seide ys scwyer a word anon ryht,
"Sire, we beth dede, ne helpeth hit no wyht,"—
(Thomas de Boys the scwyer wes to nome)—
"Nou ychot oure wajour turneth us to grome,
so y-bate."
Y do ou to wyte,
Here heved wes of smyte
byfore the Tour gate.

This wes on oure Levedy even, for sothe ych understonde,
The justices seten for the knyhtes of Scotlonde,
Sire Thomas of Multone, an hendy knyht ant wys,
Ant Sire Rauf of Sondwyche that muchel is told in pris,
ant Sire Johan Abel;
Mo y mihte telle by tale,
Bothe of grete ant of smale,
ʒe knowen suythe wel.

they took him in hold,—whatever betide.—Sorry was he then,—when he might know him—to ride through the town.

Then said his squire a word anon right,—" Sir, we are dead, there is no creature to help us ;"—(the squire was named Thomas de Bois)—"now I wot our wager turns to our sorrow,—so bet."—I give you to know,—their heads were smitten off—before the gate of the Tower.

It was on our Lady's eve, for truth I understand,—the justices sat for the knights of Scotland,—Sir Thomas de Multon, a gentle knight and wise,—and Sir Ralph de Sandwich, who is much esteemed in worth,—and Sir John Abel; —more I might tell by reckoning,—both of great and of small,—ye know very well.

Thenne saide the justice, that gentil is ant fre,
" Sire Simond Frysel, the kynges traytour hast thou be,
In water ant in londe, that monie myhten se :
What sayst thou thareto ? hou wolt thou quite the ?
          do say."
      So foul he him wiste,
      Nede waron truste
        for to segge, nay.

Ther he wes y-demed, so hit wes londes lawe,
For that he wes lord-swyke, furst he wes to-drawe,
Upon a retheres hude forth he wes y-tuht :
Sum while in ys time he wes a modi knyht,
        in huerte.
      Wickednesse ant sunne,
      Hit is lutel wunne
        that maketh the body smerte.

For al is grete poer, ʒet he wes y-laht ;
Falsnesse ant swykedom, al hit geth to naht ;
Tho he wes in Scotlond, lutel wes ys thoht
Of the harde jugement that him wes bysoht

Then said the justice, who is gentle and free,—" Sir Simon Fraser, the king's traitor hast thou been,—on water and on land, as many may see :—what sayest thou thereto ? how wilt thou clear thyself?—do say."—He knew himself to be so foul,—he had not whereon to trust—to say, nay.

There he was judged, as it was the law of the land,—because he was traitor to his lord, first he was drawn,—upon a bullock's hide forth he was led :—for once in his life he was a moody knight—in heart.—Wickedness and sin,—it is little gain—that makes the body smart.

For all his great power, still he was taken ;—falseness and treachery all come to nothing ;—when he was in Scotland, little was his thought—of the hard

in stounde.
He wes four-sithe for-swore
To the kyng ther bifore,
    ant that him brohte to grounde.

With feteres ant with gyves ichot he wes to-drowe,
From the Tour of Londone, that monie myhte knowe,
In a curtel of burel a selkethe wyse,
Ant a gerland on ys heved of the newe guyse,
    thurh Cheepe ;
    Moni mon of Engelond
    For to se Symond
    thideward con lepe.

Tho he com to galewes, furst he wes an-honge,
Al quic by-heveded, thah him thohte longe,
Seththe he wes y-opened, is boweles y-brend,
The heved to Londone-brugge wes send
    to shonde :
    So ich ever mote the !
    Sum while wende he
    ther lutel to stonde.

judgment which was prepared for him—in a short time.—He was four times perjured—to the king there before,—and that brought him to the ground.

With fetters and with gyves I wot he was drawn,—from the Tower of London, that many might know,—in a kirtle of sack-cloth in strange wise,—and a garland on his head of the new guise,—through Cheap ;—many a man of England—to see Simon—thither began to leap.

When he came to the gallows, first he was hanged,—beheaded all alive, though it seemed to him long,—afterwards he was opened, his bowels burnt,— the head to London Bridge was sent—for disgrace :—As I may ever thrive !— at one time he thought—little there to stand.

He rideth thourh the sité, as y telle may,
With gomen and wyth solas, that wes here play,
To Londone-brugge hee nome the way,
Moni wes the wyves chil that theron laketh a day,
              ant seide, alas !
          That he wes i-bore,
          Ant so villiche for-lore,
              so feir mon ase he was.

Nou stont the heved above the tu-brugge,
Faste bi Waleis, soth for te sugge ;
After socour of Scotlond longe he mowe prye,
Ant after help of Fraunce wet halt hit to lye,
              ich wene.
          Betere him were in Scotlond
          With is ax in ys hond
              to pleyen o the grene.

Ant the body hongeth at the galewes faste,
With yrnene claspes longe to laste ;
For te wyte wel the body, ant Scottyshe to garste,
Foure ant twenti ther beoth to sothe ate laste

They ride through the city, as I may tell,—with game and with solace, that was their play,—to London Bridge they took the way,—many was the woman's child that thereon lacks-a-day,—and said, alas !—that he was born,—and so vilely undone,—so fair a man as he was.

Now stands the head above the twi-bridge,—fast by Wallace, to say the truth ; —after succour from Scotland long they may pray,—and after help from France what profits it to wait, (?)—I ween.—It were better for him in Scotland—with his axe in his hand—to play on the green.

And the body hangs fast on the gallows,—with iron clasps long to last ;—to guard well the body, and the Scotch to drive away (?),—four-and-twenty there are

by nyhte.
ʒef eny were so hardi
The body to remuy
al so to dyhte.

Were Sire Robert the Bruytz y-come to this londe,
Ant the Erl of Asseles, that harde is an honde,
Alle the other pouraille, for sothe ich understonde,
Mihten be ful blythe ant thonke Godes sonde,
wyth ryhte :
Thenne myhte uch mon
Bothe riden ant gon
in pes withoute vyhte.

The traytours of Scotlond token hem to rede,
The barouns of Engelond to brynge to dede ;
Charles of Fraunce, so moni mon tolde,
With myht ant with streynthe hem helpe wolde,
his thonkes !
Tprot, Scot, for thi strif !
Hang up thyn hachet ant thi knyf,
Whil him lasteth the lyf
with the longe shonkes.

for sooth at least—by night.—If any one were so hardy—the body to remove—
immediately to attack them.

If Sir Robert the Bruce were come to this land,—and the Earl of Athol that
is hard in hand,—all the rest of the common people, for truth I understand,—
might be full blith, and thank God's sending,—with right :—then might each
man—both ride and go—in peace, without fighting.

The traitors of Scotland took counsel with themselves,—to bring the barons of
England to death ;—Charles of France, as many a one said,—with might and with
strength would help them,—thanks to him !—Tprot, Scot, for thy strife !—hang
up thy hatchet and thy knife,—while life lasts to him—with the long shanks.

The following song, remarkable for the playfulness of its metres and rhymes, gives us a strong picture of the extortions committed at this period of our history upon the weak and defenceless, by the magistrates and the officers connected with the courts of law.

SONG ON THE VENALITY OF THE JUDGES.

[From MS. Harl. No. 913, fol. 59, r°. of the beginning of the 14th century. This song is in the MS. written as prose.]

Beati qui esuriunt
Et sitiunt, et faciunt
    justitiam,
Et odiunt et fugiunt
    injuriæ nequitiam ;
Quos nec auri copia
Nec divitum encennia
    trahunt a rigore,
    nec pauperum clamore ;
Quæ sunt justa judicant,
Et a jure non claudicant
    divitum favore.
    Sed nunc miro more
Multos fallit seculum,
Et trahit in periculum,
    mundi ob favorem,
    ut lambeant honorem.

TRANSLATION.—Blessed are they who hunger and thirst, and do justice, and hate and avoid the wickedness of injustice ; whom neither abundance of gold nor the jewels of the rich draw from their inflexibility, or from the cry of the poor ; they judge what is just, and do not fall off from the right for the sake of the rich. But now the age deceives many in a wonderful manner, and draws them into danger, for love of the world, that they may lick up honours.

Hoc facit pecunia,
Quam omnis fere curia
    jam duxit in uxorem.

Sunt justitiarii,
Quos favor et denarii
    alliciunt a jure;
Hii sunt nam bene recolo,
Quod censum dant diabolo,
    et serviunt hii pure.
    Nam jubet lex naturæ,
Quod judex in judicio
Nec prece nec pretio
    acceptor sit personæ;
    quid, Jhesu ergo bone,
Fiet de judicibus,
Qui prece vel muneribus
    cedunt a ratione?

Revera tales judices
Nuncios multiplices
    habent;—audi quare.
    Si terram vis rogare,

The cause of this is money, to which almost every court has now wedded itself.
    There are judges, whom partiality and bribes seduce from justice; these are they, I remember well, that pay toll to the devil, and they serve him alone. For the law of nature commands, that a judge in giving judgment should not be an acceptor of anybody either for prayer or money; what therefore, O good Jesus, will be done with the judges, who for prayers or gifts recede from what is just?
    In fact such judges have numerous messengers;—listen for what purpose. If you wish to claim land, a messenger will come to you, and speaks in confidence,

Accedet ad te nuncius,
Et loquitur discretius,
 dicens, " Amice care,
 vis tu placitare ?
Sum cum justitiario
Qui te modo vario
 possum adjuvare ;
 si vis impetrare
Per suum subsidium,
Da michi dimidium,
 et te volo juvare."

Ad pedes sedent clerici,
Qui velut famelici
 sunt, donis inhiantes ;
 et pro lege dantes,
Quod hii qui nichil dederint,
Quamvis cito venerint,
 erunt expectantes.

Sed si quædam nobilis,
Pulcra vel amabilis,
 cum capite cornuto,
 auro circumvoluto,

saying, " Dear friend, do you wish to plead ? I am one who can help you in various ways with the judge ; if you wish to obtain anything by his aid, give me half, and I will help you."

At his feet sit clerks, who are like people half-famished, gaping for gifts ; and proclaiming it as law, that those who give nothing, although they come early, will have to wait.

But if some noble lady, fair and lovely, with horns on her head, and that

Accedat ad judicium,
Hæc expedit negotium
 ore suo muto.

Si pauper muliercula,
Non habens munuscula,
 formam neque genus,
  quam non pungit Venus,
Infecto negotio
Suo pergit hospitio,
 dolendo corde tenus.

Sunt quidam ad hanc curiam,
Qui exprimunt juditiam ;
 dicuntur relatores ;
 cæteris pejores.
Utraque manu capiunt,
Et sic eos decipiunt
 quorum sunt tutores.
  Et quid janitores ?
Qui dicunt pauperibus
Curiam sequentibus,

encircled with gold, come for judgment, such a one despatches her business without having to say a word.

If the woman be poor, and has no gifts, neither beauty nor rich relationship, whom Venus does not stimulate, she goes home without effecting her business, sorrowful at heart.

There are some at this court, who express judgment ; whom they call relaters, worse than the others. They take with both hands, and so deceive those whose defenders they are. And what shall we say to the ushers ? who say to the poor that follow the court, " Poor man, why do you trouble yourself ? why

" Pauper, cur laboras ?
     Cur facis hic moras ?
Nisi des pecuniam
Cuique ad hanc curiam,
          in vanum laboras.
     Quid, miser, ergo ploras ?
Si nichil attuleris,
          stabis omnino foras."

De vicecomitibus,
Quam duri sunt pauperibus,
          quis potest enarrare ?
     Qui nichil potest dare,
Huc et illuc trahitur,
Et in assisis ponitur,
          et cogitur jurare,
          non ausus murmurare.
Quod si murmuraverit,
Ni statim satisfecerit,
          est totum salsum mare.

Hoc idem habent vitium,
Cum subeunt hospitium

do you wait here ? unless you give money to everybody in this court, you labour
in vain. Why then, wretch, do you lament ? If you have brought nothing,
you will stand altogether out of doors."

Concerning the sheriffs, who can relate with sufficient fulness how hard
they are to the poor ? He who has nothing to give is dragged hither and
thither, and is placed in the assises, and is obliged to take his oath, without
daring to murmur. But if he should murmur, unless he immediately make
satisfaction, it is all salt sea.

The same people have this vice, when they enter the house of some country-

cujusdam patriotæ,
vel abbathiæ notæ,
Quo potus et cibaria,
Et cuncta necessaria,
   eis dentur devote.
Nil prosunt sibi talia,
Nisi mox jocalia
      post prandium sequantur,
      et cunctis largiantur,
Bedellis, garcionibus,
Et qui sunt secum omnibus.
      Nec adhuc pacantur,
      nisi transmittantur
Robæ suis uxoribus
Ex variis coloribus.
         Si non clam mittantur,
         Et post sic operantur;
Quotquot habent averia
Ad sua maneria
      cum impetu fugantur,
      et ipsi imparcantur
Quousque satisfecerint,
Ita quod duplum dederint ;
      tunc demum liberantur.

man, or of a famous abbey, where drink and victuals, and all things necessary,
are given to them devoutly. Such things are of no avail, unless by and by the
jewels follow after the meal, and are distributed to all, bedels and garçons, and
all who are with them. Nor even yet are they paid, unless robes of various
colours are transmitted to their wives. If these are not sent privately, then
they proceed as follows ; whatever cattle they find, are driven off violently to
their own manors, and the owners themselves are put in confinement until they
make satisfaction, so that they give the double : then at length they are liberated.

Clericos irrideo
Suos, quos prius video
  satis indigentes,
  et quasi nil habentes,
Quando ballivam capiunt ;
Qua capta mox superbiunt,
  et crescunt sibi dentes,
  collaque erigentes,
Incipiunt perpropere
Terras et domos emere,
  et redditus placentes ;
  nummosque colligentes,
Pauperes despiciunt,
Et novas leges faciunt,
  vicinos opprimentes ;
  fiuntque sapientes.
In hoc malum faciunt,
Et patriam decipiunt,
  nemini parcentes.

I laugh at their clerks, whom I see at first indigent enough, and possessing next to nothing, when they receive a bailiwick ; which received they next show themselves proud, and their teeth grow, and holding up their necks they begin very hastily to buy lands and houses, and agreeable rents ; and amassing money themselves, they despise the poor, and make new laws, oppressing their neighbours ; and they become wise men. In this they do wickedness, and deceive their country, sparing no one.

The next song was doubtlessly considered as very libellous at the time when it was composed, and professes to have been written in the wild wood; the means of publication being to drop it on the high road, that it might fall into the hands of passengers. It is directed against one of the king's ordinances.

THE OUTLAW'S SONG OF TRAILLEBASTON.

[MS. Harl. No. 2253, fol. 113, v°. of the reign of Edw. II.]

Talent me prent de rymer e de geste fere
D'une purveaunce qe purveu est en la terre;
Mieux valsit uncore que la chose fust à fere :
Si Dieu ne prenge garde, je quy que sourdra guere.

Ce sunt les articles de Trayllebastoun ;
Salve le roi meismes, de Dieu eit maleysoun
Qe a de primes graunta tiel commissioun !
Quar en ascuns des pointz n'est mie resoun,

Sire, si je voderoi mon garsoun chastier
De une buffe ou de deus, pur ly amender,
Sur moi betera bille, e me frad atachier,
E avant qe isse de prisone raunsoun grant doner.

TRANSLATION.—I am seized with the desire to rhyme and to make a story,—of a purveyance which is provided in the land ;—it would be much better if the thing were still undone :—if God does not avert it, I think that there will arise war.

It is the articles of Traillebaston ;—except the king himself, may he have God's curse—whoever first granted such a commission !—For there is little reason in any of the points of it.

Sire, if I wished to chastise my lad—with a slap or two, to amend him,—he will ask a bill against me, and will cause me to be arrested,—and to give a great ransom before I escape from prison.

Quaraunte souz pernent pur ma raunsoun,
E le viscounte vint à son guerdoun,
Qu'il ne me mette en parfounde prisoun.
Ore agardez, seigneurs, est-ce resoun ?

Pur ce me tendroi antre bois sur le jolyf umbray ;
Là n'y a fauceté ne nulle male lay ;—
En le bois de Belregard, où vole le jay,
E chaunte russinole touz jours santz delay.

Mès le male doseynes, dount Dieu n'eit jà pieté !
Parmi lur fauce bouches me ount enditée
De male robberies e autre mavestée,
Que je n'os entre mes amis estre receptée.

J'ai servi my sire le roy en pées e en guere,
En Flaundres, Escoce, en Gascoyne sa terre ;
Mès ore ne me sai-je point chevisaunce fere ;—
Tot mon temps ay mis en veyn pur tiel honme plere.

Si ces maveis jurours ne se vueillent amender,
Que je pus à mon pais chevalcher e aler,

Forty shillings they take for my ransom,—and the sheriff comes for his fee,—
that he may not put me in deep prison.—Now consider, lords, is this right ?

For this cause I will keep myself among the woods, in the beautiful shade ;
—where there is no falseness and no bad law ;—in the wood of Beauregard,
where the jay flies,—and where the nightingale sings always without ceasing.

But the bad idlers, on whom may God have no pity !—with their false mouths
have indited me—of ill robberies and other delinquency,—so that I dare not be
received among my friends.

I have served my lord the king in peace and in war,—in Flanders, Scotland,
and his land of Gascony ;—but now I do not know how to make any expedient
for myself ;—all my time I have spent in vain to please such a man.

If these wicked jurors will not amend,—that I may be able to ride and go at

Si je les pus ateindre la teste lur froi voler,
De touz lur manaces ne dorroi un dener.

Ly Martyn et ly Knoville sunt gent de pieté,
E prient pur les povres qu'il eyent sauveté ;
Spigurnel e Belflour sunt gent de cruelté,
Si il fuissent en ma baylie ne serreynt retornée.

Je lur apre[n]droy le giw de Traylebastoun,
E lur bruseroy l'eschyne e le cropoun,
Les bras e les jaunbes, ce serreit resoun,
La lange lur tondroy e la bouche ensoun.

Qy cestes choses primes comença,
Jà jour de sa vie amendé ne serra ;
Je vus di pur veyr, trop graunt pecché en a,
Quar pur doute de prisone meint laroun serra.

Ytel devendra leres que ne fust unque mès,
Que pur doute de prisone ne ose venir à pes ;

my peace,—if I can reach them I will make their heads fly off,—I would not give a penny for all their threats.

The Martin and the Knoville are people of piety,—and pray for the poor that they may have safety ;—Spigurnel and Belflour are people of cruelty,—if they were in my keeping they should not be returned.

I would teach them the game of Trailebaston,—and would break their backbone and their crupper,—their arms and their legs, it would be but right,—I would cut their tongues and their mouths likewise.

He who first commenced these things,—never in his life will he be amended ;—I tell you for truth, he has committed therein too great a sin,—for out of the fear of prison there will be many a robber made.

He will become a robber who was never so before,—who for fear of prison

Vivre covient avoir chescum jour adès ;
Qy ceste chose comenca, yl emprist grant fes.

Bien devoient marchaunz e moygnes doner maliçoun
A tous iceux que ordinerent le Traillebastoun ;
Ne lur vaudra un ayle le roial proteccioun,
Que il ne rendrount les deners sauntz regerdoun.

Vus qy estes endité, je lou, venez à moy,
Al vert bois de Belregard, là n'y a nul ploy,
Forque beste savage e jolyf umbroy ;
Car trop est dotouse la commune loy.

Si tu sachez de lettrure, e estes coroucé,
Devaunt les justices serrez appellée ;
Uncore poez estre à prisone retornée,
En garde de le evesque, jesque seiez purgée,
E soffryr messayse e trop dure penaunce,
E par cas n'averez jamès delyveraunce.

Pur ce valt plus ou moi à bois demorer,
Q'en prisone le evesque fyerge gyser.

dare not come to peace ;—it is necessary to have livelihood every day as it comes ;
—he who commenced this thing, undertook a great task.

Well may merchants and monks bestow a curse—on all those who ordained
the Trailebaston ;—the royal protection will not be worth a garlic to them,—if
they do not repay the pence without recompense.

You who are indited, I advise you, come to me,—to the green wood of
Beauregard, there where there is no plea,—except wild beast and beautiful
shade ;—for the common law is too much to be feared.

If thou knowest letters, and art enraged,—thou shalt be called before the
justices ;—again you may be returned to prison,—in keeping of the bishop,
until you be cleansed ;—and suffer mis-ease and too hard penance,—and perchance you will never have deliverance.

Therefore it is better to dwell with me in the wood,—than to lie cast in

Trop est la penaunce e dure à soffrer ;
Quy le mieux puet eslyre, fol est qe ne velt choyser.

Avant savoy poy de bien, ore su-je meins sage ;
Ce me fount les male leis par mout grant outrage,
Qe n'os à la pes venyr entre mon lignage ;
Les riches sunt à raunsoun, povres à escolage.

Fort serroit engager ce qe ne puet estre aquytée,
C'est la vie de honme que taunt est cher amée.
E je n'ay mye le chatel de estre rechatée ;
Mès si je fusse en lur baundoun à mort serroi lyverée ;

Uncore attendroy grace e orroi gent parler,
Tiels me dient le mal que me ne osent aprochier.
E volenters verroient mon corps ledenger ;
Mès entre myl debles Dieu puet un honme sauver.

Cely me pust salver que est le fitz Marie ;
Car je ne su coupable, endité su par envye ;

the bishop's prison.—Too much is the penance, and hard to suffer ;—he who has the opportunity to select what is better, is a fool if he does not make the choice.

Before I knew little what was good, now I am less wise ;—the bad laws cause this by very great outrage,—so that I dare not come to the peace among my kindred ;—the rich are put to ransom, the poor to prison.

It would be penible to engage what cannot be acquitted ;—that is the life of man which is so dearly loved ;—and I have not at all the goods wherewith to be bought off ;—but if I were in their power I should be put to death.

Yet if I should expect grace and hear people talk,—those would say evil to me who dare not approach me,—and would willingly see my body disgraced.—But God can save a man in the midst of a thousand devils.

He can save me, who is the son of Mary ;—for I am not culpable, I am in-

Qy en cesti lu me mist, Dieu lur maldie !
Le siècle est si variant, fous est qe s'affye.

Si je sei compagnoun e sache de archerye,
Mon veisyn irra disaunt, " cesti est de compagnie,
De aler bercer à bois e fere autre folie ;"
Que ore vueille vivre come pork merra sa vye.

Si je sache plus de ley qe ne sevent eux,
Yl dirrount, " cesti conspyratour comence de estre faus,"
E le heyre n'aprocheroy de x. lywes en d'eus ;
De tous veysinages hony seient ceux.

Je pri tote bone gent qe pur moi vueillent prier,
Qe je pus à mon pais aler e chyvaucher ;
Unqe ne fu homicide, certes à moun voler,
Ne mal robberes pur gent damager.

Cest rym fust fet al bois desouz un lorer,
Là chaunte merle, russinole, e cyre l'esperver ;
Escrit estoit en parchemyn pur mout remenbrer,
E gitté en haut chemyn, qe um le dust trover.

dited out of malice ;—God's curse be on those who drove me to this place !—
The world is so variable, that he is a fool who trusts in it.

If I am a companion and know archery,—my neighbour will go and say, " This
man belongs to a company,—to go hunt in the wood and do other folly ;"—so
now I will live as a pig will lead his life.

If I happen to know more law than they know,—they will say this conspirator
begins to be treasonable,—and I will not approach home within ten leagues of
them ;—of all neighbourhoods cursed be those.

I pray all good people that they will pray for me,—that I may be able to go
and ride to my country ;—I was never a homicide, at least by design,—nor an
ill robber to do people damage.

This rhyme was made in the wood beneath a bay tree,—there sings the thrush,
the nightingale, and the hawk cries (?) ;—it was written on parchment to be
better remembered,—and cast in the highway, that people may find it.

The following song is a satire upon the numerous retinues of the nobles and rich people, whose idle attendants and servants preyed upon the produce of the industrious peasantry. It shows us how great were the pride and ostentation of the courtiers of the latter years of Edward the First.

A SONG AGAINST THE RETINUES OF THE GREAT PEOPLE.

[MS. Harl. 2253, fol. 124, vº ; of reign of Edw. II.]

Of ribaudz y ryme
    Ant rede o mi rolle,
Of gedelynges, gromes,
    Of Colyn ant of Colle,
Harlotes, hors-knaves,
    Bi pate ant by polle;
To devel ich hem to-lvyre
    Ant take to tolle !

The gedelynges were gedered
    Of gonnylde gnoste;
Palefreiours ant pages,
    Ant boyes with boste;
Alle weren y-haht
    Of an horse thoste :
The devel huem afretye,
    Rau other a-roste !

TRANSLATION.—Of ribalds I rhyme—and read in my roll,—of gadlings, grooms,—of Colin and of Colle,—scoundrels, horse-boys,—by pate and by poll; —to the devil I them deliver—and give for toll.

The gadlings were gathered—of .... ;—palfrey-keepers and pages,— and boys with boast ;—all were ...... —of a horse .... :—may the devil devour them—raw or roasted !

The shuppare that huem shupte,
To shome he huem shadde,
To fles ant to fleye,
To tyke ant to tadde ;
So seyth Romaunz,
Whose ryht radde,—
Fleh com of flore,
Ant lous com of ladde.

The harlotes bueth horlynges,
Ant haunteth the plawe :
The gedelynges bueth glotouns,
Ant drynketh er hit dawe.
Sathanas huere syre
Seyde on is sawe,
Gobelyn made is gerner
Of gromene mawe.

The knave crommeth is crop,
Er the cok crawe ;
He momeleth ant moccheth,
Ant marreth is mawe ;
When he is al for-laped,
Ant lad over lawe,

The maker that made them,—he shed them to shame,—to fleas and to fly,—
to tyke and to toad;—so saith Romanz,—whoever read right,—fly comes of
flower,—and louse comes of lad.
The rogues are horelings,—and haunt the play :—the gadlings are gluttons,
—and drink before it dawns.—Satan their sire—said in his saying,—Goblin
made his garner—of the grooms' maw.
The knave crams his crop—before the cock crows ;—he mumbles and mocks,
—and marrs his maw ;—when he is all weary of lapping (?),—and laid over

A doseyn of doggen
Ne myhte hyre drawe.

The rybaudz a-ryseth
Er the day rewe ;
He shrapeth on is shabbes,
Ant draweth huem to dewe.
Sene is on is browe
Ant on is eʒe-brewe,
That he louseth a losynger,
And shoyeth a shrewe.

Nou beth capel-claweres
With shome to-shrude ;
Hue bosketh huem with botouns,
Ase hit were a brude ;
With lowe lacede shon
Of an hayfre hude,
Hue pyketh of here provendre
Al huere prude.

Whose rykeneth with knaves
Huere coustage,
The luthernesse of the ladde,
The prude of the page,

law,—a dozen of dogs—could not draw him.

The ribalds arise—before the day breaks ;—they scrape on their scabs,—and draw themselves to the dew.—Seen it is on his forehead—and on his eye-brows, that he looseth a flatterer,—and shoeth a shrew.

Now are horse-clawers—shamefully clothed ;—they busk them with buttons —as it were a bride :—with low laced shoes—of a heifer's hide,—they pick out of their provender—all their pride.

Whoever reckons with knaves—their expense,—the perverseness of the lad,

Thah he ȝeve hem cattes-dryt
To huere companage,
ȝet hym shulde a-rewen
Of the arrerage.

Whil God wes on erthe
And wondrede wyde,
Whet wes the resoun
Why he nolde ryde ?
For he nolde no grom
To go by ys syde,
Ne grucchyng of no gedelyng
To chaule ne to chyde.

Spedeth ou to spewen,
Ase me doth to spelle ;
The fend ou afretie
With fleis ant with felle !
Herkneth hideward, horsmen,
A tidyng ich ou telle,
That ȝe shulen hongen,
Ant herbarewen in helle !

—the pride of the page,—though he give them cats' dirt—for their sustenance,
—yet he shall rue—of the arrears.

While God was on earth—and wandered wide,—what was the reason—why
he would not ride ?—Because he would not have a groom—to go by his side,—
nor the grudging of any gadling—to jaw or to chide.

Haste you to spew,—as men do to spell (talk) ;—may the fiend devour you—
with flesh and with skin !—Harken this way, horsemen,—a tiding I tell you,—
that ye shall hang,—and be lodged in hell.

REIGN OF EDWARD II. 1307—1327.

Edward the First quitted the stage at a period when wars from without and internal troubles were gathering fast over his country. His son and successor, a weak and ill-advised prince, was little calculated to repel the one or to calm the other; and the following song shows us that, contrary to the general rule in such cases, the people were more sorrowful for their loss than pleased with the novelty of a new monarch.

LAMENT ON THE DEATH OF EDWARD I.

[MS. Bibl. Publ. Cantab. Gg. I. 1, fol. 489, of the reign of Edw. II.]

Seigniurs, oiez, pur Dieu le grant,
    Chançonete de dure pité,
De la mort un rei vaillaunt;
    Homme fu de grant bounté,
    E que par sa leauté
Mut grant encuntre ad sustenue;
    Ceste chose est bien prové;
De sa terre n'ad rien perdue.
    Priom Dieu en devocioun
    Que de ses pecchez le face pardoun.

TRANSLATION.—Lords, listen, for the sake of God the great,—a little song of grievous sorrow,—for the death of a precious king;—a man he was of great goodness,—and who by his loyalty—has sustained many a great encounter;—this thing is proved well;—of his land he lost none.—Let us pray God with devotion—that he pardon him his sins.

De Engletere il fu sire,
　E rey qe mut savoit de guere ;
En nule livre puet home lire
　De rei qe mieuz sustint sa tere.
　Toutes les choses qu'il vodreit fere,
Sagement les tinst à fine.
　Ore si gist soun cors en tere :
Si va le siècle en decline.

Le rei de Fraunce grant pecché fist,
　Le passage à desturber
Qe rei Edward pur Dieu emprist,
　Sur Sarazins l'ewe passer.
　Sun tresour fust outre la mere,
E ordine sa purveaunce
　Seint eglise pur sustenire :
Ore est la tere en desperaunce.

Jerusalem, tu as perdu
　La flour de ta chivalerie,
Rey Edward le viel chanu,
　Qe tant ama ta seignurie.

Of England he was lord,—and a king who knew much of war ;—in no book can we read—of a king who sustained better his land.—All the things which he would do,—wisely he brought them to an end.—Now his body lies in the earth ; —and the world is going to ruin.

The King of France did great sin,—to hinder the voyage—which King Edward undertook for God's sake,—to pass the water against the Saracens.—His treasure was beyond the sea,—and he ordains his purveyance—to sustain holy church :—now is the land in despair.

Jerusalem, thou hast lost—the flower of thy chivalry,—King Edward the old and hoary,—who loved so much thy lordship.—Now he is dead ; I know not

Ore est-il mort ; jeo ne sai mie
Toun baner qi le meintindra :
   Sun duz quor par grant druerie
Outre la mere vous mandera.

Un jour avant que mort li prist,
   Od son barnage voleit parler ;
Les chivalers devant li vist,
   Durement commenca de plurer.
   " Jeo murrai," dist, " par estover,
Jeo vei ma mort que me vent quere ;
   Fetes mon fiz rey corouner,
Qe Dampnt-Dieu li don bien fere !"

A Peiters à l'apostoile
   Une messager la mort li dist ;
E la Pape vesti l'estole,
   A dure lermes les lettres prist.
   " Alas !" ceo dist, " comment ? morist
A qi Dieu donna tant honur ?
   A l'alme en face Dieu mercist !
De seint eglise il fu la flour."

at all—who will maintain thy banner :—his gentle heart for great love—he will send you over the sea.

One day before death took him,—he would talk with his baronage ;—he saw the knights before him,—grievously he began to weep.—" I shall die," he said, " of necessity,—I see my death which comes to seek me ;—cause my son to be crowned king,—may the Lord God give him grace to do well !"

At Poitiers to the pope—a messenger told his death ;—and the pope put on the stole,—with bitter tears he took the letters.—" Alas !" he said, " how ? is he dead—to whom God gave so much honour ?—May God grant mercy to his soul !—he was the flower of holy church."

L'apostoile en sa chambre entra,
    A pein le poeit sustenir ;
E les cardinals trestuz manda,
    Durement commenca de plurir.
    Les cardinals li funt teisir,
En haut commencent lur servise :
    Parmy la cité funt sonir,
Et servir Dieu en seint eglise.

L'apostoile meimes vint à la messe,
    Oue mult grant sollempnité ;
L'alme pur soudre sovent se dresse,
    E dist par grant humilité :
    " Place à Dieu en Trinité,
Qe vostre fiz en pust conquere
    Jerusalem la digne cité,
E passer en la seinte tere !"

Le jeofne Edward d'Engletere
    Rey est enoint e corouné :
Dieu le doint teil conseil trere,
    Ki le pais seit gouverné ;

The pope entered in his chamber,—he could scarcely support it ;—and he sent for all the cardinals,—grievously he began to weep.—The cardinals made him desist,—aloud they begin their service ;—they cause the bells to be rung through the city,—and God's service to be performed in holy church.

The pope himself came to the mass,—with very great solemnity ;—he often applies himself to absolve the soul,—and said in great humility :—" May it please God in Trinity,—that your son may effect the conquest—of Jerusalem the noble city,—and pass into the Holy Land !"

The young Edward of England—is anointed and crowned king :—may God grant that he follow such counsel,—that the country may be governed ;—and

E la coroune si garder,
Qe la tere seit entere,
  E lui crestre en bounté,
Car prodhome i fust son pere.

Si Aristotle fuste en vie,
  E Virgile qe savoit l'art,
Les valurs ne dirr[ai]ent mie
  Del prodhome la disme part.
  Ore est mort le rei Edward,
Pur qui mon quor est en trafoun ;
  L'alme Dieu la salve garde,
Pur sa seintime passioun ! AMEN.

so to keep the crown,—that the land may be entire,—and himself to increase in goodness,—for his father was a worthy man.

If Aristotle were alive,—and Virgil who knew skill,—they would not say the value—of the worthy man a tenth part.—Now is dead King Edward,—for whom my heart is in desolation ;—may God preserve his soul in safety,—for the sake of his holy passion ! Amen.

The following song, in English, on the same event, is preserved in another manuscript. It is somewhat singular that one of these songs is clearly translated from the other, the variations being comparatively small, and consisting chiefly in the transposition of some of the stanzas. The French song was probably the original.

ELEGY ON THE DEATH OF EDWARD I.

[MS. Harl. No. 2253, fol. 73, r°. of the reign of Edw. II.]

Alle that beoth of huerte trewe,
   A stounde herkneth to my song,
Of duel that deth hath diht us newe,
    That maketh me syke ant sorewe among;
   Of a knyht that wes so strong,
Of wham God hath don ys wille :
    Me thuncheth that deth hath don us wrong,
That he so sone shal ligge stille.

Al Englond ahte for te knowe
    Of wham that song is that y synge ;—
Of Edward kyng that lith so lowe,
    ȝent al this world is nome con springe.
    Trewest mon of alle thinge,
Ant in werre war ant wys,
    For him we ahte oure honden wrynge,
Of Christendome he ber the prys.

Byfore that oure kyng wes ded,
    He speke ase mon that wes in care,—

TRANSLATION.—All that are true of heart,—a while hearken to my song,—
of grief that death hath wrought us now,—which makes me sigh and sorrow in
turns.—Of a knight that was so powerful,—on whom God hath done his will ;
—methinks that death has done us wrong,—that he so soon shall lie still.

All England ought to know—of whom the song is that I sing ;—of Edward
the king that lies so low,—through all this world his name sprang.— Trewest
man of all things,—and in war wary and wise,—for him we ought our hands to
wring,—of Christendom he bare the prize.

Before that our king was dead,—he spoke as one that was in care,—" Clergy,

SONG ON THE TIMES.

[MS. Reg. 12, C. xii. fol. 7, rº. of reign of Edw. II.]

Quant honme deit parleir, videat quæ verba loquatur;
Sen covent aver, ne stultior inveniatur.
Quando quis loquitur, bote resoun reste therynne,
Derisum patitur, ant lutel so shal he wynne.
En seynt eglise sunt multi sæpe priores ;
Summe beoth wyse, multi sunt inferiores.
When mon may mest do, tunc velle suum manifestat,
In donis also, si vult tibi præmia præstat.
Ingrato benefac, post hæc à peyne te verra ;
Pur bon vin tibi lac non dat, nec rem tibi rendra.
Sensum custodi, quasi mieu valt sen qe ta mesoun ;
Thah thou be mody, robur nichil est sine resoun.
Lex lyth doun over al, fallax fraus fallit ubique ;
Ant love nys bote smal, quia gens se gestat inique.
Wo walketh wyde, quoniam movet ira potentes :
Ryht con nout ryde, quia vadit ad insipientes.
Dummodo fraus superest, lex nul nout lonen y londe ;

TRANSLATION.—When a man has to speak, let him consider what words he utters ;—he ought to pay attention to them, lest he appear a fool.—When any one speaks, unless reason rest therein,—he is laughed at, and so he shall gain little.—In holy church there are often many who hold advanced situations ;—some are wise, many are inferior.—When a man may do most, then he exhibits his will,—in gifts also, if he will he gives thee presents.—Do a kindness to an ungrateful man, and afterwards he will scarcely look at you ;—he will not even give you milk for good wine, nor will he make you any return.—Take care of thy intellect, as of a thing which is worth more than thy house ;—although thou be moody, strength is nothing without reason.—Law lies down over all, false fraud deceives everywhere ;—and there is but little love, because people conduct themselves wickedly.—Woe walks wide, since anger moves those who are powerful ;—right cannot ride, because it goes to the ignorant.—Now that fraud is alive, law will not dwell in the land ;—and since the matter is in that

Et quia sic res est, ryth may nout radlyche stonde.
Fals mon freynt covenaunt, quamvis tibi dicat, " habebis."
Vix dabit un veu gaunt, lene les mon postea flebis.
Myn ant thyn duo sunt, qui frangunt plebis amorem ;
Ce deus pur nus sunt facienda sæpe dolorem.
Tresoun dampnificat, et paucis est data resoun ;
Resoun certificat, confundit et omnia tresoun.
Pees may nout wel be, dum stat per nomina bina ;
Lord Crist, that thou se, per te sit in hiis medicina !
Infirmus moritur, thah lechcraft ligge bysyde ;
Vivus decipitur, nis non that her shal abyde
Tels plusours troverez, qui de te plurima prendrount ;
Au dreyn bien verrez, quod nullam rem tibi rendrount.
Esto pacificus, so myh thou welde thy wylle ;
Also veridicus, ant stond pro tempore stille.
Pees seit en tere, per te, Deus, alma potestas !
Defendez guere, ne nos invadat egestas.
God Lord Almyhty, da pacem, Christe benigne !
Thou const al dyhty, fac ne pereamus in igne !

position, right may not easily stand.—The false man breaks his promise, although he say to thee, " thou shalt have it."—He will scarcely give an old
glove, ... thou shalt afterwards weep.—Mine and thine are two, which break
the love of the people ;—these two for us will cause frequent grief.—Treason injures, and reason is given to few ;—reason makes sure, while treason confounds all things.—Peace may not well be, while it stands by two names ;—
Lord Christ, do thou look to it, through thee may there be a medicine for these
things !—The sick man dies, although the art of medicine lie by his side ;—the
living man is deceived, there is none who shall abide here.—You will find many
such as will take very much from you ;—in the end you will see well, that they
will return you nothing.—Be pacific, so mayest thou possess thy will ;—also a
teller of truth, and stand for the time still.—May there be peace in the land,
through thee, God, kind power !—forbid war, lest want invade us.—Good Lord
Almighty, give peace, O benignant Christ !—Thou canst do all things, hinder
us from perishing in the fire.

The following song appears to have been made in the latter end of the year 1311, on the occasion of the King's journey to the North, where he was joined by his lately banished favourite, Peter de Gaveston, and disregarded the charter which he had confirmed in the beginning of the October of that year.

ON THE KING'S BREAKING HIS CONFIRMATION OF MAGNA CHARTA.

[The Auchinleck MS. in the Advocates' Library, at Edinburgh, art. 21, of the reign of Edw. II.]

L'en puet fere et defere,
    Ceo fait-il trop sovent;
It nis nouther wel ne faire;
    Therfore Engelond is shent.
Nostre prince de Engletere,
    Par le consail de sa gent,
At Westminster after the feire
    Made a gret parlement.
La chartre fet de cyre,
    Jeo l'enteink et bien le crey,
It was holde to neih the fire,
    And is molten al awey.
Ore ne say mès que dire,
    Tout i va à Tripolay,

TRANSLATION.—A person may make, and unmake,—it is what he too often does ;—it is neither well nor fair ;—on account of it England is ruined.—Our prince of England,—by the counsel of his people,—at Westminster after the fair—made a great parliament.—The charter he made of wax,—so I understand, and I readily believe it,—it was held too near the fire,—and is all melted away. —Now I know not what more to say,—all goes to Tripoly,—hundred, chapter,

Hundred, chapitle, court, and shire,
   Al hit goth a devel way.
Des plusages de la tere
   Ore escotez un sarmoun,
Of iiij. wise-men that ther were,
   Whi Engelond is brouht adoun.

The ferste seide, " I understonde
Ne may no king wel ben in londe,
   Under God Almihte,
But he cunne himself rede,
Hou he shal in londe lede
   Everi man wid rihte.
      For might is riht,
      Liht is night,
      And fiht is fliht.
For miht is riht, the lond is laweles ;
For niht is liht, the lond is loreles ;
For fiht is fliht, the lond is nameles."

That other seide a word ful god,
" Whoso roweth aȝein the flod,
   Off sorwe he shal drinke ;

court, and shire,—all it goes the devil's way.—Of the wisest men of the land—
now listen to a discourse,—of four wise men that there were,—why England is
brought down.

   The first said, " I understand—no king may be prosperous in land—under God
Almighty,—unless he can counsel himself,—how he shall in land lead—every
man with right.—For might is right,—light is darkness,—and fight is flight.—
Because might is right, the land is lawless ;—because darkness is light, the land
is without doctrine ;—because fight is flight, the land is without reputation."

   The second said a very good word,—" Whoever rows against the flood,—he

Also hit fareth bi the unsele,
A man shal have litel hele
  Ther agein to swinke.
    Nu on is two,
    Another is wo,
    And frend is fo.
For on is two, that lond is streintheles ;
For wel is wo, the lond is reutheles ;
For frend is fo, the lond is loveles.

That thridde seide, " It is no wonder
Off thise eyres that goth under,
  Whan theih comen to londe
Proude and stoute, and ginneth ȝelpe,
Ac of thing that sholde helpe
  Have theih noht on honde.
    Nu lust haveth leve,
    Thef is reve,
    And pride hath sleve.
For lust hath leve, the lond is theweles ;
For thef is reve, the lond is penyles ;
For pride hath sleve, the lond is almusles.

shall drink of sorrow ;—thus it fares by the unfortunate,—a man shall have little strength—to labour against it.—Now one is two,—another is woe,—and friend is foe.—Because one is two, the land is without strength ;—because weal is woe, the land is without ruth ;—because friend is foe, the land is without love."

    The third said, " It is no wonder—of these heirs that go under,—when they come to land—proud and stout, and begin to yelp,—but of anything that might help—they have nought in hand.—Now lust hath leave,—thief is magistrate,—and pride hath sleeves.—Because lust hath leave, the land is destitute of morality ;—because thief is magistrate, the land is pennyless ;—because pride hath sleeves, the land is without alms.

The ferthe seide, that he is wod
That dwelleth to muchel in the flod,
   For gold or for auhte ;
For gold or silver, or any wele,
Hunger or thurst, hete or chele,
   Al shal gon to nohte.
      Nu wille is red,
      Wit is qued,
      And god is ded.
For wille is red, the lond is wrecful;
For wit is qued, the lond is wrongful ;
For god is ded, the lond is sinful.

Wid wordes as we han pleid,
Sum wisdom we han seid
   Off olde men and ȝunge ;
Off many a thinge that is in londe,
Whoso coude it understonde,
   So have I told wid tongue.

Riche and pore, bonde and fre,
That love is god, ȝe mai se ;
   Love clepeth ech man brother ;

The fourth said, " That he is mad—who dwells too much in the flood,—for
gold or for property ;—for gold or silver, or any weal,—hunger or thirst, heat or
cold,—all shall go to nothing.—Now will is counsel,—wit is wicked,—and good
is dead.—Because will is counsel, the land is full of revenge ;—because wit is
wicked, the land is full of wrong ;—because good is dead, the land is full of sin."
   With words as we have played,—some wisdom we have said—of old men and
young ;—of many a thing that is in land,—whoever might understand it,—thus
have I told with tongue.
   Rich and poor, bond and free,—that love is good, ye may see ;—love calls

For it that he to blame be,
Forȝif hit him *par charité,*
   Al theih he do other.

Love we God, and he us alle,
That was born in an oxe stalle,
   And for us don on rode.
His swete herte-blod he let
For us, and us faire het
   That we sholde be gode.

Be we nu gode and stedefast,
So that we muwen at the last
   Haven hevene blisse.
To God Almihti I preie
Lat us never in sinne deie,
   That joye for to misse.

Ac lene us alle so don here,
And leve in love and god manere,
   The devel for to shende ;
That we moten alle i-fere

---

every man brother ;—for that for which he may be to blame,—forgive it him in charity,—although he do other.

Love we God, and may he love us all,—who was born in an oxe's stable,—and for us placed on the cross.—His sweet heart's blood he shed—for us, and bade us fairly—that we should be good.

Be we now good and steadfast,—so that we may at last—have the bliss of heaven.—To God Almighty I pray,—let us never die in sin,—to miss that joy.

But grant us all so to do here,—and live in love and good manner,—the devil

Sen him that us bouhte dere,
In joye withoute ende. AMEN.

for to shame ;—that we may all in company—see him that bought us dearly,—
in joy everlasting. AMEN.

Edward's wretched favourite, Peter de Gaveston, was beheaded by the Barons in the May of 1312. The two following
songs exhibit the general feeling of exultation which attended
this execution. It is scarcely necessary to say that they are
parodies on two hymns in the old church service.

SONGS ON THE DEATH OF PETER DE GAVESTON.

[MS. Trin. Coll. Cambr. O. 9. 38. 15th cent. on paper.]

I.

De Petro de Gaverstone.

Vexilla regni prodeunt,
　　fulget cometa comitum,
Comes dico Lancastriæ
　　qui domuit indomitum ;
Quo vulneratus pestifer
　　mucronibus Walensium,
Truncatus est atrociter
　　in sexto mense mensium.
Impleta sunt quæ censuit
　　auctoritas sublimium ;

TRANSLATION.—I. The banners of the kingdom go forth, the comet of Earls
shines, I mean the Earl of Lancaster, who tamed him whom nobody else could
tame ; whereby the pestiferous one being wounded by the blades of the Welsh,
was disgracefully beheaded in the sixth month. What the authority of the

Mors Petri sero patuit,—
    regnavit diu nimium.
Arbor mala succiditur,
    dum collo Petrus cæditur :—
Sit benedicta framea
    quæ Petrum sic aggreditur !
Beata manus jugulans !
    beatus jubens jugulum !
Beatum ferrum feriens
    quem ferre nollet sæculum !
O crux, quæ pati pateris
    hanc miseram miseriam,
Tu nobis omnem subtrahe
    miseriæ materiam !
Te, summa Deus Trinitas,
    oramus prece sedula,
Fautores Petri destruas
    et conteras per sæcula ! Amen.

powers above willed has been fulfilled ; the death of Peter at last has been effected,—he reigned much too long. The bad tree is cut down, when Peter is struck on the neck :—Blessed be the weapon which thus approached Peter ! Blessed be the hand which executed him ! blessed the man who ordered the execution ! blessed the steel which struck him whom the world would not bear any longer ! O Cross, which allowed to be suffered this wretched misery, do thou take from us all the material of misery. Thee, highest God in Trinity, we pray earnestly, destroy and crush for ever the maintainers of Peter. Amen.

II.

Pange, lingua, necem Petri qui turbavit Angliam,
Quem rex amans super omnem prætulit Cornubiam ;

II. Celebrate, my tongue, the death of Peter who disturbed England, whom

Vult hinc comes, et non Petrus, dici per superbiam.

Gens est regni de thesauri fraude facta condolens,

Quando Petrus de thesauro prodige fit insolens,

Quid ventura sibi dies pariat non recolens.

Hoc opus nostræ salutis, quod Petrus interiit;

Multiformis proditoris ars tota deperiit;

Ex nunc omen cor lætetur, quia væ præteriit.

Quando venit apta rei plenitudo temporis,

Est præcisum caput ei de junctura corporis;

Turbans turbas intra regnum nunc turbatur a foris.

Nulli volens comparari, summo fastu præditus,

Se nolente subdit collum passioni deditus;

De condigna morte cujus est hic hympnus editus.

Perdit caput qui se caput paribus præposuit:

Rite corpus perforatur cujus cor sic tumuit:

Terra, pontus, astra, mundus, plaudant quod hic corruit.

Trux, crudelis inter omnes, nunc a pompis abstinet;

Jam non ultra sicut comes, vel ut rex, se continet;

the king in his love for him placed over all Cornwall; hence in his pride he will
be called Earl, and not Peter.—The people of the kingdom was made sorrowful
for the fraud upon the treasure, when Peter becomes wastefully insolent with
the treasury, not bearing in mind what the future day may produce for him.—
This is the work of our salvation, that Peter is dead; all the artfulness of the multifarious traitor has perished; henceforth let the good omen rejoice our hearts, for
sorrow is past.—When the fulness of time which was fit for the thing came, his
head is cut off from the juncture of the body; he who raised troubles within
the kingdom is now troubled from without.—He who was unwilling to have an
equal, clothed in the extreme of pride, against his will bends his neck to the
executioner; of whose merited death this hymn is set forth.—He who placed
himself as a head above his equals, loses his own head; justly his body is
pierced, whose heart was so puffed up; both land, sea, stars, and world, rejoice
in his fall.—Ferocious and cruel among all men, he ceases now from his pomp;
now he no longer behaves himself like an earl, or a king; the unworthy man,

Vir indignus, morte dignus, mortem dignam sustinet.
Flexis ramis arbor illa ruit in proverbia ;
Nam rigor lentescit ille quem dedit superbia ;
Sic debet humiliari qui sapit sublimia.
Ædes Petri qua tenetur non sit fulta robore ;
Sit prophanus alter locus, sit et in dedecore,
Quem fœdus cruor fœdavit fusus Petri corpore !
Gloria sit creatori ! gloria comitibus
Qui fecerunt Petrum mori cum suis carminibus !
A modo sit pax et plausus in Anglorum finibus ! AMEN.

worthy of death, undergoes the death which he merits.—This tree with its branches bent falls into a proverb ; for the stiffness which pride gave is softened ; thus ought the ambitious and aspiring man to be humbled.—May the house of Peter, in which he is held, not be supported in strength ; may the other place be profane, and may it be in disgrace, which the filthy gore spilled from Peter's body has defiled !—Glory be to the Creator ! Glory to the Earls who have made Peter die with his charms ! Henceforth may there be peace and rejoicing throughout England ! AMEN.

————————

The events of the Scottish war during the reign of Edward II. were not of a character to draw forth the songs of triumph which had attended the campaigns of his father. The loss of his father's conquests, and the reverses of his own arms, while they produced universal dejection, only tended to widen the breach which his own folly had made between himself and his people. The following song was made in 1313, immediately after the disastrous battle of Bannockburn, where the Earl of Gloucester was slain. The writer, while he laments the humiliation to which his country had been reduced, glances from time to time at the evil counsels which had led to it.

THE BATTLE OF BANNOCKBURN.

[From MS. Cotton. Titus, A. xx, fol. 68 rᵒ. written in the reign of Ed. III.]

Quomodo comes Gloverniæ fuerat occisus apud Strivelyn,
et Anglici victi.

Me cordis augustia cogit mira fari,
Scotiæ quod Anglia cæpit subjugari :
Nova jam prodigia dicitur patrari,
Quando matri filia sumit dominari.
    Regionum Anglia plurium matrona,
Cuï tributaria jam dabantur dona,
Proth dolor! nunc cogitur nimis esse prona
Filiæ, qua læditur materna corona.
    Exiit per Angliam edictum vulgare,
Admonendo quempiam arma præparare,
Ut adiret Scotiam phalanx vendicare
Jura, vel injuriam posse vindicare.
    Ad quod thema debeam nimis protelare :
Rex cæpit militiam suam adunare,
Inconsultus abiit Scotos debellare.
Ira sponte rediit nolens plus obstare.

TRANSLATION.—Perplexity of heart compels me to tell wonderful things, that England begins to be subjected to Scotland : it is said that new prodigies are now performed, when the daughter takes upon her to lord it over the mother.—England the matron of many regions, to whom tributary gifts were given, is now, alas! constrained too much to be prostrate to the daughter, by whom the maternal crown is injured.—A general proclamation went through England, admonishing everybody to take up arms, that the army might go to Scotland to vindicate our rights, or to be able to avenge our injury.—To which theme I ought to procrastinate very much ; the king began to assemble his troops, unadvisedly he went to make war on the Scots : his anger voluntarily subsided, unwilling longer to hold out.—There were in the army many nobles,

Erant in excercitu plures generosi,
Milites in exitu nimis et pomposi;
Cum ad bellum venerant tot impetuosi,
Satis promti fuerant hostes animosi.

Animosi fuerant et hoc apparebat;
Cum partes certaverant, illa permanebat
Stabilis, sed fugiit quæ superbiebat.
Inproba succubuit, astuta vincebat.

Inauditus ingruit inter hos conflictus;
Primitus prosiliit Acteus invictus,
Comes heu! Gloverniæ dans funestos ictus;
Assistens in acie qui fit derelictus.

Hic phalangas hostium disrupi coegit,
Et virorum fortium corpora subegit;
Sed fautor domesticus sibi quem elegit,
Hic non erat putitus quando factum fregit.

Hic est proditorius vir Bartholomeus,
In cunctis victoriis quem confundat Deus!
Domino quod varius fit ut Pharisæus.
Hinc Judæ vicarius morte fiet reus.

knights who were too showy and pompous; when so many impetuous men
came to the conflict, the courageous enemies were ready enough.—They were
courageous, as will appear; when the two sides engaged, that one remained firm,
but that which had shown so much pride fled. The wicked party succumbed,
the cunning one conquered.—An unheard-of battle thickened between them;
first rushed forward the unconquered Actæus, the Earl of Gloucester, alas! giving
fatal blows; who, standing in the thick of the battle, is deserted.—He compelled
the troops of the enemy to break, and subdued the bodies of strong men; but
one of his own chosen retainers, he was not a fool when he ruined the affair.—
This is the traitorous man, Bartholomew, whom in all victories may God confound! Because he has been to his master as changeable as a Pharisee. Hence as
the representative of Judas he shall be condemned to death.—Seeing the enemy's

Videns contra dominum hostes desævire,
Fingit se sex seminum longius abire ;
Domino quod renuit suo subvenire,
Proditor hic meruit tormenta obire.

Plures sunt quem perperam comes est seductus,
Ut ovis ad victimam et ad mortem ductus,
Qui [sunt] per quos oritur tam vulgaris luctus,
Hoc satis cognoscitur per eorum fructus.

Quorum virus Anglia tota toxicatur ;
Vulgaris justitia sic et enervatur ;
Regale judicium per hos offuscatur ;
Ex hoc in exilium fides relegatur.

Victa jacet caritas, et virtus calcatur ;
Viret ingratuitas, et fraus dominatur ;
Quicquid in hiis finibus mali perpetratur,
Dictis proditoribus totum inputatur.

Iste deceptorius vir non erat solus,
Per quem proditorius jam fiebat dolus ;
Alter sed interfuit, quem non celet polus,
Et fiat ut meruit infernalis bolus.

---

rage against his master, he pretends that he had been out more than six weeks ; because he refused to come to his master's support, this traitor has deserved to be put to the rack.—Many are they whereby the Earl was seduced, led like a sheep to the sacrifice and to death ; through whom such common lamentation arises, is sufficiently known by their fruits.—With whose venom all England is poisoned ; and thus common justice is weakened ; by these the royal judgment is darkened ; in consequence of this, faith is driven into exile.—Charity lies subdued, and virtue is trodden down ; ingratitude flourishes, and fraud rules ; whatever of evil is perpetrated in this country, is all the work of the aforesaid traitors.—This deceitful man was not the only one by whom the art of treason was now exercised; but there was another concerned in it, whom may heaven not conceal, and may he become,

Hujusmodi milites, regno pervicaces,
Sathanæ satellites, sunt nimis rapaces;
Regis si sint judices undique veraces,
Destruent veneficos suos et sequaces.

Capitis sententiam pati meruerunt,
Cum sponte militiam talem prodiderunt;
Qui fuerunt rustici, sicut permanserunt,
Comitis domestici fugam elegerunt.

Hii fraude multiplica virum prodiderunt,
Inpia gens Scotica quem circumdederunt;
Ipsum a dextrario suo prostraverunt,
Et prostrati vario modo ceciderunt

Fideles armigeri qui secum fuerunt;
Milites et cæteri secum corruerunt;
Cum sui succurrere sibi voluerunt,
Hostibus resistere tot non valuerunt.

Sic comes occubuit præ cunctis insignis,
Qui sua distribuit prædia malignis;
Sibi quisque caveat istis intersignis,
Jam fidem ne præbeat talibus indignis.

as he deserves, a morsel of hell.—Knights such as these, obstinate against the
kingdom, retainers of Satan, are too rapacious ; if the King's judges every where
are true, they will destroy the enchanters and their followers.—They deserved to
suffer judgment of decapitation, since voluntarily they have betrayed such a sol-
diery ; the Earl's domestics, who were clowns, as they have remained, took to
flight.—These by a multifarious treason betrayed their lord, whom the impious
people of Scotland surrounded ; they struck him down from his steed, and the
faithful esquires who were with him fell struck down in different ways ; the
knights and others fell along with him ; when his friends tried to succour him,
they were not able to resist so many enemies.—Thus died an Earl who was
distinguished above all others, who had given his property to wicked men ; let
every one have a care to himself, after these examples, that he give not hence-

Ex hoc illi comites actibus periti,
Adhuc qui superstites sunt, fiant muniti,
Alias in prælio cum sistant uniti,
Ne sic proditorio telo sint attriti.
Cruciatur Anglia nimio dolore,
Tali quod versutia privatur honore,
Muniatur cautius mentis cum labore,
Error ne novissimus pejor sit priore.
Consulo comitibus adhuc qui sunt vivi,
Quod sint proditoribus amodo nocivi;
Sic et per industriam omnes sint captivi:
Anglici ad Scotiam fiant progressivi.
Credo verum dicere, non mentiri conor;
Jam cæpit deficere nostri gentis honor;
Comitem cum lividus mortis texit color,
Angliæ tunc horridus statim crevit dolor.
Nostræ gentis Angliæ quidam sunt captivi;
Currebant ab acie quidam semivivi;
Qui fuerunt divites fiunt redemptivi;

forth trust to such unworthy people.—By this let those Earls who are still alive,
learning from experience, be on their guard, when at another time they stand
united in battle, that they be not thus bruised by the weapon of treason.—England is tormented with very much grief, that she is deprived of her honour by
such craftiness; let her be fortified more cautiously, with labour of mind, that the
last error be not worse than the former.—I advise the Earls who are still alive,
that henceforward they destroy traitors; and thus by their industry let them all
be made prisoners; let the English thus make their way into Scotland.—I believe that I tell the truth, I endeavour not to say what is false; now the honour
of our nation begins to decline; when the livid colour of death spread itself
over the Earl, then immediately grew the terrible grief of England.—Of our
people of England some are in captivity; some ran away from the battle half
dead; they who were rich are made ransom; because the nobles go mad, the

Quod delirant nobiles plectuntur Achivi.

Mentes ducum Angliæ sunt studendo fessæ,
Nam fœdus justitiæ certo caret esse ;
Ergo rex potentiæ stirps radice Jessæ,
Fautores perfidiæ ducat ad non esse !

Quando sævit aquilum, affricus quievit ;
Et australi populo dampnum mortis crevit.
Anglia victoria frui consuëvit,
Sed prolis perfidia mater inolevit.

Si scires, Glovernia, tua fata, fleres,
Eo quod in Scotia tuus ruit hæres ;
Te privigni capient quorum probra feres ;
Ne te far . . facient, presens regnum teres.

Facta es ut domina viro viduata,
Cujus sunt solamina in luctum mutata ;
Tu es sola civitas capite truncata ;
Tuos casus Trinitas fæcundet beata !

common people are the sufferers.—The minds of the chieftains of England
are weary with studying, for the league of justice is without any certain existence ; may therefore the King of power, who sprang from the root of Jesse,
destroy utterly the maintainers of perfidy !—When the north-east wind rages, the
south-west wind dropped ; and to the people of the south the pain of death increased. England used to obtain victory, but by the treachery of the offspring
the mother hath lost her savour.—If you knew, Gloucester, your fate, you
would weep, because your heir perishes in Scotland ; thy sons-in-law will take
thee, from whom thou wilt suffer disgrace ; lest they should make thee ......
thou will bruise the present government.—Thou art made as a lady widowed of
her husband, whose comfort is changed into weeping ; thou art a solitary city
deprived of thy head ; may the blessed Trinity amend thy fortune !

The last piece in our collection is rather different in character from those which have preceded it. One of the most unpopular acts of this weak reign was the execution of the Earl of Lancaster in 1322. The love which the people bore towards him, led them to sanctify his memory. A martyr in what was loudly proclaimed to be the cause of God, his countrymen believed that he testified his unshaken love for those in whose defence he had fallen by miracles performed at his tomb, and a regular form of service was composed for his worship.

THE OFFICE OF ST. THOMAS OF LANCASTER.

[MS. Reg. 12, c. xii. fol. 1, r°. of the end of the reign of Edward II., or beginning of that of Edw. III., written all as prose.]

Ant.—Gaude Thoma, ducum decus, lucerna Lancastriæ,
Qui per necem imitaris Thomam Cantuariæ;
Cujus caput conculcatur pacem ob ecclesiæ,
Atque tuum detruncatur causa pacis Angliæ;
Esto nobis pius tutor in omni discrimine.

Oratio.—Deus, qui, pro pace et tranquillitate regnicolarum Angliæ, beatum Thomam martyrem tuum atque comitem gladio persecutoris occumbere voluisti, concede propitius, ut omnes qui ejus memoriam devote venerantur in terris, præmia condigna cum ipso consequi mereantur in cœlis, p. đn. ñ.

TRANSLATION.—*Anthem.*—Rejoice, Thomas, the glory of chieftains, the light of Lancaster, who by thy death imitatest Thomas of Canterbury; whose head was broken on account of the peace of the Church, and thine is cut off for the cause of the peace of England; be to us an affectionate guardian in every difficulty.

Prayer. O God, who, for the peace and tranquillity of the inhabitants of England, willed that the blessed Thomas thy martyr and Earl should fall by the sword of the persecutor, grant propitious, that all who devoutly reverence his memory on earth, may merit to obtain worthy reward along with him in heaven, through our Lord.

Prosa.—Sospitati dat ægrotos precum Thomæ fusio;
Comes pius mox languentum adest in præsidio;
Relevantur ab infirmis infirmi suffragio.
Sancti Thomæ quod monstratur signorum indicio,
Vas regale trucidatur regni pro remedio.
O quam probat sanctum ducem morborum curatio!
Ergo laudes Thomæ sancto canamus cum gaudio;
Nam devote poscens illum, statim proculdubio
sospes regreditur.

Sequentia.—Summum regem honoremus,
dulcis pro memoria
Martyris, quem collaudemus
summa reverentia.
Thomas comes appellatur,
stemmate egregio;
Sine causa condempnatur,
natus thoro regio.
Qui cum plebem totam cernit
labi sub naufragio,

Prosa. The pouring out of prayers to Thomas restores the sick to health; the pious Earl comes immediately to the aid of those who are feeble; they are relieved from their infirmities by the suffrage of one who was infirm. So that it is shown by the evidence of the miracles of St. Thomas, that the royal vessel is beheaded for the cure of the kingdom. O how the cure of diseases declares the sainted leader! Therefore with rejoicing let us sing praises to St. Thomas; for he who asks him devoutly, immediately without doubt he will return healed.

Sequence. Let us honour the highest King, for the memory of the sweet martyr, whom we join in praising with the utmost reverence. He is called Earl Thomas, of an illustrious race; he is condemned without cause, who was born of a royal bed. Who when he perceived that the whole commons were falling into wreck, did not shrink from dying for the right, in the

Non pro jure mori spernit,
lætali commercio.
O flos militum regalis,
tuam hanc familiam
Semper conserves a malis,
perducens ad gloriam! AMEN.

Pange, lingua, gloriosi comitis martyrium,
Sanguinisque præciosi Thomæ floris militum,
Germinisque generosi laudis, lucis comitum.
De parentis utriusque regali prosapia
Prodit Thomas, cujus pater proles erat regia,
Matrem atque sublimavit reginam Navarria.
Dux fidelis suum gregem dum dispersum conspicit,
Æmulumque suum regem sibi motum meminit,
Mox carnalem juxta legem in mirum contremuit.
Benedicti benedictus capitur vigilia,
Agonista fit invictus statim die tertia,
Diræ neci est addictus, ob quod luget Anglia.
Proht dolor! acephalatur plebis pro juvamine,

fatal commerce. O royal flower of knights, preserve ever from evils this thy family, bringing them to glory! AMEN.
    Declare, my tongue, the martyrdom of the glorious Earl, and of the precious blood of Thomas the flower of knights, and of the praise of the noble sprout, the light of Earls.—Thomas sprang from a royal race by both his parents, whose father was the son of a king, and whose mother Navarre raised to be a queen.—The faithful leader when he saw that his flock was dispersed, and he called to mind that his king was moved with jealousy towards him, soon according to the law of the flesh he trembled wonderfully.—The blessed man is taken on the vigil of St. Benet, on the third day he is suddenly made an unconquered champion, he is delivered to dire death, on account of which England mourns.—Alas! he is beheaded for the aid of the commons, he is deserted by the company of his

Suorumque desolatur militum stipamine,
Dum dolose desiandatur per sudam Hoylandiæ.
    Ad sepulcrum cujus fiunt frequenter miracula,
Cæci, claudi, surdi, muti, membra paralytica,
Prece sua consequuntur optata præsidia.
    Trinitati laus et honor, virtus et potentia
Patri, proli, flaminique sacro sit per sæcula,
Quæ nos salvat a peccatis Thomæ per suffragia! Amen.

O jam Christi pietas,
Atque Thomæ caritas
    palam elucescit!
Heu! nunc languet æquitas,
Viget et impietas,
    veritas vilescit!
Nempe Thomæ bonitas,
Ejus atque sanctitas,
    indies acrescit;
Ad cujus tumbam sospitas
Ægris datur, ut veritas
    cunctis nunc clarescit.

knights, whilst he is treacherously deserted by Robert de Hoyland.—At whose tomb are frequently performed miracles; the blind, the lame, the deaf, the dumb, and paralytics, by his prayer obtain the help they desire.—Praise and honour, virtue and power be to the Trinity, Father, Son, and Holy Ghost, for ever, which preserve us from sin through the intercession of Thomas! Amen.

O now the piety of Christ, and the charity of Thomas, shine openly! Alas! equity now pines away, and impiety flourishes, truth is made vile! Yet the goodness of Thomas, and his sanctity, daily increase; at whose tomb health is given to the sick, that the truth may now be clear to all.

Copiosæ caritatis
   Thoma pugil strenue,
Qui pro lege libertatis
   decertasti Angliæ,
Interpella pro peccatis
   nostris patrem gloriæ,
Ut ascribat cum beatis
   nos cœlestis curiæ. AMEN.

O Thomas, strenuous champion of plentiful charity, who didst combat for the law of England's liberty, intercede for our sins with the Father of Glory, that he may give us a place with the blessed in the heavenly court. AMEN.

APPENDIX.

EXTRACTS FROM PETER LANGTOFT'S CHRONICLE.

EDWARD THE FIRST'S WAR WITH SCOTLAND IN 1294.

[From a MS. in the Public Library of the University of Cambridge, Gg. I. 1, fol. 337, written early in the reign of Edw. II.—The Collations are from MS. Cotton. Julius, A. v. fol. 137, vº. (*C.*), of about the same age; and MSS. Reg. 20, A. II. fol. 123, rº. (*R.* 1), and 20, A. XI. fol. 105, rº. (*R.* 2), both of the fourteenth century.]

* * * * *

Gales soit maldit de Deus e de Saint Symoun !
Car tuz jours ad esté pleins de tresoun.

E SCOCE soit maldit de la Mere Dé !
E parfount à diable Gales enfoundré !

VARIOUS READINGS.—The two first lines are wanting in C.—1. *Dieu*, R. 1 and 2.—2. *plein*, R. 1 and 2.—3. *maudite*, C.

TRANSLATION.—May Wales be accursed of God and of St. Simon !—for it has always been full of treason.

May Scotland be accursed of the mother of God !—and may Wales be sunk

En l'un ne en li autre fust unkes verité.
Car si toust en Gales guere est comencé,
Et de Aquitaine le covenaunt taillé
Fu par le rai de Fraunce rumpu e refusé,
E Edward e Philippe comencent medlé,
10 Li fol rai de Escoce, Jon Baliol nomé,
Qe par le ray Edward al regne est aproché,
Par l'enticement de sun faus barné,
Encuntre sun homage e encuntre sa fealté,
Ad la court de Rome ad messagers maundé,
A Celestine la pape, ke al houre tint le sé,
Par suggestioun ad fausement demustré
Qe le regne d'Escoce ouf la dignité
Dait de li tenir par antiquité,
Et li rais Edward par poer e posté
20 Li fist fere homage encuntre volonté ;

VARIOUS READINGS.—5. *ne l'autre fu,* C.—9. *Et Sir Eduuard,* C. *co-
menscait,* R. 1.—10. *Bayllolf,* C. *Baylliolf,* R. 1. *Johan Baillol,* R. 2.—12.
Par le consail . . . . fol b., C.—15. *que cel h.,* R. 2.—16. *ount . . . . moustré,*
C. *ad . . . . moustré,* R. 1 and 2.—19. *le rei,* R. 2.

---

down deep to the devil !—In neither of them was there ever truth.—For as soon
as war was commenced in Wales,—and the covenant which had been cut out in
Aquitaine—was broken and refused by the King of France,—and Edward and
Philip began hostilities,—the foolish King of Scotland, named John Baliol, —
who was brought to the kingdom by King Edward,—by the seductions of his
false baronage,—against his homage and against his fealty,—sent messengers to
the court of Rome—to pope Celestin, who at the time held the see,—by a
trick falsely showed—that the kingdom of Scotland with the dignity—ought
to hold of him by testimony of ancient times,—and that King Edward by force
and might—made him do homage against his will ;—and prays that he may be

E prie q'il seit assolz e devolupé
De la fay le ray, à ki il fu joré.
La pape Celestine, trop desayvisé,
Assolt le rai d'Escoce par lettre enbullé.
Si toust cum en Escoce [la] chose est nuncié,
Les barnez unt fest ad lour hounteté
Duze peres d'Escoce, et sunt counsaillé
Desheriter Edward de la souverainté.
Pour le graunt honur ke Edward le sené
30 Fist à Johan Bailloil, tele est la bounté
  Dunt le rays Edward
  Du ray Johan musard
    est regwerdoné.
  De Escoce sait cum pot,
  Parfornir nus estoet
    la geste avaunt parlé.

QUANT Morgan est renduz, e Madok est pris,
 Le ray revient à Loundres, par cunsail des amys.

VARIOUS READINGS.—22. *la fay ly roys*, R. 1.—23. *fu trop*, R. 2.—25. *la chose*, C., R. 1.—27. *en Escoce*, C.—28. *Sire Edward à la s.*, R. 1.—30. *Bayllof*, C., R. 1.—32. *mosard*, R. 1.—37. *Morgar*, R. 2.

---

absolved and delivered—from his faith to the king, to whom he was sworn.—
Pope Celestin, too unadvised,—absolves the King of Scotland by his bull.—As
soon as the thing is announced in Scotland,—the barons have made to their
disgrace—twelve peers of Scotland, and have taken counsel—to disinherit Edward of the sovereignty.—For the great honour which Edward the prudent—
did to John Baliol, such is the goodness—with which King Edward—by King
John the sleeveless—is rewarded.—With Scotland let it be as it may,—it is needful for us to complete—the history before mentioned.

When Morgan has submitted, and Madoc is taken,—the king returns to

Deus chardinals de Rome la pape i ad transmys,
40 Ke ouf le ray de Fraunce parleint à Parys;
Del amur entre eus la pape est entremys.
Les chardinals al rai ount dist lur avis;
Edward e Philippe ount durement requis
Reposer une pesce chascoun en son pais,
Issint qe bone gent de poer e de pris,
Qe ad nule parte se facent enemys;
Ou la pape meissme sait par là justis,
Ad parfere l'acorde de quant qe sait mespris.

TAUNT cum les cardinales de la pes parlaint,
50   Les gens de Normendie suz Dover arivaint,
En la compaignie les Kauleys estaint.
En la vile de Dover sodainement entraint,
E parti du burge arder comensaynt;

VARIOUS READINGS.—40. *plaint*, R. 1.—41. *ad entremys*, R. 1. *s'est entremis*, R. 2.—42. *al rays*, C. *le reis*, R. 1.—43. *Sir Eduuard*, C. *E Edward*,
R. 2.—45. *Issi ke*, C., R. 1. This line is omitted in R. 2.—47, 48. *soit*, R. 2.
—50. *suth Dover*, C.—51. *les Kalays*, C. *Calays*, R. 1 and 2.

London by the advice of his friends.—Two cardinals of Rome the pope has sent
there,—who had talked with the King of France at Paris;—the pope has interfered to establish love between them.—The cardinals have stated their object
to the king;—pressingly they have requested Edward and Philip—to remain in
peace each in his country,—like good people of power and value,—who on no
side make themselves enemies;—or that the pope himself should be their judge,
—to effect the reconciliation wherever might be the trespass.

Whilst the cardinals were talking of the peace,—the people of Normandy
came to Dover,—along with them were those of Calais.—They entered suddenly into the town of Dover,—and began to burn a part of the town;—of young

Des joevenes e des vels .xiii. homes tuaynt.
Quant vindrent à la cunte .x. pur un lessaint.
Li gardain du chastel e cels qe manaynt,
En meismes de la celle, ke bien se gwiaint,
Se pristrent à defense, e les escriaint ;
Normaunz e Picards, ke forfet avaint,
60 Furent degagés ; les chapels demorraint
Ouf le chef des uns, le[s] autres s'en alaint.
Un moygne i fu pur veir, à ki .xx. enclinaint,
E si les assolt, mot plus ne savaint.
Les cardinals après ad Paris repeiraint ;
Ne sai leqel respouns du ray enportaint.
Noun pur ceo plusurs entre els disaint,
Qe toutes les parlaunces à drein descendaint,
Ke Edward e Philippe lur gent sustrarraint,

VARIOUS READINGS.—54. *i tuaynt*, C.—55. *.xx. pur un*, R. 1.—56. *del chastel et cel ke la m.*, C.—57. *Et moynes de la c.*, C. *E moignes*, R. 1 and 2. —59. *Pikard*, C. *forfez*, R. 1.—61. *Of les chefs*, C., R. 1 and 2.—62. *Un moyne de la celle à ky*, C.—63. *Et cyl les .... sonaynt*, C., R. 1 and 2.—65. *Ne sai quels respouns*, C., R. 2. *Ne say quel respons*, R. 1. *reportaient*, R. 2. 67. *Qe totes .... descendraint*, R. 1.—68. *lur genz suthrayeraynt*, C., R. 2. *gentz*, R. 1.

---

and old they killed thirteen men.—When they came to the reckoning, they left ten for one.—The keeper of the castle and those who remained,—and the monks of the cell, who bare themselves well,—took to their defence and cried out upon them ; —Normans and Picards who had put themselves in debt,—were let out of pledge ; the hats remained—with the heads of some, the others went away.—There was a monk in truth, to whom twenty bowed down,—and he absolved them all, they knew not a word more.—The cardinals afterwards repaired to Paris ;—I do not know what answer they carried from the king.—Nevertheless divers among them said,—that all the conversations would come to this at last,—that Edward and Philip should withdraw their people,— so that people should go by sea

Issi qe genz par mer et par tere irraint
70 En soffraunce de pesse, ke amys purraint ;
Parfournir l'acorde les Englais volaint,
Et les Alemaunz ad sei se assentiraint.

TAUNT cum les cardinals se sunt entremis
De reformer la pes, e fere les rays amis,
Thomas de Turbevile, ke ad Rouns fu pris,
Taunt ad parlé al provost de Parys,
Ke fet l'ad soun homage, et hostages mys
Ses deuz fiz en garde, e seurement promis
Aler en Engletere espier le pais,
80 E dire al ray Edward k'il vent futifs,
Eschapé de prisoun par mi ses amys.
Le provost l'ad graunté, e fet en ses escris
Cent lievre de tere par autel devis ;

VARIOUS READINGS.—69. *ou par tere*, R. 1. *Issint que gent*, R. 2.—71.
le volaynt, C. *la volaint*, R. 1.—72. *à ço se as.*, C. *Si les A. . . . à ceo*, R. 1.
—74. *De perfornir*, R. 1.—75. *Tourbevyle- . . à Ryouns*, C. *à Riouns*, R. 1 and
2.—76. *en taunt . . of le p.* C. *En taunt*, R. 1.—77. *hostage*, C., R. 2.—80.
al rays . . . . ke il vynt, C.—81. *Eschapa de p. par my ses enemys*, C. *enemys*,
R. 1 and 2.—83. *liverez*, C. *liveres*, R. 2.

---

and by land,—in sufferance of peace, as friends could ;—the English would perform the agreement,—if the Germans would agree with them.

Whilst the cardinals are interfering—to re-establish the peace, and to make
the kings friends, — Thomas de Turbevile, who was taken at Rion,—has
talked so much to the Provost of Paris,—that he has done his homage to him,
and given as hostages—his two sons in keeping, and solemnly promised—to go
to England to spy the country,—and to say to King Edward that he came a
fugitive—escaped from prison among his enemies.—The Provost agreed to it,
and put in his writing—a hundred pounds of land on such a devise ;—and

Et Thomas l'affiaunce sur les evangelis,
Ke tut Engletere e Walays e Marchis,
E du regne d'Escoce quanke sunt de pris,
Serrunt enclinaunz à Philippe fiz Lowis.

ESCOTEZ ore coment la grace Jhesu Crist
Li gentil rays Edward de la traisoun garnist.
90 Thomas en Engletere vint ad rais e dist,
Ke hors de la prisoun nutauntre issist,
E pur amur Sire Edward à tel peril se prist.
Curtaise assez li ray li countrefist ;
Et Turbevile après de jour en jour enquist
L'estate de la tere, et sun aler purvist
De leu en leu enqueir de graunt e de petist,
Coment as Englais peut fere tel despit,
Ke li rais Edward sa tere perdisist.

VARIOUS READINGS.—86. *kant ke*, C.—87. *enclynaunt*, C., R. 1 and 2.—
89. *Ly gentiz ray Ed.*, C. *rei*, R. 2.—90. *al ray*, C. *au rei*, R. 2.—91. *nuyt
auntre issist*, C. *nutaunte*, R. 2.—92. This line is omitted in C. *l'amur Edward à tielle se p.*, R. 1 and 2.—93. *Curtaisye .. li rays*, C., R. 1. *Curtaisie,*
R. 2.

Thomas pledges on the Gospels,—that all England, and Wales and the Marches,
—and all who are of value in the kingdom of Scotland,—shall bow to Philip
the son of Louis.

Hear now how the grace of Jesus Christ—warned the gentle King Edward of
the treason.—Thomas came to England and said to the king,—that he had escaped out of prison by night,—and that he had run so great a risk out of love
to Sir Edward.—The king showed him in return courtesy enough ;—and afterwards Turbeville inquired day by day—the state of the land, and provided for
his going—from place to place to seek of great and of little,—how he could do
such injury to the English,—that King Edward should lose his land.—The

L'estate de tote part, tel cum entendist,
100 Of les cardinals par un de sons tramist
Al provost de Paris, ke joie assez en fist.
Li cleirs ke la lettre ad Turbevile escrit,
Ad plus privé le rais l'entente descoverist.
Li lers l'aparcust, ad fust tost se mist,
Un serjaunt as armes, ke plus près suist,
Le tierz jour après le Turbevile surprist.

L E traitour est pris, e à Lundres remené,
    Ouf mult grant fausine ke sur lui fust trové.
Chose[s] que sunt dites, quels il ad graunté,
110 Par volunté le rai sunt mis desuz pié,
Jeskes seo sècle seit autrement turné.
Turbeville en curt cum traitur est jugé ;
Par my la vile de Lundres primes fu trainé,

VARIOUS READINGS.—99. *Les estat de tote parz*, C. *L'estat de totes partz*,
R. 2.—102. *Li clerk*, C.—103. *le rei*, R. 2.—104. *Ly leers tost l'ap.*, R. 1.—
106. *Le tierce jour après le traytour soupryst*, C.—109. *Choses*, C., R. 1 and
2.—110. *le rays*, C., R. 1. *mis suth pé*, R. 2.—111. *Jekes à ço. .... chaunyé*,
C., R. 1. *chaungé*, R. 2.—113. This line is omitted in C.

---

condition of every part, as he understood it,—he sent over with the cardinals
by one of his own servants—to the Provost of Paris, who made joy enough
about it.—The clerk who wrote the letter for Turbeville,—made known its contents to the king's most secret counsellor.—The thief got to know this, and
immediately took to flight ;—a serjeant at arms, who followed him very closely,
—surprised Turbeville the third day after.

   The traitor is taken, and brought to London,—with very great wickedness which
was found upon him.—The things which are aforesaid, which he had agreed to do,
—by the king's will are put under foot,—until the world is otherwise turned.—
Turbeville is judged in the court as a traitor ;—he was first drawn through the

E puis pendu cum lers, pur sa malfeté.

Pur nostre rais Edward mult ad Deus overé

Ore et autre fiez ad sa sauveté.

QUANT de Turbeville fet est la vengaunce,
   Les cardinales de Rome repeirez en Fraunce

Ont ouf le rei Phelippe sovent eu parlaunce,

120 Et sovent requis li rais des Alemaunce,

E par clers e leys ount fet demoustraunce

Ad gentil rais Edward, ke dure est les destaunce

Dunt li e Philippe sunt en descordaunce ;

Par ount il unt fet une tele ordinaunce,

Ke li e les deus rais enverrount sanz tarjaunce

A Kaumbré clers e lays de grant conyssaunce,

Ad trere de la pees, e juger la grevance,

VARIOUS READINGS.—114. *E pendu .. malveté*, R. 1. *maveisté*, R. 2.—115. *rei*, R. 2.—118. *repairent*, C.—120. *ly ray*, C. *del Almaunz*, R. 1. *le rei*, R. 2.—122. *rey*, R. 1 and 2.—125. *Ke ly e ly altre env.*, R. 1 and 2.—126. *à Kaumbray*, C. *Kambrai*, R. 1. *Kaunbrai*, R. 2.—127. *d treter*, C., R. 1 and 2.

---

town of London,—and then hanged like a thief, for his malpractices.—For our King Edward God has interfered much—now and at other times for his safety.

When vengeance is done upon Turbeville,—the cardinals of Rome, who had repaired to France—have had frequent conversation with King Philip,—and have often besought the King of Germany,—and have demonstrated by clerks and laymen—to the gentle King Edward, that the variance is hard—about which he and King Philip are at discord ;—whereby they have so ordained the matter,—that he and the two kings shall send without delay—to Cambrai clerks and laymen of great knowledge,—to treat of the peace, and to

E fere les amendes de la contrariaunce.

Ly rays Edward s'assent en bone affiaunce ;

130 A Kaumbray ad maundé saunz nule delaiaunce

Eveskes e barouns de graunt apparaunce :

Les garde de tresoun Dieu par sa puissaunce !

TAUNT cum cels seignurs sunt alez cel message,

Sire Edmund frere le rai de gentil corage,

Le counte de Nincole ouf toute sun menage,

Sir Willeam de Vescy, chivaler prus e sage,

.Barouns e vavasours de gentil linnage,

Chivalers e serjaunce ouf lur cosynage,

Genz à pié saunz noumbre de more e de boscage,

140 E Galais qe sevent combatir par usage,

Sunt alez en Gascoyn, e entrés en passage,

Ouf .xxx. et .vi. baners de meillur escuage

Ke feust en Engletere, salve le vacellage

VARIOUS READINGS.—134. *le rays*, C. *ly roys*, R. 1.—135. *Nicole of tote
ses menages*, C.—139. *gent*, R. 2.—142. *Of .xxvj. baneresce del m.*, C. *Ouf
.xx. et .vj.*, R. 1. *od vint e sis*, R. 2.—143. *vassellage*, R. 1 and 2.

---

judge the grievances,—and to make the amends for the war.—King Edward
agrees to it with good faith ;—to Cambrai he has sent without any delay—
bishops and barons of great account.—May God by his power guard them from
treason !

While these lords are gone upon this message,—Sir Edward the brother of the
King of gentle spirit,—the Earl of Lincoln with all his retainers,—Sir William de
Vescy, a good and prudent knight,—barons and vavasors of gentle lineage,—
knights and sergeants with their cousinage,—footmen without number from moor
and wood,—and Welshmen who know how to fight from frequent practice,—are
gone into Gascony, and entered on the passage,—with thirty-six banners of the
best escuage—that was in England, except the vassalage—of those who now

De cels qe ore ne faillent ad lour seignurage.
Car cels qe sunt remis garder lur heritage,
Ad le rei requis e pris en sun veiage
Sur le ray d'Escoce e sur sun fals barnage,
Ke ad ray Edward dedient lur homage.
Le primer jour de Marce, en tot le graunt orage,
150 Vint le ray Edward à trop grant costage
A Novechastel-sur-Tyne, pur le graunt utrage
Ke les fels mastins ount bracé par folage.
Nostre rays Edward ait la male rage !
Et ne les prenge e tiènge si estrait en kage,
Ke rien lour demourge après sun taliage,
Fors soul les rivelins et la nue nage.

R OBERT de Ros de Werke des Englais s'en fuist,
E ouf les genz d'Escoce à la gwere se mist.
Li rais Sire Edward sun chastel seisist,

VARIOUS READINGS.—146. *en son menage*, R. 1.—147. *et sun fol barnage*,
C.—148. *ke al rays*, C.—150. *ly rois*, R. 1.—151. *Newechaustel*, R. 1.—152.
ke les fols, C. *bracez*, R. 1.—153. *rays Sir Eduuard*, C.—154. *Si il ne les*, R.
1. *S'il ne les*, R. 2.—156. *rivelinges*, C. *à la nue n.*, R. 1.—158. *od le rei se
mist*, R. 2.—159. *le rei*, R. 2.

---

perform their seignorage.—For those who are left to guard their inheritance,—the
king has required and taken into his expedition—against the King of Scotland
and his false baronage,—who have withdrawn their homage from King Edward.—
The first day of March, in all the great storm,—comes King Edward with very
great purveyance,—to Newcastle-upon-Tyne, for the great outrage—which the
wicked dogs have effected in their folly.—May our King Edward suffer the "male
rage,"—if he does not take them and hold them so fast in cage,—that nothing shall
remain after his taillage,—except only their rivelings and their bare backsides.

Robert de Ros of Wark fled from the English,—and entered into the war
with the people of Scotland.—The King Sir Edward seized his castle,—held

160 La feste de pasche y tint, après s'en partist
  Devers Berwike-sur-Twede, e la vile assist.
  Le people maluré al primour surprist
  Deus navez des Englais, e tuer le fist.
  Li rays Edward l'oit dire, les portes assailist ;
  Les fossés passait li Englais sanz respit.
  Le vendredi de pasche ad truele conquist
  La vile de Berwike ; li Englais lo occist
  Quatre mile de Escoce, e autres plus perdist.
  Chivaler un saunz plus Sire Edward i perdist,
170 Richard de Cornewalle, un Fleming li ferist
  Hors de [la] sale rouge d'u[n] quarel qu'il tendist.
  Tost fu la sale pris, le fu en fist tut quist.
  Li gardein du chasteil quant la force vist,
  Le chastel saunz assalt al rais Edward rendist.

VARIOUS READINGS.—160. *de la paske,* C. *departist,* R. 1.—161. *Vers B.,*
R. 1.—163 *les fist,* C.—165. *les Englais,* C.—166. *al releve conquyst,* C. *al
revele,* R. 1. *au relevée,* R. 2.—167. *i occyst,* C. *Les Englais oc.,* R. 2.—168.
e ankes plus, C., R. 1 and 2.—171. *du sale,* C. *de la sale,* R. 1 and 2. *d'un,*
R. 2.

----

the festival of Easter there, and afterwards went—towards Berwick-on-Tweed,
and besieged the town.—The ill-fated people at first surprised—two ships of
English, and put them to death.—King Edward heard of it, and attacked the
gates ;—the English passed the ditches without respite.—On Easter Friday in
the afternoon he conquered—the town of Berwick ; the English slew there—
four thousand Scotchmen, and many others perished.—Sir Edward lost there
one knight and no more,—Richard de Cornwall [was he], a Fleming struck
him—with an arrow which he shot out of the red hall.—Soon was the hall
taken, the fire cleared the way.—The keeper of the castle when he saw the
necessity,—delivered the castle to King Edward before it was assaulted.—Wil-

Willeam de Douglasse dedens esteit elist,
E Ricard Fresel, pur fere al ray despit;
Le ray les ad prisoune, merci Jhesu Crist!

L̤I quens de la Merche, Patrik li renomé,
    Ad la pes le rays se rendist de gré;
180 Gilbert de Umfravile avaunt fust demoré
Ouf le rais Edward, à ki il fu joré;
Sire Robert de Brus of toute sa mesné
Vers le rais Edward tint tuz jours sa fealté,
Encuntre les Escotes amurs li ad mustré.
Quant Berwike fu pris, [de]denz estait trové
Or e argent saunz noumbre, des altres metals plenté,
E toute la nobley ke apendait à cité.
Ly Bailloill ad perdu li issu e l'entré
De la plus noble vile qe fust en sa poesté.
190 Le rais Edward la tent conquis par l'espé,

VARIOUS READINGS.—176. *Richard Fres'*, C. *Simoun Fresel*, R. 1. *Simon Fresele*, R. 2.—177. *prisouns*, C., R. 1 and 2. *merciez*, R. 2.—179. *le rei.*— 181. *al rays*, C. *od le rei*, R. 2.—183. *vers le roy*, R. 1 and 2.—185. *dedenz estayt*, C., R. 1 and 2.—186. *or, argent assez, des*, C.—187. *la noblye*, C.— 188. *Balliolf*, C.

---

liam Douglas was chosen in it,—and Richard Fraser, to do injury to the king; —the king has them prisoners. Jesus Christ be thanked!

The Earl of the March, the famous Patrick,—of his own free will came in to the king's peace;—Gilbert de Umfraville before remained—with King Edward, to whom he was sworn;—Sir Robert de Bruce with all his household—holds always his fealty to King Edward,—and has shown him love in his wars against the Scots.—When Berwick was taken, there was found within it—gold and silver without measure, and plenty of the other metals,—and all the nobility which belonged to a city.—The Baliol has lost the issue and entry—of the noblest town that was in his power.—King Edward holds it conquered by the

La fet environner de fossé large e lé,
En restrovant l'Escote k'ad de li chaunté,
E par mokerie en Englais rymaié.
    Piket hym and diket him,
    On scorne saiden he,
        hu best hit mai be.
    He pikes and he dikes,
    On lengthe alle him likes,
        als hy mowe best y-se.
200   Scatered heir the Scotes,
    Hodred in the hottes,
        never thai ne the :
    Ritht if y rede,
    Thay toumble in Twede
        that woned bi the se.

VARIOUS READINGS.—191. This line is omitted in C.—192. *reprovant*, C.,
R. 1 and 2.—193. *rymeyé*, C., R. 1 and 2.—194. *Pykit*, C. *Pikit* ·· *dikit*, R.
2.—195. *scoren sayd*, C. *in scoren*, R. 1. *in scorn*, R. 2.—196. *best may*, C.
Where this line is given in place of line 199, which is omitted. It is the same
in R. 1 and 2.—197. *He dikes, he pikes*, C., R. 1 and 2.—198. *On lenche als
hym*, C. *On leyhe als hym*, R. 1. *als*, R. 2.—200. *Skaterd he the*, C. *Scatird
er*, R. 1. *are the Scottis*, R. 2.—201. *Hoderd in thar*, C. *Hodird in thaire*, R.
1. *Hodered in their*, R. 2.—202. *nevere*, R. 2.—203. ȝ*if*, R. 2.—204. *tumbed*,
C., R. 2. *toumbe*, R. 1.—205. *be*, R. 2.

----

sword,—causes it to be surrounded with a ditch large and broad,— in reproof
of the Scot who had sung of him,—and made rhymes in English for mockery.—
Let him pike and let him dike,—they said in scorn,—how it may best be.—He
pikes and he dikes,—in length as he likes,—as they may best see.—Scattered are
the Scots,—huddled in their huts,—they never thrive :—Right if I read,—they
tumble in Tweed—who dwelt by the sea.

TAUNT cum Sire Edward ouf cuntes e barouns
Fist Berwiche enclore de fossez envirrouns,
Issuz sunt d'Escoce trais countes, par nouns
De Mar, de Ros, de Montesce, [of] .xl. mile felouns ;
210 Estaint en la rute alaunt en tapisouns,
Tyndale unt destruite en cendres e carbouns,
La vile de Corbridge e deuz religiouns
De Exillesham e Lanercost en unt destruite par
arcouns,
Du people du pais ount fet occisiouns,
Enporté les biens, en chacé les chanouns.
Après la ravine cum foles e bricouns
Sunt alez de Dunbar à lur confusiouns.
Le chastel unt pris, estendent pavillouns,
Ad Counte de la Marche esteint les mesouns.

VARIOUS READINGS.—209. *De Mare, de Rosse, de Menethet, of .xl.*, C.
De Ros, Assetle, de Menetz, R. 1. *De Ros, Ascetel, de Menetest,* R. 2.—210.
alaunz, C.—211. *En passan unt d.,* R. 1. *En passaunt,* R. 2.—213. *De Hex-*
hilesham et Lanercost ennentiz par arsouns, C. *De Exilsham e Lanertoft enenty,*
R. 1. *De Exilham* .... *anenti,* R. 2.—215. *Emportez,* R. 1. *emportez* ....
enchacez, R. 2.—216. *ravye cum fols,* C.—217. *à Dunbar,* C., R. 1 and 2.—
218. *estendi,* R. 1.—219. *al counte,* C.

Whilst Sir Edward with earls and barons—caused Berwick to be surrounded
with ditches,—there are issued from Scotland three earls, by name—Mar, Ross,
and Menteith, with forty thousand rascals ;—they were going in the route in
parties,—they reduced Tindale to ashes and cinders,—the town of Corbridge
and the two monasteries—of Hexham and Lanercost they have destroyed by
fire,—they have made slaughter of the people of the country,—carried off their
goods, driven away the canons.—After the ravage like fools and miserable wretches
—they are gone to Dunbar to their confusion.—They have taken the castle, and
erect their tents,—the houses belonged to the Earl of the March.—King Edward

220 Le rais Edward l'oit dire, fet fere les somouns
Dunbar pur recovre, e prendre les larouns,
Ke de seint eglise unt fet destrucciouns.
Poy avaunt cel houre parmis les regiouns
Revint le cardinal de Kaumbrai ouf respouns,
E du ray de Fraunce, cum après orrums ;
Sire Amy de Sauvaye, quens de graunt renouns,
Vint en la compagnie, e Otes de Graunt-souns.
Cil vint hors de Cypre e ses compaignouns,
Ke quant Acres fu pris, la mer as [a]virrouns
230 En passaunt eschapaint, sanz autres acheisouns.
Avaunt vus ai cunté quels mals e quels tresouns
Sunt fet à seinte eglise à tort e saunz reisouns ;
E oy avez sovent en les sainz sermouns
Ke Deus est dreitureles en tuz sels werdouns :

VARIOUS READINGS.—220. This line is omitted in C. *Le rei*, R. 2.—225. *en orroums*, R. 2.—226. *Sir Emery de Sauvay*, C.—227. *Othes*, R. 1. *Sire Otes*, R. 2.—228. *de ses*, R. 1 and 2.—229. *avyrouns*, C., R. 1 and 2.—232. *Sont feez*, R. 1. *fez*, R. 2.—234. This line is omitted in R. 2.

---

heard tell of it, and issued summonses—to recover Dunbar, and take the thieves —who had made destruction of holy church.—A little before this time, through the regions,—the cardinal returned from Cambrai with an answer—of the King of France, as we shall hear afterwards ;—Sire Amy de Savoy, a count of great renown,—came in his company, and Otho de Grauntsoun.—The latter came with his companions from Cyprus,—who, when Acres was taken, escaped—by passing the neighbouring sea, without other accidents.—I have told you before what evil and what destruction—were done to holy church wrongfully and with-out reason ;—and you have often heard in the holy sermons—that God is just in

Ore oiez de Dunbar où saunz evasaiouns
Les enemys Deus sunt pris en faude cum motouns.

A N le meis de May, le mardi primer,
Ad Berwike-sur-Twede ouf le ray parler,
Coment les foles felouns, ke feseint arder
240 Exillisham e Lanercost, n'esparnaynt muster,
Pris avaint Dunbar, chastel sur la mer,
Ouf li quens Patrik tint sa mulier.
Li rais Sire Edward par taunt i fist maunder
Le counte de Garenne ouf tute sun poer,
Le counte de Warwik e Huge le [De]spencer,
Barouns e vavasours, chivaler, esquier ;
Sorrais e Norrais i alaint de bon quer ;
Assez de gent à pié i menent al mester,
E venent à Dunbar li chastel asseger.

VARIOUS READINGS.—236. *Deu,* C., R. 1 and 2.—237. *En le mays de May,* C., R. 1 and 2.—238. *oyst le ray,* C. *oit,* R. 2.—240. *Hexlesham,* C. *Exilsham e Lanertoft,* R. 1. *Exilham,* R. 2.—245. *le Despenser,* C. W. *Sire Hughe le Despenser,* R. 1. *e* is also omitted in R. 2.—247. *Surays et Norays,* C. *Sorais e Norais il a.,* R. 1. *Surrais,* R. 2.—248. *de genz .. et menent,* C. *gentz .. il m.,* R. 1.

---

all his dealings :—Now hear of Dunbar, where without evasions—the enemies of God are caught in a fold like sheep.

On the first Monday in the month of May,—at Berwick-upon-Tweed the king heard say,—how the foolish rascals, who had burnt—Hexham and Lanercost, nor spared the monasteries,—had taken Dunbar, the castle by the sea,—where the Earl Patrick kept his wife.—The King Sir Edward forthwith caused to be sent there—the Earl of Warenne with all his power,—the Earl of Warwick and Hugh le Despenser,—barons and vavasours, knights, squires ;—Southerns and Northerns went there right courageously ;—they take there footmen enough for their need,—and come to Dunbar to besiege the castle.—They prepared for the

250 Se atirent al saut, ne volent demorer.
Les foles felouns dedenz espairent ayde aver;
Se sotillent coment les Englais enginner.
Sire Richard Syward, ke solait demorer
Ouf nostre rays Edward ad robe e à dener,
Maundent par descayt ouf nos Englais treiter;
Si les vent, e dist, ke mult tres volenter
Les fra le chastel rendre, si il volent graunter
Treis jours de respit, ke il puissent consailler
Li ray de Ballioll, e lur estate maunder.
260 E si il cel houre ne venge le sege remover,
Le chastel renderunt sanz plus par là targer.
Hostage par taunt i mette, e fet nuncier
Al hoste de Escoce en meisme la maner,
Cum vus orrez après, le fet recorder.

VARIOUS READINGS.—250. *al assaut* .. *esparnyer,* C.—254. *rei,* R. 2—
255. *à nos,* C.—256. *Cyl les vynt,* C.—259. *Le rays de Bayllof et lur maun-*
der, C.—260. *E si cel h.,* R. 1 and 2.

---

attack, and would not delay.—The foolish felons within hoped to have aid ;—they plotted together how to trick the English.—Sir Richard Syward, who used to dwell—with our King Edward, at robe and pay,—they send deceitfully to treat with our English ;—so he comes to them, and says, that very willingly—he will cause the castle to be delivered to them, if they will grant—three days' respite, that they may consult—the King Baliol, and tell him their condition.—And if he at that time do not come to raise the siege,—they will deliver the castle without further delay.—Forthwith he gives hostages, and causes to be announced—to the host of Scotland in the same manner,—as you will hear after, he caused it to be recorded.

L I messager s'en va, e tost aprochait
Al ray Johan e al hoste ke ouf li estait,
Lur dist cum li Siward enfourmez l'avait.
"Sire rais, vos barouns demourent en dure plait
En la chastel de Dunbar, en chaunce les chascait ;
270 Car quant li rais Edward lur estre là saveit,
Parti de sun hoste illeukes maunder fesait.
Li Englais quant là vint le chastel assegait.
Sire Richard Siward, ke tuz les conussait,
Issist du chastel e taunt bien parlait,
Qe treve pur treis jours li Englais li otrait.
Pour quai la compaignie, ke illoek par vus alait,
Ad vus cum à seignur aler me commandait,
E dire veraiment ke home ne set ne vait
Dunt vus les porrez vendre, si non par descait,

VARIOUS READINGS.—266. *Al ray Jon Bayllof là ou il estayt,* C.—267.
enfourmé, R. 1.—268. *dur esplayt,* C., R. 1. *sire rei,* R. 2.—269. *en chauns,*
C.—272. *quant vynt,* C.—274. *taunt cum il porrait,* C. *taunt beel parlait,* R.
1.—275. *Pur trewe de .iij. . . grauntait,* C.—276. *par quai,* C.—279. Omitted
in R. 2.

The messenger goes, and soon came to—King John and to the host which
was with him,—he said to them as Siward had instructed him :—" Sir King,
your barons remain in hard strait—in the castle of Dunbar, in danger of being
driven out.—For when King Edward knew of their being there,—he caused part
of his host to be sent thither.—The Englishman, when he came there, besieged
the castle.—Sir Richard Siward, who knew them all,—issued from the castle,
and talked them over so well,—that the English gave him a truce for three days.
—Wherefore the company, who were there on your part,—commanded me to
go to you as to their lord,— and to say truly, that the man neither sits nor goes,
—who can hinder your coming, unless by some deceit,—within the term of

280   Dedenz le terme de treve ke l'Englais nus grauntait.
A demayn cele hour k'em manghehust e bait,
Alez de ceste part hastivement l'andrait;
Les nos du chastel vous verrunt par agait;
Istrunt sur li Englais ke lour venir ne creit;
Happés-les entre vous, si tenés-les si estreit,
Ke mès en champ ne venent fere à les voz surfait.
Vous ne avez autre vaie qe valer vous dait.
Ore armez-vous, si aloums, nul alme ne se trait
Qe nos enemis quant serrunt pris merci nul en ayt.
290   Ferrez du braund;
        Northumberlaund
            le vostre ert de drait;
       Tote Engletere
       Par ceste guere
            volez qe perdu sait:
       Unkes Albanie
       Par coup d'espeie

VARIOUS READINGS.—280. All which follows, to line 354, is omitted in R.
1.—281. *k'em mangeust,* C.—284. *sur les,* C.—286. *pur fere les voz,* C.—
288. *ne se retrayt,* C.—289. *qe serrunt.... n'eit* R. 2.—295. *voyliez,* C.

---

truce which the English has granted us.—To-morrow at the hour when people
eat and drink,—go hence hastily straight there ;—ours in the castle will watch
for you ;—they will issue upon the English who do not expect their coming,—
entrap them between you and hold them so tight,—that they shall no more
come in the field to do annoyance to yours.—You have no other way that will
avail you.—Now arm, and let us go, and may no soul survive—who shall have
any mercy on our enemies when they are taken !—Strike with the sword—Northumberland—will be yours by right ;—All England—by this war—you will
that it be lost :—Never did Albania—by stroke of the sword—do so great an

fist si bon esplait."
On grene,
300   That kindrede kene
gaderid als gait;
Y wene
On sum it is sene,
ware the bit bait.

A L dit le messager la route de rascaylle
Arenger se comence al foer de bataille.
Sir Richard Siward, qe dona ceste counsaille,
Vent à nos Englais, dis[t], " Si Dieu me vaille !
Jeo voy gent venir de mult grant apparaille,
310 Cum batailler vousissent, saunz numbre de pittaille.
Je vois, si vous [loez], feir .i. desturbaille,
Ke plus [près] ne venent." Les nos dient, " nun
kaille,"
E pernent li Siward, ke plus avaunt n'i aille;

VARIOUS READINGS.—299. on the g., R. 2.—300. kynered, C. kinred,
R. 2.—301. als the gait, R. 2.—303. summe it es, C. summe is it, R. 2.—
304. whar, C. whare, R. 2.—305. al route, C.—308. et dist si, C.—309.
genz, C.—311. vus loez fere .i. d., C.—312. plus près, R. 2. noun kaylle,
C., R. 2.

---

exploit."—On the green—that keen generation—gathered like goats ;—I reckon
—on some it is seen,—where the bit bit.

At the saying of the messenger the rout of vagabonds—begin to arrange themselves in order of battle.—Sir Richard Siward, who gave this counsel,—comes
to the English, and says, " God help me !—I see people coming in very great
apparel,—as though they would give battle, without number of footmen.—I go,
if you think well, to hinder them,—that they may not come nearer."—Our people
say, " Do not trouble yourself !"—And they take Siward, that he may proceed

Establient gardayns al porte e al muraille ;
Umfray de Boune le jovene tent le garde en baille,
Ke aide du chastel lur rergarde ne assaille ;
E mountent les destrers, les brouchent al mountaille,
Ke plus tost peust coure avaunt li altre saille.
L'Escote les vait venir, la cowe les turne cum quaille,
320 En enfuaunt se vole al vent cum fet la paille.
Les Englais après les chacent cum owaille,
Cum feust quant veit le lowe venir de boscaille.
Li surquider Escote quide ke countrevaille
Le duk sire Corynée, qe conquist Cornwaille.
De taunt des genz as armes mult ai grant mervaille
Ke nes un de tuz al fet vaut un maille,
Fors Patrick de Graham, ke demourt e daille
Del espé furbie, mes tuez est saunz faille.
Dis mil .l. et .iiij. sunt tuez al travaille ;

VARIOUS READINGS.—316. *lur'* ne regard ne, C. *rereward*, R. 2.—320.
S'en vole, C.—322. *Ke fuist*, C.—323. *surquiders*, C.—325. *De taunz de gens
armez*, C., R. 2.

no further ;—they place guards at the gate and at the wall ;—Humphrey de
Bohun the younger is keeper of the guard,—to hinder aid from the castle from
attacking their rear ;—and they mount their steeds, and spur to the hill ;—he
who can run fastest springs before the others.—The Scot sees them come, and
turns his tail like a quail,—he flies away as straw does before the wind.—The
English pursue them like a sheep—when it flies at the sight of the wolf issuing
from the wood.—The proud Scot imagines that he is as good as—the Duke
Sir Corineus, who conquered Cornwall.—Of so many men at arms I marvel very
much—that there is not one of them all worth a farthing in action,—except
Patrick de Graham, who remains and strikes—with the burnished sword, but
he is slain without fail.—Ten thousand and fifty-four are slain in the engage-

330 Trestuz sunt d'Escoce, le noumbre ai par taille.
   Cels furent les cheitifs [qe] demaglaynt le aumaille
   Par mi Northumberlaund, as chiens lessaint le[n]traille;
   Escomegez estaint al livre e kaundaille,
   Pur ceo ke saint eglise, ne prestre, ne clerjaille,
   Nent plus esparnent ke four ou toraille.
   Pecché les ad chacé à tele arivaille,
   Ke perduz unt al champ le chief oufveke l'oraille.
       The fote folke
       Puth the Scotes in the polke,
340   and nakned their nages :
       By waie
       Herd i never saie
              of prestre pages,
       To pike
       The robes of the riche

VARIOUS READINGS.—331. *les cheftayns ke demaglerent* C. *qe de.*, R. 2.—
332. *l'entraylle*, C., R. 2.—337. *les chefs of le oraylle*, C.—338. *fotfolk*, R.
2.—339. *That the*, R. 2.—340. *nackened thair nages*, C. *nakid their nages*, R.
2.—341. *By wai | her I nevere sai | of prestere p.*, R. 2.—343. *prester*, C.—
345. *rike*, C., R. 2.

---

ment ;—they are all Scots, I have the number by reckoning.—These were the
caitiffs who butchered the cattle—in Northumberland, and left the entrails to the
dogs.—They were excommunicated by book and candle,—because neither holy
church nor priest or clergy—they spared no more than bake-house or barn.—Sin
has driven them to such a hap—that they have lost in the field the head with the
ears.—The foot-people—put the Scots in the poke,—and made bare their backsides :—By way—heard I never tell—of readier pages,—to pick—the robes off

that in the felde felle.
Thai token ath tulke ;
The roglre raggi sculke
    rug ham in helle !

350 DE bataille ne puingce feust unkes recordez,
        Ke taunt de genz si tost estaient outraiez,
    N'ensint saunz defence lez renes rethornez.
    Corfs ayent les cors, les almes les malfez
    De trestuz k'esint gweres ount gwiez !
    Car de cele part fut unkes une fez,
    Deinz vile ne dehors, un bon fet esprovez,
    Mès for gopiller e robber les vilez,
    Arder seint eglise, tuer les ordinez,
    Cil Dieu sait loé k'ad Dunbar l'ad vengez !
360 Les countes qe avaint fet les malvestez,
    Si toust cum savoint e furent avisez

VARIOUS READINGS.—346. For this line and the three following, R. 2 has
—*And in the dik souue | Thou wiffin | Scot of Abrenityn, | cloutid is thi houue.*
—348. *roghe raggy sculke*, C.—351. *Ke taunz*, C.—352. *Ne issynt*, C.—353.
seient sauvez, R. 2.—354. *ke issint*, C.

---

the men,—who in the field fell.—They took of each man ;—the rough ragged
devil—tear them in hell !
    In battle or encounter it was never recorded—that so many people were de-
stroyed so soon,—or thus turned their backs without making any defence.—May
the crows have the bodies, and the devils the souls—of all that thus have conducted
the wars !—For of this part there was never once,—within town or without, a good
action proved,—but only prowling and robbing the towns,—burning holy church,
killing the clergy,—may God be praised who has revenged it at Dunbar !—The earls
who had done the wicked deeds,—as soon as they knew and were aware—of the

De la desconfiture sur lur parentez,
As Englais quant repairent le chastel ount liverez,
E saunz condiciouns els memes obligez
Al ray Sire Edward, dunt fere ses voluntez.
Li rais lendemayn i vint à ses barnez,
Le[s] prisouns ke sunt pris li unt presentez,
Treis countes, treis barouns, treis banerés nomez,
E saunz eus .xxviij. chivalers adubbez,
370 Ouf .v. vinz gentilles homes ke illeukes sunt trovez;
Deus clers e deus Pikards par entre sunt numbrez.
A la Tour de Loundres les countes sunt maundez.
Les uns de[s] baro[uns] les sunt associez;
A diverse chasteles les autres ad envoiez,
Par deus e deus ensemble une hakenai muntez,
Les uns en charrettes enfirgez les peez;
En tel pleit de carole lour jue est terminez!
Par my Engletere en toutes les countrez,

VARIOUS READINGS.—362. *de lur*, R. 1.—365. *Al ꞓeis*, R. 1.—366. *e ses
b.*, R. 1.—367. *les prisouns* .... *li sunt p.*, C., R. 1 and 2.—373. *Les uns des
barons*, R. 1 and 2.—375. *sur hakenays*, R. 1.—378. This line is omitted in C.

---

defeat of their kindred,—have delivered the castle to the English on their return,—and without conditions obliged themselves—to the King Sir Edward, to
do his will.—The king next day came there to his baronage,—the prisoners who
are taken they have presented to him,—three earls, three barons, three bannerets,
—and besides them twenty-eight dubbed knights,—with five score gentlemen
who were found there;—two clerks and two Picards are counted among them.—
The Earls are sent to the Tower of London.—Some of the barons are associated with them;—the others are sent to different castles,—two by two
mounted together on a hackney;—some with their feet fettered in carts;—in such
kind of dance their game ended!—Throughout England in every country—

De lur surquideri ert tuz jours parlés
380 Taunt cum le siècle dure, lour fet les ad mokés.
    For S[c]ottes
    Telle I for sottes,
                and wirches unwarre;
    Unsele
    Dintes to dele
                thaim drohg to Dunbarre.

DES ore est tens à dire du compassement
    Les .xii. peres d'Escoce, qe quidaint seurement
Engletere destrure, bien vous dirrai coment.
390 Quant le ray de Fraunce, après le dayllement
De cele mariage dunt fu parlé sovent,
Volait tenir Gascoyn par abatement;
E le rays Edward illok maunda sa gent,
E partie par gwere de su Frauncays reprent;
Li rai Johan d'Escoce, par l'enticement

VARIOUS READINGS.—380. *fet ad mokez*, R. 2.—381. *For Scottes*, C., R.
1. *For the Scottis*, R. 2.—383. *And wrecches unwar*, C. *wreches*, R. 1.
wecchis unwar, R. 2.—386. *tham drohu to Dunbar*, C. *droght*, R. 1. *drouh
to Dunbar*, R. 2.—390. *le dallyement*, C. *daliement*, R. 1.—394. *yuere sur
Fr.*, C. *sur Francais*, R. 1 and 2.

---

people will always talk of their pride—as long as the world lasts, people have
scoffed at their action.—For the Scots—I reckon for sots,—and wretches un-
wary;—ill luck—to give blows—drew them to Dunbar.
    Now it is time to tell the plot—of the twelve peers of Scotland, who thought
surely—to destroy England, I will just tell you how.—When the King of France,
after the breaking off—of that marriage which was often talked of,—would
retain Gascony by abatement,—and King Edward sent thither his people,—and
re-took a part by war from the French ;—King John of Scotland, by the entice-

De countes e barouns, de clers ensement,
Ad maundez en Fraunce par commune assent
L'eveske de Seint Andreu, par ki procurement
Frere le rai de Fraunce, Charles nomément,
400 Pur fiz le ray d'Escoce ad fet aliement,
Dount marier sa fille, e après par serment
Fraunsays e les Escoce irraint uniement
En Engletere destrure de Twede jekes en Kent ;
E ke le rai de Fraunce prendrait arivement
Qe l'houre q'il vousist, en Twede prestement,
Parunt Northumberlaund prendrait sodainement,
E peus la tere toute sanz desturbement ;
Ne larrait home en vie, ne pere ne parent.
La faus purparlauns saunz espleit attent ;
410 Le seneschall d'Escoce est venu bonement
Al rays sire Edward, auf quanke à li apent,

Various Readings.—397. *maundé*, R. 1.—400. *Pur le fiz*, C.—402. *les Escoz*, R. 1.—403. *En*, at the beginning of this line, is omitted in C., and R. 1 and 2.—406. *prendraynt*, C.—408. *ne frere*, R. 2.—410. *venu fayntement*, C. *venuz b.*, R. 1.

---

ment—of earls and barons, and of clerks also,—sent to France by common agreement—the bishop of St. Andrew's, by whose procurement—the brother of the King of France, namely, Charles,—made an alliance for the son of the King of Scotland,—who was to marry his daughter, and afterwards by oath—the French and Scots should go conjointly—into England to destroy from the Tweed to Kent ;—and that the King of France should land,—when he would, suddenly in the Tweed,—forthwith he should suddenly take all Northumberland,—and then all the land without hindrance ;—that he should not leave a man alive, neither father nor kindred.—The traitorous negotiation being entered upon without completion,—the seneschal of Scotland is come in without more ado—to the King Sir Edward, with all that belongs to him,—earls and barons and bishops

Countes e barouns e esveskes pleinement,
Sunt venuz à sa pes tut à sun talent.
Le ray Johan e sun fiz, saunz tere e tenement,
Sunt menez à Lundres à tenir jugement.
Ore ad li rays Edward Escoce enterement,
Cum Albanak l'avait al comencement.
  Galays, Yrays,
  Ad nos Englais
420   aident durement.
  Dunt les Escoz
  Ount par les noz
    emprisounement;
  Et cele tere
  Par ceste gwere
    est perdu finablement.
  Les Galais sunt repairés,
  E les Irrays retournez
    al sigle e al vent.

VARIOUS READINGS.—413. *encountre lur talent,* C.—415. *attender juge-*
ment, C.—416. *le rei,* R. 2.—417. Omitted in R. 2.—425. *par cel gwere,* R.
1.—426. *finablement,* C. *finalment,* R. 1 and 2.—427. *Les Walays,* C. *qe*
sont, R. 1.

---

fully,—are come to his peace all at his desire.—King John and his son, without
land or tenement,—are led to London to support judgment.—Now King Edward
possesses Scotland entirely,—like Albanac had it at the beginning.—The Welsh
and Irish—to our English—aid doughtily.—Whereby the Scots—have through
ours—imprisonment;—and that land—by this war—is lost for ever.—The
Welsh are gone home,—and the Irish returned—with sail and with wind.—You

430 Vous Englais i demorrez ;
  Devoutement prier devez
    ke Dampne-Deu defent,
  Aman recosilier,
  E Mardocheum exiler
    en regal parlement.
  Edward, par my tuz vos reisuns,
  Volez penser des arsouns
    du temple Deu omnipotent,
  Ad Exlysham, où cel hoste
440 De la croiz fesait roste,
    figure de humaine salvement.
  Herodes i fert, l'emphle mourt,
  En ceste anguisse Rachel plourt ;
    Edward, or fa le vengement.
  Tu averas jugé, jugez à dreit ;
  Soffrez qu'il pent ke pendre deit,

VARIOUS READINGS.—431. *Doucement*, C.—432. *Dampne Deu omnipotent*, C.—434. *E Marche*, R. 2.—436. *vos respons*, R. 2.—437. *Voilliez*, C.—438. *En temple*, R. 1.—439. *Hexelesham*, C. *Exilsham*, R. 1.—440. *de la croice fesaint*, C. *croice fesaunt*, R. 1.—442. *emphele*, R. 1. *Herodes fert, l'enfant murt*, R. 2.—445. *avera*, R. 1.—446. *suffrez pendre*, R. 2.

English remain there ;—you ought to pray devoutly—that the Lord God forbid, —to take Aman into favour again,—and exile Mardocheus,—in royal parliament.—Edward, amid all your accusations,—please to remember the burnings,— of the temple of God Almighty,—at Hexham, where that host—of the cross made roast,—the figure of human salvation.—Herod strikes there, the child dies,— in this anguish Rachael weeps ;—Edward, wreak vengeance for it.—Thou wilt be judge, judge according to right ;—let him hang who ought to hang,—the law

la ley le vol[t] certeinement.
La peine est dure e cruele,
Car ele est perpetuele,
450   à tuz qe jugent autrement.
Vos enemys ore chastiez,
K'il ne se movent altre fez,
en un novele torment.
Home dait mercy aver ;
Mès à traitour ne dait valer,
ilokes la ley la suspent.
Pur amy ne pur dener
Ray ne dait esparnier,
k'il ne juge owelement.
460   Si li ray volt Dieu servir,
La lei le convient maintenir ;
si noun, il pecche e mult mesprent.
Pur veir quant Johan Balliolle
Leissa sun livre e l'escole,

VARIOUS READINGS.—448. *molt cruele,* C.—453. *turnayment,* R. 1. *un
novel turnement,* R. 2.—456. *la lei les,* R. 2.—460. *Si li rays,* C.—463. *J. de
Bailliole,* R. 1.—464. *sun liver à l'escol,* C.

---

wills it certainly.—The punishment is hard and cruel,—for it is everlasting,—
for all who give judgment otherwise.—Now chastise your enemies,—that they
may not stir again—in a new mischief.—We ought to have mercy ;—but that
ought not to avail a traitor,—there the law suspends it.—For love nor for
pence,—a king ought not to spare,—so as not to judge equally.—If the king
will serve God,—it is right he should maintain the law ;—if he does not, he
sins and errs very much.—In truth when John Baliol—left his book at school,

desceu fut trop malement.

¶ For boule bred in his boke,

Whenne he tint that he toke

with the kinge-dome ;

For he haves ovirhipped,

470   Hise typeth is typped,

hise tabard es tome.

He loghe wil him liked,

His paclir es thurck piked,

he wende e were liale ;

Begkot an bride,

Rede him at ride

in the dismale.

O RGOYL en pays est urtille en herber,

Ke surcrest la rose e la boute arer ;

480 Einsint est du Baliol, ke par li [li] .xii. per

Sunt chay aval pur lur vil mister,

VARIOUS READINGS.—466. *bredde*, R. 1. *his book*, R. 2.—467. *Wen*, R.
1. *Whan* .. . *took*, R. 2.—468. *kyngdome*, R. 1. *kingdom*, R. 2.—469. *over-
hippede*, R. 1. *has*, R. 2.—470. *tipet*, C., R. 1 and 2. *typpede*, R. 1.—
472—477. These six lines are omitted in C., and R. 1 and 2.—478. *urtiz*,
R. 2.—479. *suztret*, C. *reboute*, R. 2.—480. This line is omitted in R. 1 and 2.
—481. This line is omitted in C.

—he was too ill deceived.—¶ For bale bred in his book,—when he lost what he
took—with the kingdom ;—for he has over-hopped,—his tippet is tipped,—his
tabard is empty.—He laughed while it pleased him,—his pack (?) is pierced
through,—he thought he was loyal ;—.............

Pride in a country, is like a nettle in the garden,—which overgrows the
rose and pushes it back ;—so it is with Baliol, that, by him the twelve peers—are
fallen down for their wicked proceeding,—he has lost his realm, and is gone to

Perduz ait realme, e va sojorner
A la Tour de Loundres sur autri dener.
Li reis Sire Edward eces fet garder;
Li quens Jon de Gwarenne est chief justicer,
E Henri de Perci aid Galwei à gwier;
A Berwick-sur-Twede a la cheker,
Et Huge de Cressingham illokes est tresorer;
Et li Amundisham Walter est chanceler.
490 Li reis puis pes norir baunc i fet crier,
Et justis .v. le rei à guverner.
Viscuntes e baillifs sunt mis al mester
Des Engleis qe sevent e voleint dreit juger.
La garde est establi si bon e si enter,
Ne Flemyng ne Fraunceis de quer avera poer
Entrer en Escoce, si non pur marchaunder.
De tuz les mels vanez ke deivent demorer

VARIOUS READINGS.—484. *Escoce fet g.*, C., R. 1. *Le rei . . . Escoce*, R.
2.—485. *quens de G. i est*, C. *q. Johan de G. i est j.*, R. 1.—487. *Twede assise
est le escheker*, C. *assise ad l'esc.*, R. 1 and 2.—489. *Hamundesham*, C. *Ay-
mundesham*, R. 2.—490. *pur pes . . . baunk*, C., R. 1 and 2.—491. *la lay à g.*,
C., R. 1 and 2.—495. *dès ore n'avera*, C. *dès or av.*, R. 1.

---

lodge—in the Tower of London, at another's expense.—The King Sir Edward
makes guard enough;—the Earl John de Warenne is chief justice,—and Henry
de Percy has Galway to rule;—at Berwick-upon-Tweed is established the exchequer,—and Hugh de Cressingham is treasurer there;—and Walter de Amundisham is chancellor.—The King to nourish the peace causes his bench to be
proclaimed there,—and five judges to govern the law.—Sheriffs and bailiffs
are established for the need—of the English who could and would judge according to right.—The guard is established so good and so perfect,—neither Fleming
nor Frenchman henceforth shall have the power,—to enter into Scotland,
unless it be for commerce.—Of all those of most account who were to remain—

Pris sunt les homages, li reis le[s] fist jurer,
Ke leals li seront par tere e par mer.
500 Ki comensaint la gwere e li consailler
Sunt maundés delà la Trent en sew à repoter,
Taunt cum en Gascoyne la gwer deit durer.
Issint deit li sires ses homes chacer.
Le eveske de Duram, ke mout fet à loer,
En conquerant la tere fu tuz jours li primer ;
Ne fussent ses enprises e hardiment de quouer,
Choses or chyviaus serraint à comencer.
   Les duze peres
   S'en vount as freres
510   els confesser ;
   Le jugement
   Ke les attent
      purrount doter.
  Kambynoy
  Se tent tut coy,

VARIOUS READINGS.—498. *les fist*, C., R. 1. *pris unt*, R. 2.—501. *re-poser*, C., R. 1. *delà Tr. en southe reposer*, R. 2.—503. *li sire, ... chastier*, R. 2.—506. *quer*, R. 1.—507. *ore chevyes*, C., R. 1 and 2.—510. *pur els*, C., R. 2.—513. *il doter*, C.

---

the homages are taken, the King makes them swear—that they will be loyal by land and by sea.—They who began the war and the advisers of it—are sent beyond the Trent to repose in the south,—so long as the war lasts in Gascony.—Thus ought the lord to chastise his men.—The bishop of Durham, who did much worthy of praise,—in conquering the land was always the first,—were it not for his activity and boldness of heart,—things now finished would be to begin.—The twelve peers—go away to the friars—to confess them,—the judgment—which awaits them—they may fear.—Kambynoy—holds himself all coy,

ne volt aider.
La sorcerye
De Albanye
  ne pout valer.
520 Andreu se dort,
Ou il est mort
  al mouster.
L'Escos ke fra,
Quant il orra
  le rei parler,
A seint Edmon,
Et de tresoun
  apeler
Count e baroun,
530 Ke par arsoun
  destruit l'a[u]ter ?
Plus loins ne pout,
Illokes l'estoet
  ester cum ler ;
E par agard
Li rais Edward
  determiner.

VARIOUS READINGS.—520, 521. *Andreu est mort, ou il se dort,* C.—528. *le appeller,* R. 2.—531. *destrut l'autr'er,* R. 1. *l'auter,* R. 2.—536. *le rey,* R. 1 and 2.

—he will not help.—The sorcery—of Albania—cannot avail.—Andrew sleeps, —or he is dead—at the monastery.—What will the Scot do,—when he will hear —the King talk,—at St. Edmund's,—and of treason—accuse—earl and baron, —who by burning—destroys the altar?—He can go no further,—there he must—stand like a thief;—and by judgment—King Edward — determine.—

And swa mai man kenne
The Scottes to renne,
540   and wer biginne.
Sum es left na thing
Boute his rivyn riveling,
to hippe thar-hinne.
Thair kinges scet of Scone
Es driven ovir doune,
to Londen i-led.
In toun herd I telle,
The baghel and the belle
ben filched and fled.

550 **D**EUS ! cum Merlins dist sovent veritez
En ses propheciez ! si cum vous lisez,
Ore sunt le deus ewes en un arivez,
Ke par graunt mountaignes ount esté severez ;

VARIOUS READINGS.—538. *men*, R. 2.—540. *werre*, C. *were*, R. 1 and 2.
—541. *somme*, C. *is lest*, R. 2.—542. *bot his rough*, C. *bot his riven*, R. 1.
but the riven r., R. 2.—543. *thar ynne*, C. *inne*, R. 1 and 2.—544. *sette*, C.
thar king set ous Sc., R. 1. *The kinges sete*, R. 2.—545. *over done*, C., R. 1
and 2.—546. *i-ledde*, C., R. 1.—547. *In toune*, C., R. 2.—548. *Thair b. and
thair*, C.—549. *fledde*, C. *fliched and fledde*, R. 1. *bien*, R. 2.—550. *Ha
Deus ke Merlyn*, C. *E ! Deus com Merlyn*, R. 1. *A ! Dieu cum Merlin*, R. 2.
—552. *les .ij.*, C., R. 1.

And so may man teach—the Scots to run,—and begin war.—To some is left
nothing—but his torn riveling—to hop therein.—Their King's seat of Scone—
is driven over down,—and led to London.—In town I heard tell,—the ....
and the bell—are stolen and fled.

O God ! how often Merlin said truth—in his prophecies ! As you read,—
now are the two waters come into one,—which have been separated by great

Et un realme est fet [de] deus diverse regnez,
Ke solaint par deus rays estre governez.
Ore sunt les insulanes trestuz assemblez,
Et Albanye rejoynte à les regaltez,
Des quels li rais Edward est seignur clamez ;
Cornewale e Galez sunt en ses poestez,
560   E Irlaunde la graunte à sez voluntez.
Reis n'i ad nent plus de tut les cuntrez
Fors li rais Edward k'ensi les ad visitez.
Arthur n'i avait unkes si plainement les fez.
Dès ore n'ait ke fere for porver ses alez,
Sur le ray de Fraunce conquer sez heritez,
E puis porter la croiz où Jhesu Crist fu nez.
       Ses enemys,
       Deu mercis !
     sunt chatiez ;

VARIOUS READINGS.—554. *Et une r. fet de diverse regnez,* C. *E un r.,
de d.,* R. 1 and 2.—561. *ad ne prince de tuz les,* C. *a. n. p. de totes,* R. 1.
Rei n'i ad ne p., R. 2.—562. *fors le ray ... joustez,* C. *li ad justicez,* R. 1
and 2.—568. *Deus mercys,* C.

---

mountains ; and one realm is made out of two different kingdoms,—which
used to be governed by two kings.—Now are the islanders all brought together,
—and Albania is rejoined to its regalities,—of which King Edward is proclaimed lord ;—Cornwall and Wales are in his power,—and Ireland the great
is at his will.—There is no longer any king of all the countries—except King
Edward who has thus visited them.—Arthur had never so fully the feudalities.—
Henceforth he has nothing to do but to look after his goings,—to conquer his
inheritance from the King of France,—and then to carry the cross where Jesus
Christ was born.—His enemies,—thank God !—are chastised ;—they are all

570   Trestuz sunt maz,
            Et pris cum raz,
                    enlachés.
            Il ad corouns
            E combatons
                    bien assez,
            Od deuz rays
            Ad un fays,
                    et utraés ;
            Celi de sà
580   Ore aille de là,
                    od ses barnés.
            Jon e Thomas
            Li lerount pas
                    desaydés ;
            Cuthbert li vent,
            Ke od li tent
                    en les medlez.
            En Deu vous die,
            Merlin de li
590   ad prophetez ;

VARIOUS READINGS.—572. *enlacez*, C., R. 1 and 2.—573, 574. *coruz* | *Et combatuz*, C., R. 1. *coru* | *e cumbatu*, R. 2.—582. *Johan e Thomas*, R. 1 and 2.—587. *ses medlez*, C.

---

vanquished,—and taken like rats,—and bound.—He has run about—and fought —quite enough,—with two kings—at one time,—and overthrown them ;—the one on this side—now goes to that side—with his baronage.—John and Thomas—will not leave him—unassisted ;—Cuthbert comes to him,—who holds with him—in the combats.—In God, I tell you,—Merlin of him—prophesied ;

Trais regiouns
En ses baundouns
          Serrount waynez ;
Ne sait blemy
La prophecie
          par pecchez ;
Sire Deus omnipotent
Ad seint Edmound al parlement
          li consaillé,
600   E sur li faus Phelippe de Fraunce,
Par ta vertu aver vengeaunce,
K'il jamès ne seit avaunce
          pur sa pure fauseté.

A L burk de Seint Edmond le jour est establie,
  Sunt venuz les eveskes, ouf la compaignie
De lais e clers, ad quels li ray prie
Des biens de seint eglise aydé e curtaysie,
Einsint cum els pramistrent auntane en l'abie

VARIOUS READINGS.—597. *Sire Deu*, R. 1 and 2.—599. *consaillez*, R. 1
and 2.—602. This line is omitted in C., and R. 1 and 2.—603. *Ly grantez*, R.
1 and 2.—604. *jour establye*, C., R. 1 and 2.—606. *Des ercedenes et clers* . . .
li rays, C., R. 1. *Des ercediakenes*, R. 2.

—three regions—in his possession—shall be gained.—Let not be blamed—
the prophecy—sinfully ;—Lord God Almighty,—at St. Edmund's at the parliament—give him counsel.—And on false Philip of France—by thy virtue to
have vengeance,—that he may never be advanced—for his mere falseness.

To the borough of St. Edmund, on the day which was fixed,—are come the
bishops, with the company—of laymen and clerks, of whom the king prays—
aid and courtesy of the goods of holy church,—as they had promised before in

De Westmoster, par quai li rais de ceo s'affye
610 En socour de sa guere, ke n'est pas finie.
Countes e barouns à la chivalerie
Pur eus e pur le people grauntent en aie
[Le disime dener, et pur la marchaundye]
Le setim par my aide sa tresorie.
E li erceveske, ke tent la primacie
Deu sé de Canturbirs, sur respouns estudie,
E par deus eveskes al ray signefie
L'estat de seint eglise, ke mult est empoverie.
Le erceveske après al rais va e die,
620 " Sire, pur Deu ! là sus ne te greves mie,
Pur tut seint eglise [je te certefye,
Desuz Deus en terre est nul alme en vye
Ke ad sur saint eglise] por ne mestrie,
For la pape de Rome, qe tent la vicarie

VARIOUS READINGS.—610. This line is omitted in R. 1 and 2.—611. *e la chiv.*, C., R. 2. *ly grant en aye*, R. 1.—612. The following line is not found in the Cambridge MS.—613. *parmye à sa tresorye*, C., R. 1 and 2.—616. *sur respouns estodye*, C., R. 1 and 2.—617. *al reis*, R. 1.—619. *al ray*, C.—620. *eglise je te certefye*, C.—622. *Qe south Dieu*, R. 2.—623. *poesté et mestrye*, C.

---

the abbey—of Westminster, whereby the king trusts to it—for the help of his war which is not finished.—Earls and barons, with the knights,—for themselves and for the people grant in aid—the tenth penny, and for the merchants—the seventh part for the aid of his treasury.—And the archbishop, who holds the primacy—of the see of Canterbury, studies for an answer,—and explains to the king by two bishops—the condition of holy church, which is much impoverished.—The bishop afterwards goes to the king and says,—" Sire, for God's sake, do not grieve yourself at all about that,—for all holy church, I certify thee,—under God there is no soul alive in the world—who has over holy church power or mastery,—except the pope of Rome, who holds the vicary

Qe seint Pere li apostoille avoit en baillie.
La pape est nostre chef, il nous garde e guye,
E estatute ad fet qe durement nous lie,
Sur privaciune de rent e de prelacie,
Ke disme, ne .v.time, ne moité, ne partie
630 A tei ne à nul autre nul de nous otrie
Saunz sun maundement en avowerie,
Sur le sollempnement escomege e maldie
Trestuz le fiz de mere qe par seignurie
Aserveint seint eglise, ke Deus aide en fraunchie."
" Sire cler," dit li rais, " tu as parlé folie ;
Promis est dette due, si fay ne seit oublie ;
Mès ke joe te wais de boule saysie
Einsint tuz li autre, par le fiz Marie !
Ne puriez de ceste ayde estre desublie."

VARIOUS READINGS.—627. *Estatute ad*, C.—629. *vintime*, C., R. 1 and 2.
—630. *à ly altre*, C., R. 1.—632. *Sur co*, C., R. 1.—633. *les fiz*, C., R. 1.—
634. *Deus ad f.*, C. *ad enf.*, R. 1 and 2.—635. *Sire clers*, R. 1 and 2.—
636. *promesse*, R. 1 and 2.—637. *jeo te vaise de la bulle s.*, R. 1. *jeo vei de la
bulle s.*, R. 2.—638. *Ansint tuz les altres*, C.—639. *ne purrai*, R. 2.

—which St. Peter the apostle had in keeping.—The pope is our head, he keeps
and rules us,—and he has made a statute which binds us closely,—on privation
of rent and of prelacy,—that neither tenth, nor twentieth, nor half, nor part—
none of us give to thee or to any other,—without his commandment and allow-
ance,—upon it he solemnly excommunicates and curses—every son of a mother
that by lordship—injures holy church, which may God help in its freedom ! "
—" Sir clerk," said the King, " thou hast talked folly ;—promise is debt due, if
faith be not forgotten ;—but if I saw thee here in possession of the bull—as well
as all the others, by the son of Mary !—you should not be relieved of this aid."

640 " SIRE," dit le erceveske, " mout trevolunter
        Ad tei cum al seignur volums tuz aider
Par geongé de la pape, si tu le volez maunder
Par un de tes clers ouf nostre messager,
Ke toun estate e nostre li purroit cunter ;
E sur ceo qe la pape nous fra remaunder,
Volum solum nos aises curtaisement ayder."
" Sire clers," redit li rais, " jeo n'ai pas mester
De ceo qe tu me dais la pape consailler ;
Mès si tu vols respit en ceo kas aver,
650 Fa quant tu vodras tes clers assembler,
Enparlés du promesse, e tretez ent du quer ;
Après la Seint Hillari venez à Westmouster,
E fras la respouns sanz plus à parler."
" Sire," dist le erceveske, " pur Deu e Seint Richer !
Volez si e là tes gens comander,

VARIOUS READINGS.—642. *congé,* C., R. 1.—644. *porrount moustrer,* C.,
R. 1 and 2.—645. *Et soulom ço ke,* C.—646. *Voloums souloum,* C. *Volums nus
de nostre aider e prester,* R. 1 and 2.—651. *Perfournir la pr. . . enparler,* C.
—653. *fetez, . . . en parler,* R. 1 and 2.—655. *Voylliez,* C.

" Sire," said the Archbishop, " very willingly—thee as our lord we will all
aid—with the leave of the pope, if thou wilt send to him—by one of thy clerks
with our messenger,—who could relate to him thy condition and ours ;—and
according to the message which the pope shall send us back,—we will as far as
our abilities go courteously aid thee."—" Sir clerk," says the King again, " I
have no need—for thee to advise me to consult the pope ;—but if thou wilt
have respite in this case,—cause thy clerks to assemole when thou wilt,—talk
to them of the promise, and treat heartily of it ;—after St. Hilary's day come
to Westminster,—and make the answer without more talk ! "—" Sire," said
the Archbishop, " for the sake of God and St. Richard !—please to command

Ke sunt tes ministres ad .xii. dener,
Ke nous ne nos tenaunz facent molester,
Ne nos temperaltez ouf les lays taxer."
"Sire," respount li rays, "ceo n'estut doter;
660 Car ben ne mal ne frunt ad nule de ton poer.
Noun pur ceo, bel sire, jeo prie e requer,
Par my ta deocise comandez prier
Pur moy e pur le[s] menz, e Deu mercier,
Ke largement pur nous fet ad cea en arer."
Le erceveske otrie, e fet sun dever.
Poi avaunt cel houre revint le tresorer
Water de Langetoune, ke fu passé la mer
Ouf le cardinale de la pes treter.
Respouns qu'els i port ne pot nule home saver,
670 Fors cels du consaille qe ne l'osent reveler.
Messagers après vindrent nuncier
Al rays Sire Edward forme de amourer

VARIOUS READINGS.—657. *ne facent*, C.—659. *ço dist le rais*, C.—661.
li rays li prie, C.—663. *les mens*, R. 2.—664. *fet sla*, C. *fet ad ça*, R. 1. *fet
de scea*, R. 2.—665. *l'ottrye, e fet*, R. 1 and 2.—668. *les chardinals*, C.

---

here and there thy people,—who are thy agents for the twelfth penny,—that
they cause to be molested neither us nor our tenants,—nor tax our tempo-
ralities along with the layman."—"Sir," answers the King, "you need not
fear it,—for they shall do neither well nor ill to none of thy power.—Nevertheless, fair Sir, 1 pray and require,—that throughout thy diocese thou com-
mandest to pray—for me and mine, and to thank God,—who has done largely
for us in our recent affairs."—The Archbishop grants it, and does his duty.—
A little before this time returned the treasurer—Walter de Langton, who had
passed the sea—with the cardinal, to treat of the peace.—The answer which
they bring no man can know,—except those of the council who dare not
reveal it.—Messengers afterwards came to announce—to the King Sir Edward a

Contek de Gascoyne, e fet acorder
Li ouf le Rey Phellipp sanz plus guerrer,
Si cum les cardinals ount fet ordiner.
Li Rays Edward par taunt ad fet retorner
Water de Langetoun, e Hugue le Despenser,
E Jon de Beruik, clerk avertik ber.
Counduire les face Dieus, e bien remener !

680   L ES barouns d'Escoce à cel parlement
      Ne fu resoun rendu, ne doné jugement,
Ly rais est si corteis, de si pitouse talent,
E de si graunt merci, jeo crei certeinement
Ke sa misericorde serra sauvement
A cels ke ount la mort deservi plainement,
E des fez attainz felonousement.
La grant pité du quer q'il ad eu sovent
Des felons de Gales, en parlent tote gent,

form of arranging—the strife of Gascony, and to cause him to agree—with King Philip, without further war,—as the cardinals had caused it to be ordained.—King Edward forthwith sent back—Walter de Langton and Hugh le Despenser,—and John de Berwick, a clerk and a valiant knight.—May God conduct them there, and bring them well back again !

Of the barons of Scotland, at this parliament—reason was not rendered, nor judgment given.—The King is so courteous, so full of pity,—and of so great mercy, I believe certainly—that his mercy will be the saving—of those who have fully deserved death,—by their deeds attainted of felony.—The great pity of heart which he has often had—upon the felons of Wales, every body talks of

Quan[t] plus ad eu affer pur son avancement,
690 Meuz li ount la gwere, e fet desturbement,
Dunt ses alez aillours laisser li covient.

A PRES le Seint Hillori, quant le rays quidait
    Parlement à Loundres, cum ordinez aveit,
Noveles li vindrent par cil ke les estayt
Venuz de Kaumbray, e li nunciait
Ke la parlance de pez se fist pur nul esplait.
Par quey le rais Edward demourt e se purvait
Par mer e par tere ke trahi ne sait ;
En Westmouster de ses gens equait
700 Treter de sour quel ayde la clergie li frait.
Ly Sire de Canturbir sur ceo se tint etrahit,
Pur luy e sa paroche à Seint Thomas vouait
Ke nul de sa eglise taillé plus ne serrait,

VARIOUS READINGS.—691. *ses alers*, R. 1.—693. *tenir à L.*, C.—694. *lors
estait*, C., R. 1 and 2.—697. *le rei*, R. 2.—698. *Par tere et par mer*, C. *mer
ne par t.*, R. 2.—699. *en vait*, C., R. 1 and 2. *E à W.*, R. 1.—700. *Treter sur
quele aide*, C., R. 1.—702. *et pur sa p.*, C.

---

it ;—when he was most occupied for his advancement,—they made war upon
him, and cause a diversion,—whereby he was obliged to leave his goings elsewhere.

After the day of St. Hilary, when the King thought (to hold)—parliament
at London, as he had ordained,—news came to him by him who was then
—come from Cambrai, and announced to him—that the talk of peace was made
with no intention of coming to an end.—Wherefore King Edward remained
and prepared—by sea and by land that he might not be betrayed ;—at Westminster he collected his people—to treat about what aid the clergy should give
him.—The Lord of Canterbury held himself very rigid on this matter,—he
vowed to St. Thomas for him and his parish,—that no one of his church should

Ne mis en servage taunt cum il viverait,
Saunz maundement la pape, ke governer le deit.
Li sire de Nichole ataunt se [a]cordait ;
Oliver li eveske, ke flecher ne solait.
Li rais vers la clergie par taunt se corucait,
E hors de sa pese juguer la comaundait.
710 Mès meintenaunt après cele fet repellait.
Co feceint les eveskes ki volunté chascait
Aider à lur seignur dunt recoverir soun drait,
A seinte eglise defendre de hounte e de fourfait.
L'elyt de Everwyke, ke pes desirrait,
Dit ke volunters pur quanke li tuchait,
Dount saint eglise defendre le quint dener mettrait.
Des Escoz chaitifs nule alme i parlait :
Demorez sunt suz garde en autel plait,
Cum avaunt estaient, Dunbar les achascait.

VARIOUS READINGS.—705. *les dait*, C., R. 1.—713. *Et sainte*, C., R. 1.
surfait, R. 1.—718. *sunt uncore suz g. en a. esplait*, C. *sont en garde mult à
lour deshait*, R. 1. *tut à lour desheit*, R. 2.—719. This line ends in C., and R.
1 and 2, with the words *escotez ke ço dayt*, and the English lines following
are omitted.

---

be any more taxed,—nor placed in servage as long as he lived,—without command of the pope, who ought to govern them,—The Lord of Lincoln agreed to
this,—Bishop Oliver, who was not used to bend.—The King was so enraged
against the clergy,—that he commanded them to be judged out of his peace.—
But now afterwards he repealed that decree.—This did those bishops who
willingly consented—to aid their lord whereby to recover his right,—to defend
holy church from shame and loss.—The elect of York, who desired peace,—
said that willingly as far as concerned him—he would give the fifth penny
wherewith to defend holy church.—Not a soul spoke there of the caitiff Scots :—
they remained in keeping in the same care,—as they were before, Dunbar caused

720   For thar wer thai bal brend,
             He kauged ham thidre kend,
                 aut dreved to dote.
             For Scottes at Dunbar
             Haved at thayre gau char
                 schame of thar note.
             Wer never dogges there
             Hurled out of herre
                 fro coylthe ne cotte.

them vexation.—For there were they burnt .... —he .... them thither,—and
drove to dote.—For Scots at Dunbar—had at their .... —shame of their note.
—Never were dogs there—hurled out of ......

THE TRAILEBASTONS, AND EXECUTION OF WALLACE.

[From MS. Cotton. Julius A. v. fol. 162, vᵒ. collated with MS. Reg. 20, A. ɪɪ.
fol. 144, rᵒ. (R. 1.) ; and with MS. Reg. 20, A. xɪ. fol. 125, rᵒ. (R. 2.)]

E N Septembre après Estrivelyn est rendu ;
    Ly reys Sire Edwarde ses travayls ad sentu,
Vers Brustewik sur Humbre son chemyn ad tenu,

VARIOUS READINGS.—2. au rei, R. 2.—3. est meu, R. 1. en son ch. est
meu, R. 2.

TRANSLATION.—In September after Stirling was delivered ;—the King Sir
Edward was fatigued with his labours,—he held his way towards Burstwick on

Sugiour une pece i prist pur sa salu.
Sire Jon de Warenne, count been conu,
Mortz fu lors et prest à mette en sarcu.
Ly reys, ke Deu garde ! en alaunt vers le su,
Par my Lendesey enquist de lu en lu,
Taunt com en Escoz en sa guere fu,
10 Ky out sa pees enfraynt, ki out sa pees tenu ;
Pur taunt com il volait, remede fu purveu
Sur cil ke fust ataynt de sa pees rumpu.

R ESPOUNS ount fet au reys gentz de been
voyllance,
Coment parmy la tere fet est grant grevaunce
Par comune contekours, ke sunt par fiaunce
Obligez ensemble à une purviaunce ;
Traylbastouns sunt nomez de cel retenaunce,
En fayres et marchez se proferent fere covenaunce,

VARIOUS READINGS.—5. *Johan ... counte,* R. 1 and 2.—6. *mort,* R. 2.—
7. *le rei, le sieu,* R. 2.—8. *Lyndesey,* R. 1.—10. *qi l'ount tenu,* R. 2.—11.
volait, R. 1. *cum avolait,* R. 2.—13. *au rei,* R. 2.—15. *comuns,* R. 2.

Humber,—he remained there a while for his health.—Sir John de Warenne,
an Earl well known,—was then dead and ready to be put in his coffin.—The
King, whom God keep ! in going towards his own,—through Lindsey inquired
from place to place,—whilst he had been in Scotland in his war,—who had
broken his peace, and who had held it ;—straight at his will, remedy was provided—for him who was attainted of having broken his peace.

People of good will have made answer to the King,—how a great grievance
is made in the land—by common squabblers, who are by oath—obliged together
to a purveyance ;—this company are called Trailebastons,—they offer to make

Pur treys souz ou .iiii., ou pur la valiaunce,
20 Batre un prodomme ke unk fist nosaunce
A cors Cristiene, par nuli temoygnaunce.
Si homme countredye à nul de l'aliaunce,
Ou marchaund de ses merz li vee fere creaunce,
En sa mesoun demené, sauntz altre daliaunce,
Batuz serrait been, ou pur l'acordaunce
Dora de ses deners et prendre aquitaunce.
Si en la riot ne seit fet desturbaunce,
Une commune guere se levera par chaunce.
Entendu ad ly reys la plaint et la parlaunce,
30 Escutez ore coment purveu est la vengaunce.

PARMY Engletere gentz de graunz resouns
    Assignez sunt justizes sur les traylbastouns ;
Les uns par enquest sunt jugez à prisouns ;

VARIOUS READINGS.—19. *voillaunce*, R. 1.—20. *ne fist*, R. 2.—23. *vee de er.*, R. 2.—26. *prendra*, R. 2.—31. *grant resons*, R. 1. *gent de grant*, R. 2.

---

conventions at fairs and markets,—for three or four shillings, or merely to show their courage,—to beat a good man, who never did hurt—to any Christian body, by the testimony of no one.—If a man contradict any one of the alliance,—or a merchant will not trust them for his merchandise,—taken in his own house, without other interference,—he shall be well beaten, or by agreement—he shall give of his money and take acquittance.—If there were no hindrance made to their riot,—a war among the commons would by chance arise.—The King has heard the complaint and the talk,—now hear how the punishment is provided.

Throughout England men of great account—are assigned as judges on the Trailebastons ;—some by inquest are judged to prisons ;—others to go to the

Li altre alez à fourches à pendre envirouns ;
Plusours sunt privez de [lour] possessiouns;
Ke meyns mesfesaynt sunt passez par raunsouns.
Si chastiment ne fust de ribaldes et bricouns,
Osé ne serrait homme vivre en mesouns.
O ! cum Deus est bons de drayturels guerdouns,
40 Ke taunt sovent nous ad vengé de felouns !
Novel avoms oy entre compaygnouns
De William le Walays, mestre de larouns ;
Sire Jon de Meneteft li suist à talouns,
Enprès de sa puteyne li prist en tapisouns ;
A Loundres le menait en ferges et laceouns,
Où jugez esteit sur cels condiciouns ;
En primer à fourches fust trayné pur tresouns,
Pendu pur roberyes et pur occisiouns,

VARIOUS READINGS.—34. *altres*, R. 1 and 2.—36. *passé*, R. 2.—39. *est draiturels e de bone*, R. 1.—40. *vengés*, R. 2.—41. *Novels*, R. 1.—42. *des barouns*, R. 1.—43. *Johan de Menetest*, R. 1. *Mentest*, R. 2.—44. *Semprès de sa*, R. 2.

---

gallows, to hang there about ;—many are deprived of their possessions ;—those who had done least ill are obliged to pay fines. If there was not chastisement of ribalds and rascals,—people would not dare to live in their houses.—O ! how God is good in his just dealings,—who has so often revenged us of felons !— We have heard news among companions—of William Wallace, the master of the thieves ;—Sir John de Menteith followed him close at his heels,—and took him in bed beside his strumpet ;—he brought him to London in fetters and bonds,—where he was judged on the following conditions :—first to be drawn to the gallows for his treasons,—to be hung for robbery and for slaughter,—

Et pur ceo k'il avait ennenty par arsouns.
50 Viles et eglises et religiouns,
   Avalez est de fourches, et overt les ventrouns,
   Le quoer et la bowel brullez en carbouns,
   Et copé la teste par tels mesprisiouns,
   Pur ceo ke il avait par ces havyllouns
   Maintenuz la guere, doné protecciouns,
   Seysye seygnurye en ses subjecciouns
   De altri realme par ses entrusiouns.
   Copé li fust le cors en quatre porciouns,
   Chescun pende par say en memor de ses nouns,
60 En lu de sa banere cels sunt ces gunfanouns.
       Pur finir sa geste,
       A Loundres est sa teste,
           du cors est fet partye
       En .iiii. bones viles,
       Dount honurer les ylles

VARIOUS READINGS.—55. *meintenu*, R. 2.—56. *en sa*, R. 1.

---

and because he had destroyed by burning—towns and churches and monasteries,—he is taken down from the gallows, and his belly opened,—the heart
and bowels burnt to ashes,—and his head cut off for such faults,—because he
had by these .... .,—maintained war, given protections,—seized lordship into
his subjection—of the realm of another by his intrusions.—His body was cut
into four parts,—each hung by itself in memory of his name,—instead of his
banner these are his standards.—To finish his history,—at London is his head,
—his body is divided—in four good towns,—whereby to honour the isles—that

ke sunt en Albanye.
And tus may you here,
A ladde to lere
  to bigken in pais.
70 It falles in his eghe,
That hackes ovre heghe,
  wit at Walays.

VARIOUS READINGS.—67. *thus*, R. 1 and 2. *mai men*, R. 2.—68. *te lere*,
R. 2.—69. *biggen*, R. 1. *biggin*, R. 2.—70. *fallis . . . iȝe*, R. 2.—71. *hagges*,
R. 1. *hakkis . . . hie*, R. 2.—72. *with that Waleis*, R. 2.

---

are in Albania.—And thus may you hear,—a lad to learn—to build in peace.—
It falls in his eye,—who hacks too high,—with the Wallace.

POEM ON THE EVIL TIMES OF EDWARD II.

[From the Auchinleck MS. fol. 328, rº. written in the beginning of the reign of Edw.
III. in the Advocates Library, at Edinburgh.]

The Simonie.

WHII werre and wrake in londe and manslauht is i-come,
 Whii hungger and derthe on eorthe the pore hath undernome,
Whii bestes ben thus storve, whii corn hath ben so dere,

GLOSSARY.—1. *werre and wrake*, war and mischief.—2. *undernome*, undertaken,
seized upon.—3. *storve*, starved, perished.

ȝe that wolen abide, listneth and ȝe muwen here
                                    the skile.
I nelle liȝen for no man, herkne who so wile.

God greteth wel the clergie, and seith theih don amis,
And doth hem to understonde that litel treuthe ther is;
For at the court of Rome, ther treuthe sholde biginne,
Him is forboden the paleis, dar he noht com therinne   10
                                    for doute;
And thouh the pope clepe him in, ȝit shal he stonde theroute.

Alle the popes clerkes han taken hem to red,
If treuthe come amonges hem, that he shal be ded.
There dar he noht shewen him for doute to be slain,
Among none of the cardinaus dar he noht be sein,
                                    for feerd,
If Symonie may mete wid him he wole shaken his berd.

Voiz of clerk is sielde i-herd at the court of Rome;
Ne were he nevere swich a clerk, silverles if he come,   20
Thouh he were the wiseste that evere was i-born,
But if he swete ar he go, al his weye is lorn
                                    i-souht,
Or he shal singe *si dedero*, or al geineth him noht.

For if there be in countre an horeling, a shrewe,
Lat him come to the court hise nedes for to shewe,

GLOSSARY.—4. *wolen*, will (pl.). *muwen*, may.—5. *skile*, cause, reason.—6. *nelle liȝen*, will not lie.—7. *theih*, they.—10. *paleis*, palace.—11. *doute*, fear.—12. *clepe*, call.—13. *han*, have (pl.). *red*, counsel.—19. *voiz*, voice. *sielde i-herd*, seldom heard. —20. *swich*, such.—22. *ar*, before.

And bringe wid him silver and non other wed,
Be he nevere so muchel a wrecche, hise nedes sholen be spede
                           ful stille,
For Coveytise and Symonie han the world to wille.   30

AND erchebishop and bishop, that ouhte for to enquere
      Off alle men of holi churche of what lif theih were,
Summe beth foles hemself, and leden a sory lif,
Therfore doren hii noht speke for rising of strif
                           thurw clerkes,
And that everich biwreied other of here wrecchede werkes.

But certes holi churche is muchel i-brouht ther doune,
Siththen Seint Thomas was slain and smiten of his croune.
He was a piler ariht to holden up holi churche,
Thise othere ben to slouwe, and feinteliche kunnen worche,   40
                           i-wis;
Therfore in holi churche hit fareth the more amis.

But everi man may wel i-wite, who so take ȝeme,
That no man may wel serve tweie lordes to queme.
Summe beth in ofice wid the king, and gaderen tresor to hepe,
And the fraunchise of holi churche hii laten ligge slepe
                           ful stille;
Al to manye ther beth swiche, if hit were Godes wille.

GLOSSARY.—27. *wed*, pledge.—28. *muchel a wrecche*, great a wretch. *sholen be*, shall be.—29. *stille*, quietly.—34. *doren hii*, dare they.—35. *thurw*, through.—36. *everich*, every one. *biwreied*, accused.—38. *Siththen*, since.—39. *piler*, pillar.—40. *slouwe*, slothful. *kunnen*, know how.—41. *i-wis*, truely, in truth.—43. *i-wite*, know. *ȝeme*, care (*take ȝeme*, pay attention).—44. *queme*, pleasure.—45. *gaderen*, gather. *to hepe*, in a heap.

A ND thise ersedeknes that ben set to visite holi churche,
  Everich fondeth hu he may shrewedelichest worche;   50
He wole take mede of that on and that other,
And late the parsoun have a wyf, and the prest another,
                              at wille;
Coveytise shal stoppen here mouth, and maken hem al stille.

For sone so a parsoun is ded and in eorthe i-don,
Thanne shal the patroun have ʒiftes anon;
The clerkes of the cuntré wolen him faste wowe,
And senden him faire ʒiftes and presentes i-nowe,
                              and the bishop;
And there shal Symonye ben taken bi the cop.   60

Coveytise upon his hors he wole be sone there,
And bringe the bishop silver, and rounen in his ere,
That alle the pore that ther comen, on ydel sholen theih worche,
For he that allermost may ʒive, he shal have the churche;
                              i-wis,
Everich man nu bi dawe may sen that thus hit is.

And whan this newe parsoun is institut in his churche,
He bithenketh him hu he may shrewedelichest worche;
Ne shal the corn in his berne ben eten wid no muis,

GLOSSARY. — 49. *ersedeknes*, archdeacons.—50. *fondeth*, seeketh, endeavours. *shrewedelichest worche*, work most cursedly.—51. *mede*, bribe.—52. *late*, let.—54. *stoppen*, stop.—55. *sone so*, as soon as.—57. *wowe*, woo, court.—58. *i-nowe*, enough. —60. *cop*, head.—62. *rounen*, whisper. *ere*, ear.—63. *on ydel*, fruitlessly, to no avail. —64. *allermost*, most of all.—66. *nu bi dawe*, now-a-days.—68. *hu*, how.—69. *muis*, mouse.

But hit shal ben i-spended in a shrewede huis ;   70
                              if he may,
Al shal ben i-beten out or Cristemesse-day.

And whan he hath i-gadered markes and poundes,
He priketh out of toune wid haukes and wid houndes
Into a straunge contré, and halt a wenche in cracche ;
And wel is hire that first may swich a parsoun kacche
                              in londe.
And thus theih serven the chapele, and laten the churche stonde.

He taketh al that he may, and maketh the churche pore,
And leveth thare behinde a theef and an hore,   80
A serjaunt and a deie that leden a sory lif ;
Al so faire hii gon to bedde as housebonde and wif ;
                              wid sorwe
Shal there no pore lif fare the bet nouther on even ne on morwe.

And whan he hath the silver of wolle and of lomb,
He put in his pautener an honne and a komb,
A myrour and a koeverchef to binde wid his crok,
And rat on the rouwe bible and on other bok
                              no mo ;
But unthank have the bishop that lat hit so go.   90

For thouh the bishop hit wite, that hit bename kouth,
He may wid a litel silver stoppen his mouth ;

GLOSSARY.—70. *huis*, house.—74. *priketh*, rideth.—75. *cracche*, properly a manger,
perhaps here, a cradle.—76. *wel is hire*, it is well for her.—81. *deie*, dairymaid.—85.
lomb, lamb.—86. *pautener* ...... *honne*, ... —87. *koeverchef*, kerchief. *crok*, crook.
—88. *rat*, reads. *rouwe*, rough.—89. *mo*, more.—91. *bename kouth*, could take in
hand. (?)

He medeth wid the clerkes, and halt forth the wenche,
And lat the parish for-worthe ; the devel him adrenche
                      for his werk !
And sory may his fader ben, that evere made him clerk.

And if the parsoun have a prest of a clene lyf,
That be a god consailler to maiden and to wif,
Shal comen a daffe and putte him out for a litel lasse,
That can noht a ferthing worth of god, unnethe singe a masse   100
                      but ille.
And thus shal al the parish for lac of lore spille.

For riht me thinketh hit fareth bi a prest that is lewed,
As bi a jay in a kage, that himself hath bishrewed ;
God Engelish he speketh, ac he wot nevere what ;
No more wot a lewed prest in boke what he rat
                      bi day.
Thanne is a lewed prest no betir than a jay.

But everi man may wel i-wite, bi the swete rode !
Ther beth so manye prestes, hii ne muwe noht alle be gode.   110
And natheles thise gode men fallen oft in fame,
For thise wantoune prestes that pleien here nice game,
                      bi nihte,
Hii gon wid swerd and bokeler as men that wolde fihte.

GLOSSARY.—93. *medeth*, takes bribe.—94. *for-worthe*, go to nought. *adrenche*, drown.—96. *ben*, be.—97. *prest*, priest.—99. *daffe*, fool. *lasse*, less.—100. *unnethe*, hardly.—102. *for lac of lore spille*, be ruined for want of teaching.—104. *bishrewed*, cursed.—105. *wot*, knows.—106. *rat*, reads.—109. *rode*, cross, rood.—110. *muwe*, may.

Summe bereth croune of acolite for the crumponde crok,
And ben ashamed of the merke the bishop hem bitok ;
At even he set upon a koife, and kembeth the croket,
Adihteth him a gay wenche of the newe jet,
sanz doute ;
And there hii clateren cumpelin whan the candel is oute. 120

A ND thise abbotes and priours don aȝein here rihtes ;
 Hii riden wid hauk and hound, and contrefeten knihtes.
Hii sholde leve swich pride, and ben religious ;
And nu is pride maister in everich ordred hous ;
i-wis,
Religioun is evele i-holde and fareth the more [amis.]

For if there come to an abey to pore men or thre,
And aske of hem helpe *par seinte charité,*
Unnethe wole any don his ernde other ȝong or old,
But late him coure ther al day in hunger and in cold, 130
and sterve.
Loke what love ther is to God, whom theih seien that hii serve !

But there come another and bringe a litel lettre,
In a box upon his hepe, he shal spede the betre ;
And if he be wid eny man that may don the abot harm,
He shal be lad into the halle, and ben i-mad full warm
aboute the mawe.
And Godes man stant ther oute ; sory is that lawe.

GLOSSARY.—115. *crumponde crok*, crumpled crook (?).—116. *bitok*, gave, delivered
to.—117. *kembeth*, combs.—*croket*, curl or lock of hair.—118. *Adihteth him*, fits himself with.—121. *don aȝein*, do against.—126. *evele i-holde*, evil held, in ill repute.—
127. *to*, two.—129. *ernde*, errand. ȝong, young.—130. *coure*, cower.—134. *hepe*,
pack (?).

Thus is God nu served thurwout religioun ;

There is he al to sielde i-sein in eny devocioun ;   140

His meyné is unwelcome, comen hii erliche or late ;

The porter hath comaundement to holde hem widoute the gate,

in the fen.

Hu mihte theih loven that loverd, that serven thus his men ?

This is the penaunce that monekes don for ure lordes love :

Hii weren sockes in here shon, and felted botes above ;

He hath forsake for Godes love bothe hunger and cold ;

But if he have hod and cappe fured, he nis noht i-told

in covent ;

Ac certes wlaunknesse of wele hem hath al ablent.   150

Religioun was first founded duresce for to drie ;

And nu is the moste del i-went to eise and glotonie.

Where shal men nu finde fattere or raddere of leres ?

Or betre farende folk than monekes, chanons, and freres ?

In uch toun

I wot non eysiere lyf than is religioun.

Religioun wot red I uch day what he shal don ?

He ne carez noht to muche for his mete at non ;

For hous-hire ne for clothes he ne carez noht ;

GLOSSARY.—140. *to sielde i-sein*, too seldom seen.—141. *meyné* (*maisné*, Fr.), household, people. *erliche*, early.—145. *ure*, our.—146. *Hii weren*, they wear. *shon*, shoes. *botes*, boots.—148. *But if*, unless. *hod*, hood. *fured*, furred. *he nis noht i-told*, he is not reckoned, or esteemed.—150. *wlaunknesse*, pride. *wele*, weal. *ablent*, blinded.—151. *duresce*, hardness. *drie*, bear, suffer.—152. *nu*, now. *moste del*, greatest part.—153. *raddere of leres*, redder of complexion.—155. *uch*, each.—156. *wot*, know. *eysiere*, more easy.

But whan he cometh to the mete, he maketh his mawe touht   160
     off the beste ;
And anon therafter he fondeth to kacche reste.

A ND ʒit ther is another ordre, Menour and Jacobin,
  And freres of the Carme, and of Seint Austin,
That wolde preche more for a busshel of whete,
Than for to bringe a soule from helle out of the hete
     to rest.
And thus is coveytise loverd bothe est and west.

If a pore man come to a frere for to aske shrifte,
And ther come a ricchere and bringe him a ʒifte ;   170
He shal into the freitur and ben i-mad ful glad ;
And that other stant theroute, as a man that were mad
     in sorwe ;
ʒit shal his ernde ben undon til that other morwe.

And if there be a riche man that evel hath undernome,
Thanne wolen thise freres al day thider come ;
And if hit be a pore lyf in poverte and in care,
Sorwe on that o frere that kepeth come thare
     ful loth ;
Alle wite ʒe, gode men, hu the gamen goth.   180

And if the riche man deie that was of eny mihte,
Thanne wolen the freres for the cors fihte.

GLOSSARY.— 160. *touht*, full. — 162. *fondeth to kacche*, seeketh to take.—163. *ʒit*, yet.—168. *loverd*, lord.—169. *shrifte*, confession.—170. *ʒifte*, gift.—171. *freitur*, refectory. *i-mad*, made.—172. *stant*, stands.—173. *sorwe*, sorrow.—174. *ernde*, errand. *morwe*, morrow.—175. *undernome*, undertaken.—178. *o*, one. *that kepeth*, that cares.—180. *wite ʒe*, know ye. *gamen*, game.

Hit nis noht al for the calf that kow louweth,
Ac hit is for the grene gras that in the medewe grouweth
                                             so god.
Alle wite ȝe what I mene, that kunnen eny god.

For als ich evere brouke min hod under min hat,
The frere wole to the direge, if the cors is fat ;
Ac bi the feith I owe to God, if the cors is lene,
He wole wagge aboute the cloistre and kepen hise fet clene   190
                                             in house.
Hu mihte theih faire forsake that hii ne ben coveytouse ?

AND officials and denes that chapitles sholden holde,
    Theih sholde chastise the folk, and theih maken hem bolde.
Mak a present to the den ther thu thenkest to dwelle,
And have leve longe i-nouh to serve the fend of helle
                                             to queme ;
For have he silver, of sinne taketh he nevere ȝeme.

If a man have a wif, and he ne love hire noht,
Bringe hire to the constorie ther treuthe sholde be souht,   200
And bringge tweye false wid him and him self the thridde,
And he shal ben to-parted so faire as he wole bidde
                                             from his wif ;
He shal ben holpen wel i-nouh to lede a shrewede lyf.

GLOSSARY.—183. *Hit nis*, it is not. *louweth*, lows.—184. *Ac*, but.—186. *kunnen*, know.—187. *als*, as. *brouke*, use, hold.—192. *theih*, they.—193. *chapitles*, chapters. —195. *ther*, where.—196. *i-nouh*, enough. *fend*, fiend.—197. *queme*, pleasure.—198. *ȝeme*, care.—200. *constorie*, consistory. *souht*, sought.—202. *to-parted*, separated. *bidde*, ask.

And whan he is thus i-deled from his rihte spouse,
He taketh his neiheboures wif and bringeth hire to his house ;
And whiles he hath eny silver the clerkes to sende,
He may holde hire at his wille to his lives ende
                                        wid unskile ;
And but that be wel i-loked, curs in here bile.   210

A ND ȝit ther is another craft that toucheth the clergie,
    That ben thise false fisiciens that helpen men to die ;
He wole wagge his urine in a vessel of glaz,
And swereth that he is sekere than evere ȝit he was,
                                        and sein,
" Dame, for faute of helpe, thin housebonde is neih slain."

Thus he wole afraien al that ther is inne,
And make many a lesing silver for to winne.
Ac afterward he fondeth to comforte the wif,
And seith, " Dame, for of thin I wole holde his lyf,"   220
                                        a[n]d liȝe ;
Thouh he wite no more than a gos wheither he wole live or die.

Anon he wole biginne to blere the wives eiȝe ;
He wole aske half a pound to bien spicerie ;
The .viij. shillinges sholen up to the win and the ale ;
And bringe rotes and rindes bret ful a male
                                        off noht ;
Hit shal be dere on a lek, whan hit is al i-wrouht.

GLOSSARY.—205. *i-deled*, parted.—209. *wid unskile*, with wrong.—210. *here*, their.
—215. *sein*, say.—218. *lesing*, falsehood.—219. *he fondeth*, he tries.—221. *liȝe*, lie.
—222. *gos*, goose.—223. *eiȝe*, eyes.—224. *bien*, buy.—226. *bret ful*, broad full, filled
up. *male*, chest, pannier.—228. *on a lek*, for a leek. (?)

He wole preisen hit i-nohw, and sweren, as he were wod,

For the king of the lond the drink is riche and god;   230

And ȝeve the gode man drinke a god quantité,

And make him worsse than he was; evele mote he the !

                    that clerk,

That so geteth the silver, and can noht don his werk.

He doth the wif sethe a chapoun and piece beof,

Ne tit the gode man noht therof, be him nevere so leof;

The best he piketh up himself, and maketh his mawe touht;

And ȝeveth the gode man soupe, the lene broth that nis noht

                    for seke;

That so serveth eny man, Godes curs in his cheke!   240

A ND thilke that han al the wele in freth and in feld,

   Bothen eorl and baroun and kniht of o sheld,

Alle theih beth i-sworne holi churche holde to rihte;

Therfore was the ordre mad for holi churche to fihte,

                    sanz faille;

And nu ben theih the ferste that hit sholen assaille.

Hii brewen strut and stuntise there as sholde be pes;

Hii sholde gon to the Holi Lond and maken there her res,

And fihte there for the croiz, and shewe the ordre of knihte,

And awreke Jhesu Crist wid launce and speir to fihte   250

                    and sheld;

And nu ben theih liouns in halle, and hares in the feld.

GLOSSARY.—229. *wod*, mad.—231. ȝ*eve*, if.—232. *evele mote he the !* ill may he thrive!—234. *don*, do.—235. *doth*, causeth. *sethe*, to boil.—236. *tit*, touches. *leof*, dear (*i. e.* have he ever so much desire).—238. *nis noht*, is nothing.—241. *freth*, wood.—247. *strut and stuntise*, strife and debate?—248. *her res*, their assault, onset. —249. *croiz*, cross.—250. *awreke*, revenge.

Knihtes sholde weren weden in here manere,
After that the ordre asketh also wel as a frere ;
Nu ben theih so degysed and diverseliche i-diht,
Unnethe may men knowe a gleman from a kniht,
        wel neih ;
So is mieknesse driven adoun, and pride is risen on heih.

Thus is the ordre of kniht turned up-so-doun,
Also wel can a kniht chide as any skolde of a toun.   260
Hii sholde ben also hende as any levedi in londe,
And for to speke alle vilanie nel nu no kniht wonde
        for shame ;
And thus knihtshipe [is] acloied and waxen al fot lame.

Knihtshipe is acloied and deolfulliche i-diht;
Kunne a boy nu breke a spere, he shal be mad a kniht.
And thus ben knihtes gadered of unkinde blod,
And envenimeth that ordre that shold be so god
        and hende ;
Ac o shrewe in a court many man may shende.   270

A ND nu nis no squier of pris in this middel erd,
     But if that he bere a babel and a long berd,
And swere Godes soule, and vuwe to God and hote ;
But sholde he for everi fals uth lese kirtel or kote,

GLOSSARY.—253. *weden*, garments. — 255. *degysed*, arrayed. *i-diht*, arranged, clothed.—256. *unnethe*, scarcely.—258. *micknesse*, meekness.—261. *hende*, gentle. *levedi*, lady.—262. *nel*, will not. *wonde*, stay.—264. *acloied*, debased. *fot lame*, lame of foot.—265. *deolfulliche i-diht*, lamentably arrayed.—270. *o*, one. *shende*, ruin.— 271. *middel erd*, world, middle earth.— 272. *bere*, carry. *babel*, fool's bauble (?).— 273. *vuwe*, vow. *hote*, promise.—274. *uth*, oath.

I leve,
He sholde stonde starc naked twye o day or eve.

Godes soule is al day sworn, the knif stant a-strout,
And thouh the botes be torn, ʒit wole he maken hit stout;
The hod hangeth on his brest, as he wolde spewe therinne,
Ac shortliche al his contrefaiture is colour of sinne,   280
                    and bost,
To wraththe God and paien the fend hit serveth allermost.

A newe taille of squierie is nu in everi toun;
The raye is turned overthuert that sholde stonde adoun;
Hii ben degised as turmentours that comen from clerkes plei;
Hii ben i-laft wid pride, and cast nurture awey
                    in diche;
Gentille men that sholde ben, ne beth hii none i-liche.

A ND justises, shirreves, meires, baillifs, if I shal rede aricht,
      Hii kunnen of the faire day make the derke niht;   290
Hii gon out of the heie wey, ne leven hii for no sklaundre,
And maken the mot-halle at hom in here chaumbre,
                    wid wouh;
For be the hond i-whited, it shal go god i-nouh.

If the king in his werre sent after mihti men,
To helpe him in his nede, of sum toun .ix. or .x.,

GLOSSARY.—275. *I leve*, I believe.—276. *twye*, twice.—277. *a-strout*, sticking out (?).—282. *allermost*, most of all.—283. *newe taille*, new cut.—284. *raye*, cloth, garment. *overthuert*, crosswise.—286. *ben i-laft wid*, have separated from, or have sent away.—289. *shirreves*, sheriffs.—290. *kunnen*, know how, they can.—292. *mot-hall*, hall of meeting, the justice-hall.—293. *wouh*, wrong.—294. *i-whited*, whitened.

The stiffeste sholen bileve at hom for .x. shillinges or .xii.,
And sende forth a wrecche that may noht helpe himselve
                                        at nede.
Thus is the king deceyved, and pore men shent for mede.   300

And if the king in his lond maketh a taxacioun,
And everi man is i-set to a certein raunczoun,
Hit shal be so for-pinched, to-toilled, and to-twiht,
That halvendel shal gon in the fendes fliht
                                        off helle ;
Ther beth so manye parteners may no tunge telle.

A man of .xl. poundes-worth god is leid to .xii. pans rounde ;
And also much paieth another that poverte hath brouht to grounde,
And hath an hep of girles sittende aboute the flet.
Godes curs moten hii have ! but that be wel set   310
                                        and sworn,
That the pore is thus i-piled, and the riche forborn.

Ac if the king hit wiste, I trowe he wolde be wroth,
Hou the pore beth i-piled, and hu the silver goth ;
Hit is so deskatered bothe hider and thidere,
That halvendel shal ben stole ar hit come togidere,
                                        and acounted ;
An if a pore man speke a word, he shal be foule afrounted.

GLOSSARY.—297. *bileve*, remain.—300. *shent*, ruined. *mede*, reward, bribery.—
303. *for-pinched*, pinched to pieces. *to-toilled*, laboured away. *to twiht*, twitted away.
—304. *halvendel*, one half.—307. *god*, goods. *pans*, pence.—309. *flet*, floor.—312.
i-piled, robbed.—315. *deskatered*, scattered about.—318. *afrounted*, accosted (French,
affronter).

Ac were the king wel avised, and wolde worche bi skile,
Litel nede sholde he have swiche pore to pile ;   320
Thurfte him noht seke tresor so fer, he mihte finde ner,
At justices, at shirreves, cheiturs, and chaunceler,
                                        and at les ;
Swiche mihte finde him i-nouh, and late pore men have pes.

For who so is in swich ofice, come he nevere so pore,
He fareth in a while as thouh he hadde silver ore ;
Theih bien londes and ledes, ne may hem non astonde.
What sholde pore men [ben] i-piled, when swiche men beth in
                                        so fele ?   [londe
Theih pleien wid the kinges silver, and breden wod for wele.   330

Ac shrewedeliche for sothe hii don the kinges heste ;
Whan everi man hath his part, the king hath the leste.
Everi man is aboute to fille his owen purs ;
And the king hath the leste part, and he hath al the curs,
                                        wid wronge.
God sende treuthe into this lond, for tricherie dureth to longe.

AND baillifs and bedeles under the shirreve,
      Everich fondeth hu he may pore men most greve.
The pore men beth over al somouned on assise ;
And the riche sholen sitte at hom, and ther wole silver rise   340
                                        to shon.
Godes curs moten hii have, but that be wel don !

GLOSSARY.— 319. *skile,* reason, right.—320. *swiche,* such.—321. *thurfte him,*
need he. *ner,* near.—322. *cheiturs,* escheators.—324. *pes,* peace.—327. *bien,* buy. *ledes,*
possessions. *astonde,* withstand. —329. *fele,* many.—330. *wod,* wood.—331. *heste,* command.—332. *leste,* least.—338. *fondeth,* tries, endeavours.—341. *shon,* to be shewn,
to be seen.——342. *moten,* may.

And countours in benche that stondeth at the barre,
Theih wolen bigile the in thin hond, but if thu be the warre.
He wole take .xl. pans for to do doun his hod,
And speke for the a word or to, and don the litel god,
      I trouwe.
And have he turned the bak, he makketh the a mouwe.

Attourneis in cuntré theih geten silver for noht;
Theih maken men biginne that they nevere hadden thouht; 350
And whan theih comen to the ring, hoppe if hii kunne.
Al that theih muwen so gete, al thinketh hem i-wonne
      wid skile.
Ne triste no man to hem, so false theih beth in the bile.

A ND sumtime were chapmen that treweliche bouhten and solde;
 And nu is thilke assise broke, and nas noht ꝛore holde.
Chaffare was woned to be meintened wid treuthe,
And nu is al turned to treccherie, and that is muchel reuthe
      to wite,
That alle manere godnesse is thus adoun i-smite.   360

Unnethe is nu eny man that can eny craft,
That he nis a party los in the haft;
For falsnesse is so fer forth over al the londe i-sprunge,

GLOSSARY.—345. *pans*, pence.—348. *mouwe*, mow, contemptuous gesture.—352. *muwen*, may. *i-wonne*, won.—353. *skile*, reason. 354. *triste*, trust. *beth*, are.—355. *chapmen*, merchants. *treweliche*, truly.—356. *nas noht ꝛore holde*, has not been held a long time.—357. *Chaffare*, traffic.—358. *muchel reuthe*, great pity.—361. *can*, knows. —362. *party los in the haft*, ...

That wel neih nis no treuthe in hond, ne in tunge,
                              ne in herte;
And tharfore nis no wonder thouh al the world it smerte.

Ther was a gamen in Engelond that durede 3er and other;
Erliche upon the Monenday uch man bishrewed other;
So longe lastede that gamen among lered and lewed,   369
That nolde theih nevere stinten, or al the world were bishrewed,
                              i-wis;
And therfore al that helpe sholde, fareth the more amis.

So that for that shrewedom that regneth in the lond,
I drede me that God us hath for-laft out of his hond,
Thurw wederes that he hath i-sent cold and unkinde;
And 3it ne haveth no man of him the more minde
                              ariht;
Unnethe is any man aferd of Godes muchele miht.

God hath ben wroth wid the world, and that is wel i-sene;
For al that whilom was murthe, is turned to treie and tene.   380
He sente us plenté i-nouh, suffre whiles we wolde,
Off alle manere sustenaunce grouwende upon molde
                              so thicke;
And evere a3eines his godnesse we weren i-liche wicke.

GLOSSARY.—367. *gamen*, game. *3er and other*, a year and an other, *i. e.* two
years.—369. *lered and lewed*, learned and unlearned, clergy and laity.—370. *nolde
theih*, they would not. *stinten*, desist. *or*, before. *bishrewed*, accursed.—373. *shrewedom*, cursedness.—374. *for-laft*, dismissed.—375. *Thurw*, through. *wederes*, wea-
thers.—380. *treie and tene*, vexation and sorrow.—382. *grouwende*, growing. *molde*,
earth.—384. *i-liche wicke*, equally wicked.

Men sholde noht sumtime finde a boy for to bere a lettre,
That wolde eten eny mete, but it were the betre.
For beof ne for bakoun, ne for swich stor of house,
Unnethe wolde eny don a char, so were theih daungerouse
                  for wlaunke ;
And siththen bicom ful reulich, that thanne weren so ranke.   390

For tho God seih that the world was so over gart,
He sente a derthe on eorthe, and made hit ful smart.
A busshel of whete was at foure shillinges or more,
And so men mihte han i-had a quarter noht ȝore
                  i-gon;
So can God make wane, ther rathere was won.

And thanne gan bleiken here ble, that arst lowen so loude,
And to waxen al hand-tame that rathere weren so proude.
A mannes herte mihte blede for to here the crie
Off pore men that gradden, " Allas ! for hungger I die   400
                  up rihte !"
This auhte make men aferd of Godes muchele miht.

And after that ilke wante com eft wele i-nouh,
And plenté of alle gode grouwende on uch a bouh.
Tho god ȝer was aȝein i-come, and god chep of corn,
Tho were we also muchele shrewes as we were beforn,

GLOSSARY.—388. *don a char*, do a turn, or task.—389. *wlaunke*, pride.—390.
siththen, since. *reulich*, pitiful.—391. *tho*, when. *over gart*, over proud.—394-95.
noht ȝore i-gon, not long ago.—397. *gan bleiken here ble*, their complexion turned
pale. *arst lowen*, formerly laughed.—398. *rathere*, earlier, before.—400. *gradden*,
said lamentingly.—403. *eft*, again.—405-6. *Tho . . . tho*, when . . . then.

                                                  or more ;
Also swithe we forȝeten his wreche and his lore.

Tho com ther another sorwe that spradde over al the lond ;
A thusent winter ther bifore com nevere non so strong.   410
To binde alle the mene men in mourning and in care,
The orf deiede al bidene, and maden the lond al bare,
                                                  so faste,
Com nevere wrecche into Engelond that made men more agaste.

And tho that qualm was astin[t] of beste that bar horn,
Tho sente God on eorthe another derthe of corn,
That spradde over al Engelond bothe north and south,
And made seli pore men afingred in here mouth
                                                  ful sore ;
And ȝit unnethe any man dredeth God the more.   420

And wid that laste derthe com ther another shame,
That ouhte be god skile maken us alle tame.
The fend kidde his maistri, and arerede a strif,
That everi lording was bisi to sauve his owen lyf,
                                                  and his god.
God do bote theron, for his blessede blod !

Gret nede hit were to bidde that the pes were brouht,
For the lordinges of the lond, that swich wo han i-wrouht,

GLOSSARY.—408. *wreche*, punishment. *lore*, teaching.—409. *sorwe*, sorrow.—
412. *orf deiede al bidene*, cattle died all forthwith.—414. *wrecche*, punishment.—
415. *qualm*, mortality. *astint*, stopped.—418. *seli*, simple. *afingred*, hungry.—422. *god
skile*, good reason.—423. *fend*, fiend, devil. *kidde*, showed. *arerede*, raised.—424.
bisi, busy.—426. *do bote*, make a remedy.—427. *bidde*, pray.

That nolde spare for kin that o kosin that other;
So the fend hem prokede uch man to mourdren other   430
                wid wille,
That al Engelond i-wis was in point to spille.

Pride prikede hem so faste, that nolde theih nevere have pes
Ar theih hadden in this lond maked swich a res,
That the beste blod of the lond shamliche was brouht to grounde,
If hit betre mihte a ben, allas ! the harde stounde
                bitid,
That of so gentille blod i-born swich wreche was i-kid.

Allas ! that evere sholde hit bifalle that in so litel a throwe,
Swiche men sholde swich deth thole, and ben i-leid so lowe.   440
Off eorles ant of barouns baldest hii were;
And nu hit is of hem bicome riht as theih nevere ne were
                i-born.
God loke to the soules, that hii ne be noht lorn !

Ac whiles thise grete lordinges thus han i-hurled to hepe,
Thise prelatz of holi churche to longe theih han i-slepe;
Al to late theih wakeden, and that was muchel reuthe;
Theih weren ablent wid coveytise, and mihte noht se the treuthe
                for mist.   449
Theih dradden more here lond to lese, than love of Jhesu Crist.

GLOSSARY.—430. *prokede*, urged.—432. *spille*, to be ruined, spoilt.—434. *Ar*, before. *swich a res*, such a rage.—438. *wreche*, destruction. *i-kid*, shown.—440. *thole*, undergo, bear. *i-leid*, laid.—444. *lorn*, lost.—445. *i-hurled to hepe*, thrown on a heap.—448. *ablent*, blinded.—450. *dradden*, dreaded. *lese*, lose.

For hadde the clergie harde holden to-gidere,
And noht flecched aboute nother hider ne thidere,
But loked where the treuthe was, and there have bileved,
Thanne were the barnage hol, that nu is al to-dreved
          so wide ;
Ac certes Engelond is shent thurw falsnesse and thurw pride.

Pride hath in his paunter kauht the heie and the lowe,
So that unnethe can eny man God Almihti knowe.
Pride priketh aboute, wid nithe and wid onde ;
Pes and love and charité hien hem out of londe   460
          so faste,
That God wole for-don the world we muwe be sore agaste.

Alle wite we wel it is oure gilt, the wo that we beth inne ;
But no man knoweth that hit is for his owen sinne.
Uch man put on other the wreche of the wouh ;
But wolde uch man ranczake himself, thanne were al wel i-nouh
          i-wrouht.
But nu can uch man demen other, and himselve nouht.

And thise assisours, that comen to shire and to hundred,
Damneth men for silver, and that nis no wonder.   470
For whan the riche justise wol do wrong for mede,
Thanne thinketh hem theih muwen the bet, for theih han more
   nede

GLOSSARY.—451. *to-gidere*, together.—452. *flecched*, wavered.—453. *bileved*, remained.—454. *barnage*, baronage. *hol*, whole, entire. *to-dreved*, separated, driven to pieces.—456. *shent*, ruined. *thurw*, through.—457. *paunter*, pantry. *heie*, high.—459. *priketh*, rideth. *nithe*, strife. *onde*, envy.—460. *hien*, hie, haste.—462. *for-don*, destroy. *muwe*, may. *agaste*, afraid.—463. *wite*, know. *wo*, woe.—465. *Uch*, each. *wreche*, blame. *wouh*, wrong.—868. *demen*, judge.—471. *mede*, bribe.—472. *bet*, better.

to winne.

Ac so is al this world ablent, that no man douteth sinne.

But bi seint Jame of Galice, that many man hath souht !
The pilory and the cucking-stol beth i-mad for noht,

  *   *   *   *   *

GLOSSARY.—474. *douteth*, feareth.

NOTES.

Page 1, *line* 10, *Savary of Mauleon.*—For an interesting article on this Baron and his poems, see the eighteenth volume of the Histoire Littéraire de France, pp. 671—682. His name is of frequent occurrence in the English rolls and charters of the reigns of John and Henry III.

—— *l.* 20, *laxait Bordelois.*—Alphonso VIII. King of Castille, married Alianor, daughter of Henry II. of England, and in her right he claimed Gascony, in opposition to King John, and invaded it. In 1206, he laid siege to Bourdeaux. See Dom. Bouquet, Collect. des Historiens de France, tom. xviii. p. 245.

P. 3, *l.* 2, *lois* is the Latin *laudes.*

—— *l.* 19, *par presen.*—It has been suggested that this may mean *as though he were present;* but I think the translation adopted is preferable.

P. 4, *l.* 6, *Lo rei Richard.*—Richard I. was in Aquitaine when he received the wound which caused his death.

—— *l.* 17, *Lozoics* .... *Guillelme* .... *ad Aurenga.*—The allusion, I suppose, is to the inedited romance of Guillaume d'Orange.

P. 5, *l.* 20, *Cadoing.*—Perhaps *Cadomum,* or Caen, as here translated. But there was also a place called Cadoing near Perigueux, which had a celebrated abbey.

It may be observed, as a peculiar characteristic of the Provençal songs of this class, that the poet generally introduces an address to a lady, although she has nothing to do with the subject.

P. 6, *l.* 11. Song on the Bishops.—Since this part of the volume was printed, I have found among the manuscripts of the British Museum (MS. Reg. 7 F, V, fol. 1, r°, written in a contemporary hand) a copy of this song, containing important variations, which would have enabled me to give the text more correctly. In this manuscript the lines are arranged thus in each stanza :—

> Complange tuum, Anglia, melos suspendens organi ;
> Et maxime tu, Cantia, de mora tui Stephani.
> Thomam habes sed alterum, secundum habes iterum
> Stephanum, qui trans hominem induens fortitudinem signa facit in populo.
> Dolos doles metropolis quos subdoli parturiunt,
> Orbata tuis incolis, dolose quos ejiciunt,
> Largos emittis gemitus, patre privata penitus.
> Sed cum habebis Stephanum, assumes tibi tympanum, chelym tangens sub modulo.

The following are the various readings offered by this MS.—*P.* 6, *l.* 1, *tuum.* —*P.* 7, *l.* 4, *doles.*—15, *vel legem.*—17, *quis Nathan David.*—19, *vel postibus;* —21, *jam liberetur.*—*P.* 8, *l.* 2, *exurge.*—4, *ancilla.*—5, *jam superductis aliam.* —7, *Portæ prævalent inferi,* with *Tartari* written over the last word.—8, *nam ludo.*—16, *Scriptis* omitted.—19, *Patet interpretatio | et arduis et infimis, | Nam regni,* &c.—*P.* 9, *l.* 2, *et sacerdos,* with *et* erased and *nam* written over it. —3, *concurrit ad.*—7, *sudet.*—12, *eos.*—15, *et deicit.*—20, *debent et suum fundere.*—22, *jactant.*—*P.* 10, *l.* 8, *in hac.*—11, *clamet.*—16, *dum.*—17, *perit.* —20, *sedet ad.*—22, *Euvangelium.*—23, after this line should come the following, *Ad nummos vertit oculum.*—*P.* 11, *l.* 1, *lucro lucam.*—2, *Marcum marca.*—3, *librum libra.*—8, *Amplectuntur.*—13, *sunt appositi | Sed longe.*— 20, *ob hoc.*—*P.* 12, *l.* 1, *In canes nostri.*—10, *Eliensis.*—11, *datus.*—12, *Eli et ensis.*—14, *Elios.*—16, *Et Babilonis.*—19, *Wlstani.*—*P.* 13, *l.* 1, *Wlstani.* —4, *Effot, mitram, et anulum.*—8, *et* is omitted.—9, *Hinc est, et hinc a latere | Et pauper.*—13, *non causatur.*—14, *des. Cantia.*

—— *l.* 16, *tui Stephani.*—Stephen Langton, whom the Pope had appointed to the archbishopric of Canterbury, in opposition to the election of the monks and the King. He was archbishop from 1207 to 1229.

P. 7, *l.* 17, *natum* should be *Nathan;* see the above various readings for this as well as for some other necessary corrections, which would have rendered the translation less difficult.

P. 8, *l.* 3, *Agar* .. *filium.*—The marginal note in Flacius says, Joannem Graye Episcopum Nordovicensem intelligit. It is not said whether these side-notes are given from the MS. which Flacius used, or are of his own making.

P. 1, *l*. 14.—The same side-notes tell us the *scribentem digitum* means the Pope—Papam intelligit.

P. 9, *l*. 12, *Non est qui.*—The allusion, according to the side-note, is to Pandulph the legate. This explanation is, however, rather doubtful.

P. 10, *l*. 1, *præsuli Bathoniæ.*—Joceline de Welles, Bishop of Bath and Wells from 1205 to 1242. He fled out of England with the Bishops of London, Ely, and Worcester, who had published the interdict.

—— *l*. 10, *Norwicensis bestia.*—John Graye, Bishop of Norwich, who was designed by the King to the see of Canterbury. The three Bishops who took part with the King, whom Matthew Paris calls "tres episcopi curiales," were those of Norwich, Winchester, and Durham.

—— 15, *Cato quondam tertius.*—I do not quite understand the allusion. It occurs again at the end of the *Apocalypsis Goliæ*—

> De cælo cecidi ut Cato tertius,
> Nec summi venio secreti nuncius,
> Sed meus michi quod inscripsit socius,
> Hoc vobis dicere possum fidelius.

—— *l*. 19, *Wintoniensis armiger.*—Peter de Rupibus, Bishop of Winchester, from 1204 to 1238. He was a native of Poitiers in France, and had been a knight before his consecration. He, with the Bishops of Durham and Norwich, supported the party of the King against the Pope. In 1214 he was made chief-justice of England, and he was protector of the realm during the minority of Henry III. See *Godwin, de Præsulibus.*

P. 11, *l*. 1, *lucro Lucam* .... *Marco marcam* .... *libræ librum.*—These puns are frequently repeated in the satirical poetry of the thirteenth century. They will be found further on in the present volume, pp. 16 and 31, as well as in some of the poems of Walter Mapes. Giraldus Cambrensis uses a similar pun in relating his journey to Rome, where he says he differed in one particular from others who went there, for he offered *libros, non libras*. *Libra* in the song should probably be translated *a pound*, as at p. 31, not *the scales*.

P. 12, *l*. 1, *Joannes* .... *decanus.*—For Joannes, the King's MS. has *canes*, which is perhaps right, as *canus* and *canit* in the following line seem to be continued puns upon the word.

P. 12, *l.* 10, *Heliensis.*—Eustace, Bishop of Ely, from 1197 to 1214. As has been observed, he was one of the three who published the pope's interdict.

—— *l.* 19, *Wolstani subambule.*—Maugerius, Bishop of Worcester, from 1200 to 1212. He was also one of those who published the interdict, and having like the others fled to the Continent, he died in exile at Pontiniac, in 1212. It is hardly necessary to observe that St. Wolstan had held the see of Worcester in the eleventh century.

P. 13, *l.* 6, *De Roffensi episcopo.*—Gilbert de Glanville, Bishop of Rochester, from 1185 to 1214. Between him and his monks there was perpetual conten - tion, and he diminished much the goods of his church. See Godwin.

—— *l.* 10, *pauper Sarisburiæ.*—Robert, Bishop of Salisbury, who seems to have lived in obscurity. Godwin says he could find no other information re- lating to him, except the date of his being bishop.

—— *l.* 15, *I Romam.*—Flacius Illyricus gives here the following side-note— " Golias ad librum, vel Gualterus Mapes."

P. 14, *l.* 6—10.—This information is conveyed in two side-notes in Flacius Illyricus, who has printed this Song imperfectly ; but whether these notes were composed by the editor, or found in the manuscript, we are not told. There are no circumstances in the Song itself which would lead us to fix it to this date rather than to any other in the first half of the thirteenth century. The two notes are at the beginning,—" Leo, Joannes Rex ; aselli, episcopi sunt ;"—and at the end, " Jupiter Rex Joannes est : Pluto, Romanus pontifex." On refer- ence, however, to Bale, I find that he speaks of Mapes as calling King John sometimes a lion and sometimes Jupiter, and as designating the Pope by the name of Pluto, and the bishops as asses, which seems to prove that he had read these side-notes, perhaps in the manuscript from which Flacius's transcript was made. It is not indeed improbable that the latter obtained it from Bale himself, who was perhaps the author of the side-notes.

—— *l.* 11, *Song on the Times.*—Flacius has printed this Song in his *Varia Doctorum, etc. Poemata*, p. 406, with the omission of the three first stanzas, which he had previously given as a separate song at p. 159. The text now printed is made up from a comparison of the manuscript with the printed text. The variations are as follows :—*L.* 1, *utor,* Flacius.—3, *deaurati belli,* Fl.—9, *Facies in opere,* MS.—10, *Tegunt partem an.,* Fl.—*P.* 15, *l.* 2, *congruit ramum in,* Fl.—3, *caput mundi*, Fl.—5. *Trahit enim* .... *et sec.*, Fl.—7, *singula*, Fl.—9, *Romæ sunt v.*, Fl.—11, *In hoc cons.*, Fl.—17, *petunt quando petis*, Fl.—18, *seminas, eadem tu metis*, Fl.—*P.* 16, *l.* 4, *Munus al. pollet sing.*, Fl.—6, *rot. placet, totum pl.*—7, *Et c. ita pl.* .... *Romanis*, Fl.—10, *objiciat*, Fl.—12, *transeunt, ut bursa det g.*, Fl.—13, *Romam avaritiæ vitet manus p.*, Fl.—16, *At est*, MS.—*P.* 17, *l.* 1, *non sit*, Fl.—2, *Respondet, hæc tybia non est michi tanti*, MS.—4, *pappare*, Fl.—5, *nomen Gallicum*, Fl.—6, *Paies, paies, dist le mot*, Fl.—7-10, These four lines are not found in the MS.—11, *Da istis, da aliis, addas*, Fl.—*P.* 18, *l.* 1, *Burse*, Fl.—4, *Ut cum fiat vacuus, magis imp.*, Fl.—6, *habet Pl.*, Fl.—In Fl. the two last tetrastichs are transposed.

P. 16, *l.* 6, *crux placet.*—The face of the coin was marked with a cross.

P. 20, *l.* 1, *prima rabies.*—The insurrection of the Barons.

—— *l.* 2, *altera belligeras Francorum.*—The expedition of Prince Louis to help the Barons, who were hard pressed by John's foreign auxiliaries.

—— *l.* 3, *Scottorum tertia.*—*l.* 4, *Flexit quarta Galenses.*—Both the Scots and Welsh joined actively in the war, or rather took that occasion of invading the kingdom.

—— *l.* 6, *turres.*—The MS. has *turmas* in the text, and " vel turres " in the margin.

P. 22, *l.* 13.—The writer evidently intended a pun, or rather a double meaning, in the word *parentis* at the end of the line.

P. 23, *l.* 5, *viri*, *i. e.* Gualo the legate. The poem was evidently written by a strong partizan of the Pope.

—— *l.* 10, *truces.*—The MS. has *traces.*

—— *l.* 15, &c.—Louis and his party were at London, which they quitted in the November after King John's death, in order to march towards the North. On the 6th December they took Hertford Castle, and that of Berkhampstead on the 20th, and proceeded to St. Alban's. A truce was then agreed to, which continued till after Easter.

P. 24, *l.* 2, *Montique Sorello.*—When hostilities recommenced, the Barons of the king's party laid siege to Mount Sorrel, in Lincolnshire, but were obliged to retreat by the approach of a part of the army of Louis under the command of the Comte de Perche.

—— *l.* 7, *Cestrensis clipeus ;*—Ranulph de Blundeville, Earl of Chester, one of the most powerful Barons on the king's party, who now commanded the army which had besieged Mount Sorrel, and which soon afterwards defeated the Comte de Perche at Lincoln.

P. 24, *ll.* 8, 9, 10, in the margin, opposite these three lines respectively, the original scribe has written, " S. Notingham. Trente. Nicole." The *nobilis matrona* was Nichola, widow of Gerard de Camville, who defended Lincoln Castle against the French.

—— *l.* 11.—It may be well to point out the remarkable alliteration in this line and the following.

—— *l.* 14, *signa.*—The MS. has *singna*, a form not uncommon in such words.

—— *l.* 15, *ora.*—The MS. has *hora.*

P. 25, *l.* 2, *Sabbatum.*—Saturday, May 20, 1217. The next day was Trinity Sunday.

P. 28, *l.* 11, *Sabinæ.*—Sabina was a very common term for a modest woman in low Latin, just as Thais was for a strumpet. See on the latter word a note in the *Early Mysteries and other Latin Poems*, p. 131.

—— *l.* 12, *Arabes.*—Arabia, the land of gems and spices, was believed to contain inexhaustible stores of riches.

P. 33, *l.* 4, *Refert ad focariam.*—*Focaria* was the name given to the wives or concubines of the priests and clergy, who had been recently proscribed. It occurs again in the *Apocalypsis Goliæ*—

> Seductam nuncii fraude præambuli,
> Capit *focariam*, ut per cubiculi
> Fortunam habeat fortunam loculi,
> Et per vehiculum omen vehiculi.

I have rendered the word, according to its derivation, by *fire-side woman*, for it is explained in an old gloss as *meretrix foco assidens.* See *Ducange in v.* Fuller (Church Hist. p. 27, folio edit.) makes very needless difficulties on the meaning of this word, apparently for the sake of introducing some equally needless jokes. The following article in the *decreta* of Pope Alexander, printed in the History of Henry of Huntingdon (Scriptores post Bedam, fol. 1601), p. 589, which one would think must have passed under his eyes, left little room for doubt ;—

"*Ne clerici in sacris ordinibus constituti* focarias *habeant.*

"Clerici in sacris ordinibus constituti, qui mulierculas in domibus suis sub incontinentiæ nota tenuerint, aut abjiciant eas et continenter vivant, aut beneficio et officio fiant ecclesiastico alieni."

In the statutes of Stephen, Archbishop of Canterbury, MS. Cotton. Julius D. II. fol. 167, r°, we find also a chapter—

"*De* focariis *amovendis.*

"Sacerdotibus vero præcipue et spiritualiter in virtute Spiritus Sancti et sub periculo beneficii districte præcipimus quod continenter vivant et honeste, concubinas suas a domibus suis procul expellant, et nullam familiaritatem cum eis de cætero habeant, nec in propriis domibus nec in alienis, nisi volunt simul beneficiis et officiis contra hoc agendo privari," etc.

And again, just after, we have the following title :—

"*De pœna et satisfactione* focariarum.

"Concubinæ sacerdotum frequenter moneantur ab archidiaconis, et præcipue a sacerdotibus in quorum parochia morantur, vel ut contrahant, vel ut claustrum ingrediantur, vel sicut publice peccaverunt publicam agant pœnetentiam."

The word *focaria* is often used by Giraldus Cambrensis. Speaking of a priest on the Borders of Wales, he says, "More sacerdotum parochialium Angliæ fere cunctorum damnabili quidem et detestabili, publicam secum habebat comitem individuam et *in foco focariam* et in cubiculo concubinam." (Wharton, Anglia Sacr. vol. ii. p. 525.) From this passage it is clear that the name *focaria* was given to them because they lived publicly with the priests in their houses, and *shared their fire-sides ;* and from some other circumstances mentioned in Giraldus, it appears that they were in reality married to the priests, though the stricter party considered the marriage to be uncanonical.

P. 36, *l.* 2, *Omina.*—The MS. has *Homina.*

——— *Bernard de Rovenac.*—For all that is known of this poet, see the *Histoire Littéraire de France,* tom. xviii. p. 667.

P. 48, *ll.* 7—10, *Regnat nunc impietas,* &c. These four lines resemble very closely the first four lines of another song, in MS. Sloane, No. 1580, fol. 160, v°, which will be printed among the Poems of Walter Mapes—

Captivata largitas longe relegatur,
Exulansque probitas misere fugatur,
Dum virtuti veritas prave novercatur,
Inperat cupiditas atque principatur.

P. 49, *l.* 8, *Wandelardus.*—Perhaps *a Vandal.*

—— *ll.* 15—18. With the little information given in the song, it is difficult
to ascertain who were the four brothers the writer intended to satirise. This
punning way of deriving and explaining proper names was by no means uncommon during the middle ages. In a splendid Bible in three volumes folio, written
in England early in the twelfth century, and now preserved in the Library of
St. Geneviève at Paris, the scribe gives the following very curious account of
his family. Its being previously inedited will be a sufficient excuse for inserting
it here.

" Hanc Bibliothecam scripsit Mainerus scriptor Cantuariensis. Sed ne ab
ignorantibus parentelam suam putaretur nothus, sive spurius, placuit ei nomen
proprium suum et nomen propinquorum parentum suorum scribere et ethimo-
logizare. Ipse itaque scriptor inter suos recto nomine Mainerus nominabatur,
quod nomen ei desienter datum est ; Mainerus enim interpretatus est, imitata
in sua manu gnatus, quia peritus fuit et gnarus in arte scribendi. Pater
ejus Wimundus nominabatur, quod nomen interpretatum Latine sonat *hodie
mundus ;* poterat enim de eo dici cotidie quod mundus esset, quod mundus in
mundo munde vixit, ad Creatorem suum sine immunditia migravit. Nomen
matris suæ dicebatur Anglice Livena, quod Latine sonat *lætitia ;* fuit enim
mulier hylaris, facie decora, moribus ornata et pudica, et semper in largiendo
bona sua pro Dei amore datrix hilaris ; sana et incolumis per .lxxx. annos et
plus feliciter vixit. Avus suus nominabatur Ulgerus, i. ulnas gerens ; fuit
enim vir magnus et fortis, qui magnas habebat ulnas. Nomen aviæ suæ
dicebatur Anglice Elvera, quod interpretatur *Dei vidua,* quæ et in bona
viduitate diu vixit. Quatuor habuit fratres et unam sororem, quorum primus
vocabatur Radulphus, i. ratus et adustus, i. firmus in adolescentia ; fortis enim
valde juvenis fuit. Secundus dicebatur Robertus, quia a re nomen habuit,
spoliator enim diu fuit et prædo. Tertius nuncupabatur Giroldus, girovagus
enim fuit omnibus diebus vitæ suæ. Quartus nominabatur Johannes, quod
nomen interpretatum sonat *Dei gratia ;* et iste gratiam Dei gratia Dei

adeptus est; fuit enim juvenis ætate, senex moribus, virgo castitate, vita beatus. Soror ipsius dicebatur Dionisia, id est Deo nitens; nitebatur enim semper bonis operibus ad Deum venire. Animæ omnium istorum et animæ omnium fidelium defunctorum per misericordiam Dei requiescant in pace! Amen!"

P. 51. SONG UPON THE TAILORS.—It is scarcely necessary to say that the three lines which form the theme of this song, are the commencement of Ovid's Metamorphoses. Llewellin, Prince of Wales, invaded the Marches in 1263.

P. 53, *l.* 3, *capucium.*—The name capuce was given sometimes to a separate piece of apparel with which the head was covered, and at others to the upper part of the tunic of the monks which covered the head. In the present instance it must be taken in the former sense. A full account of the different senses of the word will be found in Ducange.

—— *l.* 6, *almucium.*—The aumuce was a separate article of clothing which covered both head and shoulders. One of the articles of the canons for the behaviour of the monks, given by Pope Clement V., was, " ut almutiis de panno nigro, vel pellibus, caputiorum loco, uterentur."

—— *l.* 14, *Tyeis.*—The French and Anglo-Norman form of the Latin *Teutonicus.* It is the origin of the name of several old English families.

P. 57, *l.* 4, *Cernite.*—The MS. has *scernite.*

P. 58, *l.* 2, *Frollo.*—This personage is a famous character in the fabulous history of Arthur, and is there said to have been King of Paris under the Romans. When hard pressed by Arthur, who had conquered "all France and all Germany," he took refuge in Paris, and was besieged there. The people in the city beginning to feel the effects of famine, persuaded Frollo to engage Arthur in single combat. The battle was said to have taken place in the " isle" (insula Parisiensis), the part of the French capital included between the two branches of the Seine, in which, at the present day, stand Nôtre-Dame and the Palais de Justice, with its beautiful Sainte-Chapelle. The story of Arthur and Frollo is told at length in Geoffrey of Monmouth.

—— *ll.* 10, 11, *Arthurus.*—King Arthur, the hero of so many romances. *Broinsius.* (?) *Constantinus.*—Constantine the Great, whose mother Helena was said to have been a British lady. *Brennius :* the conqueror of Rome, who, according to the British history, was a Briton.

P. 58, *ll.* 13, 14, *Karolum*—Charlemagne; *Ricardum*—Richard Cœur-de-Lion: both of whom were the heroes of romances and popular songs. The same two heroes of French and English fable are mentioned in a curious passage of the Polychronica of Ralph Higden : " Quemadmodum Græci suum Alexandrum, Romani suum Octavium, Angli suum Ricardum, Franci suum Karolum, sic Britones suum Arthurum præconiantur." P. 225, in Gale's Scriptores.

P. 59. THE SONG OF THE BARONS.—The transcript of this curious fragment was communicated to me by Sir Frederick Madden. The original is written in a contemporary hand on a roll twenty-two inches long, by three broad, and was evidently intended to be carried about by the minstrel who was to sing it. On the reverse had been written a curious interlocutory poem in English of a later period, entitled, " Interludium de Clerico et Puella." It was, in 1838, in the possession of the Rev. Dr. Richard Yerburgh, Vicar of Sleaford, in Lincolnshire.

Such rolls appear to have been in common use. A very curious vellum roll of the fifteenth century, containing chiefly religious songs with the music, and, among the rest, a copy of the well-known song on the battle of Agincourt printed by Percy, has been recently deposited in the Library of Trinity College, Cambridge. I am informed that another, of the thirteenth century, has been lately found among the archives of Sir John Hanmer, Bart., containing an Anglo-Norman romance previously unknown, on the adventures of Melors, son of Melians of Cornwall. Among the Sloane MSS. in the British Museum (No. 809), is an early copy of the curious poem of Walter de Biblesworth, designed for the instruction of children in the French language, written in a similar manner on a roll of parchment, evidently for the purpose of being more easily used in a school.

——— *l.* 1, *de Warenne ly bon quens .. en Norfolk.*—John, Earl of Warenne, a staunch supporter of the royal party, in whose cause we shall soon afterwards find him fighting at Lewes.

——— *l.* 7, *Sire Jon Giffard.*—Sir John Giffard, of Brimsfield, in Gloucestershire, a firm adherent of the Barons. When Sir Roger de Clifford delivered Gloucester to Prince Edward, Giffard fortified his castle of Brimsfield, and greatly annoyed the royalist garrison of the former place. For an account of his exploits at this time, see Robert of Gloucester's Chronicle, pp. 538, 539. He was on the Barons' party at the battle of Lewes, and was taken prisoner there; but afterwards, when Simon de Montfort was in the height of his power, Giffard deserted him. See Robert of Gloucester, p. 550.

P. 60, *l.* 1, *Sire Jon Dayvile.*—Sir John Dayvile, or D'Ayvile (Robert of Gloucester calls him in one place De Eivile) does not appear very prominent in these troubles till after the death of Simon de Montfort at Evesham. He then headed those of the Barons who established themselves at Chesterford in the Peak, and afterwards was the chief of those who held the Isle of Ely against the King. Knighton calls him " homo callidus et bellator fortis." See Knighton (in Twysden), col. 2454 ; Chron. Thomæ Wikes (Gale), pp. 81, 82 ; Robert of Gloucester, p. 564.

—— *l.* 7, *De Cliffort ly bon Roger.*—Roger de Clifford first took part with the Barons, but early in the war deserted them, and delivered Gloucester castle, which he held for them, to Prince Edward. He was with the King at North-ampton.

—— *l.* 13, *Sire Roger de Leyburne . . . ses pertes que Sire Edward le fist.*— Sir Roger de Leyburn was at first a partizan of the Barons, and had been taken prisoner at Rochester Castle, and committed to the custody of John Mareschall. It was on this occasion, probably, that he was visited with the penalties alluded to in the song. He was afterwards seduced by the royal party, and made Warden of the Cinque Ports. He was with the King at the taking of North-ampton, at the defence of Rochester, where he was wounded, and at Lewes.

P. 61, *l.* 16, *Ly eveske de Herefort.*—Peter de Egueblanche, Bishop of Here-ford, a staunch adherent to the King, and, by his oppressions, exceedingly obnoxious to the Commons. In 1263, the Barons seized and imprisoned him, and confiscated his treasures. He was a native of Savoy.

P. 62, *l.* 1, *ly pastors de Norwis.*—Simon de Wanton, Bishop of Norwich, from 1257 to 1265, chaplain to King Henry III., and one of his justices.

—— *l.* 7, *Sire Jon de Langelé.*—According to the Annales de Dunstaple, the estates of *G.* de Langley were plundered soon after the arrest of the Bishop of Hereford :—" idem facientes de maneriis G. de Langele et ejus bonis." Vol. *i.* p. 354. Perhaps this was the same person.

P. 62, l. 13, Sire Mathi de Besile.—We should perhaps read *Machi;* Robert of Gloucester and Stow call him *Macy.* He was a French knight, who had been made Sheriff of Gloucester, after the King had sworn to the articles of Oxford. The Barons ejected him, and put another sheriff in his place; Sir Macy came with a body of armed men and the authority of the King, reinstated himself by force, and drove away his rival. Sir Roger de Clifford and Sir John Giffard came against him, besieged and took Gloucester Castle, and imprisoned him along with the " Freinss bissop " of Hereford, whom they seized immediately afterwards. Robert of Gloucester mentions the confiscation of his property:—

> " And Sir Jon Giffard nom to him is quic eiȝte echon,
> And al that he fond of is, and nameliche at Sserton."

The song here printed was evidently written just after this event, and previous to the subsequent desertion of Clifford and others mentioned in it.

——— *l.* 18, *treget.*—It has been suggested that this word represents the Latin *treugellum,* a little truce.

——— *l.* 19, *mi Sire Jon de Gray.*—John de Gray held on the King's party, and was rewarded for his loyalty by the grant of various high offices. The circumstance alluded to in the song is thus told in the Annales de Dunstaple (Ed. Hearne, vol. i. p. 357); it occurred in the disturbances in London in 1263.— " Quo perpetrato facinore, cives Londoniarum contra ipsum et alios de consilio regis in civitate commorantes, insurrexerunt; in tantum quod hospitium Johannis de Grey extra Ludgate invaserunt, et equos ejus triginta duo et alia quæcunque ibidem inventa abduxerunt: ipso Johanne cum difficultate maxima ultra alveum de Flete fugam arripiente. Idem fecerunt de domibus et bonis Simonis Passelewe."

——— *l.* 21, *que must,* quod movit.

P. 63, l. 4, Sire Willem le Latimer.—Sir William le Latimer was a firm adhérent of the King, and held at different times several offices of trust. He suffered considerable losses in the Barons' wars. He afterwards appears to have accompanied Prince Edward to the Holy Land, and was at the siege of Carlaverock in 1300. He died in 1305, at a very advanced age. Knighton calls him *miles strenuissimus.*

P. 63. SONG OF THE PEACE WITH ENGLAND.—It has been suggested to me that the word *cul* in this song is only a form of *col* (collum); and I am told that among the titles of some fables in the same manuscript there is one of the stork "au long *cul.*" In this song, however, I am inclined to think such an interpretation not admissible. It is a rude burlesque not only upon the event to which it relates, but upon the English in general, and contains much coarse humour such as is not uncommonly used at the present day. The grammatical construction is, evidently by design, a complete confusion of tenses, numbers, and genders. It appears to me that not a little of the effect it was intended to produce, depended upon the coarse play upon words involved in the use of the expression above mentioned. When the reciter introduced King Henry to his auditors, and they expected he was going to sigh from his heart, instead of completing the sentence *il suspire de cœur* (p. 65), *i. e.* ille suspirat de corde, he introduces another word beginning with the same letter, and says *il suspire de cul* (ille suspirat de culo). That *Trichart* in the preceding line was intended for a pun upon *Richard*, we may conjecture from the rhymes in the English song on the same person's name, p. 69. Again, at p. 66, it would naturally be expected that he would place his lance against his enemy's *cœur ;* the blow was to be so strong, that if his opponent did not give way, he would himself suffer in that part which was in communication with the saddle, and where, of course, the resistance was concentrated. These jokes must have been extremely diverting to the class of people for whom this song was designed.

The Song of the Peace with England had been previously printed by Mons. Achille Jubinal, well known for his numerous publications of early French literature, in a very curious volume entitled " Jongleurs et Trouvères," 8vo. Paris, 1835. M. Jubinal also gave a translation into modern French of this song, as well as of the piece I am now going to mention, in the " Journal de l'Institut Historique," Jan. 1835, which has been reproduced in the Histoire de Saint Louis, by the Marquis de Villeneuve-Trans, 8vo. Paris, 1839, vol. iii. p. 614. In the manuscript from which this song is printed, it is accompanied by a piece in prose on the same event, and of a similar character, entitled *Le Chartre de la Pais aus Anglois*, which I venture to reprint here from M. Jubinal's book, as the latter is now out of print, and very scarce. It will be observed that the same style of gross joking which is found in the song, runs through the charter ; a double meaning was evidently intended, for example, in the words *qu'il fu fet*

.i. gros pes entre, etc., which might be taken as signifying, in this broken French, either *grossa pax*, or *grossus peditus*.

La Chartre de la Pais aus Anglois.

" Ce sache sil qui sont et qui ne sont mi, et qui ne doivent mi estre, qu'il fu fet *.i. gros pes entre* ce rai Hari d'Ingleter, et ce riche homme Loys à Parris, sarra forretier de ce grant forrest à Normandi. Et quant ce rai Hari d'Ingleter voudra vauchier par son terre, ce riche homme Loys à Parris voudra donier à ce rai Hari meismes *.ii. poronssores* à mester soz son houses, por ester plus minet; et quant ce rai Hari voudra aler de mort à vie, cestui riche homme Loys à Parris, devra donier à d'Adouart sa fils cesti chos meism, souz vise quitement, francement di-je, c'avant c'arier. C'est donques à saver *.i. poronssores* quant il voudra vauchier par son terre à meter soz son houses, por ester plus minet aussinc comme à sa piere. Et por ce que je véele que ce chos fout fiens en estable, je véele pendez ma saiele à ce cul par derrier, avoecques la saiele à mi barons d'Ingleter. L'an de l'incarnacion nostres sinors Jesoucriet mimes qui souffri mort à la crucefimie por nous, m. cc. lx. i. ij. et iij., à ce jodi assolier, derrière ce vendredi, à orre que Marri Masalaine chata ce honissement à honissier les *.v.* plais Jesoucriet nostre sinors mimes, qui souffra mort à la croucefin por nous, et Marri Mauvaise-alaine portez ce honnissement à la Saint Supoucre ; et Marri Mauvaise-alaine véez l'angiel, et l'angiel pona : " Marri ! Marri ! quei quieré vous quei ?" Et Marri pona : " Je queres Jhesum qui fout à la crucefimie." Et l'angel pona à Marri : " Marri ! Marri ! aléici, aléici : il ne fout pas çi, il fout alé cestui matin à Galerrie."

P. 64, l. 6, choison ; from *choir* (cadere).

P. 65, l. 6, gondre Glais grondier, contra Anglos grunnire.

—— *l. 9, à l'art.*—Perhaps it should be *alart*, and is derived from the Latin *alacriter.*

—— *l. 11, la conte à Clocestre.*—Gilbert de Clare, who succeeded his father in the Earldoms of Hereford and Gloucester in 1262, and was a zealous partizan of the Barons, until he deserted Simon de Montfort before the battle of Evesham.

—— *l. 15, la cont Vincestre.*—Roger de Quincy, Earl of Winchester. Why his name is introduced so prominently, does not seem clear. He died in the year following (1264), and the title became extinct.

P. 67, l. 3, Rogier Bigot.—Roger Bigod, Earl of Norfolk.

P. 67, *l.* 18, *Saint Amont,* means, probably, St. Edmund.

P. 69. SONG AGAINST THE KING OF ALMAIGNE.—This song was first printed in Percy's Reliques of Ancient English Poetry.

—— *l.* 2, *Kyn of Alemaigne.*—It is hardly necessary to say that this was Richard Earl of Cornwall, the King's brother.

—— *l.* 3, *Thritti thousent pound.*—The Barons had offered him this sum, if he would by his intermediation persuade the King to agree to a peace with them, and at the same time accept the terms they demanded.

—— *l.* 10, *Walingford.*—The honour of Wallingford had been conferred on Richard in 1243.

—— *l.* 12.—Windsor was the stronghold of the royal party, and had been garrisoned by foreigners.

—— *l.* 15, *mulne.*—" After the battle was lost, Richard, King of the Romans, took refuge in a windmill, which he barricadoed, and maintained for some time against the Barons, but in the evening was obliged to surrender. See a very full account of this in the Chronicle of Mailros." *Percy.*

P. 70, *l.* 8.—The Earl of Warenne escaped from the battle, and fled into France.

—— *l.* 20, *Sire Hue de Bigot.*—Hugh Bigod escaped with the Earl of Warenne to Pevensey, and from thence to France. He was cousin to the Hugh Bigod who took part with the Barons, and was slain at Lewes.

P. 71, *l.* 6, *lyard.*—This word (in low Latin *liardus*) means, properly, a dapple-grey horse; but it is often used, like several other similar words, as a common name for a horse in general. I have interpreted it as meaning a hack; but probably the passage implies a sneer at Edward, who had been more than once with his army to Dover, in the hope of taking the castle from the Barons, and the word may mean simply his horse.

P. 72, *l.* 13.—The battle of Lewes was fought on Thursday, (?) May 14, 1264.

P. 73, *l.* 36, *in claustro.*—A great part of those of the King's party who quitted the field, took shelter in the abbey of Lewes, where they were besieged by the Barons.

P. 74, *l.* 47, *apud Northamptoniam.*—Northampton had been taken by the King on the third of April preceding.

P. 74, *l.* 55, *monasterium, quod Bellum vocatur.*—I have not found any notice elsewhere of the contributions forced from the abbies of Battle and Robertsbridge.

P. 75, *l.* 1, *monachi Cystercii de Ponte-Roberti.*—There was an abbey of Cistertian monks at Robertsbridge, in Sussex.

—— *ll.* 73—77.—With these lines may be compared a passage in Knighton's Chronicle (ap. Twysden), col. 2445 :—" Et sicut Simon Machabæus surrexit pro fratre suo Juda, ut pro populo Dei et lege paterna certaret ad mortem ; sic et Simon de Monteforti pro Anglia erexit se, ut pro legibus et libertatibus ejus usque ad mortis perniciem dimicaret."

P. 76, *l.* 94, *intumuit.*—In the MS. the scribe has written *intimuit* in the margin, either as a various reading, or as an improvement of his own.

P. 78, *l.* 128, *bellici.*—The MS. has *vellici.*

P. 79, *l.* 145, *gaudii.*—The MS. has *gladii* in the text, with *gaudii* written in the margin.

P. 81, *l.* 193, *S. divina gratia præsul Cycestrensis.* — Stephen de Berkstead, Bishop of Chichester. He was excommunicated for his staunch adherence to the party of Simon de Montfort.

P. 88, *l.* 325, *movisset.*—The MS. has *novisset.*

—— *l.* 330, *for* proponerat, *read* proponeret.

P. 89, *l.* 252, *invenire.*—The MS. has *inveniere.*

P. 94, *l.* 437, *Testis sit Glovernia.*—Alluding to the delivery of Gloucester to Prince Edward, and his treatment of the town.

P. 102, *l.* 609, *regis et.*—The MS. has *regisset.*

P. 104, *l.* 635, *Unius rex, etc.*—This line appears to be very corrupt, as are one or two others in the poem.

P. 114, *l.* 833, *Nec libertas proprie debet nominari,* | *quæ permittit inscie stultos dominari.* — The reader will hardly fail to call to mind the similar sentiment expressed in the line of Milton—

" Licence they mean, when they cry liberty."

P. 115, *l.* 858, *p'rat.*—The MS. has p̃rat, the meaning of which is by no means clear.

P. 116, *l.* 875, *Veritas, lux, caritas, calor, urit zelus.*—Perhaps the commas should be omitted after *veritas* and *caritas*, and the whole be translated, " Truth is light, charity is warmth, zeal burns."

P. 117, *Regis esse noveris nomen relativum.*—It would be by no means unin-teresting to collect the expressions of the popular doctrine concerning the kingly character held by our forefathers at different periods. Perhaps it may not be considered altogether foreign to the subject to point out here a few of them.

I.—In a MS. of the tenth century (MS. Cotton. Nero, A. i., fol. 71, r°.) we have, among some other things of a similar kind, the following sketch of the opinion of the Anglo-Saxons on this subject, said to be from the pen of Alfric :—

Cristenum cyninge ge-byreð on cristenre þeode, þæt he sy eal swa hit riht is folces frofer, ꝝ rihtwis hyrde ofer cristene heorde, ꝝ hym ge-by-reð þæt he eallum mægene cristendom ræ¯re, ꝝ Godes cyrcan æghwar georne fyrðrie ꝝ friðrie, ꝝ eal cristen folč sibbie ꝝ sehte mid rihtre lage, swa he geornost mæge, ꝝ þurh ælc þing riht-wisnesse lufie, for Gode ꝝ for wo-rolde. For þam þurh þæt he sceal sylf fyrmest ge-þeon, ꝝ his þeodscype eac swa, þe he riht lufige, for Gode ꝝ for worolde. ꝝ him ge-byreð þæt he geornlice fylste þam þe riht willan, ꝝ á hetelicest yre þam þe þryres wyllan.

He sceal mán dæde men þreagean þearle, mid woroldlicre steore ; ꝝ he sceal ryperas ꝝ reaferas ꝝ worold-stru-deras hatian ꝝ hynan ; ꝝ eallum

It behoves a Christian King in a Christian people, that he be all as it is right the people's protector, and a just shepherd over the Christian flock, and it behoves him that he with all his might raise Christendom, and advance and protect God's church everywhere diligently, and pacify and reconcile with just law all Christian people, as he most earnestly may, and love justice in every thing, before God and before the world. Because by that he shall profit himself in the first place, and also his people, whom let him love rightly, before God and before the world. And it behoveth him that he diligently help those who wish for justice, and ever most hatefully per-secute those who wish for wrong.

He shall punish men severely for evil deeds, with secular punishment ; and he shall hate and put down thieves and robbers and oppressors of the

Godes feondum styrnlice wiðstandan;
꒟ ægðer he sceal beon mid rihte ge
milde ge reðe, milde þam godum, ꒟
styrne þam yfelum. Ðæt bið cyninges
riht, ꒟ cynelic ge-wuna, ꒟ þæt sceal
on þeode swyþost ge-fremian. La!
þurh hwæt sceal Godes þeowum ꒟
Godes þearfum frið ꒟ fultum cuman,
butan þurh Crist ꒟ þurh cristenne
cyning? Ðurh cyninges wisdom folc
wyrð ge-sælig, ge-sundful, ꒟ sigefæst,
꒟ þy sceal wis cyning Cristendom ꒟
cynedom miclian ꒟ mærsian, ꒟ á he
sceal hæþendom hindrian ꒟ hyrwan.

He sceal boc-larum hlystan swyþe
georne, ꒟ Godes beboda geornlice
healdan, ꒟ ge-lome wið witan wisdom smeagan, gyf he gode wile
rihtlice hyran. ꒟ gif hwa to þam
stræt sy ahwar on þeode, þæt riht nelle
healdan swa swa he scolde, ac Godes
lage wyrde, oððe folc lage myrre,
þonne cyþe hit man þam cynge, gif
man þæt nyde scyle, ꒟ he þonne sona
ræde ymbe þa bote ꒟ ge-wylde hine
georne, to þam þe his þearf sy huru
unþances, gif he elles ne mæge. ꒟
do swa him þearf is, clænsige his
þeode, for Gode ꒟ for worolde, gif
he Godes miltse ge-earnian wylle.

world; and sternly resist all God's
enemies; and he shall be with justice
both mild and severe, mild to the good
and stern to the bad. This is the
king's right, and the manner of a
king, and this shall be most efficient
in the people. Lo! through what
shall peace and help come to God's
servants and to God's poor, except
through Christ and through a Christian king? Through the king's wisdom
the people shall be happy, prosperous,
and victorious, and on that account
shall a wise king enlarge and increase
Christianity and royalty, and ever he
shall hinder and persecute heathen-
dom. He shall listen very diligently
to scholars, and diligently hold God's
commandments, and frequently search
wisdom from his witans, if he will
rightly hear what is good. And if any
one openly be any where in the
people, that will not hold justice as he
should, but infringes God's law, or
obstructs the law of the people, then
let people declare it to the king, if they
would extinguish that violence, and
there let them soon take counsel for the
amends, and subdue him diligently,
until that he be reduced at last by force,
if he may not otherwise. And let him
do as it is needful for him, purify his
people, before God and before the
world, if he will earn God's mercy.

And again, a little further on (fol. 72, r⁰.)—

Ælc riht cynestol stent on þrim stapelum, þe fullice ariht stænt. An is *Oratores*, ⁊ oðer is *Laboratores*, ⁊ þridde is *Bellatores*. *Oratores* syndon gebedmen, þe Gode scylan þeowian, ⁊ dæges ⁊ nihtes for ealne þeodscype þingigan georne. *Laboratores* syndon weorc-men, þe tilian scylan þæs þe eal þeodscype big sceal libban. *Bellatores* syndon wig-men, þe eard scylon werian, wiglice mid wæpnum. On þyssum þrim stapelum sceal ælc cynestol standan mid rihte on Cristenre þeode. ⁊ awacie heora ænig, sona se stol scylfð; ⁊ ful berste heora ænig, þonne hryst se stol nyþer, ⁊ þæt wyrð þære þeode eal to unþearfe.	Every just throne stands on three props, that stands perfectly right. One is *Oratores*, and the other is *Laboratores*, and the third is *Bellatores*. The *Oratores* are the men of prayer, who shall serve God, and by day and night intercede for the whole nation. The *Laboratores* are the workmen, who shall labour in order that all the nation shall live thereby. The *Bellatores* are the men of war (*i. e.* knights), who shall defend the land, valiantly with weapons. On these three props shall every throne stand with justice among Christian people. And if any of them become weakened, soon the throne wavers; and if any one of them fail entirely, then the throne falls down, and that will be the entire ruin of the
Ac staþelige man ⁊ strangige and trymme hy georne, mid wislicre Godes lage ⁊ mid rihtlicre worold lage, þæt wyrð þam ðeodscype to langsuman ræde. ⁊ soð is þæt ic secge, awacie se Cristendom, sona scylfð se cynedom; ⁊ arære man un-laga ahwar on lande oððon únsida lufige ahwar to swyþe, þæt cymð þære þeode eal to un-þearfe. Ac do man swa hit þearf is, alecge man un-riht, ⁊ rære up Godes riht, þæt mæg to þearfe for Gode ⁊ for worolde. *Amen.*	people. But let man establish and strengthen and confirm them diligently, with the wise law of God and just law of the world, that will be to the nation for a lasting counsel. And it is true what I say, if Christendom be weakened, soon royalty wavers; and if people raise lawlessness everywhere in the land, or love everywhere wickedness too much, that brings the people entirely to ruin. But let people do as it is needful, let people put down injustice, and raise up God's justice, that may bring it to prosperity before God and before the world. *Amen.*

II. In the curious poem of the proverbs of Alfred, composed perhaps in the twelfth century, and which is here quoted from a MS. of the earlier part of the thirteenth century (MS. Trin. Coll. Cambridge, B. 14, 39) is the following account of the duties of King and People.

¶ þus quad Alfred,	Thus saith Alfred,
Englene frovere :	the protector of the English :
May no riche king	There may no just king
ben onder Crist selves,	be under Christ himself,
bote þif he be booc-lerid,	unless he be book-learned,
ꝛ he writes wel kenne,	and he know well writings,
ꝛ bote he cunne letteris,	and unless he know letters,
lokin himselven	to look himself
wu he sule his lond	how he shall his land
laweliche holden.	hold with good laws.
¶ þus quad Helfred :	Thus saith Alfred :
þe herl ꝛ þe heþeling	The Earl and the Atheling
þo ben under þe King,	they are under the King,
þe lond to leden	the land to lead
mid lauelich i-dedin,	by example of lawful deeds,
boþe þe clerc ꝛ þe cnit	both the clerk and the knight
demen evenliche rict.	to judge impartially right.
For after þat mon souit,	For according as a man sows,
als inpich sal he mouin,	so shall he mow,
ꝛ everiches monnes dom	and every man's judgment
to his oge dure cherricd.	falls at his own door.
¶ þus quad Alfred :	Thus saith Alfred :
þe cnith biovit	It behoves the knight
kerliche to cnouen	carefully to know
for to weriin þe lond	how to defend the land
of here ꝛ of here-gong,	from army and from invasion,
þat þe riche habbe gryt,	that the rich may have peace,
ꝛ þe cherril be in frit,	and the churl be in tranquillity,

his sedis to souin,	his seeds to sow,
his medis to mowen,	his meadows to mow,
his plouis to drivin,	to drive his ploughs,
to ure alre bi-lif.	for the sustenance of us all.
þis is þe cnichs lage,	This is the knights' law,
loke þat hit wel fare.	see that it goes well.

III. In the middle of the thirteenth century, at the period of the Barons' wars, we have the passage to which this forms a note.

IV. In the reign of Edward III. the writer of Piers Ploughman gives us the following description of the relative duties of the different orders of society.

Thanne kam ther a kyng,	Then came there a king,
knyȝthod hym ladde,	knighthood led him,
miȝt of the communes	the power of the commons
made hym to regne.	made him to reign.
And thanne cam kynde wit,	And then came natural sense,
and clerkes he made,	and he made clerks,
for to counseillen the kyng,	in order to counsel the king,
and the commune save.	and to be a safeguard to the com-
The kyng and knyȝthod,	The king and knighthood, [mons,
and clergie bothe,	and clergy along with them,
casten that the commune	determined that the commons
sholde hemself fynde.	should find themselves.
The commune contreved	The commons contrived
of kynde wit craftes,	arts by means of natural sense,
and for profit of al the peple	and for the profit of the people
plowmen ordeyned,	ordained ploughmen,
to tilie and to travaille,	to till and to labour,
as trewe lif asketh.	as true life requires.
The kyng and the commune,	The king and the commons,
and kynde wit the thridde,	and natural sense the third,
shopen lawe and leauté,	created law and loyalty,
ech man to knowe his owene.	each man to know his own.

V. We may compare all these with the Alliterative Poem on the Deposition of Richard the Second, p. 23, to which, as it is one of the Publications of the Camden Society, I need do no more than refer.

P. 120, *l.* 947.—This line cannot be construed as it stands, and is evidently corrupt.

P. 121. *William de Rishanger* was a monk of St. Alban's, and is said to have been the King's historiographer (historiographus regius) after Matthew Paris's death. He died in 1312. He tells us that this song was written before, and not after, the battle of Lewes ; and that it was the defection of some of the Barons mentioned in the song at p. 59, which gave rise to it. It is, therefore, probably placed wrongly after the battle of Lewes.

P. 122, *l.* 19, *O Comes Gloverniæ.*—This was Gilbert de Clare, who was extremely active in the cause of the Barons, and distinguished himself at the battle of Lewes.

P. 123, *l.* 3.—The second line of this tetrastich seems to be lost.

—— *l.* 10, *Comes le Bygot.*—This was Roger Bigod, Earl of Norfolk, whom the Barons made Governor of Orford in Suffolk, after the battle of Lewes.

P. 124, *l.* 3, *nobis.*—A mere error of the press for *vobis.*

P. 125. THE LAMENT OF SIMON DE MONTFORT.—This song was printed privately, with some other Anglo-Norman poems from the same MS., by Sir Francis Palgrave, in 1818, in a collection which is now extremely rare. It was also inserted in the second edition of Ritson's Ancient Songs (1829), where it is accompanied with a translation in English verse by George Ellis.

—— *l.* 8, *Tot à cheval.*—The Barons were surprised at Evesham before they were joined by their foot soldiers, and when therefore they were unprepared for this decisive conflict.

P. 126, *l.* 4, *Sire Hue le fer, ly Despencer, tresnoble justice.*—Hugh Despencer, appointed justiciary of England by the Barons. He fell at Evesham.

—— *l.* 6, *Sire Henri .... fitz le cuens de Leycestre.*—The eldest son of Simon de Montfort ; he fell in the battle.

—— *l.* 7, *par le cuens de Gloucestre.*—After the battle of Lewes, the Earl of Gloucester, becoming jealous of Simon de Montfort's popularity, deserted to the King, and fought against his former associates at Evesham.

—— *l.* 14, *une heyre.*—I suppose this refers to Guy de Montfort, Simon's second son, who was taken prisoner at Evesham, but afterwards escaped and fled to the Continent.

P. 126, *l.* 15, *les faus ribaus.*—As this word, *ribaldus, ribaus, ribaud,* occurs frequently in our Songs, both in Latin, Anglo-Norman, and English, it may be worth while to say something about it.

It is one of those curious words of which the origin and primary signification are very doubtful. It was certainly applied to a particular class of people, and a class which seems to have been dependant on the household of the great. Giraldus Cambrensis, when telling his various troubles and persecutions (Wharton, Anglia Sacra, vol. iii. p. 575), speaks thus of the witnesses brought against him by his enemies :—" Archidiaconus (*i. e.* Giraldus himself) autem statim, productis testibus illis coram auditoribus ad jurandum, proposuit in singulorum personas se dicturum ; in canonicos Menevenses tanquam perjuros et excommunicatos, in monachos tanquam trutannos et domorum suarum desertores, in *ribaldos* tanquam vilissimos et, sicut cæteri cuncti, mercede conductos." And again, on the next page, " Et testium multitudinem de garcionibus et *ribaldis* partis adversæ, qui omnes jurare parati fuerant et testificare .... trutannus ille vilissimus id totum faciebat ; qui et *ribaldos suos* cunctos ad hoc probandum simul cum ipso mittebat....... Videns igitur archidiaconus *ribaldos illos* ad nutum *dominorum suorum* quidlibet probare paratos..... Sciens itaque si *probatio ribaldica* procederet ...... *ribaldica multitudo,* etc." They seem to have been the lowest class of retainers, perhaps men without any certain appointment, who had no other mode of living than following the courts of the Barons, and who were employed on all kinds of disgraceful and wicked actions. One authority quoted by Ducange couples " parasitos atque *ribaldos.*" A story quoted from a MS. at Berne, by Sinner (Catalogus, tom. i. p. 272), shows us that a *goliard* belonged to the class of *ribalds :* now a *goliard* seems to have been only another name for a *jongleur* (joculator), or one who attended the tables of the rich to amuse the guests by jokes, buffoonery, and mountebank tricks. An ecclesiastical statute quoted in Ducange (v. Goliardus) says, " item præcipimus quod clerici non sint *joculatores, goliardi,* seu *bufones;*" and another commands, " quod clerici *ribaldi,* maxime vero qui dicuntur *de familia goliæ,* per episcopos .... tondere præcipiantur." Matthew Paris, sub an. 1229, says, " quidam famuli, vel mancipia,

vel illi quos solemus *goliardenses* appellare, versus ridiculos componebant."
In this last passage we find them classed with the famuli, or household retainers.   This class appears, at least in France, to have enjoyed certain popular
rights or privileges.   In a very curious charter of the year 1380, printed in
Ducange, we find one Antony de Sagiac " se *gerens pro ribaldo*, et se dicens
de ordine seu de statu goliardorum, seu buffonum," claiming a fine of five
pence upon incontinent women, and accused of trying to extract money from
a woman, whom he accused wrongfully, on this account, " de talique et alio
vili questu, quem sub umbra *ribaldiæ, goliardiæ*, seu *buffoniæ* ejusmodi ......
vivebat."   In the household of the King of France there was a *rex ribaldorum*,
whose office was to judge disputes, &c. which might occur among the retainers
of his class, and who had also a jurisdiction over the public stews.   As the
lives of this class of men were set at a small value by their masters, they were
commonly exposed to the first brunt of battle in the wars, and the name is
sometimes given to the body which is now called the *forlorn hope* in the
attack of a town.   The *ribaldi* who accompanied the army were also employed
in plundering and destroying the country.   As they were people of vile life
and condition, the term *ribald* came gradually into use as a common appellation for a low and infamous person, and was used, as in the present instance,
as an epithet of contempt and degradation.

   P. 128, *l.* 1, *pepulere.*—The MS. has *pepulare.*

   P. 130, *l.* 8, *Plebs devicta fremit.*—Alluding to the rising at Chesterfield,
the occupation of the Isles of Axholme and Ely, and other insurrections.

   —— *l.* 11, *Urbs Londoniensis.*—The Earl of Gloucester, dissatisfied with the
King's proceedings after the battle of Evesham, had taken up arms and established himself at London, the citizens of which joined his party readily, as
they were themselves enraged against the King for having deprived them of their
charter.

   P. 131, *l.* 2, *Francorum regis germanus rex Siculorum.*—Prince Edward
left England in July, 1270, to join the King of France, Saint Louis, in his
expedition to the Holy Land.   Louis was persuaded by his brother, Charles,
then King of Sicily, to turn aside, in order to make war on the Bey of Tunis,
from whom he claimed a tribute.   Louis died at Carthage of a disease produced by the climate ; and when Prince Edward and his English army arrived,

they found their ally dead, and the King of Sicily, who had made advantageous terms with the Bey, ready to return home. Charles, who hastened to take possession of the throne of France, refused to proceed in the crusade, and Edward, who was obliged to go alone, went over to Sicily, and wintered at Trapeni. Here, on the night of December 23, the day after their arrival, occurred the terrible storm alluded to in the Poem. Early in the spring, Edward, with his small army, proceeded on their voyage, and landed at Acre.

P. 132, *l.* 5, *Accon respirat.*—Acre was besieged by Bondocar, Sultan of Babylon, who was preparing to take the place by assault, at the moment when Edward arrived to raise the siege.

—— *l.* 9, *Assessinus Veteris de Monte.*—On the Old Man of the Mountain, and the Assassins, or Assessins, much information will be found in a popular form, in the Marquis of Villeneuve-Trans, Histoire de St. Louis.

—— *l.* 16.—This seems to be a new testimony against the truth of the story which makes Edward's Queen suck the poison from his wound. A song made on the occasion would hardly have failed to mention such a circumstance, if it had been known.

—— *l.* 17, *Thomam de Wyta.*—This writer's name is not found in Tanner.

P. 135, *l.* 13, *comencent.*—Probably an error of the scribe for *comencement.*

P. 136, *l.* 4, *vironum.*—The MS. has *virronum.* *Viro* i given by Ducange as synonymous with *baro,* and is supposed to be derived from *vir.*

P. 137, *ll.* 15, 16, *sonne .. prodhonme.*—In old manuscripts it is quite impossible to say whether the scribe meant *n* or *u,* unless we know otherwise which it ought to be, and the *n* in words of the form of those just quoted may perhaps be intended for *u.* But I am rather inclined to think such was not the case.

P. 138, *l.* 34, *Sympringham.*—The order of Sempringham, commonly called Gilbertine canons, was founded by Sir Gilbert de Sempringham, in the first half of the twelfth century. One of its peculiarities was the establishment of monks and nuns in the same house, though their different habitations were carefully separated, and all intercourse between them strictly forbidden.

Nigellus Wireker speaks of this as a newly established order, and satirizes the near collocation of nuns and monks in a spirit similar to that of our song :—

Canonici missas tantum, reliquumque sorores
Explent; officii debita jura sui.
Corpora, non voces, murus disjungit, in unum
Psallant directe psalmitis absque metro.

And again, in describing his own order, he says, archly,—

Quid de Semplingama? quantum? vel qualia sumam?
Nescio, nam nova res me dubitare facit.
Hoc tamen ad præsens nulla ratione remittam,
Namque necem nimis fratribus esse reor;
Quod nunquam nisi clam, nullaque sciente sororum,
Cum quocunque suo fratre manere licet.

P. 139, *l.* 61, *De Beverleye.*—The monks of Beverley were Franciscans.

P. 140, *l.* 71, *De Hospitlers.*—The order of Knights Hospitalers, founded during the first crusades, was introduced into England about the year 1100. They were laymen, and, from an humble beginning, they became exceedingly rich and proud. In the Patent Rolls (45 Edw. III.) we find that the King " constituit Ricardum de Everton visitatorem Hospitalis S. Joannis Jerusalem in Anglia ad reprimendam religiosorum insolentiam, et ad observandam religiosorum honestatem." See Ellis's Dugdale, vol. vi. p. 786.

——— *l.* 79, *De Chanoynes.*—The regular canons were a less strict order than the other monks in general, and followed the rule of St. Augustine. One of the rules of their order was expressed simply thus—" Carnem vestram domate jejuniis et abstinentia escæ quantum valetudo permittit." They appear to have been particularly enjoined frequent abstinence from flesh. However, at the time when this song was written, they seem not to have observed their rule in this respect very strictly. Rutebeuf says of them (Jubinal's Rutebeuf, vol. i. p. 239)—

En l'ordre des canoines qu'on dist Saint-Augustin,
Ils vivent à plenté, sans noise et sans hustin.
Je lo que leur soviègne au soir et au matin
Que la chars bien nourie porte à l'âme venin.

P. 141, *l.* 95, *de Moyne Neirs.*—The Black Monks were the Benedictines.

P. 142, *l.* 115, *Des Chanoygnes Seculers.*—The luxury of the secular canons is often alluded to by the early satirists. Nigellus Wireker says of them—

Illud præcipue tamen instituere, tenendum
    Omnibus in tota posteritate sua,
Lex vetus ut suasit, ne quilibet absque sua sit,
    Et quod quisque suas possit habere duas.
Hi sunt qui mundum cum flore cadente tenentes,
    Ne sic marcescat, sæpe rigare student.
Hi sunt qui faciunt quidquid petulantia carnis
    Imperat, ut vitiis sit via prona suis.

Rutebeuf (ed. Jubinal, vol. i. p. 239) says that there were many of them—

—————— qui ont grant signorie,
Qui poi font por amis et assés por amie.

P. 143, *l.* 133, *Gris Moignes.*—Perhaps the Cistercians. In a poem on the Grey Monks, *De Grisis Monachis* (MS. Cotton. Vespas. A. xix. fol. 56, rº), which will be found among the works of Walter Mapes, they are ridiculed for the same arrangement of clothing,—

    Carent femoralibus partes turpiores,
    Veneris ut usibus sint paratiores,
    Castitatis legibus absolutiores ;
    In cunctis hominibus nulli sunt pejores.

The *Albi Monachi* are similarly satirized by Nigellus Wireker for going without breeches. The Friars de Sacco wore no breeches under their robes.

P. 144, *l.* 154, *l' Ordre de Cilence.*—Perhaps the Carthusian monks, a branch of the Benedictines, whose order, which was peculiarly strict, was introduced into England by Henry II. They were enjoined to live in separate cells, and to keep very strict silence, and have little communication with each other.

—— *l.* 169, *Les Frere Menours.*—The Friars Minors were better known as Franciscans, and in France as the Cordeliers. Their order enjoined, above all things, poverty and humility. They were not to ride when travelling, unless some manifest necessity or infirmity obliged them. See Dugdale, vi. 1505.

P. 145, *l.* 188.—The MS. has *en autre*, which seems to be a mere error for *ne autre*.

P. 146, *l.* 194, *des Prechours.*—The preaching friars were the Dominicans, called, in France, Jacobins. This order was introduced into England in 1221. Rutebeuf says that instead of adhering to their primitive humility and poverty, the Jacobins became the richest and most overbearing of all the orders. Jubinal, vol. i. pp. 152, 175—179.

P. 148, *l*. 240, *devyns* seems to be a mere variation of *devys*, thus spelt in order to accommodate the rhyme.

P. 149. SONG OF THE HUSBANDMAN.—This Song is in many parts extremely difficult to translate, from the numerous words in it which do not occur elsewhere, as well as from the abruptness of the phraseology. The same may be said of one or two other songs printed from the same manuscript.

P. 154, *l*. 14, *halymotes*.—This word means literally *holy meetings*. It is translated *sabbath*, in the supposition that there is some allusion to the popular notion of the festive meetings of the devils and the witches.

P. 160. SONG ON THE SCOTTISH WARS.—The copy of this Song preserved among the manuscripts of Clare Hall was first pointed out by Mr. Hunter, in the Appendix to the last Report of the Record Commission. I have obtained a copy of part of it by the kindness of Mr. Halliwell, who was unable from different circumstances to continue his transcript beyond the 72nd line. The Oxford MS. I only know through Mr. Halliwell's description of it : to judge by the articles contained in this MS., I should be inclined to think they were mostly copied from the Cottonian MS. Titus A. xx. In the Cottonian MS., Claudius D. vi. this poem bears the title " Commendatio Gentis Anglorum et processus guerræ inter Anglos et Scotos." In the Clare Hall MS. the Song is attributed to the " Prior de Blithe." The Prior of Blythe, in Nottinghamshire, at this time, was William Burdon. See Ellis's Dugdale, iv. 621. The MS. in the Sloane Library seems to be a transcript from a monastic register, perhaps of Alnwick, in Northumberland, for the reference in the margin is, " Regist. Prem. fol. 59, a." It is there attributed to the Prior of Alnwick. The original title seems to have been " Rithmus bonus de bello Scotiæ ad Dunbarre ;" which the transcriber had first copied, and then, after erasing it, substituted the following, " Prioris Alnwicensis de Bello Scotico apud Dunbarr, tempore regis Edwardi I., dictamen sive rithmus Latinus ; quo de Willielmo Wallace, Scotico illo Robin Whood, plura, sed invidiose, canit." Ritson, in his preface to Robin Hood, was misled by this latter title, and cites it as a proof that this hero was popular in the thirteenth century. In MS.

Cotton. Titus A. xx. a hand of the sixteenth century ascribes this poem to Robert Baston.

It will already have been observed by the reader, that, in verse of this kind, the fourth line of each tetrastich is an hexameter (sometimes a pentameter), taken from some poet then popular, and often from a classic writer. In the MS. from which the Sloane transcript was made, the authorities for the hexameters, in the present Song, were indicated in the margin. They are as follows :—*ll.* 4, *Morus.*—8, *Cato.*—†8, *Cato.*—†12, *Poetria.*—†16, *Oracius.* —12, *Cato.*—16, *Doctrinale.*—20, *Doctrinale.*—24, *De proprio.*—28, *Doctrinale.*—32, *Cartul.*—36, *Urbanus.*—40, *Doctrinale.*—44, *Morus.*—48, *Theodorus.*—52, *De proprio.*—56, *Vulgat.*—60, *Pu* . . . .—64, *Vulgat.*—68, *Buliardus.*—72, *Oracius.*—76, *Oracius.*—80, *Oracius.*—84, *Cato.*—88, *Ovidius.*—92, *Doctrinale.*—96, *Cato.*—100, *Cato.*—104, *Ovidius.*—108, *Cato.*— 112, *Cato.*—116, *Cato.* (?)—120, *Cato.*—124, *Cato.*—128, *Cato.*—132, *Doctrinale.*—136, *Cato.*—140, *Cato.*—144, *Poeta.*—148, *Poeta.*—152, *Orasius.*— 156, *Virgilius.*—160, *Statius.*—†164, *Oratius.*—†168, *Teodorus.*—164, *Omerus.*—168, *Ovid. Omer.*—172, *Cartul.*—176, *Veritas evangelica.*—180, *De proprio.*—184, *Ovidius.*—188, *Vulgat.*—192, *Doctrinale.*—196, *Vulgat.*—200, *Doctrinale.*—204, *Idem.*—208, *Oracius.*—212, *De Vulg.*—216, *Doctrinale.*— 220, *Amianus.*

In the above list of names, *Poetria* refers to the celebrated work of Galfridus de Vinesauf. *Poeta* seems to be a mere error of the scribe for *Poetria.* *Doctrinale* is here only another name for the *Parabolæ* of Alanus de Insulis. *Cato* refers to the well-known *Disticha.* *De proprio* means that the verse is of the author's own making.

P. 164, *l.* 44, *Joannis,* John Baliol.— In the Cottonian MS. Claudius D. vi. the following lines are here inserted, which evidently do not belong to the poem :

> " *Exprobratio Scotorum.*
> Caude causantur, regnarunt, apocapantur ;
> Privantur caude, fas fandi, Scotia, plaude.
> *Responsio Anglorum.*
> Scotia scotabit strebæ, Scotus vix latitabit ;
> Anglia, jam pange, fas fandi, Scotia, plange."

P. 168, *l.* 102, *Johannem Warenniæ.*—This was the same John de Warenne, Earl of Surrey, who, staunch to the party of Henry III., had escaped from the battle of Lewes. He commanded the English army at the battle of Dunbar, was afterwards made Governor or Guardian of Scotland, and was again at the head of the English forces when they were defeated at Stirling.

P. 169, *Quod Trentam non transient.*—The King had carried with him to London the Scottish knights whom he most suspected, and, before he went to Flanders, he exacted from them solemn oaths that during his absence they would not repass the Trent without his permission.

P. 170, *l.* 138, *ad Strivelyne.*—The battle of Stirling was fought on Thursday the 11th of September, 1297.

P. 171, *l.* 141, *comes dux Anglorum.*—The Earl of Surrey (Warenne).

—— *l.* 147, *Levenax et Ricardus Lundi.*—For an account of this reverse, and the part which the Earl of Levenax (Lennox) and Richard Lundi acted, see Knighton, in Twisden, coll. 2516, et seq.

P. 172, *l.* 163.—This line is evidently corrupt ; but, as it is only found in one MS., I have no means of correcting it.

P. 173, *l.* 163, *Cremare Northumbriam.*—The invasion of Northumberland and the burning of Hexham and Corbridge are told by Matthew of Westminster, p. 427. See also Peter Langtoft, in the present volume, p. 287 ; and Knighton, coll. 2520, et seq. None of them mention the damages done at Alnwick.

—— *l.* 167, *Vesey, Morley, Somervile, Bertram.*—The poet seems to refer to members of those families who had distinguished themselves in opposing the inroads of the Scots at different periods, but who were dead at the time of this invasion.

—— *l.* 186, *Willelmo datum est militare pignus.*—On his return from the expedition into England, Wallace was solemnly installed Guardian of Scotland.

P. 176, *l.* 205, *die Magdalenæ.*—The battle of Falkirk, so fatal to the Scots, was fought on St. Mary Magdalen's day, the 22nd of July, 1298.

—— *l.* 211, *trutannus.*—This word is the origin of the modern word *truant.* Its primary meaning has not been accurately ascertained, but it seems to have been most generally used for a person who wandered about, and gained his living by false pretences, or passed himself under a different character to that which really belonged to him. It is applied sometimes to abbots or priors who lived abroad and neglected their monasteries, or to monks who had quitted their houses, as in the passage of Giraldus, quoted at p. 369.

P. 178, *l.* 234, *Margaretam reginam.*—Edward married, in second nuptials, Margaret, sister of the King of France.

—— *l.* 243, *Comyn, Karryk, Umfraville.*—Three of the most active leaders of the Scots in their opposition to Edward. The Earl of Karrik was Robert Bruce. Gilbert de Umfraville, Earl of Angus, had been one of Edward's Commissioners for manning and fortifying the castles in Scotland.

P. 183, *l.* 11, *collectio lanarum.*—The oppressive duty upon wool, which was the staple of English commerce at that period, was severely felt and complained of. In 1296, the King seized all the wool in the merchants' warehouses, and sold it for his own profit, paying for it, as usual, with tallies, and promises to repay them to the full. " Ministri regis omnes saccos lanæ, quinarium numerum excedentes, datis talliis, acceperunt ad opus regis, et ab unoquoque sacco, numerum quinarium non excedente, ab ipsis eorum dominis, nomine *malæ totæ*, xl. solidos extorserunt." Hemingford, p. 110.

P. 186, *l.* 11, *de fust manger* (de fusto manducare).—In low Latin, *fustum* was a generic name for everything made of wood. It need hardly be said that it means here the plates and other utensils of the table, which among the lower classes were generally of this material. It would be more reasonable, says the writer of the song, if the court would eat out of wooden vessels, and pay for their provisions with silver, than to live sumptuously with plate, and only pay their victuals with wooden tallies.

—— *l.* 13, *Est vitii signum pro victu solvere lignum.*—The King's purveyors were a great grievance to the peasantry. In the curious poem of " King Edward and the Shepherd " (printed by Hartshorne from a MS. in the University Library, Cambridge), the latter personage is made to say :—

> " In Wynsour was I borne ;
> Hit is a myle but here beforne,
>   The town then maist thou see.
> I am so pyled with the Kyng,
> That I most fle fro my wonyng,
>   And therefore woo is me.
> I hade catell, now have I non ;
> Thay take my bestis, and don thaim slon,
>   And payen but *a stick of tre.*"

And when the King, in disguise, promises to obtain redress, the Shepherd proceeds—

" Sir," he seid, " be seynt Edmonde,
Ther is owand .iiii. pounde
   And odd twa schillyng.
A stikke I have to my witnesse,
Off hasill I mene that hit is,
   I ne have non other thyng.
      *   *   *   *
Thei do but gode, the kynges men,
Thei ar worse then sich ten
   That bene with hym no dell.
Thei goo aboute be .viij. or nyne,
And done the husbondes mycull pyne,
   That carfull is their mele.
Thei take geese, capons, and henne,
And alle that ever thei may with renne,
   And reves us our catell.
Sum of them was bonde sore,
And afturwarde honget therfore,
   For soth as I you say.
ʒet ar ther of them nyne moo ;
For at my hows thei were also,
   Certis, ʒisturday.
Thei toke my hennes and my geese,
And my schepe with all the fleese,
   And ladde them forth away.
Be my doʒtur thei lay al nyʒt.
To come agayne thei have me hyʒt ;
   Of helpe I wolde yow pray.
With me thei lefte alle their thyng,
That I am sicur of theire comyng,
   And that me rewes sore.
I have fayre chamburs thre ;
But non of them may be with me
   While that thei be thore.
Into my cart-hows thei me dryfe ;
Out at the dur thei put my wyfe,
   For she is olde gray-hare."

P. 187. Song on the Flemish Insurrection.—This Song was printed by Ritson, in his *Ancient Songs.*

P. 188, *l.* 16, *Peter Conyng.*—Peter Coning (in English, Peter King,) was a weaver of Bruges. A brief account of this insurrection is given in Matthew of Westminster, p. 444. See, for a more complete narrative, Michelet's Histoire de France, vol. iii. p. 76.

P. 189, *l.* 8, *avowerie.*—This is the low Latin *advocaria.* See Ducange, in voce.

—— *l.* 11, *hou.*—The MS. has *hout.*

P. 189, *l.* 17, *to clynken huere basyns of bras.*—This circumstance occurred on the 21st March, 1302, at the beginning of the insurrection. In the towns of Flanders, as in the boroughs in England, the people were called up in an insurrection by the sound of the church bell. There was a famous distich on the bell of Roland, at Bruges—

> Roelandt, Roelandt, als ick kleppe dan ist brandt,
> Als ick luye, dan ist storm in Vlaenderlandt.

On the present occasion, the people dared not go to their bell, on account of their French governors, so they beat their brass basins :—cumque ad campanam civitatis non auderent accedere, pelves suas pulsantes .... omnem multitudinem concitarent. Meyer, Annal. in a. 1301, p. 90.

P. 191, *l.* 9, *Conyng.*—This word, in English, meant a *rabbit,* and is here made the subject of a pun. In Flemish, it signified *king.*

P. 193, *ll.* 17, 18, *Awey thou ʒunge pope !* .... *Thou hast lore thin cardinals.—P.* 194, *l.* 2, *Do the forth to Rome.*—An allusion to the dissensions between the Pope and the family of the Colonnas.—" Illis etiam diebus, dominus papa, fidei et orationum quæ erant beati Petri oblitus, assumens quæ non erant ejus, tam aurum videlicet a viduis et orphanis quam argentum, non viduis et orphanis, sed militibus bellicosis illud erogare curavit, contra schema quorundam cardinalium, eos denique degradando, et contra regem Siciliæ guerram movendo. Sed dicti regis exercitus de galeatis turmis domini papæ multa millia viriliter necaverunt." Matthew of Westminster, p. 432. This was the famous Pope Boniface VIII., who suffered so much from the persecutions of the King of France.

—— *l.* 7, *fot lome,* probably means *foot-lame,* lame of foot. It occurs again in p. 335 of the present volume.

P. 195. A SONG ON THE TIMES.—The MS. from which this song is taken, MS. Harl. No. 913, was written in Ireland, about the year 1308, by an English monk. For a detailed description of it, see Mr. Crofton Croker's *Popular Songs of Ireland.*

P. 196, *l.* 19, *hoblurs.*—The name *hoblurs* (hobellarii) was given properly to a kind of light-armed soldiers.

P. 198, *l.* 14, *geet.*—This word should probably be translated *goats*, rather than *kids.*

P. 199, *l.* 7, *anone.*—In the MS. this word is explained by the original scribe in the margin as " at one time."

P. 206. SONG AGAINST THE SCHOLASTIC STUDIES.—In the Cottonian MS. from which this song is taken, a hand of the 16th century has written in the margin that it was the work of Robert Baston.

The Oxford MS. was pointed out to me by Mr. Halliwell, but I have not been able to obtain a collation.

P. 207, *l.* 2, *propere.*—The MS. has p͠pe, the meaning of which is not clear.

—— *l.* 10, *Sicut servus Stichus.*—This name was given to a servant in the Roman comic writers. It is introduced here for the sake of rhyme.

P. 208, *l.* 2, *nullus.*—The MS. has *unus.*

—— *l.* 10, *Thebanas* .... *vel Trojanas cædes.*—Referring to the Thebaid of Statius, and the poem *De bello Trojano* of Joseph of Exeter, both of them at that period popular reading books.

—— *l.* 16, *Telluris.*—The MS. has *Celurus.*

P. 209, *l.* 4, *agro* .... *positis.*—The MS. has *ager* and *positus.*

P. 212. SONG ON THE EXECUTION OF SIR SIMON FRASER.—This song was printed by Ritson, in his *Ancient Songs.*

P. 213, *l.* 6, *The Waleis.*—Wallace was taken prisoner at the second battle of Dunbar, in 1305, and was executed at London on the Eve of St. Bartholomew, (Aug. 24) 1306. The places to which his quarters were sent were Newcastle, Berwick, Perth, and Aberdeen.

—— *l.* 10, *Simond Frysel.*—This was the original form of the name of Fraser, and is the way in which it is spelt in all the English documents.

P. 215, *l.* 14, *kyng of somere.*—Matthew of Westminster gives a popular story, that Bruce's queen had told him in derision, he was but a *summer king*, and that his kingdom would scarcely last in the winter. See Holinshed, p. 314.

P. 215, *l.* 9, *Sire Edward of Carnarvan.*—The Prince of Wales.

P. 216, *l.* 10, *Sir Emer de Valence.*—Aylmer de Valence, second Earl of Pembroke, a Baron who was frequently occupied in the Scottish wars, and who was appointed by Edward to be one of the guardians of his son, Edward II.

—— *l.* 19, *the batayle of Kyrkenclyff.*—Fought, according to Holinshed, on the next Sunday after Midsummer day, 1306.

—— *l.* 15, *Sire Thomas of Multone.*—Thomas de Multon, of Egremond, in Cumberland. He was active in the Scottish wars of this reign.

P. 218, *l.* 17, *Sire Herbert of Morham.*—Apparently a mere error of the scribe for Norham. Matthew of Westminster relates the same anecdote.

P. 219, *l.* 13, *oure Levedy even.*—The seventh of September, 1306.

—— *l.* 16, *Sire Rauf of Sondwyche.*—Ralph de Sandwich was constable of the Tower of London *(constabularius turris London).*

P. 221, *l.* 7, *a curtel of burel.*—*Burellus*, in low Latin, *bureau* or *burel* in old French, was a kind of coarse and common cloth.

P. 222, *l.* 9, *tu-brugge.*—Perhaps this word means a drawbridge. It occurs again in Robert of Gloucester, p. 543 :—

> " And the castel brugge out of the med he barnde fram then ende
> To the tu-brugge along, vor me ne ssolde out wende."

Which means probably that he burnt all that part of the bridge on the meadow side up to the place where its communication with the rest was cut off by the raising of the drawbridge.

P. 223, *l.* 6, *Erl of Asseles.*—John de Strathbogie, Earl of Athol. He also was captured and executed.

—— *l.* 18, *Tprot, Scot, for thi strif!*—The word *tprot* appears to be a mere exclamation of contempt. In a poem on "The Propertees of the Shyres of Engelond," printed by Hearne in the Introduction to the fifth volume of Leland's Itinerary, we find it used, as here, against the Scots :—

> " Northumbrelond hasty and hoot ;
> Westmerlond *tprut Scotte !*"

It will be found similarly used in a passage quoted in a note further on (p. 391).

In Sir Thomas de la More's Chronicle, it is applied to King Edward II. :—
" *Tprut !* Sire King !" It seems to be taken from the French : in Jean Bodel's
Jeu de S. Nicolas (Théatre Français au Moyen-Age, edited by MM. Mon-
merqué and Michel) it is put in the mouths of the common gamblers in a
public-house :—

> " *Tproupt ! tproupt !* bevons hardiement ;
> Ne faisons si le coc emplat."—(p. 183.)

And again, immediately after (p. 184) :—

> " *Tproupt ! tproupt !* où que soit passé, Diex !"

P. 223, *l.* 21, *with the longe shonkes.*—King Edward, still known popularly
as Edward Long-shanks.

P. 224. Song on the Venality of the Judges.—After this song was
printed, I found another copy of it in MS. Reg. 12, c. xii. fol. 1, v°. of reign
of Edw. II., written likewise as prose, which presents the following variations :
—*P.* 224, *ll.* 1, 2, *esuriunt | Et faciunt justitiam | et od.*—7, *exhennia.*—9, this
line is omitted, and the following begins *Sed quæ.*—11, *et aure non.*—13, *Sed
modo miro more.*—15, *ad peric.*—17, *ambiant.*—*P.* 225, *l.* 1, *hæc.*—7, *nam* is
omitted.—8, *Qui sensum.*—9, *ei pure.*—14, *Quid ergo Jhesu bone.*—*P.* 226, *l.* 1,
accedit.—2, *secretius.*—7, *potest.*—*ll.* 12-18 are placed after *l.* 10 in the next
page.—14, *dona.*—15, *et hoc pro l.*—17, *quamvis prius.*—19, *Si quædam pulcra
nobilis | decora vel am.*—*P.* 227, *l.* 2, *hoc.*—12, *ut exprimant.*—13, *vocantur.*—
14, *priores.*—18, *Sed quid.*—*P.* 228, *l.* 1, *quid laboras.*—2, *quid facis.*—8, *ibis
Omere, foras.*—9, *De vinctibus.*—11, *enumerare.*—19, *Est salsum totum.* This
MS. ends with this verse.

——— *l.* 7, *encennia.*—This word answers as nearly as may be to the modern
word *jewels.* The other MS., of which the variations are given above, reads
exennia, i. e. *treasures.*

P. 225, *l.* 17, *cedunt.*—In the MS. the scribe has written over this word
" i. re," that is, " i. e. recedunt."

P. 226, *l.* 21, *cum capite cornuto.*—The head dress of the ladies of rank and
fashion at this period was arranged in the form of two horns.

P. 227, *l.* 13, *relatores,* " qui querelam ad judices referunt." Ducange.

P. 229, *l.* 13, *transmittantur.*—The MS. has *transmutantur.*

P. 229, *l.* 18, *averia.*—The term *averium* is commonly used to signify all kinds of moveable property ; but more particularly to signify cattle and horses.

P. 230, *l.* 1, *clericos.*—The scribe has written above this word, in the MS. " i. pauperes."

P. 231. THE OUTLAW'S SONG OF TRAILEBASTON.—This song also was printed by Sir Francis Palgrave in the collection mentioned in a former note. The notion that the judges were called Trailebastons on account of the hastiness of their proceedings, is quite incorrect. The term was applied not to the judges, but to the persons judged, who received this name because they carried with them long staffs. An account of the origin of the Trailebastons will be found in the extract of Peter Langtoft, at p. 318 of the present volume. The proceedings against them led to many abuses, and were often made the means of gratifying personal revenge. The statute against the Trailebastons was continued in force through the reigns of Edward II. and Edward III.

P. 232, *l.* 1, *souz.*—In old French and Anglo-Norman, the word *sous* was not used in its present sense, but represented the Latin *solidos.*

—— *l.* 7, *le bois de Belregard.*—Perhaps a fictitious name, invented by the poet.

P. 233, *l.* 3, *ly Martyn.* .... *ly Knoville.*—*l.* 5, *Spigurnel* .... *Belflour.*— By the following commission, given in Rymer, we find that these Barons were the commissioners appointed to judge the Trailebastons in the western counties of England. There can be little doubt that *Belflour* in the song is meant for the name which in the commission is *Bellafagus.* This document is curious, both for the light it throws on the subject, and for the circumstance that it fixes the period at which the song was written ; it bears date at Westminster, April 6, 1305.

" *De transgressionibus nominatis Trailbaston audiendis et terminandis per totum regnum.*—Rex delectis et fidelibus suis, Wilielmo Martyn, Henrico Spigurnell, Wilielmo de Knovill, Rogero de Bellafago, et Thomæ de la Hyde, salutem.—Quia quamplures malefactores, et pacis nostræ perturbatores, homicidia, deprædationes, incendia, et alia dampna quamplurima nocte dieque perpetrantes, vagantur et discurrunt in boscis, in parcis, et aliis locis diversis, tam infra libertates quam extra, in comitatibus Cornubiæ, Devoniæ, Sumersetiæ, Dorsetiæ, Herefordiæ, Wygorniæ, Salopiæ, Staffordiæ, Wiltes', et Suthamptoniæ, et ibidem receptantur, in maximum periculum tam hominum per partes illas transeuntium, quam ibidem morantium, et nostri contemptum, ac pacis nostræ læsionem manifestam, ut accepimus : Per quorum incursus poterunt pejora prioribus de facili evenire, nisi remedium super hoc citius apponatur : Nos, eorum malitiæ in hac parte obviare, et hujusmodi dampnis et periculis præcavere volentes, assignavimus vos justiciarios nostros : Ad inquirendum, per sacramentum tam militum quam aliorum proborum et legalium hominum de comitatibus prædictis, tam infra libertates quam extra, per quos rei veritas melius sciri poterit, qui sunt illi malefactores, et eorum scienter receptatores, et eis consentientes, vim et auxilium præbentes, seu dictas transgressiones fieri procurantes et præcipientes : Et etiam ad inquirendum de illis, qui pro muneribus suis pactum fecerunt et faciunt cum malefactoribus, et pacis nostræ perturbatoribus, et eos conduxerunt et conducunt ad verberandum, vulnerandum, male tractandum et interficiendum plures de regno nostro, in feriis, mercatis, et aliis locis, in dictis comitatibus, pro inimicitia, invidia, malitia, et etiam pro eo quod in assisis, juratis, recognitionibus, et inquisitionibus factis de feloniis, positi fuerunt, et veritatem dixerunt : unde per conductionem hujusmodi malefactorum, juratores assisarum, juratorum recognitionum, et inquisitionum iilarum, præ timore dictorum malefactorum et horum minarum, sæpius veritatem dicere seu dictos malefactores indictare minime aussi fuerunt, et sunt : Et etiam ad inquirendum de illis qui hujusmodi munera dederunt et dant : et quantum et quibus : et qui hujusmodi munera receperunt et recipiunt : et a quibus, et qualiter, et quo modo : et qui hujusmodi malefactores in sua malitia fovent, nutriunt, et manutenent in comitatibus prædictis : Et etiam de illis, qui, ratione potestatis et dominii sui, aliquos in eorum protectionem et advocationem pro suo dando susceperunt, et adhuc suscipiunt : Et de illis qui pecuniam ab aliquo, per graves minas ei factas, malitiose extorserunt : Et ad felonias et transgressiones illas audiendas et terminandas secundum legem et consuetudinem regni nostri, et juxta formam ordinationis per nos et consilium nostrum super hoc factæ, et vobis in parliamento nostro liberatæ : Et etiam ad omnes felonias et transgressiones, de quibus inquisitiones coram dilectis et fidelibus nostris, Henrico de Cobeham, Thoma Paynel, Hugone de Sancto Philiberto, et Johanne Randolf, in prædictis comitatibus Wiltes' et Suthamtoniæ factæ sunt, et per vos, si necesse fuerit, faciendæ, audiendas et terminandas in forma prædicta :" etc.

P. 235, *l.* 6, *escolaye,* answers probably to a low Latin word *excollectionem.*

P. 237. A SONG AGAINST THE RETINUES OF THE GREAT PEOPLE.—Half of this song is written in the original in short lines, and the other half in long lines, to suit the convenience of the MS. It contains numerous popular words and phrases, the meaning of which it is now very difficult to ascertain.

P. 242, *l.* 9, *Le rei de Fraunce.*—Edward seems to have long cherished the design of embarking in a new crusade, which had been strongly advocated by the Pope, but he had been hindered by his continued wars and embarrassments, which the writer of the song attributes to the intrigues of the King of France.

P. 243, *l.* 13, *A Peiters à l'Apostoile.*—Pope Clement the Fifth, who was constantly in hostilities with his Italian subjects, and little more than a dependent on France, resided a great part of his pontificate at Poitiers.

P. 245, *ll.* 5, 6, *Si Aristotle . . . e Virgile.*—Aristotle and Virgil were names in great repute in the popular literature of the middle ages, and were the subject of much legend and romance.

P. 246. ELEGY ON THE DEATH OF EDWARD I.—This song had been already printed in Percy's Reliques of Ancient English Poetry.

P. 253. ON THE KING'S BREAKING HIS CONFIRMATION OF MAGNA CHARTA.—This curious poem is reprinted from an interesting little volume of early poetry, edited and printed privately by David Laing, Esq. and W. B. D. D. Turnbull, Esq. under the title of " Owain Miles, and other Inedited Fragments of Ancient English Poetry." 8vo. Edinburgh, 1837.

—— *l.* 7, *the feire.*—Probably the fair of St. Bartholomew.

P. 254, *l.* 5, *Of .iiij. wise-men.*—This was a very popular story, and found its way into the celebrated Gesta Romanorum. It also occurs frequently in a separate and different form in manuscripts of the fourteenth and fifteenth centuries. The sentences of the wise men were popular sayings independent of the tale, and are sometimes found separately. They varied at different periods, both as they are found separately, and as they are given in the different recensions of the story. It would be a curious and interesting work to collect together such popular political proverbs in chronological order. I have met with this story in a MS. in the British Museum contemporary with the present song, in which, if I remember right, both the sayings and the explanations of them are given in full both in English and Latin, but I have unfortunately mislaid my reference to it. The following is taken from MS. Reg. 5 A. vi. fol 83 r°, of the end of the 14th or beginning of the 15th cent. A more modern copy, with rather larger commentary, will be found in MS. Harl. No. 206, fol. 38, v°.

" Legitur quendam Regem quondam fuisse qui habuit 4ᵒʳ Philosophos in regno suo. In quo regno multæ plagæ, multa infortunia, et multi defectus fiebant in populis. Rex autem videns se ipsum nullo peccato mortali vulne- ratum, mirabatur valde, et diligenter inquirebat a prædictis 4ᵒʳ Philosophis qua de causa hæc infortunia magis agebantur in populis in tempore suo quam in tempore prædecessorum suorum.

" Primus Philosophus dixit, *Miȝt is riȝt;* Unde illud Ysaiæ, 69, Conversum est retrorsum judicium, et justitia longe stetit; corruit in platea veritas, et æquitas non potuit ingredi. *Liȝt is nyȝt;* unde Ewang., Væ homini illi per quem scandalum venit! Per eum scandalum venit qui alios malo exemplo cor- rumpit. Dominus in Levetico dixit: Time, inquit, Dominum Deum tuum, ut vivere possit frater tuus apud te; hoc est, ut sic vivas quod frater tuus per tuum exemplum vitam possit habere non mortem. *Fiȝt is fliȝt;* unde Augustinus: Bene agere et illicita non prohibere consensus erroris est. Gregorius: Facientis proculdubio culpam habet qui quod potest corrigere negligit emendare.

" Secundus Philosophus dixit, *One is too;* unde Ewang. : Omne regnum in se divisum desolabitur. Ambrosius: Sicut sine via nullus pervenit quo tendit, sic sine caritate, quæ dicta est via, non ambulare possunt homines, sed errare. *Frend is foo;* hoc potest intelligi quando homines et præcipue potentes veram pacem vel justitiam aut Dei ecclesiam strangulant, quibus principaliter propter Deum militare deberent. *Weele is woo;* Gregorius: Qui bona mundi diligit, velit nolit timori et dolori bene succumbit. Seneca: Avarus nisi dum moritur nichil bene facit.

" Tertius Philosophus dixit, *Lust has leve* ; unde Paulus: Si secundum car- nem vixeritis, moriemini. Jeronimus: Qui post carnem ambulant, in ventrem et libidinem proni, quasi irrationalia jumenta reputantur. *Thef is refe;* unde Jeremias: Væ qui ædificant domum suam non in justitia! Robertus Lincolni- ensis: Væ illis qui dicunt, faciamus mala, ut veniant bona, quorum damnatio justa est! *Pride has slef;* unde in Ps. : Irritaverunt eum in adinventionibus suis, et multiplicata est in eis ruina. David autem dixit : Non habitabit in medio domus meæ qui facit superbiam.

" Quartus Philosophus dixit, *Wille is red;* unde per Psalmistam dicitur : Noluit intelligere ut bene aget. Prover. 12 : Via stulti recta in oculis ejus; qui autem sapiens est audit consilium. *Wytte is qued;* unde P. : Erit enim tempus cum sanam doctrinam non sustinebunt. Augus. : Juventuti malorum hominum venenum est quidquid virtus præcipit, esca vero quidquid diabolus suggerit. *Good is ded;* unde in psalmo : Universa vanitas omnis homo vivens, i. vivens secundum hominem, non secundum Deum. Augus. : Sicut mors corporalis separat animum a corpore, ita peccatum mortale animam a vera vita, quæ est Deus."

In the following, which is taken from the common printed Gesta Romanorum, cap. 144, the English is translated.

" Fertur de quodam Rege cujus regnum in tam subitam devenit mutationem, quod bonum in malum, verum in falsum, forte in debile, justum in injustum est mutatum. Quam mutationem Rex admirans, a quattuor Philosophis sapientissimis causam hujus quæsivit ; qui, inquam, Philosophi post sanam deliberationem ad quattuor portas civitates pergentes quilibet eorum tres causas ibi scripsit. Primus scripsit, Potentia est justitia, ideo terra sine lege ; dies est nox, ideo terra sine via ; fuga est in pugna, ideo regnum sine honore. Secundus scripsit, Unum est duo, ideo regnum sine veritate ; amicus est inimicus, ideo regnum sine fidelitate ; malum est bonum, ideo terra sine pietate. Tertius scripsit, Ratio habet licentiam, ideo regnum sine nomine ; fur est præpositus, ideo regnum sine pecunia ; corabola vult esse aquila, ideo nulla discretio in patria. Quartus scripsit, Voluntas est consiliarius, ideo terra male disponitur ; denarius dat sententiam, ideo terra male regitur ; Deus est mortuus, ideo totum regnum peccatoribus est repletum."

In the moralisation, these sentences are applied to the time in which it was written. In the English *Gesta Romanorum* (edited by Sir Frederick Madden for the Roxburghe Club in 1838, and which it is to be regretted is not published in a popular form), p. 397, we have the following version of the story.

" This is redde in the Cronycles of Rome, that in the tyme of Antynyane the Emperour, in the citie of Rome befille a grete pestilence of men and bestes, and grete hungre in alle the empire. The comons risene agayne her lordes, and agayne her Emperour. The Emperour desirede to wete the cause of the tribulacions and diseases, and disposede hym for to putte a remedie agayne the foresaide disease. He callede to hym iiij. wise Philisophers, for to shew hym the cause of the grete vengeaunce; of the whiche Philisophers the first saide thus, ' Gifte is domesman, and Gile is chapman; the grete holde no lawe, and servauntes have none awe.' The seconde saide, ' Witte is turnede to trechery, and love into lechery; the holy day into glotonye, and gentrie into vilanie.' The thirde saide, ' Wise men are but scornede, and wedowes be sore yernede; grete men are but glosede, and smale men borne downe and myslovede.' The fourthe saide, ' Lordes wexen blynde, and kynnesmen ben unkynde; dethe out of mynde, and trewthe may no man fynde.''

The sentences in this last version are also found frequently in MSS. in a separate form. An imperfect copy of them will be found in the *Reliquiæ Antiquæ*, (Pickering, 1839,) p. 58. I have met recently with a much more complete copy, agreeing closely with the sentences in the above tale from the English *Gesta*, but I have also unfortunately lost the reference to it, and cannot recall it to mind at the present moment. In MS. Cotton. Vespas. E. xii. fol. 100, r°., of the end of the fourteenth century, is given another Latin version of this story, where the scene is laid at Carthage, the King is Hannibal, and instead of the four wise men we have Virgil, and the sayings are again different from the others. This version is important both for the history of the story, and for its connexion with the fable of the legendary Virgilius.

P. 256, l. 9, god is ded.—It will have been observed in the foregoing note that one of the versions of the story interprets *god* by *Deus ;*—God is dead,— which is most probably right, and the former editors have very properly given the word with a capital.

P. 258. SONGS ON THE DEATH OF PETER DE GAVESTON.—Both these songs are parodies upon hymns in the Romish ritual.

P. 260, l. 1, Vult hic comes, et non Petrus, dici.—The favourite was, indeed, extremely angry because people persisted in calling him Peter, and obtained a Royal decree that no one should be permitted to call him otherwise than Earl of Cornwall in future.

P. 262. THE BATTLE OF BANNOCKBURN.—The text of this poem is extremely corrupt. It appears, from Mr. Halliwell's description of the MS., that there is another copy of it at Oxford, MS. Rawl. B. 214. This poem is attri- buted to Robert Baston, a carmelite, who, according to a popular story, was present at the battle, and was taken prisoner by the Scots. We are told that he was liberated on condition of composing a poem to celebrate the valour of the Scots : the song here printed is of quite a different character.

P. 262, *l.* 6, *dabantur.*—*Debantur* in the MS.

—— *l.* 10, *præparare.*—The MS. has *portare*, with "p'p'are" written above.

P. 263, *l.* 9, *conflictus.*—The MS. had *consultus*, which is changed into *conflictus*.

—— *l.* 10, *Comes heu ! Gloverniæ.*—Gilbert de Clare, son of that Earl of Gloucester who was so active in the Barons' wars of the reign of Henry III. On his death, at Bannockburn, the title became extinct.

—— *l.* 17, *proditorius vir Bartholomeus.*—Perhaps Bartholomew de Badlesmere, who was Steward of the King's household, and attended the King in these wars.

P. 264, *l.* 2, *sex seminum.*—This word evidently represents the French *semaines*.

P. 265, *l.* 2, *nimis.*—The MS. has *nims*.

—— *l.* 4, *veneficos.*—The MS. has *venifices*.

—— *l.* 9, *multiplica.*—In middle-age Latin, the form *multiplicus* is frequently used for *multiplex*.

—— *l.* 14, *corruerunt.*—The scribe has written *sub* over the first syllable of this word in the MS., as though he would correct it to *subruerunt*.

P. 266, *l.* 16, *horridus.*—The MS. has *oridus*, and just afterwards it seems to have *quievit* for *crevit*.

P. 267, *l.* 4, *stirps radice.*—The MS. has *radix*, with *ortus* written over it ; from which it may be conjectured that the original from which the scribe copied had the reading which I have given, and that the word *ortus* was written over it, or in the margin, to supply the construction—*stirps ortus radice Jessæ*.

—— *l.* 12, *far.....*—The MS. has *far*⁹.

P. 268. THE OFFICE OF ST. THOMAS OF LANCASTER.—Popular heroes and patriots were frequently canonised by the people after their death. Such was the case with Simon de Montfort. See p. 124 of the present volume. A very curious story of this kind will be found in William of Newbury, l. 5, cc. 20, 21. The King, in the present instance, was obliged to issue a proclamation forbidding the worship of Earl Thomas of Lancaster.

P. 268, *l.* 2, *Thomam Cantuariæ.*—All the popular heroes were compared to St. Thomas of Canterbury. We have seen the comparison used in the case of Simon de Montfort, see p. 125 of the present volume.

P. 270, *l.* 11, *pater proles erat regia.*—Thomas Plantagenet, Earl of Lancaster, was son of Edmund, younger brother of Edward I.

—— *l.* 12, *matrem* .... *reginam Navarria.*—Blanche, daughter of Robert, Earl of Artois, and widow of Henry, King of Navarre, who was espoused in second marriage to Edmund Plantagenet.

—— *l.* 16, *Benedicti capitur vigilia* .... , *l.* 17, *die tertia.*—After the battle of Boroughbridge (March 15, 1322), the Earl of Lancaster took refuge in a chapel, where he was taken on the 20th, brought to Pontefract on the 21st, tried on the 22nd, and beheaded the same day. The 20th of March was the eve of St. Benet.

P. 271, *l.* 2, *Hoylandiæ.*—Robert de Hoyland (the father of Thomas de Holand, Earl of Kent, the first husband of Joan, Princess of Wales,) had been sent to collect forces in Lancashire, to assist the Earl of Lancaster, but when he had gotten them together, he deserted the Earl, and went over with them to the King's party.

——— *sudam* appears to be an error for some other word.

P. 273. PETER LANGTOFT'S CHRONICLE.—The Cambridge MS. contains only the history of Edward I., which is given as a complete work, with the title, " Içi commence le Brut coment li bon rei Edward gaigna Escotz e Galis." The Fairfax MS. seems also to have given the same portion of Langtoft's Chronicle. Since my text was printed, Sir Frederick Madden has kindly given me his transcripts of the English fragments as they stand in the Fairfax MS. No. 24, in the Bodleian Library, at Oxford, and in the Arundel MS. No. 14, in the College of Arms. The numerous variations in these lines, and the frequent recurrence of lines in one MS. which are omitted in another, seem clearly to prove they were fragments of popular songs interwoven into the Chronicle by its writer. I ought to say that, at the time the extracts in the present volume were printed off, it was not in my power to have the sheets collated with the original. It may also be observed, that it has not been thought proper to correct the text by the various readings, but the translation is frequently made from the latter, when the text is evidently wrong.

P. 274, *l.* 15, *Celestine la pape.*—Pope Celestin the Fifth, who was elected in July, 1294, and abdicated in the December following.

P. 275, *l.* 50, *suz Dover.*—An account of this attack upon Dover will be found in Matthew of Westminster, p. 424, and in Knighton, col. 2502.

P. 278, *l.* 75, *Thomas de Turbevile.*—See, on this affair, Matthew of Westminster, p. 425, Knighton, col. 2502, Hemingford, p. 58.

—— *l.* 83, *Cent lievre de tere.*—Robert de Brunne's version has a hundred pounds of land, *i. e.* lands of that yearly value.

P. 280, *l.* 106, *Le tierz jour.*—Robert de Brunne says—

> Opon the thrid day, at a toun hamelet,
> Thomas was his pray, as he to mete was set.

—— *l.* 112, *cum traitur est jugé.*—Robert of Brunne has given more details of Turbeville's trial than are found in the original.

P. 282, *l.* 135, *Le counte de Nincole.*—Henry de Lacy, Earl of Lincoln and Salisbury.

—— *l.* 136, *Sir Willeam de Vescy.*—William de Vescy, Lord of Alnwick, and governor of Scarborough Castle.

—— *l.* 153, *la male rage.*—" *Male rage:* Faim extraordinaire, enragée ; *mala rabies.*" Roquefort.

—— *l.* 156, *rivelins.*—Apparently a kind of rough boots worn by the Scots, so called perhaps on account of their ragged and torn appearance.

——— *la nue nage.*—*Nage* is the Latin *nates.* The Fairfax and Arundel MS. have here a line or two of the French which is not found in the other copies, with the following fragments of English—

> (*F.*) Tprut ! Skot riveling,
> In unseli timing
> crope thu out of cage.

> (*A.*) Tprut ! Scot riveling,
> With mikel mistiming
> crop thu ut of kage.

—— *l.* 157, *Robert de Ros de Werke.*—Robert de Ros was an English Baron, but, falling in love with a Scottish lady, he deserted to the Scots, for which his possessions were confiscated. See Hemingford, p. 85.

P. 284, *l.* 168, *quatre mile.*—The English version makes it *forty thousand*—

> In the non tyme felle this cas, that slayn was ilk a man,
> That were in Berwik, fourti thousand and mo.

—— *l.* 170, *Richard de Cornewalle.*—Holinshed, p. 298, says Sir Richard Cornwall was brother to the Earl of Cornwall. See also Hemingford, p. 91.

—— *l.* 171, *la sale rouge.*—The Red Hall was the factory of the Flemish merchants, who carried on an extensive trade with Berwick.

P. 285, *l.* 175, *Willeam de Douglasse.*—William Douglas was captain of the garrison of Berwick. See Hemingford, *ib.*

—— *l.* 176, *Ricard Fresel.*—The English has *Symoun Freselle.*

——— *l.* 178, *li quens de la Merche, Patrik.*—Patrick, Earl of Dunbar and March, served in the English army; but his Countess, who was left in the castle of Dunbar, and who hated the English, delivered the castle to the Scots.

—— *l.* 180, *Gilbert de Umfravile.*—Gilbert de Umfraville, Earl of Angus, was one of the Scottish Barons who remained faithful to the English.

P. 286, *l.* 194, *Piket him, etc.*—The Fairfax MS. has only four lines of this song :—

> Piket him and diket him,
>   in skorn seiden he ;
> Nu piketh he it and diketh it,
>   his owen for to be.

In the Arundel MS. it stands thus :—

> Pikit him and dikit him,
>   in hoker seiden he ;
> Nu pikes he it and dikes it,
>   his owen for to be.
> Skiterende Scottes
> Hodere in their hottes,
>   nevere thei ne the ;
> Rigth if I rede,
> Thei tumbled in Twede,
>   that woned bi the se.

Robert of Brunne gives the fragment as follows, with six additional lines :—

> Now dos Edward dike Berwik brode and long,
> Als they bad him pike, and scorned him in ther song.

Pikit him and dikit him
　　　　on scorne said he,
He pikes and dikes
　　in length as him likes
　　　　how best it may be.
And thou has for thi pikyng
Mykille ille likyng,
　　　　the sothe is to se.
Without any lesyng
Alle is thi hething
　　　　fallen opon the,
For scatred er thi Scottis,
And hodred in ther hottes,
　　　　never thei ne the.
Right als I rede,
Thei tombled in Tuede,
　　　　that woned bi the se.

P. 288, *l.* 227, *Otes de Graunt-souns.*—Otho had been sent into the East to the aid of the Christians by Edward I., who intended to follow him in person. An account of the loss of Acre, and the escape of the Christians to Cyprus, will be found in Hemingford, pp. 21—28.

P. 289, *l.* 245, *le counte de Warwik e Huge le Despencer.*—Guy de Beauchamp, Earl of Warwick, and Hugh Despencer, who was afterwards so famous as the favourite of Edward II.

P. 293, *l.* 299, *On grene, &c.*—In Robert of Brunne, these lines stand thus :—

Ther on that grene,
That kynrede kene
　　gadred als the gayte.
Right als I wene,
On som was it sene
　　　　ther the bit bayte.

P. 294, *l.* 324, *sire Corynée.*—The fabulous hero who was said to have killed the giant Gogmagog.

P. 295, *l.* 338, *The fote folke, etc.*—Robert of Brunne gives these lines as

follows, with an introduction of his own, in which he says distinctly that they
were rhymes which the English made on the Scots :—

> ¶ The Scottis had no grace,
>   To spede in ther space,
>   for to mend ther misse,
>   Thei filed ther face,
>   That died in that place ;
>   the Inglis rymed this.
>   Oure fote folk
>   Put tham in the polk,
>   and nakned ther nages,
>   Bi no way
>   Herd I never say
>   of prester pages,
>   Purses to pike,
>   Robis to rike,
>   and in dike tham schonne,
>   Thou wiffin
>   Scotte of Abrethin,
>   kotte is thi honne.

In the Fairfax MS. they stand thus :—

> Wel worthe swich a fot folk,
> That drof the Skottes in the polk,
>   and paiede hem here wages.
> Bi wode ne bi weye,
> Ne herd I nevere seien
>   of prestere pages,
> To pullen and to piken
> The robes of the rike
>   that in the feld fellen.
> Fi ! Skot, hu spedde ye thenne ?
> The devel I you bikenne,
>   that ragged rit in helle !

The Arundel MS. gives them thus :—

> Wel worth swich a fote folk,
> That put the Scottes in the polk,
>   . and paied tham their wages.

Bi wode ne bi weie,
Herd I nevere seie
 of prestere pages,
To pulle and to pike
The robes of the rike
 that in the feld felle.
Hou ferd the wreches thenne ?
The devel I them bikenne
 that ragged sit in helle.

In my transcript of the Cambridge MS. I had written *wages* in the third line, but, thinking it might be an error of my own, I ventured to change it to *nages*, in conformity with the readings of the other MSS. I have no doubt that *nages*, the French *nages* (see before, p. 283, l. 156, and the note), the Latin *nates*, is the right word. The other reading of the line was perhaps substituted by some one who did not understand the word.

P. 298, *l.* 380, *For Scottes, etc.*—Robert of Brunne agrees with the present text, in this song. In the Fairfax and Arundel MSS. it stands thus :—

  (*F.*) For skiterande Skottes
   Tell I for sottes,
    of wrenches unwarre.
   Hem to wrothere hele
   Dintes to dele
    driven to Dunbarre.
  (*A.*) Skiterende Scottes
   I telle for sottes,
    and wreches unwar.
   Mikel unsele
   Dintes to dele
    them drof to Dunbar.

P. 300, *l.* 417, *Albanak*, the son of Brute, who was said to have first peopled Scotland, and given it the name of Albania.

P. 303, *l.* 466, *For boule, etc.*—Robert of Brunne, like the Museum MSS., gives only the first six lines of this fragment.

—— *l.* 471, *hise tabard es tome.*—*Toom tabard* (empty tabard) was a nickname given by the Scots to their King, John Baliol, on account of his little wit. In like manner, we still vulgarly call people who possess very little sense, *empty bottles*.

P. 304, *l.* 484, *eces ;* another form of *assez.*

—— *l.* 486, *Henri de Perci aid Galwei.*—Henry de Percy, nephew of Warenne, was made keeper of the county of Galloway and the sheriffdom of Ayr.

P. 305, *l.* 504, *le eveske de Duram.*—The famous Anthony Beck, Bishop of Durham, who, at the head of his knights, attended Edward in all his invasions of Scotland, and commanded one division of the army at the battle of Falkirk.

—— *l.* 514, *Kambynoy.*—Robert of Brunne translates this passage as follows :—

> Cambinhoy
> Beres him coy,
>   that fendes whelp,
> Ther with craft
> He has tham raft,
>   it may not help.
> The Trulle the
> Drenge on se,
>   thei lenge the fendes tueye,
> The hold tham fer,
> And dar no ner
>   than Orkeneye.
> Andrew is wroth,
> The wax him loth,
>   for ther pride.
> He is tham fro,
> Now salle thei go,
>   schame to betide.
> Thou scabbed Scotte,
> Thi neck, thi hotte,
>   the develle it breke,
> It salle be hard
> To here Edward
>   ageyn the speke.
> He salle the ken
> Our lond to bren,
>   and werre begynne
> Thou getes no thing,
> Bot thi rivelyng
>   to hang therinne.

The sete of the Scone
Is driven over done,
to London led ;
I hard wele telle,
That bagelle and belle
be filchid and fled.

P. 306, *l*. 521, *Ou il est mort* | *al mouster.*—The Monastery of Hexham, which the Scots had burnt, was dedicated to their patron Saint, St. Andrew. Hemingford remarks, in a similar manner, the impiety of the Scots in burning the church of their patron. This writer, in many parts of his Chronicle, seems to paraphrase and enlarge upon the narrative of Peter Langtoft.

P. 307, *l*. 550, *Deus! cum Merlins.*—The Cambridge MS. has *Teus*, with a great T., by an error of the illuminator. Robert of Brunne, in translating this part of the Chronicle, quotes the original author, Peter Langtoft, as his authority :—

> Nou tels Pers, on his maners, a grete selcouth,
> He takis witnes, that it soth es, of Merlyn mouth, etc.

The MS. from which Hearne printed contained a marginal note, "De unione Scotiæ et Angliæ secundum dicta Petri et Bridlingtone," meaning that Bridlington had something similar in his prophecies. Hearne, not aware that it is Peter Langtoft to whom the writer refers, alters it to Petri de Bridlington ; although, if he had referred to Bale, he would have found that Bridlington's name was John, and not Peter.

P. 309, *l*. 582, *Jon e Thomas ... Cuthbert.*—John of Beverley, Thomas of Canterbury, and Cuthbert of Durham. These three saints are elsewhere spoken of in Peter Langtoft as Edward's especial patrons and aiders.

P. 310, *l*. 607, *Des biens de seint eylise.*—See, on this transaction, Matthew of Westminster, p. 428, and Hemingford, p. 107.

P. 311. I suspect that the lines here inclosed in brackets, as not found in the Cambridge MS., were missed by myself in transcribing.

—— *l*. 613, *disime dener.*—Robert of Brunne says the twelfth penny.

P. 315, *l*. 683, *jeo crei.*—The manner in which the writer here speaks, as well as other expressions in the course of the poem, seem to show that he wrote down the events as they happened.

P. 316, *l.* 701, *le Sire de Canturbir.*—Robert Winchelsey, Archbishop of Canterbury, from 1294 to 1313.

P. 317, *l.* 709, *Li sire de Nichole.*—Oliver Sutton, Bishop of Lincoln, who died in the November of 1299.

—— *l.* 714, *L'elyt de Everwyke.*—Henry de Newark, who succeeded to the Archbishopric in 1297, and died in 1299.

P. 318, *l.* 720.   These English verses are only found in the Cambridge MS.

P. 320, *l.* 19, *Pur treys souz, &c.*—Robert of Brunne translates this—

Thei profere a man to bete, for tuo schilynges or thre,
With piked staves grete beten salle he be.

We learn from this writer that it was the King who gave them the name of *Trailebastons.*

P. 321, *l.* 43, *Sire Jon de Meneteft.*—He is said to have been incited by his personal hatred of Wallace to seek out and deliver the Scottish Chieftain to his enemies.   Robert de Brunne adds something to his original in this place :—

Sir Jon of Menetest sewed William so nehi,
He tok him whan he wend lest, on nyght his leman bi.
That was thorght treson of Jak Schort his man,
He was the encheson that Sir Jon so him nam.
Jak brother had he slayn, the Waleis that is said,
The more Jak was fayn to do William that braid.
Selcouthly he endis the man that is fals,
If he trest on his frendes, thei begile him als
Begiled is William, taken is and bondon.
To Inglond with him thei cam, and led him unto London.

We may take this occasion of pointing out the impropriety of quoting Robert de Brunne as Peter Langtoft.   Mr. Tytler quotes this story of Jack Short upon Langtoft's authority, which involves two serious errors, first, making Langtoft say what he did not say, and, secondly, giving the story on better authority than that on which it really rests, for, in this respect, Robert de Brunne is certainly inferior to Langtoft.

P. 323, *l.* 67, *And tus, etc.*—Robert of Brunne has six lines of this fragment more than in the French MSS.

It is not to drede,
Traytour salle spede,

als he is worthi,
His lif salle he tyne,
And die thorgh pyne,
          withouten merci.
Thus may men here,
A ladde for to lere
          to biggen in pays.
It fallis in his iȝe,
That hewes over hie,
          with the Walays.

P. 326, *l.* 66, *nu.*—In the MS. it is written n°u. Perhaps the *o* was added by somebody who thought the orthography should be *nou.*

P. 327, *l.* 78, *serven the chapele.*—This last word, which answers to *capella* in the similar passage in the Song at the end of these notes (p. 401, l. 21), means here, perhaps, a *wardrobe.*

P. 329, *l.* 126, *amis.*– This word is added in the MS. by a later hand than that which wrote the other part.

P. 336, *l.* 285, *turmentours that comen from clerkes plei.*—Men who have performed the part of devils, or tormentors, in the miracle plays, which were performed by the clerks.

P. 338, *l.* 330, *Theih pleien wid the kinges silver, and breden wod for wele.* —They use the king's silver for their own pleasures, and produce wood, or tallies, instead of contributing to the prosperity of the people.

P. 341, *l.* 392, *a derthe.*—*l.* 403, *eft wele i-nouh.*—*P.* 342, *l.* 409, *another sorwe.*—*l.* 416, *another derthe of corn.*—Our poem was probably composed in 1321. During the preceding years, the kingdom had been visited repeatedly by dearth and famine. Holinshed remarks in 1316, a great dearth and famine, insomuch that a quarter of wheat sold for forty shillings, and at the same time a murrain among the cattle; in 1317, a "pitiful famine" with a "sore mortalitie of people;" the year 1318 seems to have been free from these visitations, and may have been that in which, according to the poem, there was "eft wele i-nouh;" in 1319, again, a great murrain of cattle; and in the latter end of the following year and in 1321, broke out the "great variaunce betwixt the lords and the Spensers," which was the cause of so much bloodshed, and which seems to be the "strif" (*l.* 423) under which the poet represents the people as then labouring.

P. 342, *l.* 418, *afingred.*—For other instances of the use of this form, see a note on " The Tale of the Basyn and the Frere and the Boy." (Pickering, 1836.)

P. 344, *l.* 457, *paunter.*—The true meaning of this word seems to be a *trap*, or *snare.* An English prose treatise of counsel for hermits, probably by Hampole (MS. Trin. Coll. Cant. B. 15, 17, of the reign of Edward III.), speaking of the snares laid by the devil to deceive people, observes, " This *panter* leyeth owre enemy to taken us with, whan we bigynne to haten wikkednesse, and turne us to goodnesse."

P. 345.—This poem is defective at the end, by the loss of the remainder of the MS., which is imperfect. The following curious Song, which was given me by Mr. Halliwell, bears a remarkable resemblance in some parts to the English poem of the Auchinleck MS. It is taken from a MS. in the University Library, Cambridge, Ee. vi. 29, of the beginning of the fifteenth century, though most, if not all, the articles it contains are compositions of a much earlier date.

> Ecce dolet Anglia luctibus imbuta !
> Gens tremit tristitia, sordibus polluta ;
> Necat pestilentia viros atque bruta.
> Cur ? quia flagitia regnant resoluta.
> 　Heu ! jam totus vertitur mundus in malignum.
> Inter gentes quæritur ubi cor benignum.
> Christus non recolitur, mortuus per lignum ;
> Ergo plebs perimitur in vindictæ signum.
> 　Pax et patientia penitus orbantur ;
> Amor et justitia domi non morantur ;
> Errores et vitia gentes amplexantur ;
> Patrum per malitia parvuli necantur.
> 　Pastorum pigritia greges disperguntur ;
> Insontes astutia mercantum falluntur ;
> Fraus et avaritia sorores junguntur ;
> Divitum nequitia pauperes plectuntur.
> 　Simonia colitur, Simon Magus vivit ;
> Æquitas opprimitur, veritas abivit ;
> Christi grex dispergitur, lupus insanivit ;
> Pestisque diffunditur, agnos deglutivit.
> 　Favor non scientia permovet rectores ;
> Intrudit potentia servos ob labores,
> Et regum clementia quosdam per favores ;
> Æs et amicitia juvant pervisores.

Fortes Christi milites modo recesserunt ;
Sathanæ satellites templum subverterunt ;
Laceras et debiles oves prodiderunt ;
Cuculi degeneres nisis successerunt.

Patres quondam nobiles pestes fugarunt,
Et in fide stabiles languidos sanarunt ;
Vita venerabiles signis coruscarunt ;
Actus per laudabiles Christo militarunt.

Tales erunt vestibus asperis vestiti ;
Ut moderni mollibus raro sunt potiti.
Hii præclaris moribus erant insigniti ;
Juvenes a sordibus sacris eruditi.

Heu ! nunc mercenarii, nec veri pastores,
Rectores, vicarii, mutaverunt mores ;
Ambitu denarii subeunt labores ;
Tales operarii merentur mœrores :

Isti pro ciliciis utuntur pellura ;
Farciunt deliciis ventres tota cura ;
Dant post[ea] spurcitiis se sine mensura ;
Suffulti divitiis vivunt contra jura.

Dum capella tegitur nobili vestura,
Sponsa Christi rapitur nudata tectura ;
Vinea destruitur porcorum ursura,
Et vitis evellitur, carens jam cultura.

Sacerdotes Domini sunt incontinentes ;
Actus suo nomini non sunt respondentes ;
Sacra dantes homini forent et docentes ;
Sui mores ordini non sunt congruentes.

Ista super æthera sanguine scribantur,
Ut patenti littera sæculis legantur ;
Ignibus cum vetera peccata purgantur,
Sua ferant onera jam qui dominantur.

En ! amor et caritas regnis refrigescunt ;
Livor et severitas gentibus ardescunt ;
Cleri plebis veritas et fides tepescunt ;
Hinc regni nobilitas et fama quiescunt.

Feminæ fragilitas omni caret laude ;
Mercantum subtilitas versatur in fraude ;
Et fratrum dolositas jungit caput caudæ.
Homo, si jam veritas te gubernat, gaude !
Explicit.

P. 14.   SONG ON THE TIMES.—Giraldus Cambrensis has inserted a copy of this Song in the Speculum Ecclesiæ, MS. Cotton. Tiberius, B. XIII. fol. 126, vº, and attributes it to the famous Golias, which is commonly supposed to be only a fictitious name for Walter Mapes.   This takes away all doubt as to its age, and the explanations given by Flacius Illyricus may be right.   There is another copy in a Cottonian MS. of the thirteenth century, Vespas. A. XIX. fol. 59, rº, where it is entitled *De veneranda justitia Romanæ curiæ.*   In Giraldus, the song commences with the 13th line, *Roma mundi caput est,* &c. In the other Cotton. MS. it begins as in our text.   The variations afforded by these two MSS. are as follow :—*P.* 14, *l.* 1, *Romanæ reb.*, C.—6, *profluit,* C. —9, the first *est* is omitted in C.—10, *Tegunt picem,* C.—*P.* 15, *l.* 12, *ramus in sap.*, C.—15, *trahit enim,* G. and C.—17, *res et sing.*, C.—21, *In hoc consistorio,* G. and C.—27, *petunt quando petis,* G. and C.—28, *eadem et metis,* C.—*P.* 16.   The first 16 lines in this page are omitted in Giraldus.—*l.* 5, *nummus,* C.—6, *rot. placet, totum pl.*, C.—7, *ita pl.* .. *Romanos,* C.—10, *obiceret,* C.—11, *Et sanc.*, C.—12, *transeunt,* C.—13, *venit parca,* C.—15, *pro munere,* C.—*P.* 17, *l.* 1, *et* .. *sit,* G. and C. *animanti,* C.—2, *Respondet hæc tibia,* G. and C.—6, *li mort,* C.—7, G. and C. have *Porta* at the beginning of this line, and *Papa* in the next.   G. omits the words *chartula quærit :* it ought to be observed that in this MS. the song is written as prose, so that such omissions are easily explained.—8, G. and C. omit the words *cursor quærit.*—9, *omnis quærit,* G. *si des si quid uni,* G. and C.—10, *Totum mare salsum est, tota,* G. and C. except that the former has *salseum* for *salsum est :* see another example of this expression in the present volume, p. 228, l. 19.—11, *Des* .. *des* .. *addas,* G.—*l.* 12, the extract in Giraldus ends here.—*P.* 18, *l.* 4, *totum impl.*, C.—6, *habet Pluto,* C.—9, *dant divitibus,* C.

P. 44, *l.* 3 of Song against the Bishops, *read* fungar vice cotis, " I will perform the part of a whetstone."

P. 282, *l.* 5 of translation, *for* Edward, *read* Edmund.

INDEX.

THE END.

London : J. B. Nichols and Son, Printers, 25, Parliament Street.